GARY GUNDERSON

John S. Friedman is a journalist and documentary filmmaker.
He produced the Academy Award–winning documentary *Hotel
Terminus: The Life and Times of Klaus Barbie* and co-directed the
documentary *Stealing the Fire*, a history of the weapons-of-mass-
destruction underground from the Holocaust to the present. He
is a regular contributor to *The Nation*, among other publications.
Friedman holds a Ph.D. in comparative literature.

3/06

Hey J:
You mentioned you
might be interested in
this book.
No hurry to ret.
Enjoy. — E.

The Secret Histories

The Secret Histories

HIDDEN TRUTHS THAT
CHALLENGED THE PAST AND
CHANGED THE WORLD

Edited by John S. Friedman

PICADOR NEW YORK

ISBN 0-312-42517-1
EAN 978-0-312-42517-3

First Edition: October 2005

10   9   8   7   6   5   4   3   2   1

FOR JULIA,

who will discover other secret histories

CONTENTS

PART IV
Cold War Secrets

PART V
Organized Crime, J. Edgar Hoover, and FBI Abuses

PART VI
Hidden Sides of the Vietnam War

PART VII
Covert Intervention, Overt Neglect

PART VIII
Health and the Environment

ACKNOWLEDGMENTS

THIS BOOK grew out of a lecture on secret history I gave in 2002 to Milton Academy high school students. I want to thank Milton faculty members David Smith, Carly Wade, and Mark Hilgendorf.

Special thanks to Joseph S. Drew for his years of friendship, and to Ariel Dorfman, Richard Fox, and Eric Nadler.

I also want to thank Roger Salloch, Hamilton Fish, Michael Mierendorf, Hugh Mackenzie, Kathy Lace, Henny Wenkart, Peter Kovler, Roger Salloch, Victor Navasky, Katrina vanden Heuvel, Karen Rothmyer, Richard McCord, Isabelle Lemonnier, Shakun Drew, Jack Kolbert, Norma Lumpkins, Ivan Weissman, Caren Plank, Barbara Solomon, Christian Bompard, and Natasha Lunn.

Research assistance was provided by Steven McGuirl and the staff of the New York Society Library, Rowena Clough of the National Cryptological Museum, William J. Leonard of the Information Security Oversight Office and by the staffs of the National Security Archive, the National Archives and Records Administration, the St. Louis Public Library, and the Wellesley Free Library.

Jane Rosenman deserves special thanks for helping me take the first steps.

I appreciate the encouragement and support of publisher Frances Coady and the assistance of others at Picador, including Courtney Randall, Kenneth J. Silver, Tanya Farrell, Katherine Monaghan, and James Meader.

One could not have a better editor than Joshua Kendall, who was a constant source of intelligent guidance and enthusiasm.

I am especially grateful for everything Deirdre Mullane, agent extraordinaire of the Spieler Agency, has done for this book.

The spirit, warmth, and friendship of Roy Friedman were an ongoing inspiration.

I want to express deep gratitude to my wife Kathleen McCaffrey Friedman for editorial advice and for years of stimulating ideas and companionship.

My mother and father, Judith and Arnold Friedman, introduced me to the world of secret history by subscribing to the first and all subsequent issues of *I. F. Stone's Weekly*.

Finally, the journalists, investigators, documentarians, and historians included in this collection prove that individuals who reveal the truth and strive for justice can change the world.

FOREWORD

James Carroll

I WAS A CHILD of the Cold War. My father was part of the National Security establishment in Washington. As a teenager, exploiting his connections, my summer jobs were at the Federal Bureau of Investigation: 1960, 1961, and 1962. Those were the peak years of crisis between the United States and the Soviet Union—the shooting down of the U-2 spy plane, the Vienna confrontation between Kennedy and Khrushchev, the Berlin Wall, Soviet missiles into Cuba. At the FBI, I held a position entitled "Cryptanalyst's Aide" in the Cryptanalysis-Translation section of the Laboratory. Mostly, I did the mind-numbing work of feeding punch cards into a room-sized computer, or counting numbers on a page. It took imagination to think of my efforts as urgent, but I did. My bosses were trying to break the codes of the diplomatic communications intercepted from Washington embassies, especially of the Communist nations. Our work was top secret.

Even our office was secret; the section was housed in a made-over garage on Capitol Hill. From the street, it still looked like a place to get your car fixed. Secrecy was more than a discipline with us. It was like a religion. I thought at the time that we were keeping our secrets from Moscow. But, of course, now I know that, as much as from the Russians, U.S. government enterprises like ours were keeping secrets from the American people.

What a long time ago. What innocence. What fear. The great contest between East and West, as we experienced it at the time, was a matter of transcendent importance because the enemy was evil and we were good.

The enemy believed, as we said, that the end justified the means. The enemy would lie and kill for the sake of what it called a higher good. But we would do no such thing. We knew that the end was embodied in the means. We knew that the higher good required a strict observance of morality. We could trust our government with its secrets, therefore, because our government would never betray that trust.

It was not true. One need not attribute malevolent intentions to the Cold War leaders of the United States to see how they twisted ends and means, and how, in opposing what they thought of as rank evil, they began to imitate it. In this volume, John S. Friedman has assembled, as it were, the record of the great American mistake. For a long time, it was a secret record because the people of the United States were convinced that such a mistake *on our side* was inconceivable. In my reading of the documents gathered here, of course, it is the particular revelations of the secret chicanery of the FBI that I find most stirring—and most instructive. The Bureau was a kind of priesthood to me—and there's the point. Not even the literal priesthood (to which, as it happens, I went next) is immune from the corruptions that take place in secret.

When corruptions are laid bare at last, there is a tendency, still, to look for self-justification—as if we the good people were victimized by our betraying government. Moscow was no longer the wicked adversary, but Washington! Washington kept its secrets from us! Or the tobacco companies did! Or IBM! Thus, the whistle-blowers and investigative journalists and truth-tellers are our new heroes, and now they are the tribunes of our virtue. Our virtue still.

But it is more complicated than that. In a democracy (as opposed to a totalitarian system), abusive secrets are often kept by means of a collaboration between the government and the governed. The media, in particular, can be an instrument of a willful not-knowing, which allows the people to look the other way. What made Seymour M. Hersh's revelations powerful at My Lai and Abu Grahib both was the way in which these particular secrets exposed something central to the larger secret of the very wars during which the uncovered "crimes" occurred. Vietnam involved an unfettered killing of civilians—not just at My Lai; torture was a passively accepted, if not fully justified, part of the new war on terror—not just at

Abu Grahib. In both instances, the American people had willfully turned away from abundant evidence that these were new facts of government policy. What made Hersh's work important—twice—was its break with the lockstep of media complicity in a broad national denial. And so with the records of I. F. Stone, Edward R. Murrow, Neil Sheehan, and a dozen others gathered here.

A reader might take this book as yet another reason to think skeptically about agencies of government and corporate economy, understanding them as prone to the abuse of power through secrecy. Even my once beloved FBI proved capable of egregious assaults on the rights of a population it was sworn to protect. If the FBI is capable of such corruption, why not the Army, or IBM? But a reader might also take this book as the occasion to ask a more difficult question about the nature of democratic polity. Suppression of information, in a free society, can be exclusively a matter of government connivance, but often—and some of the stories collected here make the point—the culture of secrecy requires a complicitous media and a passive citizenry. We do not know what we do not want to know.

The Soviets lie, while we tell the truth? Why were Americans like me so blasé, say, when Washington was caught in its blatant lie about that U-2 "weather plane"? During the Cuban Missile Crisis, it was apparent that the United States was as ready to destroy the world as the Soviet Union was—and where, exactly, was the moral difference in that? Yet the illusion of that difference underwrote nearly three more decades of nuclear arms accumulation. In another realm, the secret that the Nazi-ordered Holocaust involved the active complicity of other nations, companies, and, for that matter, churches is maintained to this day, even if the work of Marcel Ophuls, Edwin Black, and John S. Friedman points directly at larger responsibility. One might say, in yet another realm, it is no secret that smoking causes cancer, yet a smoker keeps that secret from himself every time he says just one more puff won't hurt.

The point is not to judge such denial from a moral high horse. Anymore than it is for me to look contemptuously back on my younger self, enthralled as I was with illusions about the FBI. The human condition is difficult. No one is innocent. There are secrets, therefore, that no one wants to face. The Bible says that the truth will set you free. Maybe. But experience says that first, the truth will knock you for a loop. *Then* it will set you free. In this important book, John S. Friedman has opened up the secret history that shows how that works. The truth-tellers whom he honors are true heroes. But the truth laid bare here is less about our flawed institutions than about our human selves.

WHEN THE PRACTICED EYE of the simple peasant sees the half of a frog projecting above the water, he unerringly infers the half of the frog which he does not see," Mark Twain wrote in *The Secret History of Eddypus.* "To the expert student in our great science, history is a frog; half of it is submerged, but he knows it is there, and he knows the shape of it."

Throughout history, governments and the powerful have submerged truths that do not serve their interests. Not surprisingly, most histories and news reports, which have largely determined our views of the past and influenced our perceptions of the present, have relied almost exclusively on what is visible—"above the water." But in the last seventy-five years, with World War II, the Cold War, and the Vietnam War as catalysts, historical research, investigative journalism, and congressional probes have upended our views of government and business, bringing into the open previously hidden knowledge or information, challenging established versions of events, and forcing a reevaluation of accepted beliefs. Such secret histories have revealed the submerged half of the frog. An emerging genre, secret history is well suited to our rather skeptical times.

For centuries, state secrets were predominantly concerned with military matters, such as troop movements in time of war, and issues of diplomacy. But with the rise of the modern bureaucratic state, the cult of secrecy has grown exponentially. "The concept of the 'official secret' is the specific invention of the bureaucracy, and nothing is so fanatically defended by the bureaucracy as this attitude," wrote sociologist Max Weber. To preserve its power, bureaucracy hides information about its activities.

The less lawmakers and citizens know about what the bureaucracy is doing, the less chance there is for criticism and change.

The recent growth of government bureaucracy in the United States is staggering. In 2004, the U.S. government employed approximately 4,000 people to decide on original classification guidelines; in other words, to deem what pieces of information should be a matter of secrecy. Additionally, some three million people, including those working for private defense contractors—just about anybody with a security clearance—can make classification decisions based on these guidelines. In 2004, some 15.6 million classification decisions were made—even taking September 11th into account, this is more than a 200 percent increase from 1994. Senator Daniel Patrick Moynihan, an advocate of openness and the author of *Secrecy: The American Experience,* surmised that if every newspaper in the U.S. devoted every page to printing classified documents, produced by the government on that day alone, there would be room for nothing else.

The exact price of keeping these secrets is itself unknown, only estimated. For 2004, the estimated cost for government security classification was over $7 billion (not including CIA expenses), according to the government's Information Security Oversight Office. In Moynihan's words, secrecy has become "a hidden, humongous, metastasizing mass within the government itself."

Beyond the modern burgeoning of bureaucracy, another dominant factor in the growth of secrecy was the fear, paranoia, and hysteria cast over the government by the Cold War, in ways real and imagined, with the Soviet Union. "The awful dilemma was that in order to preserve an open society, the U.S. government took measures that in significant ways closed it down," Moynihan observed. "The culture of secrecy that evolved was intended as a defense against two antagonists, by now familiar ones: the enemy abroad and the enemy within." Secrecy became a form of government regulation, but unlike other regulations, citizens had no idea what was being regulated or even how the regulations were determined.

The hall of mirrors that surrounded efforts at secrecy during the Cold War is perhaps best illustrated in the case of the Venona Project, the top secret program that decoded messages between Soviet officials abroad and Moscow. In 1946, the first decoded cable identified the principal scientists working on the development of nuclear technology at Los Alamos. Looking over the shoulder of the American cryptanalyst who deciphered the cable was a linguist, employed by the Americans but in fact a Soviet spy. The second breach of Venona secrecy occurred in 1949 when H. R. "Kim" Philby, a senior British intelligence official and longtime Soviet spy, visited the staff of the Venona project at Arlington Hall in Virginia, where American officials proceeded to give him a briefing of the project's findings. For fifty years, the Soviets knew about Venona. The U.S. army and the FBI knew that they knew and they knew that we knew. But the American people were never informed of Venona's existence. Nor, astonishingly, was President Truman. Despite these security breaches, the government bureaucracy kept the Venona Project secret until 1995, when its existence was officially revealed. Such concealment has nothing to do with national security. This is an example of what happens when there are no checks and balances to counteract the secrecy mindset: the passion for secrecy runs amok.

With the arrival of the Vietnam War, an outgrowth of the Cold War, government secrecy received another boost. The Nixon Justice Department went to great lengths in the courts to block publication of a confidential history of U.S involvement in Indochina, documents that came to be known as *The Pentagon Papers* claiming that national security would be harmed. But as far as can be determined, publication of the papers in 1971 caused no harm to national security, but rather, wrote *Times* Reporter Neil Sheehan in his introduction, *The Pentagon Papers* made "clear the deep-felt need of the government insider for secrecy in order to keep the machinery of state functioning smoothly and to maintain a maximum ability to affect the public world." Instead of trying to keep critical information from the enemy, the Nixon White House was using secrecy as a way to stigmatize outsiders and protect itself from criticism.

It is not accidental that the revelations of secret histories, reached a high point during the Nixon years, a period when power was abused to extreme ends. As a result of skepticism about the Vietnam War, the Watergate break-in, and a gnawing awareness of abuses by the CIA and FBI, the press assumed a bolder, more adversarial role. *Ramparts* magazine, for example, exposed a number of stories, including a 1967 article on the CIA's financial support of the National Student Association. In 1968, CBS began the investigative series *60 Minutes.* In 1969, Seymour Hersh uncovered the My Lai massacre; two years later *The New York Times, The Washington Post,* and other newspapers published *The Pentagon Papers;* and in 1976, investigations by the Church Committee in the Senate and the Pike Committee in the House revealed illegal acts and abuses by the CIA and FBI.

On the other side of the Cold War divide, in 1973, Aleksandr Solzhenitsyn's *The Gulag Archipelago,* a towering exemplar of secret history, was smuggled out of the Soviet Union and published in France. His description of the Soviet slave labor camps made it impossible for either the West or the Soviets to ignore the history and realities of the Communist system. These revelations helped bring about the fall of the Soviet state. The Soviet authorities responded by exiling him from Russia.

Others who published secret histories faced comparably dire consequences. In 1975, the United States expelled former CIA agent Philip Agee from five NATO countries after he published *Inside the Company: CIA Diary,* revealing agency secrets. In 1986, after providing details to the London *Sunday Times* about Israel's nuclear-bomb–making facilities, Mordechai Vanunu, an Israeli nuclear technician, was seized by Israeli security agents in Italy and taken back to Israel, where he was held for eighteen years in prison. Such actions prove secret history's threat to power.

Most serious studies of the latter half of the twentieth century or first years of the twenty-first cannot ignore secret histories. For instance, how can the Allied victory over the Axis powers be understood without knowledge of the German encryption device known as the Enigma machine and the efforts to break the code known as Ultra? How can the deportation of the Jews in the Holocaust be analyzed without considering the financial and technological role of IBM in Germany? What history of Richard Nixon's presidency could fail to mention the investigative reporting of Woodward and Bernstein?

Secrets have a special aura, providing an insider's view that has never been made public. But, as journalist John Dinges has noted, secrecy does not inoculate against inaccuracy and works that rely on secret information "are only as factual as the reporting and sourcing that went into them."

Secret histories usually reveal an unknown element of a completed event. Investigative journalism usually focuses on ongoing events. Obviously, they can overlap. As this collection tries to be inclusive, a few selections may lean more towards investigative journalism than to secret history. Often, works of secret history clarify differing historical interpretations. At other times, as seen here in the selections on the true causes of the Korean War, and FBI Director J. Edgar Hoover's private life and public actions, they stimulate debate.

Although secret history is as old as the Dead Sea Scrolls, the following collection, the first of its kind, focuses on a wide range of topics from the last seventy-five years, drawn from a number of media. Included are television documentaries, newspaper and magazine articles, selections from books, reports from Senate investigations, tape recordings, decoded cables, and an article that first appeared on the Internet. Whenever possible, the original source or initial publication is used. In deciding what topics to include, I considered the importance of the historical event or the deeds of a powerful individual, the significance and effect of the revealed secret history, and, in relevant cases, the background and skills of the investigator.

The secret history of armed conflicts, from the Second World War to Vietnam, can be found here, as well as accounts of human rights atrocities, from the Holocaust to My Lai, genocide in Rwanda to the torture of prisoners at Abu Ghraib. The passion for secrecy on both sides of the Iron Curtain during the Cold War provides a rich vein of material, from the repression of the Soviet Gulag to the domestic abuses of Nixon, J. Edgar Hoover, the CIA, and the FBI. The theft of nuclear secrets, government experiments on humans using radiation and LSD, the health effects of tobacco, oil tanker spills, and the prevalence of organized crime in America all have their own secret histories.

Foreshadowed by hidden irregularities during the 2000 presidential election in Florida and by the Iraq War, the excessive secrecy of the current administration portends still more abuses. "The Bush-Cheney secrecy and style of governing carries with it potential consequences that are far worse than any political scandal," writes John W. Dean, former counsel to President Nixon. "Their secret presidency is a dangerous threat to democracy in an age of terrorism." More than ever, there is a need for the secret histories of recent events to be revealed. The consequences are simply too great. Or as the historian Richard Gid Powers observes, "the release of government secrets has the power to redeem American history and save the national soul."

All I have is a voice
To undo the folded lie.

—W. H. Auden
September 1, 1939

PART I

World War Two: Code Breakers and Collaborators

Introduction to
F. W. Winterbotham's

The Ultra Secret

ULTRA WAS THE NAME used by the British to describe intelligence deciphered from coded German communications during World War II. The Ultra information was mostly produced by the Enigma machines, placed throughout the German army and navy. The Enigma machine was an electromechanical rotor device developed in the 1920s in Germany that employed an astronomical number of encryption combinations to transmit secret messages. Several factors enabled Enigma messages to be decoded by the British in the early years of the war: the skills of Polish and British mathematicians, including Alan Turing, one of the fathers of modern computing; captured Enigma machines and codebooks; early computers that could expeditiously analyze far more quantities of information than humans; and German carelessness.

During the Battle of Britain, Ultra intercepts played a decisive role in defending England from German attack. In North Africa, Ultra information was crucial in the defeat of General Erwin Rommel who led the German forces. Ultra was also essential in providing information that helped destroy German submarines that preyed on Allied ships and was vital to the planning of the D-day Invasion, informing the Allies where German armor and troops were located.

Historians already had some vague hints about the role of codebreaking on the course of the war, from Churchill and others, but the claims were generally discounted. In 1973, when Gustave Bertrand, a French intelligence officer, wrote a book that divulged secrets about Enigma, his work was generally ignored. In contrast, F. W. Winterbotham's revelations, in the bestselling *The Ultra Secret,* published in 1974, attracted wide attention and forced historical revisions about virtually all aspects of the war against the Germans. Winterbotham had been a British spy before World War II. During the war he was an RAF intelligence officer whose duties included deciding each day which Ultra information Churchill should receive.

After years of "smug propaganda on the subject of how the Allies routed the evil forces of Nazi Fascism," Winterbotham wrote, "it is difficult to tell people now how very nearly it never happened." The Ultra story has become part of popular culture through plays, films, and books. The effect of Winterbotham's book cannot be overestimated. Military historian Harold C. Deutsch observed that if the Ultra revelations don't "require a 'complete' rewriting of World War II history," at the least "old chapters must be rewritten and new ones added."

ADDITIONAL SOURCES

Bertrand, Gustave. *Enigma ou la plus grande enigme de la guerre 1939–1945.* Paris: Plon, 1973.

Calvocoressi, Peter. *Top Secret Ultra.* New York: Ballantine Books, 1981.

Deutsch, Harold C. "The Historical Impact of Revealing the Ultra Secret." *Cryptologic Spectrum* 8, no. 1 (winter 1978), pages 17–29.

Kahn, David. *The Codebreakers.* New York: Macmillan, 1967.

Whitemore, Hugh. *Breaking the Code.* New York: Samuel French, Inc., 1986.

F. W. Winterbotham

Science to the Rescue:
The Birth of Ultra

THE ULTRA SECRET, 1974

IN THE ALMOST static war of 1914–18 information about the enemy's operations was largely gleaned from low-level aerial photography and from trench raids, both of which proved highly dangerous and very expensive in manpower and aeroplanes. There was also the beginnings of a system of watching the volume of the enemy's wireless traffic which gave some indication of his activity, and on the naval side valuable intelligence was obtained by breaking and reading the German naval wireless signals, a triumph for the cryptographers in the famous Room 40 at the Admiralty.

Now, towards the end of 1938, the German security services had already cracked down on the cloak and dagger agents operating out of Germany. It is true they had not been of great use to my Air Section, but I had been able to balance this to some extent by my own visits to Germany and the flights of my spy plane.

Early in 1939 I set up the first Scientific Intelligence Unit in my Air Section of the Secret Intelligence Service [S.I.S.]. I had been getting queries from Robert Watson-Watt, the inventor of the British radar system, on German radar progress and other scientific devices which might be used by the Luftwaffe, and so with the help of Sir Henry Tizard, the Scientific Adviser to the Air Ministry, and Robert Watson-Watt, I was supplied with a young scientist, Dr R. V. Jones, whom I set up in an office close to my own in Broadway, near Victoria, to begin his training in the art of spotting the difference between good and bad information and evaluating such Intelligence as we could get hold of. Jones was a good choice; his early reports on enemy radar development and later on beam bombing, jet-engine experiments and Hitler's secret weapons, the V1 and V2, were classic examples of the vital role science was to play in our wartime Intelligence.

Despite our secret success with high altitude photography, I soon realized that in a war of rapid movement, such as General Reichenau had described to me back in 1934, rapid and accurate information about the enemy's intentions might well mean the difference between swift defeat and eventual victory.

Two floors below the one on which I worked were the cryptographers of the Government Code and Cypher School. I had from time to time been able to help them with aviation terms and names of aircraft types in the signals they were busy decyphering. These backroom boys were a dedicated team of highly intellectual individuals under the control of Commander Alastair Denniston who had been one of the original cryptographers in Room 40 at the Admiralty during World War I. He was a quiet, rather reserved man of about fifty, somewhat short of stature but certainly not of intellect. He had organized the present set-up, and it was from talking to him that I began to learn the enormous possibilities of the broken enemy cypher. He told me about the failures and successes of the inter-war years, the hopes and possibilities of the future and, one single fact which was to serve me in good stead later, that the only really secure cypher at that time was the one that is used only once.

Denniston explained to me that there were a number of methods used to encypher messages, mostly based on the use of books of numerals held only by the sender and the recipient, but that machines had also been tried out. The basis of encyphering was that each service up to now had used its own particular code book in which a multitude of words and phrases likely to be used by that particular service had opposite each phrase or word a numerical group. Thus 'To the Commanding Officer' might read 5473, 'The Division will move' 0842, 'on Monday' 4593. Most code books are not considered to be completely secret since they get lost or stolen or because in time the meaning of the groups becomes generally known.

In order to make the message secret, therefore, additional groups of figures known only to the sender and receiver must be added so as to make the final groups in the signal untranslatable by any third party.

The safest way to do this is for both the sender and receiver to have a sort of tear-off writing pad, on each sheet of which are columns of four digit groups printed absolutely at random.

The sender indicates the page, the column and the line where the message is to start in the first group of the signal, thus 1348 would mean page 13, column 4, line 8. Now if the next three groups on the pad are 4431, 7628 and 5016 and these are added to the ones already quoted, we find that the message reads 1348.9904.8470.9609 which means 'To the Commanding Officer, the Division will move on Monday.'

Once used the whole page of the pad is torn off and destroyed. This is known as the one-time pad system and was at that time the only known absolutely safe cypher. If, for instance, the cypher groups are in a non-destructible book form and are used over and over again, in time an enemy will work out where the groups occur in the book and be able to read the signals. This unfortunately occurred in our own naval cyphers during the war.

The one-time pad method is, however, a long and very cumber-some method to use on any very large scale. All the printing presses in Germany could hardly have coped with the numbers of tear-off pads required. It was therefore thought likely that Germany would turn to a mechanical system which could be quick and easy to operate, a system of so changing the letters of the words in the signal by progressive proliferation that only the receiver who knew the key to the system could set his own machine to unscramble the letters back to their original meaning.

I will not try to enlarge on the subject of codes and cyphers, a subject which has been so excellently covered by David Kahn in his book *The Codebreakers,* but from my talks with Denniston, it was obvious that we ought to get to know all we could about the Germans' signals set-up. It seemed evident that the great German war machine dedicated to the rapid blitzkrieg must have a secure and quick wireless signalling organiz-ation, since the laying of land lines would hardly be possible, and that the one-time cypher would be far too cumbersome and out of the question for such a volume of traffic. So enquiries had already been sent out to our agents in Europe to try to find out just what the Germans were going to do about it. What sort of cypher system would they use?

In 1938 a Polish mechanic had been employed in a factory in Eastern Germany which was making what the young man rightly judged to be some sort of secret signalling machine. As a Pole, he was not very fond of the Germans anyway and, being an intelligent observer, he took careful note of the various parts that he and his fellow workmen were making. I expect it was after one of the security checks which were made by the Gestapo on all high security factories that they discovered his nationality. He was sacked and sent back to Poland. His keen observation had done him some good, and he got in touch with our man in Warsaw. The Gestapo in Poland were active, and so he was told to lie low. Meantime, we received the information in London. It was obviously a very delicate matter, and our Chief, Admiral Sinclair, decided that the fewer people, even in our office, that knew about it, the better. He therefore put the development of the concept in the hands of his deputy, Colonel Stewart Menzies, and it was decided that only the departmental heads were to be kept in the picture.

In due course the young Pole was persuaded to leave Warsaw and was secretly smuggled out under a false passport with the help of the Polish Secret Service, he was then installed in Paris where, with the aid of the Deuxième Bureau, he was given a workshop. With the help of a carpenter to look after him, he began to make a wooden mock-up of the machine he had been working on in Germany.

There had been a number of cypher machines invented over the years and our own backroom boys had records and drawings of most of them. It didn't take them long to identify the mock-up as some sort of improved mechanical cypher machine called Enigma. The name Enigma was given to the machine by the German manufacturers. The Pole had been told not to attempt to make his wooden model to scale. In fact, the bigger the better, because he could then more easily incorporate any details he could remember. The result was rather like the top half of an upright piano, but it was enough to tell us that it would be essential to get hold of an actual machine if we were to stand any chance of trying to break into its method of operation. So, while the Pole was carefully looked after in Paris, we set about working out a scheme with our friends in Poland, who were just as keen as we were to try and grab a complete machine from Germany. We knew where the factory was and all about its security methods, and that there were still some Poles working there under German names. However, the Polish Secret Service thought the scheme might stand more chance of success if we gave them the money and they did the job. They knew the terrain and the people much better than we did, so we gladly agreed.

It was Denniston himself who went to Poland and triumphantly, but in the utmost secrecy, brought back the complete, new, electrically operated Enigma cypher machine which we now knew was being produced in its thousands and was destined to carry all the secret signal traffic of the great war machine.

It is difficult to explain this cypher machine in a few words so I do not intend to try to describe the working of the complicated system of electrically connected revolving drums around which were placed letters of the alphabet. A typewriter fed the letters of the message into the machine, where they were so proliferated by the drums that it was estimated a team of top mathematicians might take a month or more to work out all the permutations necessary to find the right answer for a single cypher setting; the setting of the drums in relation to each other was the key which both the sender and receiver would no doubt keep very closely guarded.

No wonder the Germans considered that their cypher was completely safe.

Despite the fact that we had an actual machine, were we now faced with an impossible problem? By August 1939 Denniston and his Government Code and Cypher School had moved to Bletchley Park, a secluded country house which the Chief had previously acquired as a wartime hideout; with them went the machine.

Alas, at the end of the year only months before Bletchley became fully operational, Sinclair died. To me personally it was a sad loss. He had fought the government of the day for the recognition of my 'Nazi' information; he had no need or intention of allowing anyone to corrode the absolute independence of the Secret Service, the last chief to do so. Over the years we had had many a quiet chuckle over my visits to Hitler and Co.

He seemed the only person to understand how and why I had become a confidante of the Nazi hierarchy. Somehow the Nazis seemed unable to communicate with the career diplomats, and Rosenberg, himself an amateur, preferred to explain Nazi policy to another amateur.

In my case as a 'supposed' admirer of the regime, they believed I could influence my friends in high places in London in their favour and achieve the neutrality of Britain in their coming wars.

I never attempted to conceal my association with the Foreign Office, and copies of the reports I was supposed to have submitted to the FO were described by Rosenberg as 'glowing' in a memo to Hitler.

The weeks I spent each year from 1934–8 travelling freely about Germany with Rosenberg, Rudolf Hess, Erich Koch or the ADC Rosenberg supplied me with, gave me an almost unique insight into the Nazi plans for the future and perhaps more important into the mentalities of these men, including Hitler.

If I expressed a desire to know more about any subject, then either Hitler or Rosenberg would give some expert the green light to talk to me.

It had not been an easy part to play, especially when associating with such cold sadistic characters as Himmler, but I had got away with it for four years without disaster to myself or embarrassment to my chief. He and Sir Robert Vansittart, the head of the Foreign Office, were close friends, but even together they had been unable to dent the shield of disbelief that Neville Chamberlain and Lord Halifax had erected to protect them.

Had the admiral lived to serve Churchill, he might well have helped him to better understand what we were up against in those hectic first months in office as prime minister.

To be Chief of the Secret Service, a post which by long tradition had been a gift of the monarch, was, of course, a plum job. In recent years it had been a perquisite of the navy and now the admirals were lining up. However, Colonel Stewart Menzies had other ideas. I had worked with Stewart as a colleague for the past nine years and I think all of us in the office were anxious that he should take over rather than that we should have a new broom at this critical stage. Our only misgivings were whether he carried the weight to hold on to his chair. He had been educated at Eton,

and, like so many sons of wealthy parents, he had gone into the House-
hold Cavalry. He won the DSO and served on Haig's staff during World
War I. He was a member of the exclusive White's Club and had personal
contacts with the highest in the land. He was a Scot, he had a ready smile
and the assurance which had come down with the profit from the millions
of gallons of whisky distilled by his ancestors. His family owned the lovely
Dorchester House set on an island in Park Lane, soon to become the great
yellow-white edifice of the hotel, and, back in my own home county of
Gloucestershire, his family estate sat quietly in secluded elegance next to
that of the Duke of Beaufort. He wouldn't give in easily and, by the end of
1939, realization that something very big might come out of the Enigma
cypher operation made him doubly determined to hold on. He had kept
his word and personally informed me of the progress being made. But
there were tremendous problems to be overcome.

In September 1939 the SIS were also evacuated to Bletchley Park, some
fifty miles north of London near the main road and railway to the northwest. It was one of those large and rather ornate houses of red brick with
timbered gables in the prosperous late Victorian style, probably built by
one of the wealthy owners of the many brickworks which abound in this
rich clay area. There must have been twenty or more rooms in the house,
which was a long two-storey building, entered through a pretentious
porch. There were spacious green lawns with the regulation cedar trees, a
croquet lawn and a ha-ha, a sunken boundary fence that was invisible
from the house and gave the idea of unbroken space. This was a favourite
place later on to sit and eat one's sandwich lunch.

Bletchley was only a small town. It was not beautiful; five miles away
was Woburn Park and Abbey where the Duke of Bedford lived. A number
of wooden huts had been erected on the wide lawns at Bletchley and it
was in Hut No. 3 that I and my small staff set up office. We lived, however,
in billets in the surrounding country, and it was in another big house,
which belonged to a man who owned a nearby glucose factory, that I
found I had a number of backroom boys as fellow boarders. They were a
cheerful lot, even if the conversation was at times well over the top of my
head. I had known several of them when we all worked in the same building in London. Between them there was little they did not know about

cyphers, and now that we had actually got one of Hitler's latest Enigma cypher machines, it was possible to understand with some accuracy its function and complexity. Enigma, the ancient Greek word for a puzzle, was certainly a good name for it. We could now at least get the machine accurately duplicated.

In the absence of a grey-stone quadrangle of an old university college, what remained of the green tree-studded lawns of the English country house was as good a place as any for the assembly of a pride of intellectual lions. There had come to Bletchley some of the most distinguished mathematicians of the day. Alexander, Babbage, Milner Barry, Gordon Welchman, names to whisper in the world of chess. They had been persuaded by Denniston to leave their comfortable universities and join with our own backroom boys to try to prove or disprove the theory that if man could design a machine to create a mathematical problem, then man could equally design a machine to solve it.

It was, I think, generally accepted that of our own backroom boys 'Dilly' Knox was the mastermind behind the Enigma affair. He was quite young, tall, with a rather gangling figure, unruly black hair, his eyes, behind glasses, some miles away in thought. Like Mitchell, the designer of the Spitfire fighter aeroplane which tipped the scales in our favour during the Battle of Britain, who worked himself to his death at the moment of his triumph, Knox too, knowing he was a sick man, pushed himself to the utmost to overcome the problems of Enigma variations (introduced by the Germans to further complicate their cyphers between 1940 and 1942). He, too, died with his job completed. J. H. Tiltman, another brilliant brain, had been borrowed from the army. He was tall and dark with a short, clipped, military moustache, and his regimental tartan trousers eventually gave way to green corduroy slacks which were thought slightly way out in 1939. Oliver Strachey was an individualist, tall though a little stooped, with greying hair, broad forehead; his eyes, behind his glasses, always had a smile in them, as if he found life intensely amusing, except when our billetor used to stand at the foot of the stairs on Saturday mornings collecting our cheques. Oliver was also extremely musical. I believe he played several instruments, but he most enjoyed playing duets with Benjamin Britten on the grand piano in his rather untidy London flat.

Then there was 'Josh' Cooper whom I saw fairly often, as he was primarily concerned with air force matters. He was another brilliant mathematician. Still in his thirties, he had to use powerful glasses which often seemed to get in the way of his straight black hair. Dick Pritchard, young, tall, clean-shaven, rather round of face, with a quiet voice, could talk on any subject with witty penetration. He, too, was deeply musical. It struck me at the time how often the art of undoing other people's cyphers was closely allied to a brain which could excel both in mathematics and music. It was rather frightening playing one's evening bridge with these men. It all came easily to them and the conversation was ever interesting. I could well have spent longer in our country retreat than I did, but it soon became apparent that the phoney war would last over the winter of 1939–40, so I took my small staff back to London in order to be near the Air Ministry. I missed the professorial atmosphere of Bletchley.

It is no longer a secret that the backroom boys of Bletchley used the new science of electronics to help them solve the puzzle of Enigma. I am not of the computer age nor do I attempt to understand them, but early in 1940 I was ushered with great solemnity into the shrine where stood a bronze-coloured column surmounted by a larger circular bronze-coloured face, like some Eastern Goddess who was destined to become the oracle of Bletchley, at least when she felt like it. She was an awesome piece of magic. We were, of course, all wondering whether the great experiment could really become operational, and if so, would it be in time for the hot war which we now felt was bound to break out in the spring? Hitler had given us six months' respite. Each day had, I think, been used to the full by every branch of the nation's defences. We all knew it was too little, too late, but at least in this one vital concept the possibilities were prodigiously exciting, for we had in our hands the very encyphering machine the Germans would be using in their wartime communications.

It must have been about the end of February 1940 that the Luftwaffe, the German Air Force, had evidently received enough Enigma machines to train their operators sufficiently well for them to start putting some practice messages on the air. The signals were quite short but must have contained the ingredients the bronze goddess had been waiting for. Menzies had given instructions that any successful results were to be sent immediately to him, and it was just as the bitter cold days of that frozen winter were giving way to the first days of April sunshine that the oracle of Bletchley spoke and Menzies handed me four little slips of paper, each with a short Luftwaffe message dealing with personnel postings to units. From the Intelligence point of view they were of little value, except as a small bit of administrative inventory, but to the backroom boys at Bletchley Park and to Menzies, and indeed to me, they were like the magic in the pot of gold at the end of the rainbow.

The miracle had arrived.

NOTE

Since this book was completed, Polish officers now living in Britain have stated that the Poles constructed a number of Enigma machines from information extracted from the factory in Germany coupled with the help of their own cryptographers, and that it was presumably one of these which they supplied to us. This may very well be true and certainly the Polish mathematicians and technicians displayed brilliance and great courage, but the story I have given is the one told to me at the time.

Introduction to
Edwin Black's

IBM and the Holocaust

THE ROLE of American corporations in helping to finance the Nazi war machine has been examined in a number of books, of which *IBM and the Holocaust* by Washington-based writer Edwin Black is the most revealing. Unlike Ford, General Motors, Chase National Bank (later Chase Manhattan Bank), Standard Oil, and other companies, IBM's business alliance with Hitler was overlooked. Scholars were never able to explain the speed and accuracy with which the Nazis identified and located Jews—until Black's monumental history. In *IBM and the Holocaust,* Black reveals the key role played by the IBM corporation as well as its technology in not only assisting Hitler but also in locating Jews, helping to operate Nazi railroads, and in organizing concentration camp labor. IBM and its German subsidiary custom-designed complex solutions, anticipating the Reich's needs.

For years, U.S. corporations had covered up and denied any assistance to Nazi Germany. For example, when Bradford Snell, a young Senate staff attorney told a Senate subcommittee in 1974 that "communications as well as matériel continually flowed between GM plants in Allied countries and GM plants in Axis-controlled areas," and that without the support of Ford and General Motors the Nazis would never have been able to pursue the war as long and successfully as they did, GM's lawyers succeeded in discrediting his claims as "totally false." When Ford was approached by historians researching its role in the war, the company claimed it had no archival documents of relevance. Likewise, Black writes of IBM: "Since WWII, the company has steadfastly refused to cooperate with outside authors." IBM finally gave Black what he terms "proper access" but only after repeated approaches.

The son of Polish survivors, Black surprisingly encountered some hostile criticism when *IBM and the Holocaust* was published. A senior editor at *Commentary,* writing in *The New York Times Book Review,* charged Black with avoiding "the subtle hues of genuine scholarship" and launched an ad hominem attack, accusing him of writing "techno-thrillers, and articles for a variety of popular magazines like *Mademoiselle* and *Redbook.*" One reason for such a reaction might be that Black's previous book, *The Transfer Agreement,* was an examination of a 1933 pact between Zionist leaders and the Nazis that allowed Jews to immigrate to Palestine in exchange for lifting a boycott of Nazi products. Some critics continue to fault Black for even writing about this still controversial subject.

IBM and the Holocaust is a seminal work of Holocaust history. It proves that profit dominated all else—patriotism, ethics, human rights, even life and death—in the IBM boardroom.

ADDITIONAL SOURCES

Black, Edwin. *The Transfer Agreement. The Dramatic Story of the Pact Between the Third Reich and Jewish Palestine.* New York: Macmillan, 1984.

Goldhagen, Daniel Jonah. *Hitler's Willing Executioners: Ordinary Germans and the Holocaust.* New York: Alfred A. Knopf, 1996.

Hilberg, Raul. *The Destruction of the European Jews.* New Haven, Conn.: Yale University Press, 2003.

United States Holocaust Memorial Museum, internet site: www.ushmm.org

Edwin Black

Introduction

IBM AND THE HOLOCAUST: THE STRATEGIC ALLIANCE BETWEEN NAZI GERMANY AND AMERICA'S MOST POWERFUL CORPORATION, 2001

THIS BOOK will be profoundly uncomfortable to read. It was profoundly uncomfortable to write. It tells the story of IBM's conscious involvement—directly and through its subsidiaries—in the Holocaust, as well as its involvement in the Nazi war machine that murdered millions of others throughout Europe.

Mankind barely noticed when the concept of *massively organized information* quietly emerged to become a means of social control, a weapon of war, and a roadmap for group destruction. The unique igniting event was the most fateful day of the last century, January 30, 1933, the day Adolf Hitler came to power. Hitler and his hatred of the Jews was the ironic driving force behind this intellectual turning point. But his quest was greatly enhanced and energized by the ingenuity and craving for profit of a single American company and its legendary, autocratic chairman. That company was International Business Machines, and its chairman was Thomas J. Watson.

Der Führer's obsession with Jewish destruction was hardly original. There had been czars and tyrants before him. But for the first time in history, an anti-Semite had automation on his side. Hitler didn't do it alone. He had help.

In the upside-down world of the Holocaust, dignified professionals were Hitler's advance troops. Police officials disregarded their duty in favor of protecting villains and persecuting victims. Lawyers perverted concepts of justice to create anti-Jewish laws. Doctors defiled the art of medicine to perpetrate ghastly experiments and even choose who was healthy enough to be worked to death—and who could be cost-effectively sent to the gas chamber. Scientists and engineers debased their higher calling to devise the instruments and rationales of destruction. And statisticians used their little-known but powerful discipline to identify the victims, project and rationalize the benefits of their destruction, organize their persecution, and even audit the efficiency of genocide. Enter IBM and its overseas subsidiaries.

Solipsistic and dazzled by its own swirling universe of technical possibilities, IBM was self-gripped by a special amoral corporate mantra: if it *can* be done, it *should* be done. To the blind technocrat, the *means* were more important than the *ends*. The destruction of the Jewish people became even less important because the invigorating nature of IBM's technical achievement was only heightened by the fantastical profits to be made at a time when breadlines stretched across the world.

So how did it work?

When Hitler came to power, a central Nazi goal was to identify and destroy Germany's 600,000-member Jewish community. To Nazis, Jews were not just those who practiced Judaism, but those of Jewish blood, regardless of their assimilation, intermarriage, religious activity, or even conversion to Christianity. Only after Jews were identified could they be targeted for asset confiscation, ghettoization, deportation, and ultimately extermination. To search generations of communal, church, and governmental records all across Germany—and later throughout Europe—was a cross-indexing task so monumental, it called for a computer. But in 1933, no computer existed.

When the Reich needed to mount a systematic campaign of Jewish economic disenfranchisement and later began the massive movement of European Jews out of their homes and into ghettos, once again, the task was so prodigious it called for a computer. But in 1933, no computer existed.

When the Final Solution sought to efficiently transport Jews out of European ghettos along railroad lines and into death camps, with timing so precise the victims were able to walk right out of the boxcar and into a waiting gas chamber, the coordination was so complex a task, this too called for a computer. But in 1933, no computer existed.

However, another invention did exist: the IBM punch card and card sorting system—a precursor to the computer. IBM, primarily through its German subsidiary, made Hitler's program of Jewish destruction a technologic mission the company pursued with chilling success. IBM Germany, using its own staff and equipment, designed, executed, and supplied the indispensable technologic assistance Hitler's Third Reich needed to accomplish what had never been done before—the automation of human destruction. More than 2,000 such multi-machine sets were dispatched throughout Germany, and thousands more throughout German-dominated Europe. Card sorting operations were established in every major concentration camp. People were moved from place to place, systematically worked to death, and their remains cataloged with icy automation.

IBM Germany, known in those days as Deutsche Hollerith Maschinen Gesellschaft, or Dehomag, did not simply sell the Reich machines and then walk away. IBM's subsidiary, with the knowledge of its New York headquarters, enthusiastically custom-designed the complex devices and specialized applications as an official corporate undertaking. Dehomag's top management was comprised of openly rabid Nazis who were arrested after the war for their Party affiliation. IBM NY always understood—from the outset in 1933—that it was courting and doing business with the upper echelon of the Nazi Party. The company leveraged its Nazi Party connections to continuously enhance its business relationship with Hitler's Reich, in Germany and throughout Nazi-dominated Europe.

Dehomag and other IBM subsidiaries custom-designed the applications. Its technicians sent mock-ups of punch cards back and forth to Reich offices until the data columns were acceptable, much as any software designer would today. Punch cards could only be designed, printed, and purchased from one source: IBM. The machines were not sold, they were leased, and regularly maintained and upgraded by only one source: IBM. IBM subsidiaries trained the Nazi officers and their surrogates throughout Europe, set up branch offices and local dealerships throughout Nazi Europe staffed by a revolving door of IBM employees, and scoured paper mills to produce as many as 1.5 billion punch cards a year in Germany alone. Moreover, the fragile machines were serviced onsite about once per month, even when that site was in or near a concentration camp. IBM Germany's headquarters in Berlin maintained duplicates of many code books, much as any IBM service bureau today would maintain data back-ups for computers.

I was haunted by a question whose answer has long eluded historians. The Germans always had the lists of Jewish names. Suddenly, a squadron of grim-faced SS would burst into a city square and post a notice de-manding those listed assemble the next day at the train station for depor-tation to the East. But how did the Nazis get the lists? For decades, no one has known. Few have asked.

The answer: IBM Germany's census operations and similar advanced people counting and registration technologies. IBM was founded in 1896 by German inventor Herman Hollerith as a census tabulating company. Census was its business. But when IBM Germany formed its philosophi-cal and technologic alliance with Nazi Germany, census and registration took on a new mission. IBM Germany invented the racial census—listing not just religious affiliation, but bloodline going back generations. This was the Nazi data lust. Not just to count the Jews—but to *identify* them.

People and asset registration was only one of the many uses Nazi Ger-many found for high-speed data sorters. Food allocation was organized around databases, allowing Germany to starve the Jews. Slave labor was identified, tracked, and managed largely through punch cards. Punch cards even made the trains run on time and cataloged their human cargo. German Railway, the *Reichsbahn,* Dehomag's biggest customer, dealt di-rectly with senior management in Berlin. Dehomag maintained punch card installations at train depots across Germany, and eventually across all Europe.

How much did IBM know? Some of it IBM knew on a daily basis throughout the twelve-year Reich. The worst of it IBM preferred not to know—"don't ask, don't tell" was the order of the day. Yet IBM NY officials, and frequently Watson's personal representatives, Harrison Chauncey and Werner Lier, were almost constantly in Berlin or Geneva, monitoring activities, ensuring that the parent company in New York was not cut out of any of the profits or business opportunities Nazism pre-sented. When U.S. law made such direct contact illegal, IBM's Swiss office became the nexus, providing the New York office continuous information and credible deniability.

Certainly, the dynamics and context of IBM's alliance with Nazi Germany changed throughout the twelve-year Reich. I want the full story understood in context. Skipping around in the book will only lead to flawed and erroneous conclusions. So if you intend to skim, or rely on selected sections, please do not read the book at all. If you believe that somehow the Holocaust would not have occurred without IBM, you are more than wrong. The Holocaust would have proceeded—and often did proceed—with simple bullets, death marches, and massacres based on pen and paper persecution. But there is reason to examine the fantastical numbers Hitler achieved in murdering so many millions so swiftly, and identify the crucial role of automation and technology. Accountability is needed.

What made me demand answers to the unasked questions about IBM and the Holocaust? I confronted the reality of IBM's involvement one day in 1993 in Washington at the United States Holocaust Museum. There, in the very first exhibit, an IBM Hollerith D-11 card sorting machine—riddled with circuits, slots, and wires—was prominently displayed. Clearly affixed to the machine's front panel glistened an IBM nameplate. It has since been replaced with a smaller IBM machine because so many people congregated around it, creating a bottleneck. The exhibit explained little more than that IBM was responsible for organizing the census of 1933 that first identified the Jews. IBM had been tight-lipped about its involvement with Nazi Germany. So although 15 million people, including most major Holocaust experts, have seen the display, and in spite of the best efforts of leading museum historians, little more was understood about this provocative display other than the brief curator's description at the exhibit and a few pages of supportive research.

I still remember staring at the machine for an hour, and the moment when I turned to my mother and father who accompanied me to the museum that day and promised them I would discover more.

My parents are Holocaust survivors, uprooted from their homes in Poland. My mother escaped from a boxcar en route to Treblinka, was shot, and then buried in a shallow mass grave. My father had already run away from a guarded line of Jews and discovered her leg protruding from the snow. By moonlight and by courage, these two escapees survived against the cold, the hunger, and the Reich. Standing next to me five decades later, their image within the reflection of the exhibit glass, shrapnel and bullet fragments permanently embedded in their bodies, my parents could only express confusion.

But I had other questions. The Nazis had my parents' names. How?

What was the connection of this gleaming black, beige, and silver machine, squatting silently in this dimly lit museum, to the millions of Jews and other Europeans who were murdered—and murdered not just in a chaotic split second as a casualty of war, but in a grotesque and protracted twelve-year campaign of highly organized humiliation, dehumanization, and then ultimately extermination.

For years after that chance discovery, I was shadowed by the realization that IBM was somehow involved in the Holocaust in technologic ways that had not yet been pieced together. Dots were everywhere. The dots needed to be connected.

Knowing that International Business Machines has always billed itself as a "solutions" company, I understood that IBM does not merely wait for governmental customers to call. IBM has amassed its fortune and reputation precisely because it generally anticipates governmental and corporate needs even before they develop, and then offers, designs, and delivers customized solutions—even if it must execute those technologic solutions with its own staff and equipment. IBM has done so for countless government agencies, corporate giants, and industrial associations.

For years I promised myself I would one day answer the question: How many solutions did IBM provide to Nazi Germany? I knew about the initial solution: the census. Just how far did the solutions go?

In 1998, I began an obsessive quest for answers. Proceeding without any foundation funds, organizational grants, or publisher dollars behind me, I began recruiting a team of researchers, interns, translators, and assistants, all on my own dime.

Soon a network developed throughout the United States, as well as in Germany, Israel, England, Holland, Poland, and France. This network continued to grow as time went on. Holocaust survivors, children of survivors, retirees, and students with no connection to the Holocaust—as well as professional researchers, distinguished archivists and historians, and even former Nuremberg Trial investigators—all began a search for documentation. Ultimately, more than 100 people participated, some for months at a time, some for just a few hours searching obscure Polish documents for key phrases. Not knowing the story, they searched for key words: census, statistics, lists, registrations, railroads, punch cards, and a roster of other topics. When they found them, the material was copied and sent. For many weeks, documents were flowing in at the rate of 100 per day.

Most of my team was volunteers. All of them were sworn to secrecy. Each was shocked and saddened by the implications of the project and intensely motivated. A few said they could not sleep well for days after learning of the connection. I was often sustained by their words of encouragement.

Ultimately, I assembled more than 20,000 pages of documentation from fifty archives, library manuscript collections, museum files, and other repositories. In the process, I accessed thousands of formerly classified State Department, OSS, or other previously restricted government papers. Other obscure documents from European holdings had never been translated or connected to such an inquiry. All these were organized in my own central archive mirroring the original archival source files. We also scanned and translated more than fifty general books and memoirs, as well as contemporary technical and scientific journals covering punch cards and statistics, Nazi publications, and newspapers of the era. All of this material—primary documents, journal articles, newsclips, and book extracts—were cross-indexed by month. We created one manila folder for every month from 1933 to 1950. If a document referred to numerous dates, it was cross-filed in the numerous monthly folders. Then all contents of monthly folders were further cross-indexed into narrow topic threads, such as Warsaw Ghetto, German Census, Bulgarian Railroads, Watson in Germany, Auschwitz, and so on.

Stacks of documents organized into topics were arrayed across my basement floor. As many as six people at a time busily shuttled copies of documents from one topic stack to another from morning until midnight.

One document might be copied into five or six topic stacks. A high-speed copier with a twenty-bin sorter was installed. Just moving from place to place in the basement involved hopscotching around document piles.

None of the 20,000 documents were flash cards. It was much more complex. Examined singly, none revealed their story. Indeed, most of them were profoundly misleading as stand-alone papers. They only assumed their true meaning when juxtaposed with numerous other related documents, often from totally unrelated sources. In other words, the documents were all puzzle pieces—the picture could not be constructed until all the fragments were put together. For example, one IBM report fleetingly referred to a "Mr. Hendricks" as fetching an IBM machine from Dachau. Not until I juxtaposed that document with an obscure military statistics report discovered at the Public Record Office in London did I learn who Sgt. Hendricks really was.

Complicating the task, many of the IBM papers and notes were unsigned or undated carbons, employing deliberate vagueness, code words, catchphrases, or transient corporate shorthand. I had to learn the contemporaneous lexicon of the company to decipher their content. I would study and stare at some individual documents for months until their meaning finally became clear through some other discovered document. For example, I encountered an IBM reference to accumulating "points." Eventually, I discovered that "points" referred to making sales quotas for inclusion in IBM's Hundred Percent Club. IBM maintained sales quotas for all its subsidiaries during the Hitler era.

Sometimes a key revelation did not occur until we tracked a source back three and four stages. For example, I reviewed the English version of the well-known volume *Destruction of the Dutch Jews* by Jacob Presser. I found nothing on my subject. I then asked my researchers in Holland to check the Dutch edition. They found a single unfootnoted reference to a punch card system. Only by checking Presser's original typescript did we discover a marginal notation that referenced a Dutch archival document that led to a cascade of information on the Netherlands. In reviewing the Romanian census, I commissioned the translation of a German statistician's twenty-page memoir to discover a single sentence confirming that punch cards were used in Romania. That information was juxtaposed against an IBM letter confirming the company was moving machinery from war-torn Poland into Romania to aid Romanian census operations.

In the truest sense, the story of IBM and the Holocaust has been shattered into thousands of shards. Only by piecing them all together did I erect a towering picture window permitting me to view what really occurred. That verified account is retold in this book.

In my pursuit, I received extraordinary cooperation from every private, public, and governmental source in every country. Sadly, the only refusal came from IBM itself, which rebuffed my requests for access to documents and interviews. I was not alone. Since WWII, the company has steadfastly refused to cooperate with outside authors. Virtually every recent book on IBM, whether written by esteemed business historians or ex-IBM employees, includes a reference to the company's refusal to cooperate with the author in any way. Ultimately, I was able to arrange proper access. Hundreds of IBM documents were placed at my disposal. I read them all.

Behind every text footnote is a file folder with all the hardcopy documentation needed to document every sentence in this book at a moment's notice. Moreover, I assembled a team of hair-splitting, nitpicking, adversarial researchers and archivists to review each and every sentence, collectively ensuring that each fact and fragment of a fact was backed up with the necessary black and white documents.

In reconstructing the facts, I was guided on every page by two principles: context and consequences. For instance, although I enjoyed access to volumes of diplomatic and intelligence information, I was careful to concentrate on what was known publicly in the media about atrocities and anti-Jewish conditions in Europe. For this reason, readers will notice an extraordinary reliance on articles in the *New York Times*. I quote the *New York Times* not because it was the newspaper of record in America, but because IBM executives, including Thomas Watson, were headquartered in New York. Had they lived in Chicago, I would have quoted the *Chicago Tribune*. Had they lived in Cleveland, I would have quoted the *Cleveland Plain Dealer*.

Readers will also notice that I frequently relied upon reproducing the exact words the principals themselves used in telegrams, letters, or telephone transcripts. Readers can judge for themselves exactly what was said in what context.

With few exceptions (see Bibliographical Note), the Holocaust literature is virtually devoid of mention of the Hollerith machines—in spite of its high profile display at the United States Holocaust Memorial Museum. Historians should not be defensive about the absence of even a mention. The public documents were all there, but there are literally millions of frames and pages of Holocaust documents in the leading archives of the world. Many of these materials had simply never been accessed, many have not been available, and some are based on false chronologies or appear to be corporate minutia. Others were well known, such as Heydrich's 1939 instruction on concentrating Jewish communities near railroad tracks, but the repeated references to census operations were simply overlooked.

More than the obscurity of the documents, such an investigation would require expertise in the history of the Holocaust before and after the war began, the history of post–Industrial Revolution mechanization, the history of technology, and more specifically the archaic punch card system, as well as an understanding of Reich economics, multinational corporations, and a grasp of financial collusion. In addition, one would need to juxtapose the information for numerous countries before assembling the complete picture. Just as important is the fact that until I examined the IBM documents, that half of the screen was totally obscured. Again, the documents do not speak by themselves, only in ensemble. I was fortunate to have an understanding of Reich economics and multinational commerce from my earlier book, *The Transfer Agreement,* as well as a background in the computer industry, and years of experience as an investigative journalist specializing in corporate misconduct. I approached this project as a typical if not grandiose investigation of corporate conduct with one dramatic difference: the conduct impacted on the lives and deaths of millions.

Gathering my pre-publication expert reviewers was a process in itself. I sought not only the leading historians of the Holocaust, but niche experts on such topics as Vichy France, Romania, and census and persecution. But I also consulted business historians, technical specialists, accountants, legal sources on reparations and corporate war crimes, an investigator from the original Nuremberg prosecution team, a wartime military intelligence technology expert, and even an ex-FBI special agent with expertise in financial crimes. I wanted the prismatic view of all.

Changing perspective was perhaps the dominant reason why the relationship between IBM and the Holocaust has never been explored. When I first wrote *The Transfer Agreement* in 1984, no one wanted to focus on assets. Now everyone talks about the assets. The formative years for most Holocaust scholarship was before the computer age, and well before the Age of Information. Everyone now possesses an understanding of how technology can be utilized in the affairs of war and peace. We can now go back and look at the same documentation in a new light.

Many of us have become enraptured in the Age of Computerization and the Age of Information. I know I have. But now I am consumed with a new awareness that, for me, as the son of Holocaust survivors, brings me to a whole new consciousness. I call it the Age of Realization, as we look back and examine technology's wake. Unless we understand how the Nazis acquired the names, more lists will be compiled against more people.

The story of IBM and the Holocaust is just a beginning. I could have written twenty books with the documents I uncovered, one for every country in Europe. I estimate there are 100,000 more documents scattered in basements and corporate archives around the United States and Europe. Corporate archivists should take note: these documents are related to a crime and must not be moved, tampered with, or destroyed. They must be transferred to those appropriate archival institutions that can assure immediate and undelayed access to scholars and war crimes prosecutors so the accountability process can continue (see Major Sources).

Only through exposing and examining what really occurred can the world of technology finally adopt the well-worn motto: *Never Again*.

PART II

The Korean War

Introduction to I. F. Stone's

The Hidden History of the Korean War

WHEN THE KOREAN WAR broke out in 1950, the legendary American journalist I. F. Stone at first accepted the official U.S. version of events, believing that the cause of war was unprovoked aggression by the North Koreans with the support of the Russians. But working in Paris during the winter of 1950–1951, Stone read the British and French press and noticed discrepancies between the communiqués issues by U.S. military headquarters in Tokyo and the accounts of reliable reporters. He inquired further into these discrepancies, which led him to reassess the war, concluding that the U.S. likely knew of the North Korean military buildup and that South Korea and Taiwan provoked the North to attack, arguments he put forward in his *The Hidden History of the Korean War*.

When the book was published in the U.S. in 1952, it met with an almost complete press blackout and boycott. Che Guevara later told Stone in an interview that the U.S. embassy in Mexico had bought up and junked all the copies it could lay its hands on of the Spanish translation of *Hidden History*. Historians such as Bruce Cumings have defended Stone's controversial views: "If Stone's theses remain unproved on a possible provocation of the Korean War, or a tacit agreement to let the attack happen, no honest historian today can do anything other than withhold judgment on these dangling questions."

More recently, Stone's interpretations have been brought into question by newly released documents from Soviet archives that support the theory that the attack by the North was premeditated and approved by

Stalin. Such conflicting interpretations prove how hard it is to get to the bottom of secret history.

Born in Philadelphia in 1907, in his long and distinguished career, Stone was a reporter, editorial writer, and columnist for the *Philadelphia Daily Record, PM,* the *New York Post, Star* and *Daily Compass.* In 1940 he became the Washington editor of *The Nation.* In 1953, inspired by the achievements of George Seldes and his political weekly *In Fact,* he began his own newsletter *I. F. Stone's Weekly,* which achieved an international reputation for independence and investigation until ill-health forced him to cease the weekly's publication in 1971. Author of some ten books, Stone learned ancient Greek after his retirement and wrote *The Trial of Socrates.*

ADDITIONAL SOURCES

Cottrell, Robert C. *Izzy: A Biography of I. F. Stone.* Piscataway, N.J.: Rutgers University Press, 1994.

Cumings, Bruce. *Liberation and the Emergence of Separate Regimes, 1945–1947,* vol. 1, *The Origins of the Korean War.* Princeton, N.J.: Princeton University Press, 1981.

———. *The Roaring of the Cataract, 1947–1950,* vol. 2, *The Origins of the Korean War.* Princeton, N.J.: Princeton University Press, 1990.

I. F. Stone. *I. F. Stone's Weekly Reader.* New York: Random House, 1973.

I. F. Stone

Hiding the Lull, Lost and Found,
Van Fleet Sums Up

THE HIDDEN HISTORY OF THE KOREAN WAR, 1952

HIDING THE LULL

CLAUSEWITZ'S OBSERVATION THAT war is only politics carried on by other means was never better illustrated than in Korea. Were MacArthur allowed to evacuate his troops, the humiliation of defeat would make peace almost impossible to negotiate. Were MacArthur to stay in the peninsula, however, and permit a lull in the fighting, it would become almost impossible to keep peace from breaking out. How could negotiations be prevented if public opinion at home began to realize that very little fighting was going on anyway? And how to prevail upon the United Nations to condemn the Chinese as aggressors if it began to appear that they had ceased "aggressing"?

From the moment MacArthur was ordered to stop the withdrawal, his object was to find the enemy and resume the fighting. As long as there was fighting, the "security" of his fighting forces could be cited as paramount considerations, overriding any civilian political directives. Under cover of the plea of military necessity, the commander in the field could make the decisions. But unless battle, or the appearance of battle, were maintained, the initiative would slip from his hands. This is the key to events from the about-face in January, 1951, to the second crossing of the Parallel in force early in April of that year.

One of the five principles put forward by the UN's cease-fire negotiating committee on January 11 said, "When a cease-fire occurs . . . either as a result of a formal arrangement *or . . . as a result of a lull in hostilities . . .*

advantage should be taken of it to pursue consideration of further steps to be taken for the restoration of peace." (Italics added.) The lull for which the United Nations hoped was the lull its military commander feared. MacArthur waged slow-motion war, stretching out a minimum of combat for a maximum of effect, hinting darkly every few days of enemy traps which were never sprung and enemy offensives which were never launched. "No one," he declared flamboyantly on January 20, when further retreat had been inescapably countermanded, "is going to drive us into the sea." There didn't seem to be anybody around.

This farce no doubt turned stomachs at the White House, the State Department, and even the Pentagon. Some twenty years earlier, Prussian military aristocrats and sophisticated Rhineland millionaires felt a similar distaste for the perhaps more vulgar but equally shrewd antics of Adolf Hitler. They swallowed rapidly and went along with Hitler. And in this case the White House, the State Department, and the Pentagon went along with MacArthur. During the latter half of January, the United States was threatening to withdraw from the United Nations unless the General Assembly obediently condemned Peking as an aggressor, and MacArthur was trying unsuccessfully to find some substantial body of enemy troops which might oblige with a little aggression. Though something close to a *de facto* cease-fire existed in Korea, MacArthur kept on valiantly shooting at an enemy who wasn't there, at least in any sizable quantity. Without that continual rumble in the press dispatches, the reluctant diplomats at Lake Success might not have been stampeded.

The lull was difficult to hide, but MacArthur managed, if not to hide it, then at least to confuse the public mind as to its duration and significance. On January 12, when the British Commonwealth parley urged direct talks with Stalin and Mao Tse-tung, a State Department spokesman said coldly, "We will not participate in these talks until the Chinese Communists have stopped fighting." They had. On the central front MacArthur's troops, as we have seen, were fighting North Koreans, not Chinese. And the day after the State Department spokesman rebuffed the idea of direct talks, an Eighth Army communiqué disclosed that there had been nothing but patrol action for eight days in the west. But these admissions were always phrased so as to create rather than allay apprehension. The wording was characteristic. "Despite eight days of nothing more than patrol action in the west, possibility of a major Communist attack there is not discounted." The UN troops seemed always about to be overwhelmed. Catastrophe with MacArthur, like prosperity with his old chief Herbert Hoover in the early thirties, was always just-around-the-corner.

On January 20, when MacArthur said no one was going to drive him into the sea, the communiqués still showed "little or no enemy contact." Fifth Air Force fighters and bombers complained of "a paucity of enemy troops as targets," having flown 260 sorties in the battle area and killed only forty of the enemy, an average of less than one enemy casualty for every six sorties—hardly a profitable operation. But MacArthur warned that "the entire military might of Communist China is available against this relatively small command" and "only by maneuver" could the allies "avoid the hazards confronting inferior forces in face of the masses of a determined enemy." It always seemed quite a miracle that MacArthur's little band survived at all, though these masses never seemed to move out of the headlines.

Alarms were audible in the briefings and the headlines, even when the communiqués showed that little actually was going on. Attention was focused on a "lull" only when it was—almost triumphantly—announced that it had at last been broken. The break in the lull always of course confirmed the most recent prediction of an enemy offensive, but the battle reports when read closely usually showed little sign of enemy masses "U.N. TROOPS YIELD ICHON AS LULL ENDS ON KOREAN FRONTS," the New York Times proclaimed on January 22. "ICHON, WONJU ARE GIVEN UP BY U.N. FORCES," said the Paris edition of the New York Herald Tribune the same day; "CHINESE ATTACK 12 HOURS AT ICHON IN THEIR FIRST BIG ACTION SINCE SEOUL." The first "big" action since Seoul—almost three weeks—was an attack "by an estimated three enemy platoons." The affair at Wonju was an American drive into the town against an "estimated" enemy regiment which seized Wonju the day before "but failed to follow up," said the United Press from Tokyo, "with an anticipated drive." The enemy had a habit of disappointing these anticipations; the UN column entered the town, held the Wonju air strip for three hours, exchanged fire with the enemy, and left at dusk. The three platoons at Ichon were termed Chinese, but it was again admitted that on the central front the fighting had been "carried out principally by North Korean units."

Rarely has an aggressor shown himself so perversely unwilling to advance. Never has an aggressor so stubbornly resisted victory by holding back his overwhelming hordes from the eager victim. While the United States Senate was unanimously passing a resolution on January 23 demanding that the United Nations brand China an aggressor, the UN forces were probing deep into a no man's land, reoccupying one ghost town after another without finding the aggressor. On the 25th an Allied column had penetrated past Wonju into Hoengsong only thirty-three miles below the Parallel without being able to report more than "two sharp fights with an enemy force estimated at more than one company." The lull was becoming noticeable at Lake Success. Sir Benegal N. Rau, fighting desperately for peace, said the lull "may not be without significance." There was desperation reflected in next day's headlines from the curiously unembattled battlefront: "U.N. SHIPS BOMBARD INCHON," said the *New York Times*, "AS PATROLS SEARCH FOR ENEMY." MacArthur's search for the enemy was disrupting the UN's search for peace. If someone at Lake Success had dared challenge the supreme commander's activity, even the constant plea of military necessity could hardly have covered this frantic effort to move his troops within shooting range of that elusive enemy.

While the United States put the pressure on at Lake Success to brand the Chinese as aggressors, Tokyo Headquarters was hard put to maintain the semblance of major combat. On January 28, with UN patrols only fourteen miles from Seoul, enemy opposition was said to be "hardening," and a "major clash" was said to be "in sight." On the 29th "approximately 1,000 of the enemy" actually turned up in a night attack and "MASSING OF FOE" was "REPORTED." On January 30 the United Nations forces were "seemingly coming into contact with advance posts of the Chinese and North Korean defense." Next day the Political and Security Committee of the United Nations voted 44–7 to brand China an aggressor and initiate a study of sanctions. On February 1, the day the Assembly had to vote, fighting reached a new "intensity." Along the front generally "enemy resistance" was described as "long and sporadic," while at one point an attack by "an estimated two enemy regiments" was reported, the largest concentration of enemy troops actually encountered in many days. The Air Force listed among its own exploits against aggression that day "a strike on two enemy-held villages east of Seoul" which "destroyed or damaged 1,200 bags of rice and hit several buildings." It was in the face of such mounting evidence that the Assembly formally ratified the finding of aggression. International law and order were vindicated.

Lost and Found

FOR THREE WEEKS," said the *New York Times* war summary on February 4, "UN patrols have been probing for the main body of the Chinese army. Last week—after a fifteen-mile advance through no man's land—the UN forces finally found it. The Chinese were dug in along a forty-mile line, stretching from just south of Seoul on the west, along the southern bank of the Han River, up to the central mountain spine." Tokyo Headquarters was proved wrong again. Advancing patrols found that no man's land extended to the very gates of Seoul. "YONGDUNGPO QUIET DISTURBS CAPTORS" said the *New York Times* headline on the battlefront dispatch describing the taking of Seoul's industrial suburb six days later. The troops marched unopposed "through silent empty streets, . . . past bomb-wrecked factories and shrapnel-pocked houses." When Seoul itself was entered "no enemy contact" was reported. Headquarters hinted that the enemy had probably pulled back to mass on the central front; those Chinese always seemed to be massing—in Headquarters estimates—where the fighting wasn't.

Though the enemy was difficult to find, he was being slaughtered in astronomical numbers. "Enemy troops in almost full division strength fell before the UN onslaught each day this week," said a report from Eighth Army Headquarters on February 10. "An enemy division is generally estimated to contain 6,000 troops." How were they able to kill so many when there was so little contact? The paradox was not made any clearer by an examination of the daily communiqués during this period. The day with the biggest number of announced ground casualties was February 4, when 8,635 casualties were said to have been inflicted. But the communiqué which gave this figure spoke of limited advances against "moderate resistance" at one point and "light" resistance at another. It spoke of six enemy attacks along the front, two by unspecified numbers, two by an estimated two enemy companies each, one by an estimated enemy company, and one by "two enemy platoons." In no case did the communiqué claim to have annihilated these enemy forces; it only reported that they were repulsed or contained. How, then, did MacArthur's forces manage to inflict such huge casualties?

Eighth Army Headquarters claimed to have killed or wounded 69,500 of the enemy from January 25 to midnight February 9, an average of about 4,600—or, as headquarters put it, "almost" a "full division" a day. Comparisons with the peak battles of World Wars I and II will indicate what a feat this was, if true. Divisions vary a good deal in size, but it is worth noting that in the great Battle of Verdun in 1916, one of the most terrible battles of attrition in history, the Germans lost forty-three and a half divisions from February 21 to July 1, an average of ten divisions a month. The rate claimed in those ten days before reaching Seoul would be the equivalent of thirty divisions a month.

If the figures given out that day at Lieutenant General Matthew Ridgway's Headquarters were correct, then that push through the no man's land south of Seoul must rank with the Battle of Stalingrad, the climax of World War II, the point at which the German armies began the long retreat back to defeat. The high point at Stalingrad was the twenty-day period from January 10 to January 30, when Marshal von Paulus was taken prisoner and his famous Sixth Army destroyed. The Red Army claimed in those twenty days to have killed 100,000 German officers and men. That is an average of 5,000 a day. The average of the estimates given in the communiqués for the first ten days of February before Seoul adds up just a shade better than that—to 5,510 casualties a day! Were MacArthur's generals military marvels or military Münchhausens?

These figures did not seem so strange to a newspaper-reading public in America which had been led to picture Chinese hordes "marching abreast" and "in human waves" against American guns, in supposed "Oriental" disregard of their own lives. Belief in fairy tales is not limited to childhood. The experts paused to wonder, but expert analysis does not make headlines.

MacArthur Headquarters had claimed to have killed or captured 134,616 Chinese since mid-October, about 36,000 a month—not a bad total for an army which had spent most of its time in full retreat and out of contact with the enemy. Hanson Baldwin in the *New York Times* of February 11 wrote that the "only exact" part of this estimate was the number of prisoners: "We knew we had exactly 616 Chinese Communist prisoners." He did not think that number in four months was "encouraging," comparing as it did with 8,531 Americans listed as "missing." Baldwin assumed that most of these "missing are probably prisoners." Were Americans more easily captured than Chinese? Or were there errors in the count of the casualties? Could it be that so few Chinese Communists had been taken prisoner because so few had been fighting in Korea?

Figures like these—and the obscene advertising slogan "Operation Killer" which grew out of them—were part of military operations which might have seemed almost comic, were it not for the effect on the Korean people. If there was any reality in "Operation Killer" it lay in what was happening to the Koreans and their country as MacArthur's troops maneuvered up and down the South and finally crossed the Parallel in force again in April, without once meeting that major enemy offensive which continued to be predicted "Reports of Chinese concentrations continue to come in," the military correspondent of the London *Times* reported as late as April 2. "Opinion in Washington expects a strong hostile offensive to be launched in the near future. This belief naturally damps hopes of any successful negotiation, at all events for some time to come." It must also have damped the hopes of Koreans north and south for some end to the frightful process of their liberation.

The Mongols, to whom Truman compared the Chinese Communists in calling for a "moral mobilization" against them, could not have hoped to match the depredations of Korea's liberators. Not only the industrial potential of the cities but the poorest possessions of the countryside were ravaged. "Allied troops in the Wonju sector," the London *Times* reported on January 15, "pursuing a scorched-earth policy, have burned twenty-two villages and set fire to three hundred haystacks." A policy which is truly heroic when practiced by a bravely resisting people on their own homes becomes as truly atrocious when practiced by a powerful "ally" on a helpless partner.

An article published by the London *Times* on November 16, 1950, showed that the North Korean command rejected a scorched-earth program and left the countryside over which they retreated little touched by war. The contrast recalls the legend about Solomon and the two mothers who each claimed the same child; he found the true one by suggesting that the child be cut in half and divided between them. Korean opinion, to which so little attention was paid by either side, was no doubt heartily sick of both. A *New York Times* correspondent from Taegu described it as "dislike and distrust of the Communists, with no great love for the South Korea regime." But the same correspondent noted that "when the Koreans saw that the Communists had left their homes and schools standing in retreat while the United Nations troops, fighting with much more destructive tools, left only blackened spots where towns once stood, the Communists even in retreat chalked up moral victories."

Ground troops in retreat left ghost towns in their wake, while terror rained down upon the land from the skies. As early as September 1950, Far East Air Forces Headquarters announced that the first stage of its bombing program, aimed at industrial installations, was complete, and that there was now a "paucity" of industrial targets for bombers. One of the problems which began to trouble the Air Force in Korea, judging by the communiqués, was that there was nothing left to destroy. These communiqués must be read by anyone who wants a complete history of the Korean War. They are literally horrifying.

"Crews on B-26 light bombers of the 452nd Bomb Wing," said the Fifth Air Force operational summary at 5 P.M. Tokyo time, January 31, "reported a scarcity of targets at Hamhung today." According to Staff Sergeant Clark V. Watson of Hutchinson, Kansas, "It's hard to find good targets, for we have burned out almost everything."

Other Air Force units were still managing. "The Eighth Fighter Bomber Wing F-80 jets," said the same communiqué, "reported large fires in villages in the western sector following attacks with rockets, napalm, and machine guns. A village was hard hit south of Chorwon." *Why* was not explained. Whether the village represented some military objective was not stated. Sometimes a possible military objective seemed to have been hit by accident. In the same communiqué it was announced that the navigator of one of the light bombers that attacked Pongung near Hamhung reported: "One of our napalms must have hit a gas or oil dump. It landed and there was a big belch of orange flame and black smoke." Peasants do not detonate so colorfully.

Sometimes the reason offered for bombing a defenseless village was that it was "enemy-occupied." The same communiqué said, "One flight dive-bombed the enemy-occupied village of Takchong and then rocketed and strafed the area, reporting several buildings destroyed and large fires started." Were all villages in enemy territory regarded as enemy-occupied? The ratio of civilian to soldier dead in these raids must have been very large. This same communiqué said the "largest claim of troops casualties inflicted" in the day's raids were 100 enemy troops killed or wounded by one group of planes. Even in a small village more civilians than that could be killed in one raid.

A complete indifference to noncombatants was reflected in the way villages were given "saturation treatment" with napalm to dislodge a few soldiers. George Barrett, a front-line correspondent of the *New York Times*, drew an unforgettable picture of such a village in a dispatch early in February. He was with an armored column which "took" a village north of Anyang and found what he described as "a macabre tribute to the totality of modern war":

A napalm raid hit the village three or four days ago when the Chinese were holding up the advance, and nowhere in the village have they buried the dead because there is nobody left to do so. This correspondent came across one old woman, the only one who seemed to be left alive, dazedly hanging up some clothes in a blackened courtyard filled with the bodies of four members of her family.

The inhabitants throughout the village and in the fields were caught and killed and kept the exact postures they had held when the napalm struck—a man about to get on his bicycle, fifty boys and girls playing in an orphanage, a housewife strangely unmarked, holding in *her hand a page torn from a Sears-Roebuck catalogue crayoned at Mail Order No. 3,811,294 for a $2.98 "bewitching bed jacket—coral." There must be almost two hundred dead in the tiny hamlet.*

Such were the realities behind efficient notations like the following, in Fifth Air Force operational summary February 4: "Other F-80s from the Eighth reported excellent results in attacks on villages near Chorwon, Kumchon, Chunchon, and Chunchon-ni. The villages were hit with bombs as well as rockets and napalm." The results were . . . "excellent." Not all the reports were so brisk. There were some passages about these raids on villages which reflected, not the pity which human feeling called for, but a kind of gay moral imbecility, utterly devoid of imagination—as if the fliers were playing in a bowling alley, with villages for pins.

An example was Fifth Air Force operational summary 5 P.M. Tokyo time Friday, February 2. This told how the two-man crew of a downed Mosquito patrol plane was rescued by helicopter "from the midst of an enemy troop concentration near Hongchon." Some fifty enemy troops had been sighted and between 300 and 400 foxholes reported so it was decided to give the whole area "saturation" treatment.

A mass flight of twenty-four F-51 mustangs poured 5,000 gallons of napalm over the area. The flight leader, Lieutenant Colonel James Kirkendall, of Duluth, Minnesota—the Air Force communiqués gave names, as if to foster individual pride in such handiwork—reported that "his flight hit every village and building in the area." Perhaps it was some uneasy qualm which led him to add, "There was plenty of evidence of troops living in the houses there." The evidence itself was not disclosed. It might have been hard to find, for Colonel Kirkendall added that "smoke blanketed the area, rising to over 4,000 feet when they left."

His subordinates were cheerful. Captain Everett L. Hundley of Kansas City, Kansas, who led one group of four planes, was quoted by the communiqué as saying, "You can kiss that group of villages good-bye." Captain Hugh Boniford of Montgomery, Alabama, said he saw "tracks and other evidence of enemy activity in the area." He added, "That place can really be called devastated now."

Captain Boniford's remark applies to all Korea.

Van Fleet Sums Up

A WORLD in which neither side could impose terms on the other was a world in which peaceful settlement—at least settlement without war—was dictated by military realities. As this book went to press there seemed to be a growing awareness of this in every capital but Washington. Who started the war and how was still a mystery, as it is still a mystery just how we got into the Spanish-American War. In fact, George F. Kennan, the newly appointed American Ambassador to Moscow, spoke of the Spanish-American War—in his astute and sophisticated lectures on American foreign policy at the University of Chicago early in 1951—in terms which may some day be used of the Korean War. "We can only say," Kennan declared, discussing the war and its extension to the Philippines by Dewey's attack on the Spanish fleet in Manila, "that it looks very much as though, in this case, the action of the United States government had been determined primarily on the basis of a very able and very quiet intrigue by a few strategically placed persons in Washington, an intrigue which received absolution, forgiveness, and a sort of public blessing by virtue of war hysteria." No one really seemed to know just how the United States had been drawn into the Korean War, but as it continued there was less and less doubt as to who wanted to stop it and who wanted to continue it. Chiang Kai-shek and Syngman Rhee, its principal political beneficiaries in Asia, still wanted it to continue. John Foster Dulles and Governor Dewey were campaigning for broader American involvement in the Far East, along the lines of the Pacific Pact that Chiang had long been urging. Truman and Acheson were their prisoners, sometimes eagerly, sometimes hesitantly, as in a sense the whole American economy had become the prisoner of war fever and war addiction.

An almost hysterical fear of peace made itself felt when the shooting stopped on November 28, 1951, the day after agreement on a cease-fire line, the day when Red troops played volleyball within range of UN trenches. There was an almost frantic reaction from Key West, where the president was vacationing. Truman showed himself more insistent even than General Van Fleet that the fighting in Korea must continue until every last item in the interminable negotiations had finally been thrashed out. Again there were new political obstacles. The day the negotiators finally agreed on a cease-fire line, Eisenhower in Rome was pleading with the North Atlantic Council for a speedup in Europe's rearmament. The *Wall Street Journal,* which had been carrying on an admirable fight for a saner foreign policy, dryly underscored the difficulty in an editorial on Korea and Rome: "It is understandable that peace in Korea, or even talk of peace, should make people—in the United States as well as Europe—less eager to sacrifice civilian standards for arms . . . if there is peace in Korea the position of the United States as the prime mover of European defense will be more difficult—and much more costly."

One could almost feel the relief in Washington as the truce talks bogged down again in an endless wrangle over air bases and the exchange of prisoners. A month earlier Tokyo Headquarters had been worrying noisily in public about the alleged mistreatment of American prisoners by the Reds. Now it was worrying, not about speeding up the exchange and releasing our prisoners from the enemy, but about "saving" Red prisoners who did not wish to be repatriated. Their safety seemingly took precedence over the now forgotten danger to Americans in the hands of "Communist brutes." Tokyo Headquarters was still dragging out an obscene farce while Truman in his conversations with Churchill paved the way for extension of the war to China. "The United States," the *Wall Street Journal* reported from Washington January 17, "has wrung an informal okay from reluctant Britain, for American bombing and naval blockade of Red China if Korean talks fail." The dispatch showed that American military men were still scheming toward a "limited" war with China which would somehow involve neither American ground troops nor war with Russia.

This was MacArthur's dream. "The MacArthur plan for dealing with Chinese Communists is being dusted off again by United States military planners," *U. S. News and World Report* said in its issue of February 1, 1952, "just about one year after the General was fired for suggesting it." But it was now MacArthur who lagged behind Truman. *U. S. News* added, "General MacArthur himself feels that the delay of one year, permitting Communists to build up, makes the plan he suggested out of date." Unfortunately the same political and economic factors that pressed for the Korean War now pressed for its extension. Chiang Kai-shek and Rhee still feared that peace would be the end of them. Dulles feared that peace would fatally interfere with the plan to rebuild the old Axis powers for a new anti-Soviet crusade. Truman and Acheson feared that peace would confront them anew in an election year with the need to face up to the Far Eastern problem and recognize the government of Communist China. America's allies were growing restive. Britain and France with the rest of Western Europe and practically the whole of the Middle East abstained or voted "No" when Chiang with American support put through the United Nations General Assembly in Paris a resolution condemning the Soviet Union in effect for Chiang's own richly deserved fall from power. It looked as if extension of the war, a new provocation, was necessary if the Cold War front was to be held together.

While the arms race and the attendant inflation were ruining America's allies, American leadership was still gripped by dread of the consequences of peace upon the economy. This dread was dictating the actions of the politicians and business leaders. An economy accustomed to ever larger injections of inflationary narcotic trembled at the thought that its deadly stimulant might be shut off. The road to war was more than ever the path of least resistance in 1952. If peace came in Korea, there might be new Koreas in the making in Indochina and Burma. If not there, then with American troops in Korea some new "incident" might start up the war again. The dominant trend in American political, economic, and military thinking was fear of peace. General Van Fleet summed it all up in speaking to a visiting Filipino delegation in January 1952: "Korea has been a blessing. There had to be a Korea either here or some place in the world." In this simple-minded confession lies the key to the hidden history of the Korean War.

NOTES

[Editor's Note: Reference numbers have been updated to reflect the page numbers of this anthology.]

HIDING THE LULL

Page 33, line 21. *New York Times,* January 12, 1951.

Page 34, line 5. *New York Times,* January 20, 1951.

Page 34, line 27. London *Daily Mail,* January 13, 1951. (Paris edition.)

Page 34, line 34. Release No. 124, *New York Times,* January 14, 1951.

Page 35, lines 6, 11. *New York Times,* January 21, 1951.

Page 35, line 27. *New York Times,* January 22, 1951. (Dispatch from Tokyo.)

Page 35, lines 30, page 36, line 1. *New York Herald Tribune,* January 22, 1951. (Paris edition.)

Page 36, line 8. *New York Times,* January 23 and 24, 1951.

Page 36, lines 11, 14, 16. *New York Times,* January 26, 1951.

Page 36, line 25. *New York Times,* January 28, 1951.

Page 36, line 26. *New York Times,* January 29, 1951.

Page 36, line 29. *New York Times,* January 30, 1951.

Page 36, line 34; page 37, line 2. *New York Times,* February 2, 1951.

LOST AND FOUND

Page 38, line 1. *New York Times,* "News Of The Week In Review," February 4, 1951.

Page 38, lines 11, 13. *New York Times,* February 11, 1951.

Page 38, line 18. *New York Times,* February 10, 1951.

Page 39, line 1. Release No. 170, *New York Times,* February 6, 1951.

Page 39, line 10. *New York Times,* February 10, 1951.

Page 40, line 30. *New York Times,* December 24, 1951.

Page 41, line 11. *New York Times,* February 21, 1951.

Page 41, line 21. *New York Times,* September 15, 1950.

Page 41, line 27. *New York Times,* February 1, 1951.

Page 42, line 25. *New York Times,* February 9, 1951.

Page 43, line 5. *New York Times,* February 5, 1951.

Page 43, line 13. *New York Times,* February 3, 1951.

VAN FLEET SUMS UP

Page 44, line 10. George F. Kennan, *American Diplomacy: 1900–1950* (Chicago: University of Chicago Press, 1951), p. 14.

Page 45, line 16. *Wall Street Journal,* November 27, 1951.

Page 46, line 35. United Press dispatch from Eighth Army Headquarters, *New York Journal-American,* January 19, 1952.

PART III

Atomic Secrets

Introduction to "The Venona Cables"

The February 9, 1944 Cable:
Klaus Fuchs and Harry Gold

The September 21, 1944 Cable:
The Rosenbergs and the Greenglasses

The November 12, 1944 Cable:
Theodore Alvin Hall and Saville Sax

O N FEBRUARY 1, 1943, the U.S. Army's Signal Intelligence Service, a forerunner of the National Security Agency, began a small, secret program, later codenamed Venona, to decipher messages sent by Soviet diplomats from their posts abroad back to Moscow. Within a few years, American code breakers were able decrypt parts of KGB messages and the Venona operation continued until 1980. In 1995, at the insistence of Democratic Senator Daniel Patrick Moynihan, vice chair of the Senate Select Committee on Intelligence, the National Security Agency (NSA) released the first batch of decrypted and translated messages. Approximately 3,000 Venona messages have been released so far. These messages, wrote historians John Earl Haynes and Harvey Klehr, "may change the way we think about twentieth-century American history."

Among the Venona revelations is information about Soviet attempts to gain atomic capability, particularly the role of Klaus Fuchs, a British physicist, born in Germany, who may have been the Soviet Union's most important spy. Fuchs worked on the British atomic project from 1941 to 1943, then worked for the American nuclear program at Los Alamos during the war, all the time passing top secret information to the Soviet Union. The February 1944 message from the KGB in New York to Moscow confirms that Fuchs, code-named Rest, newly arrived in the United States, had established contact with Harry Gold, code-named Gus, who was to become his courier and main liaison with the Soviets, and that Fuchs had provided information about the structure of the atomic bomb project and uranium separation. After the war, Fuchs returned to England where, relying on Venona information provided by the FBI, MI5 officers interrogated him and he confessed in 1950 to his role in supplying covert information.

Fuch's confession led the FBI to Gold, who in turn led the FBI to David Greenglass, who implicated his wife Ruth and his brother-in-law, Julius Rosenberg, code-named Liberal. Later, the Greenglasses extended the circle to Ethel Rosenberg, Julius's wife. The September 21, 1944, Venona cable reveals the step that eventually led to the arrest of the Rosenbergs, namely the recruitment of Ruth Greenglass, Ethel's sister-in-law. The Rosenbergs were the only people put to death in America for espionage during the Cold War. Their electrocution in 1953 was one of the most controversial events in American history. Defenders claimed that they were innocent victims of the anti-communist hysteria of the 1950s. Accusers insisted they had passed atomic bomb secrets to the Soviets. During the trial, the government, as in other cases, did not reveal the Venona material, fearing it would compromise the top secret project. Did Venona support the innocence or guilt of the Rosenbergs? The messages reveal that Julius participated in low-level espionage rather than in what J. Edgar Hoover called "the crime of the century" Ethel was simply an accessory to her husband's activities. Conservative historians Haynes and Klehr concluded that if the Venona information had been made public at the time, it is less likely that the Rosenbergs would have been executed.

The final cable included here is the first of eight decrypted KGB messages that mention Theodore Alvin Hall, a brilliant American physicist who passed crucial atomic information to the Soviets from Los Alamos, where he began research in 1944 when he was only eighteen years old.

Hall's case is unusual. Hall and his courier Saville Sax were never arrested. But enough information was revealed for *Washington Post* reporter Michael Dobbs to uncover Hall's identity in 1996, trace him to his home in Cambridge, England, and break the story of Hall's espionage.

In their book *Bombshell,* Joseph Albright and Marcia Kunstel quote Hall as once suggesting that he should turn himself in. "Don't pin it all on the Rosenbergs," he said, "because I was more responsible than they were."

ADDITIONAL SOURCES

Albright, Joseph and Marcia Kunstel. *Bombshell: The Secret Story of America's Unknown Atomic Spy Conspiracy*. New York: Times Books, 1997.

Benson, Robert Louis and Michael Warner, eds. *Venona: Soviet Espionage and the American Response 1939–1957*. Washington, D.C.: National Security Agency and Central Intelligence Agency, 1996.

Haynes, John Earl and Harvey Klehr. *Venona: Decoding Soviet Espionage in America*. New Haven and London: Yale University Press, 1999.

"Secrets, Lies, and Atomic Spies." *NOVA*, original broadcast, February 5, 2002.

Venona Documents Released: www.nsa.gov/docs/Venona/venona_docs.html

VENONA

~~TOP SECRET~~

USSR

Ref. No.: ▓▓▓▓▓

Issued : ▓▓▓▓ /25/6/1973

Copy No.: 301

MEETING BETWEEN "GUS'" AND "REST"; WORK ON ENORMOUS
(1944)

From: NEW YORK

To: MOSCOW

No.: 195   9th February 1944

Personal to VIKTOR[i].

    In reply to No. 302[ii].

    On 5th February a meeting took place between "GUS'"[iii] and "REST"[iv]. Be-
forehand GUS' was given a detailed briefing by us. REST greeted him pleasantly but
was rather cautious at first, [1 group unrecovered] the discussion GUS' satisfied
himself that REST was aware of whom he was working with. R.[iv] arrived in the
COUNTRY[STRANA][v] in September as a member of the ISLAND[OSTROV][vi] mission on
ENORMOUS[ENORMOZ][vii]. According to him the work on ENORMOUS in the COUNTRY is
being carried out under the direct control of the COUNTRY's army represented by
General SOMERVELL[SOMMERVILL][viii] and STIMSON[ix]: at the head of the group
of ISLANDERS[OSTROVITIANE][vi] is a Labour Member of Parliament, Ben SMITH[x].

                                                          [Continued overleaf]

VENONA

~~TOP SECRET~~

The February 9, 1944 cable.

VENONA

- 2 -

The whole operation amounts to the working out of the process for the separation of isotopes of ENORMOUS. The work is proceeding in two directions: the electron method developed by LAWRENCE[LAURENS][xi]

[71 groups unrecoverable]

separation of isotopes by the combined method, using the diffusion method for preliminary and the electron method for final separation. The work

[46 groups unrecovered]

18th February, we shall report the results.

No. 92   ANTON[xii]

Footnotes:		
[i]	VIKTOR:	Lt. Gen. P.M. FITIN.
[ii]	Not available.	
[iii]	GUS':	i.e. "GOOSE"; Harry GOLD.
[iv]	REST/R.:	Dr. Emil Julius Klaus FUCHS.
[v]	COUNTRY:	U.S.A.
[vi]	ISLAND, ISLANDERS:	GREAT BRITAIN, British.
[vii]	ENORMOUS:	a) U.S. Atomic Energy Project. b) Uranium.
[viii]	General SOMERVELL:	Lt. General Brehan Burke SOMERVELL, Commanding General Army Service Forces, War Department.
[ix]	STIMSON:	Henry Lewis STIMSON, Secretary of War.
[x]	Ben SMITH:	Rt. Hon. Ben SMITH, Minister Resident in WASHINGTON for Supply from 1943.
[xi]	LAWRENCE:	Professor Ernest Orlando LAWRENCE.
[xii]	ANTON:	Leonid Romanovich KVASNIKOV.

VENONA

Reissue (T1362)

From: NEW YORK

To: MOSCOW

No: 1340

21 September 1944

To VIKTOR[i].

Lately the development of new people [D% has been in progress]. LIBERAL[ii] recommended the wife of his wife's brother, Ruth GREENGLASS, with a safe flat in view. She is 21 years old, a TOWNSWOMAN [GOROZhANKA][iii], a GYMNAST [FIZKUL'TURNITsA][iv] since 1942. She lives on STANTON [STANTAUN] Street. LIBERAL and his wife recommend her as an intelligent and clever girl.

[15 groups unrecoverable]

[C% Ruth] learned that her husband[v] was called up by the army but he was not sent to the front. He is a mechanical engineer and is now working at the ENORMOUS [ENORMOZ][vi] plant in SANTA FE, New Mexico.

[45 groups unrecoverable]

detail VOLOK[vii] who is working in a plant on ENORMOUS. He is a FELLOWCOUNTRYMAN [ZEMLYaK][viii]. Yesterday he learned that they had dismissed him from his work. His active work in progressive organizations in the past was the cause of his dismissal.

In the FELLOWCOUNTRYMAN line LIBERAL is in touch with CHESTER[ix]. They meet once a month for the payment of dues. CHESTER is interested in whether we are satisfied with the collaboration and whether there are not any misunderstandings. He does not inquire about specific items of work [KONKRETNAYa RABOTA]. In as much as CHESTER knows about the role of LIBERAL's group we beg consent to ask C. through LIBERAL about leads from among people who are working on ENORMOUS and in other technical fields.

Your no. 4256[a]. On making further enquiries and checking on LARIN[x] we received from the FELLOWCOUNTRYMEN through ÉKhO[xi] a character sketch which says that they do not entirely vouch for him. They base this statement on the fact that in the Federation LARIN does not carry out all the orders received from the leadership. He is stubborn and self-willed. On the strength of this we have decided to refrain from approaching LARIN and intend to find another candidate in FAECT [FAKhIT][xii].

No 751   MAJ[xiii]
20 September

Notes: [a]   Not available.
Comments:
    [i]   VIKTOR: Lt. Gen. P. M. FITIN.
   [ii]   LIBERAL: Julius ROSENBERG.
  [iii]   GOROZhANKA: American citizen.
   [iv]   FIZKUL'TURNITsA: Probably a Member of the Young Communist League.
    [v]   i.e. David GREENGLASS.
   [vi]   ĖNORMOZ: Atomic Energy Project.
  [vii]   VOLOK: ████████
 [viii]   ZEMLYaK: Member of the Communist Party.
   [ix]   CHESTER: Communist Party name of Bernard SCHUSTER.
    [x]   LARIN: Unidentified.
   [xi]   ĖKhO: i.e. ECHO, Bernard SCHUSTER.
  [xii]   FAKhIT: Federation of Architects, Chemists, Engineers and Technicians. See also NEW YORK's message no. 911 of 27 June 1944.
 [xiii]   MAJ: i.e. MAY, Stepan APRESYaN.

28 April 1975

TOP SECRET

USSR

Ref. No: ▓▓▓▓▓▓

Issued: ▓▓ 25/4/1961

Copy No: 204

DECISION TO MAINTAIN CONTACT WITH THEODORE HALL (1944)

From: NEW YORK

To: MOSCOW

No: 1585   12 Nov. 44

To VIKTOR.[i]

BEK[ii] visited Theodore HALL[TEODOR KhOLL],[iii] 19 years old, the son of a
furrier. He is a graduate of HARVARD University. As a talented physicist he was
taken on for government work. He was a GYMNAST[FIZKUL'TURNIK][iv] and conducted
work in the Steel Founders' Union.[a] According to BEK's account HALL has an
exceptionally keen mind and a broad outlook, and is politically developed. At the
present time H. is in charge of a group at "CAMP-2"[v] (SANTA-FE). H. handed over
to BEK a report about the CAMP and named the key personnel employed on ENORMOUS.[vi]
He decided to do this on the advice of his colleague Saville SAX[SAVIL SAKS],[vii]
a GYMNAST living in TYRE.[viii] SAX's mother is a FELLOWCOUNTRYMAN[ZEMLYaK][ix]
and works for RUSSIAN WAR RELIEF. With the aim of hastening a meeting with a
competent person, H. on the following day sent a copy of the report by S. to the
PLANT[ZAVOD].[x] ALEKSEJ[xi] received S. H. had to leave for CAMP-2 in two days'
time. He[b] was compelled to make a decision quickly. Jointly with MAY[MAJ][xii]
he gave BEK consent to feel out H., to assure him that everything was in order and
to arrange liaison with him. H. left his photograph and came to an understanding
with BEK about a place for meeting him. BEK met S. [1 group garbled] our automobile.
We consider it expedient to maintain liaison with H. [1 group unidentified] through
▓ and not to bring in anybody else. MAY has no objection to this. We shall send
the details by post.

No. 897   [Signature missing]
11th November

Distribution   [Notes and Comments overleaf]

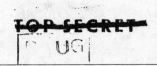

TOP SECRET

The November 12, 1944 cable.

~~TOP SECRET~~

2

Notes: [a] I.e. Trade Union [PROFSOYuZ].

       [b] I.e. ALEKSEJ.

Comments: [i] VIKTOR : Lt. Gen. P. M. FITIN.

         [ii] BEK : Sergej Nikolaevich KURNAKOV.

      [iii] HALL : Theodore Alvin HALL.

      [iv] GYMNAST : Possibly a member of the Young Communist League.

       [v] CAMP-2 : LOS ALAMOS.

      [vi] ENORMOUS: Manhattan Engineering District - U.S. Atomic Energy Project.

     [vii] SAX

    [viii] TYRE : NEW YORK CITY.

      [ix] FELLOWCOUNTRYMAN: Member of the Communist Party.

       [x] PLANT : Soviet Consulate.

      [xi] ALEKSEJ : Anatolij Antonovich YaKOVLEV, Soviet Vice-Consul in NEW YORK.

     [xii] MAY : Stepan Zakharovich APRESYaN, Soviet Vice-Consul in NEW YORK.

~~TOP SECRET~~

Introduction to
Eileen Welsome's

The Plutonium Experiment

WHILE SIFTING through documents at Kirtland Air Force Base in Albuquerque, New Mexico, Eileen Welsome, a reporter for *The Albuquerque Tribune,* discovered that between 1945 and 1947 scientists and doctors from the U.S. atomic weapons program had conducted experiments in which they injected plutonium into unwitting human guinea pigs.

Welsome learned that a story about the experiments had first been published in 1976 by a newsletter called *Science Trends,* and had been examined in a 1986 congressional report, which had attracted some press coverage. But nowhere were the victims identified by name; they were referred to only by code numbers. As she wrote in her book, *The Plutonium, Files,* Welsome wondered "who these people were; what happened to them after they left the hospital with the silvery, radioactive metal circulating in their veins—if they ever left at all." Over months and years she tried to track down the victims of the experiments, but she was repeatedly stonewalled by the Department of Energy. Five years into her investigation, she realized that the energy department had neglected to delete two words on a document that unlocked the story. Government scientists, according to the document, had written "to a physician in *Italy, Texas,* about contacting patient CAL-3. . . ."

Welsome knew CAL-3 was an African American who would have been roughly eighty years old if he were still alive. Doctors in a San Francisco hospital in 1947 had injected plutonium into his left calf. Three days later his left leg was amputated for what doctors thought was preexisting bone cancer. Pursuing this lead in Italy, Texas, near Dallas, Welsome learned that CAL-3 was a man named Elmer Allen. Through patient detective work, she discovered that CAL-3 was the last of eighteen patients injected with plutonium, and was able later to uncover the identity of other victims.

After Welsome's three part series was published in *The Albuquerque Tribune*, Energy Secretary Hazel O'Leary denounced the experiments. It turned out that thousands of human radiation experiments had been conducted during the Cold War on people who were, for the most part, poor, sick, and powerless. By exposing a half-century of cover-ups and denials and by forcing the government to admit its role in poisoning its own citizens, "The Plutonium Experiment" is a classic example of secret history. Welsome was awarded a Pulitzer Prize in 1994 for her series.

––––––––

ADDITIONAL SOURCES

Alterman, Eric. "The Plutonium Files," *The Nation*, February 28, 2000, p. 10.

Udall, Stewart. *The Myths of August: A Personal Exploration of Our Tragic Cold War Affair with the Atom*. New York: Pantheon Books, 1994.

U.S. Congress, House. Committee on Energy and Commerce, Subcommittee on Energy Conservation and Power. *American Nuclear Guinea Pigs: Three Decades of Radiation Experiments on U.S. Citizens*. Report 99th Congress, 2nd session, November 1986.

Welsome, Eileen. *The Plutonium Files: America's Secret Medical Experiments in the Cold War*. New York: The Dial Press, 1999.

Eileen Welsome

Elmer Allen Loses His Leg—and All Hope, The Plutonium Experiment

THE ALBUQUERQUE TRIBUNE, NOVEMBER 15, 1993

BACKGROUND

THE EXPERIMENT BEGAN in the hot, fretful dawn of the Atomic Age in quiet hospitals far removed from the New Mexico desert where scientists were putting the finishing touches on a "gadget" that would alter the course of history.

In the wards of the sick and dying, syringes were loaded with an ingredient so secret it was known only as "the product." Then, in quick succession, the needles were plunged into the veins of an auto accident victim in Tennessee, a cancer patient in Chicago, a house painter in San Francisco.

The product was plutonium, the highly radioactive substance that would power the brilliant mushroom cloud over Alamogordo three months later. But what did plutonium—the ingredient in a weapon that President Truman would boast harnessed the power of the universe—do in the human body? How long did it circulate in the blood? Where did it lodge in the bone? How quickly was it excreted?

The experiment was approved by the U.S. Army's Manhattan Project, the wartime machine that developed the atomic bomb. Some contemporary scientists compare the project to the human experiments conducted in Nazi Germany. Others defend it.

In all, scientists injected eighteen people with plutonium between 1945 and 1947. Even as the plutonium was being administered, the army colonel listed in documents as primarily responsible for the experiment was describing plutonium as the "most poisonous chemical known."

The patients were ordinary people with one thing in common: life-threatening illnesses that made survival beyond ten years "highly improbable." They included a boy of slight build who was just two months shy of his fifth birthday, a malnourished alcoholic, an eighty-five-pound woman suffering from widespread cancer.

With the possible exception of one patient, *The Tribune* found no written evidence that any of the patients were informed of the nature of the experiment or gave consent. Most of them probably went to their graves not knowing they had been injected with one of the most potent cancer-producing chemicals on Earth.

One patient received "many times the so-called lethal textbook dose" of plutonium. That patient and five others received radiation doses to the bone that a scientist thirty years later calculated as being high enough to cause tumors.

One-third of the patients outlived their doctors' grim predictions, and in the early 1970s, four still were living when a follow-up study began. Scientists took urine, blood and stool samples from three to measure the plutonium remaining in their bodies. Scientists also sought exhumations of deceased patients.

Neither the survivors nor the relatives of the deceased plutonium patients initially were told the real reason for the government's interest. In some cases, the relatives were lied to when permission for exhumation was sought.

"This is one of the great, dark stories of the nuclear era," said Arjun Makhijani, president of the Institute for Energy and Environmental Research in Washington, D.C., a nonprofit group that studies nuclear issues. "The public is not aware of the depths to which many universities, doctors and scientists descended."

Los Alamos National Laboratory played a major role in the experiment's first phase. The lab analyzed the excretion samples of the patients injected in a Rochester, N.Y., hospital and later published a classified report that has become the definitive source document on the experiment.

The data, some scientists say, helped protect thousands of workers at nuclear facilities from being overexposed to plutonium and did not harm the patients or contribute to their deaths. Others say the experiment was unethical and bad science because, among other reasons, the sample size was too small.

The experiment itself has received limited attention in the media. But to this day, the patients' identities have been known by numbers only.

Six years ago, *The Tribune* began a search to find them. We thought they deserved to be remembered as something more than numbers, something more than laboratory animals who contributed to science a wealth of data on how plutonium is deposited in the human body—its heart, skeleton, even its ashes.

Working with scant data from scientific reports and a few clues from government documents, we determined the identities of five of the eighteen patients.

In the next few days, *The Tribune* will tell you how these ordinary Americans unwittingly were swept up by the hot winds of the Atomic Age. We also will tell you about how their families weren't told the truth for almost fifty years.

The first patient we found was a railroad porter named Elmer Allen, identified in records as "Cal-3." Elmer was injected with plutonium in the left calf, and three days later, his leg was amputated for what was thought to be a preexisting bone cancer.

The second patient was a California house painter named Albert Stevens, known as "Cal-1." Albert received a massive dose of plutonium four days before undergoing surgery for stomach cancer. But he didn't have stomach cancer. Specimens of his spleen, rib and body tissues later show up in a report titled "A Comparison of the Metabolism of Plutonium in Man and the Rat."

The third patient was "HP-6," a man named John Mousso who suffered from Addison's disease and struggled to make ends meet in a small town outside Rochester, N.Y.

The fourth was Eda Schultz Charlton, identified as "HP-3" in official records. Eda's condition was monitored for almost thirty-five years by the University of Rochester's Strong Memorial Hospital. She underwent dozens of diagnostic tests ranging from X-rays to biopsies and barium enemas, and she developed an obsessive fear of cancer.

And finally, there was "HP-9," a man named Fred C. Sours, a political official in a Rochester suburb whose body was exhumed thirty-one years after his death and sent to a national laboratory near Chicago. His remains were kept there for more than three years.

Who are the others? The malnourished alcoholic? The auto accident victim in Tennessee?

We don't know. And the government won't say.

We've filed two legal requests under the Freedom of Information Act with the Department of Energy, the sprawling agency that eventually took over many functions of the wartime Manhattan Project.

The first was filed in 1989. The second, filed more than a year ago, was a seven-page request based on the DOE's own documents—including a 1974 report detailing an internal inquiry into the experiment conducted by its predecessor agency, the Atomic Energy Commission.

We've received some documents from the DOE, but it is still withholding many of the most important records, such as medical files and other correspondence that would identify the other patients. The DOE said it doesn't even have a copy of the findings of its own investigation—an investigation that involved teams of officials who reviewed numerous records, conducted interviews with scientists in fourteen cities and returned to Washington with 250 documents.

The plutonium experiment began in the hubris of a new age. Among its advocates and architects were some of the brilliant young scientists from Los Alamos who, from behind protective lenses, watched on the morning of July 16, 1945, when a man-made explosion outshone the New Mexico sun.

A half-century has elapsed. The Cold War is over, and the bombs are being dismantled. Still, the DOE refuses to relinquish the identities of the victims of one of its darkest secrets.

Elmer Allen Loses His Leg—and All Hope

AT 3:30 P.M. on July 18, 1947, doctors in a San Francisco hospital gathered around a patient's bed and explained an experiment they were about to perform. The patient, a railroad porter with an eighth-grade education, nodded his assent. Doctors later would describe him as "fully oriented and in sane mind."

A bull's-eye was drawn in ink on the hard, smooth calf of the man's left leg. A hypodermic needle loaded with plutonium, a silvery, man-made metal considered one of the most toxic substances on Earth, was plunged into the center. The needle sank nearly an inch. There was no bleeding when it was withdrawn and no pain or discomfort "whatsoever" six and a half hours later.

Three days later the left leg was amputated at midthigh for what was believed to be a preexisting bone cancer. Tissue samples were sent to a laboratory where researchers conducting a secret experiment were eager to find out how, among other things, plutonium distributed itself in the human body.

The patient was Elmer Allen. He was the eighteenth and last person to be injected with plutonium in an experiment conducted between 1945 and 1947.

Elmer, who was thirty-six at the time, returned with his wife to her small hometown of Italy, Texas, where a bleak future awaited him. He would suffer epileptic seizures, alcoholism and eventually be diagnosed as paranoid schizophrenic—a mental illness his family doctor said centered partly on his feelings about how he had been used.

IT WAS THE SUMMER of 1944 when Fredna Hadley met a strapping young porter named Elmer Allen in a West Texas train station. It was a romantic beginning in an era of romance—a time of sad farewells and sweet homecomings in a democracy caught up in a global war.

Fredna, a young graduate of Tillotson College in Austin, Texas, was in the El Paso train station waiting for the train that would take her to Los Angeles to see her aunt.

"People were pushing to get on the train. This woman had some children, a little baby in her arms and two small children. I stepped back and let her go in front of me, and they closed the gates," Fredna recalled.

She began to cry. Elmer, a porter for the Pullman Co., noticed her distress. "I can get you on the next train," he said.

Their love affair began. Not long after that, Elmer followed Fredna to her hometown of Italy, Texas, a small farming community forty-five miles south of Dallas.

After a brief courtship, Elmer and Fredna were married on September 10, 1944. They moved to Oakland, California, and later to nearby Richmond. Their first child, Elmerine, was born a year later. A second child, William, was born two years after that.

Elmer continued his work as a railroad porter while Fredna worked as an aide in a health clinic. Like Texas, the postwar Bay area was still segregated, but the African-American couple felt happy to be working. "We were optimistic about the future," Fredna recalled.

But an accident occurred on September 3, 1946, a minor accident really, which would set in motion events that would forever alter their lives. Elmer was trying to get off a train in Chicago when it jolted and threw him to the side, injuring his left knee.

When he got back to Oakland, a company doctor took an X-ray. The film revealed a fracture. Elmer was advised to wrap the knee in an Ace bandage and apply heat, but that didn't help. He was referred to another doctor.

A second X-ray showed a lesion in the knee area had grown. A biopsy was done. The pathologist found no evidence of abnormal growth or tumor.

"The principal picture is that of newly forming bone, organizing hemorrhage and chronic inflammation," he said.

Elmer was unable to work and the Pullman Co. refused to accept liability for the accident, saying the injury didn't appear to be "on a traumatic basis." He couldn't afford further treatment and was referred in June 1947—almost a year later—to the outpatient clinic at the University of California Hospital in San Francisco.

By then, Elmer's physical and financial situation was desperate. His knee had swollen to three or four times its original size and was so tender he couldn't put weight on it. He was taking pain medication and had been out of work for six months. According to a hospital application form, Elmer had sixty dollars in debts and twenty-five dollars in cash. (His rent alone was thirty-five dollars a month.)

Elmer's diagnosis worsened, and he later was admitted to the San Francisco hospital. His medical records show the following:

- June 25, 1947. A doctor examining one set of X-rays suggests the changes in Elmer's knee could stem from an infection superimposed on a surgical defect, but he says the possibility of bone cancer "must be seriously considered."
- July 3, 1947. The doctor examining the June 25 X-rays does another set and reverses his opinion. Elmer, he said, "probably" has a cancer in the cartilage or bone. He doesn't rule out infection.
- July 14, 1947. The hospital's pathology department does a second biopsy. Elmer definitely has a form of bone cancer, a pathologist said.

The doctors decided the only way to prevent the spread of bone cancer through his body was to amputate his leg, a treatment still used today. Bone cancer is a rare disease that is usually fatal by the time it is diagnosed. Eighty percent to 95 percent of patients who have it die within five years of its discovery.

The days and weeks after Elmer's amputation are a blur in Fredna's mind. What she remembers most is how scared she was—two babies to support and a husband with an amputated leg.

"I was so far away from my people," she said.

They were both far from home and about to be hurtled into a more alien world—an experiment conducted by scientists of the Manhattan Project, which produced the atom bomb.

WHILE SCIENTISTS at Los Alamos National Laboratory were designing the bomb itself, other research was being done at the Metallurgical Laboratory at the University of Chicago, the William H. Crocker Radiation Laboratory at the University of California in Berkeley and other labs.

Much of the health and safety research centered on new, radioactive elements that were capable of sustaining a nuclear chain reaction. Of great interest was plutonium, named after the planet Pluto.

"It realty should have been called 'plutium,'" Glenn Seaborg, a codiscoverer of plutonium and Nobel laureate, said from his Bay area home. "But we liked how 'plutonium' rolled off the tongue."

Plutonium was discovered in 1941 on the University of California campus in Berkeley. Plutonium 239 has a half-life of 24,065 years, the time it takes for half of its radioactive atoms to decay.

The military potential of plutonium, a material so secret that it was referred to during the war years as "the product," was recognized. Scores of young scientists recruited into the secret Manhattan Project went to work, trying to figure out how to manufacture plutonium and other radioactive isotopes in large enough quantities to be harnessed into an atomic bomb.

By the fall of 1942, enough plutonium had been made to be visible to the naked eye. As the amount of plutonium increased, so did concern over its toxicity.

In 1944—a year before the human experiments were to begin—eleven milligrams of plutonium (about the size of the head of a pin) were set aside for animal studies by physician and researcher Joseph Hamilton at UC-Berkeley. Col. Stafford Warren, the chief medical officer of the Manhattan Project who authorized the experiment, described plutonium in 1946 as the "most poisonous chemical known."

Plutonium had properties similar to the radioactive element radium. The human toll wreaked by radium was well-documented, and the federal government wanted to avoid a similar tragedy in its laboratories.

Young women who had worked in factories painting luminous figures on watch dials with radium-laced paint in the 1920s were developing cancer. It was discovered that many had swallowed lethal amounts of radium when licking their paint brushes.

Unlike radium, which decayed to radon and could be detected in the breath, the only way to measure plutonium in the body was through urine and stools. And the only way to extrapolate how much plutonium a person may have been exposed to, researchers figured, was through an experiment in which a known amount of plutonium would be introduced into the body and carefully measured in the urine and stools.

"Studies conducted on man involving the introduction of known quantities of the element into the human body were viewed as the only solution to the problem," states a report by the Atomic Energy Commission, which investigated the experiment in 1974.

The injections began in 1945, just three months before J. Robert Oppenheimer watched the atomic bomb near Alamogordo and recalled an ancient Hindu quotation: "I am become Death, the destroyer of worlds."

The first patient, injected on April 10, 1945, was an African American suffering from severe auto injuries and hospitalized at the Manhattan Engineer District Hospital in Oak Ridge, Tennessee. The patient walked out of the hospital several weeks later, giving rise to a long-held belief by some researchers that the plutonium actually had promoted a rapid healing of the bones. "They gave him a whopping dose of plutonium," recalled Karl Morgan, the former director of Oak Ridge's health physics division. "They were surprised a Black man who had been scheduled to die had walked out of the hospital and disappeared."

Three patients were injected at Billings Hospital at the University of Chicago; three patients, including Elmer, were injected at the University of California Hospital in San Francisco; and the remaining eleven patients were injected at Strong Memorial Hospital, the teaching hospital of the University of Rochester in upstate New York.

Wright Langham, a group leader in radiobiology at Los Alamos, went to Rochester to help coordinate the experiment on the eleven Rochester patients. Langham, who was later known as "Mr. Plutonium," may have escorted the numerous samples shipped back to New Mexico by train. Los Alamos did the chemical analyses of the urine, stool, blood and tissue samples taken from patients.

Scientists were looking for patients suffering from chronic diseases that made survival for more than ten years unlikely. Two reasons lay behind this thinking, one humane and one utilitarian:

First, they wanted to avoid the possibility of radiation effects, such as cancer, showing up later in life. Second, early death improved the chances of obtaining what a Los Alamos report called "post-mortem material"—body parts.

Livers, spleens, gonads, kidneys, hearts, ribs, intestines—virtually every organ—would be harvested and measured for plutonium in patients who died soon after the injections.

Three patients were African American, and fifteen were White. Five—including Elmer, Albert Stevens, John Mousso and Eda Schultz Charlton—lived for more than twenty years after the injections.

That alone is reason to condemn the project, some scientists say. "I find that when people play God, when they find somebody's terminal and therefore it's all right to do something to them you wouldn't do to other people, I find that rather obnoxious," said Berkeley scientist John Gofman, considered one of the world's leading experts on low-level radiation.

Had they lived fifty years, the plutonium patients would have received an average of forty-four times the radiation the average person receives in a lifetime from background and medical X-rays. But three patients received much more.

Elmer received the smallest dose, but he received plutonium 238, a "hotter" form that is more unstable and more radioactive than plutonium 239. About half remained in the amputated leg, giving Elmer about six times the radiation the average person today receives in a lifetime.

Scientists today disagree on whether the plutonium would have increased the patients' pain, worsened their conditions or hastened their deaths. "I think any of these exposures would cause excruciating pain in the person who would suffer the consequences," health physicist Morgan said.

But Roland Finston, a health physicist who just retired from Stanford University and helped *The Tribune* calculate the radiation doses, said it's unlikely the doses would have caused any immediate acute effects. The real danger, he said, would have been the development of leukemia or solid tumors in later life. "It would not have caused any measurable effect on the patients at the time or shortly thereafter," he said.

The government said later deaths were unrelated to the plutonium injections and said there was no evidence to suggest the plutonium influenced the patients' diseases or caused cancer.

"The observation that cancer did not, apparently, develop in any of these eighteen injected patients does not mean that the doses given were too small to cause cancer," said John C. Cobb, a retired physician living in Corrales. "The plutonium may indeed have caused a cancer to start in any, or all, of these patients, but the patients' own immune systems could have eliminated the cancer cells."

Cobb is a former chairman of the University of Colorado's department of preventative medicine and served on a governor's task force that looked at health effects from plutonium and other problems at Colorado's Rocky Flats nuclear weapons plant.

Cobb said plutonium's irradiation of the bone marrow also could have damaged the patients' immune systems and made them more susceptible to diseases. "Immune deficiency can contribute to a great variety of symptoms," he said.

MANY YEARS LATER, when Elmer was back in Italy, Texas, he would tell his old friend Joe Speed about the doctors who raced in and out of his hospital room the summer his leg was amputated.

"They were practicing to be doctors," Speed recalled. "They were students. Different young men would come in, telling him to do this and that.

"He told me they put a germ cancer in his leg. They guinea-pigged him. They didn't care about him getting well. He told me he would never get well."

Doctors at the clinic were immediately interested in Elmer. "Of great teaching value," a medical official wrote on Elmer's chart after an early visit.

Patricia Durbin, a scientist at Lawrence Berkeley Laboratory in California, said the patient selection was both "personalized and random."

"The bulk of the people were just people," she said.

Durbin was in a second generation of scientists who "rediscovered" the plutonium experiment and lobbied in the early '70s for follow-up studies. In 1946, she was a young student working in the lab of scientist Joseph Hamilton, one of the experiment's architects.

"They were always on the lookout for somebody who had some kind of terminal disease who was going to undergo an amputation," Durbin said. "There are not very many of them. But they had colleagues at UC-San Francisco and San Francisco General who were kind of on the alert for potential cases."

About a month before Elmer was admitted to the hospital, a Chinese boy described in documents as "CAL-A," underwent a similar injection and amputation. The sixteen-year-old boy was injected on June 10, 1947, with americium, another radioactive element, at what records described as the "Chinese Hospital" in San Francisco.

Two days later his leg was amputated. He was taken to the University of California Hospital in San Francisco for studies before and after the amputation. He died eleven months later and is buried in San Francisco. "There was no evidence of disclosure in the chart of this patient," said DOE records obtained under the Freedom of Information Act.

When asked if she knew anything about that case, Durbin said, "His guardian couldn't speak English. He got treated in a good hospital as a consequence."

ON JULY 18, 1947, the white cast placed on Elmer's left leg after the biopsy was split down the side and removed to prepare for the "tracer injection."

"Some throbbing pain but no other discomfort," a doctor wrote in Elmer's records.

At 3:30 p.m. that day, medical people gathered at Elmer's bedside. He was told of a procedure they were about to perform.

"The experimental nature of the intra-muscular injection of the radioactive tracer sample was explained to the patient, who agreed upon the procedure. The patient was in fully oriented and in sane mind," his medical records state.

Three doctors and a registered nurse witnessed the explanation, assisted in the injection and signed their names at the bottom of Elmer's consent form.

One doctor who signed his name was Bertram V.A. Low-Beer, another early nuclear pioneer who used radioactive substances in medical treatments. Low-Beer's name shows up in Elmer's medical records only on the day he was injected. The consent form also appears to have been written by Low-Beer.

Elmer is the only patient for whom there is documented evidence that he was told of the injection. The consent form, however, does not describe what he was told. Even then, Elmer's consent didn't come close to today's strict guidelines for informed consent, which require written acknowledgment by the patient after full disclosure of the research, its risks and benefits.

Fredna questioned why doctors did not include her when they discussed the experimental procedure with Elmer. "It seems like they should have told me about it," she said.

Elmer's daughter, Elmerine, said her father, with his limited education, would not have understood the explanation. "If they told my father that he was injected with plutonium, that would be like telling him he was injected with ice cream," she said. "He would not know the difference."

THE INJECTION of plutonium into Elmer was conducted despite orders to the contrary. On December 24, 1946, the Manhattan Engineer District learned "certain radioactive substances were being prepared for intravenous administration to human subjects" in Berkeley. An immediate halt was ordered.

Then, on April 17, 1947, four months before Elmer's injection, the U.S. Army Corps of Engineers, Manhattan District, sent a memo to the Atomic Energy Commission reiterating the prohibition and going one step further:

"It is desired that no document be released which refers to experiments with humans and might have adverse effect on public opinion or result in legal suits. Documents covering such work should be classified 'secret.' Further work in this field has been prohibited by the general manager."

In that same memo, officials ordered that three documents involving human experimentation be upgraded from "restricted" to "secret" and that a search be conducted to make sure no other agency had gotten any of the records.

A month later, commission officials refused to declassify a paper titled "A Comparison of the Metabolism of Plutonium in Man and the Rat," written by Hamilton and others in Berkeley. "It contains material, which in the opinion of the management of the United States Atomic Energy Commission, might adversely affect the national interest," a May 23, 1947, letter states.

SOME HISTORIANS HAVE SAID experiments with critically ill patients were common in the 1940s. And in fact, radioactive isotopes of strontium and radium, as well as massive doses of radiation to the whole body from X-rays, were given to patients at hospitals throughout the country, records show.

Scientists and doctors working for the Manhattan Project, and later under contract with the AEC, frequently stated the experimental therapies were part of the patients' normal treatment and that they were simply gathering data on physiological changes.

In one case that was similar to the plutonium experiment, eight very ill cancer patients in the early 1940s were exposed over a month to an average of 300 rads of whole-body irradiation from X-rays in a New York hospital. Five died within six months. Scientist L. F. Craver blamed their deaths on their diseases and said such doses should be "well-tolerated" by healthy people.

About 300 rads of whole-body irradiation delivered in a week or less will kill 50 percent of its subjects. Some 420 rads delivered in a one-month period will kill 50 percent of those exposed, according to Finston, a health physicist who recently retired from Stanford University.

Scientist Robert Stone, one of the experiment leaders, admitted the true purpose of the experiments with X-rays in a 1948 letter found at the Bancroft Library at UC-Berkeley:

"I freely admit that in 1942 when we started this work, I was influenced by the fact that we needed to learn as much as we possibly could concerning the effects of total-body irradiation on people with relatively normal blood pictures. At that time, I was confronted with the problem of building up the morale of the workers on the new atomic bomb project, many of whom were seriously worried about the effects of prolonged whole-body irradiation."

The records also show that scientists and doctors knew the ethics of such experiments were questionable and were sensitive about the experiment. In later documents, the AEC itself admitted that a policy of informed consent was well established by 1947.

As late as 1983, the DOE was still sensitive. In a letter to Alvin Trivelpiece, director of the DOE's Office of Energy Research, Nathaniel Barr of the office put it this way: "The issue of informed consent, if raised, will be difficult to deal with in the light of present DOE and federal policies and procedures regarding human subjects."

ELMER WAS A cooperative patient. Only a week after the amputation, he was eager to get up and around. "Has been up in wheelchair with great joy," Dr. Raymond S. Mullen wrote nine days after the surgery. Mullen was one of the doctors who witnessed the injection.

"In wheelchair most of day. No pain from stump. Eager to find work after convalescence—not depressed," Mullen wrote the next day.

Elmer was discharged from the hospital August 7. He was fitted for a prosthesis and got regular chest X-rays at an outpatient orthopedic clinic. In an entry dated May 11, 1948, a doctor wrote: "This pt. had radioactive stuff injected prior to amp." (The first four words are underlined.)

Elmer's last visit to the clinic appeared to have been July 6, 1949. "Gaining weight and feeling fine. No difficulty with stump. Walking (with) aid of cane," an entry states.

As an amputee, Elmer no longer could work as a railroad porter, so he turned to other ways of making a living. He learned how to repair shoes. He haunted the wharves in San Francisco, where he would get and sell fish.

For the rest of his life he felt phantom aches and pains in the missing limb. "He said they kept the leg. They didn't bury the leg," Fredna recalled. "When his toes would start hurting, he'd say, 'I guess they're working on that foot of mine.'"

A couple of years later, with Elmer wearing a new prosthesis from the California's vocational rehabilitation department, the couple bundled up their two young children and returned to Italy. "He wanted to make a good living for his family," Fredna said. "After he lost his leg, he just gave up all hope."

The move back to Italy, despite its boast of being the "biggest little town in Texas," demoralized Elmer. In the summer, when a furnacelike heat drives all but the heartiest behind air-conditioned doors, Italy's Main Street looks like a deserted movie set. Elmer had not wanted to leave the hills or the cool breezes that rolled in from San Francisco Bay, but he needed family support. And Italy was home to Fredna's family.

IN THE EARLY 1950S, Italy attracted national attention because of its approach to race relations: Two mayors and two city councils—one for African Americans and one for Whites. "He was disgusted. He never wanted to come back here. He had so many hopes and dreams for his family," Fredna recalled.

He cleaned bricks in nearby Dallas, repaired shoes at Goodwill Industries, upholstered chairs and sometimes plowed the rich, dark soil farmers called "black gumbo," friends said.

Mostly, it was up to Fredna to hold the family together. For thirty-five years she taught school, much of the time at Stafford Elementary, which was within walking distance of their small house.

Fredna, a poet in her spare time, thinks she never lived up to her potential, in part because of the pressure of raising two children and taking care of Elmer. "It took something away from me. I haven't done all the things I could have done."

Elmer's now-married daughter, Elmerine, said her father got the best of care. "Anything he wanted, he got it. He had an automobile to drive; it wasn't always a new one. Whatever he had, my mother provided it."

Elmer made toys for schoolchildren, kites from brown paper bags, lampshades from Popsicle sticks and flower baskets from egg cartons. His son, William, and his granddaughter, April, would go on to become engineers. "He could do anything. But there was nothing for him to do," recalled Speed, Elmer's friend.

A job at Goodwill ended when Elmer began having epileptic seizures and it was no longer safe for him to commute to Dallas. Fredna would put a tablespoon in his mouth when he had a seizure in the middle of the night. "He would chew the spoon to pieces—his tongue, too," Elmerine recalled.

He had other problems. He drank alcohol "very, very heavily" until ten or twelve years before he died, Elmerine said. He began taking Thorazine, a drug used in the treatment of various mental disorders. For some reason, it halted the drinking, she said.

David Williams, a physician in nearby Waxahachie, was Elmer's family doctor for the last twenty years of his life. Williams said he diagnosed Allen as a paranoid schizophrenic.

"This paranoia was certainly helped and did center around his feeling that he had been utilized as a younger man with this exposure to plutonium," he said.

"What I saw was a fellow who had a loss of limb and became an emotional cripple because of it. He took to the bottle and then got off that. He probably had paranoid schizophrenia all of his life. As far as doing things, I thought he was using this possible exposure as a crutch, a reason, rather than quite doing as well as I would have like to have seen him do."

Elmer told Williams on his first office visit that he had been injected with plutonium. "It was difficult to tell whether to believe him or not. I wondered," Williams said. "I also wondered if it was a portion of his paranoia and whether or not it was a crutch for him not to function as he should have functioned. His conscience needed a salve to where it was OK for his wife to be teaching and earning and so forth."

Williams said he never saw evidence that the plutonium had any physical effect on Elmer. He said he didn't encourage Elmer to talk about the experiment. "I didn't think there was a lot of gain there. Do you follow? In other words, I didn't turn him off; I'd listen, but I felt like he had other, more ongoing problems that were more pressing that we needed to deal with day to day rather than going back to that."

IT WAS THE EVENING of June 9, 1973. Elmer and Fredna were in Car 1635, Drawing Room D of the "Texas Chief," an overnight train bound for Chicago. Elmer had worked as a railroad porter many years earlier, so the sway of the train and the clacking rhythm of the rails must have cradled him like an old rocking chair.

Then there was the view from his window. Weedy back lots and wash hanging from clothes lines as the train pulled out of Fort Worth. Cows, horses and barns hurtling by. Green pastures unspooling like dreams. And later, the lights. Everything chattering of those old railroad days.

The next day, they were met in Chicago by a limousine driver at Union Station and whisked to a Ramada Inn, where a bouquet of flowers awaited them.

The Allens were on the trip of their life, a nineteen-day whirlwind that would take them to Chicago and then hundreds of miles northeast to Rochester. Limousines, fresh flowers, private train compartments and immaculate hotel rooms awaited them. And the government scientists were actually going to pay them $140 for participating in follow-up studies plus $13 a day.

On the day after their arrival in Chicago, Fredna went sightseeing. Elmer went to a sprawling national lab near Chicago. There he was placed in a whole-body counter, and his urine was collected and studied for traces of plutonium from a long-ago injection.

Against the festive backdrop, Elmer's unwitting participation in the second phase of an experiment launched almost thirty years earlier began. A new generation of researchers carried forward a cover-up initiated by the Manhattan Project scientists.

Neither Elmer nor Fredna nor their family doctor learned of the real purpose of the trip until a year later, formerly classified documents show. Eda Schultz Charlton and John Mousso, two other patients injected with plutonium many years earlier, also were unknowing participants in the follow-up studies, which involved the collection and chemical analyses of urine, stool and blood samples. Relatives of deceased patients whom scientists also wanted to exhume were duped, records show.

"My mother thought this was big stuff coming from Italy, Texas," Elmerine said of her parents' trip. "She thought she was the queen of England. It wasn't like they said, 'We're testing you guys because we injected you with plutonium.'"

CHICAGO, the place Elmer and Fredna were bound for that warm summer night, was the city where it all began. While working as a railroad porter many years earlier, Elmer fell from a train and injured his leg, which eventually led to an amputation.

Doctors said the leg had bone cancer, a disease which is normally fatal in five years. But Elmer was to live another forty-four years, which makes the original diagnosis suspect, one scientist said.

"If the diagnosis had been correct, by rights he should have been dead in five years or something like that," said retired scientist John Rundo. "Bone cancer is normally fatal, not universally, but usually. He didn't die, as you know, so one can conclude that he probably didn't have bone cancer," Rundo oversaw the chemical analyses done on the excretion samples taken from Elmer and the others in 1973.

Durbin, the scientist from Lawrence Berkeley Laboratory in California who reviewed Elmer's medical records, also said she doubted the accuracy of "CAL-3's" diagnosis.

"I think the diagnosis of the bone cancer was questionable," she said. "The cells were not convincingly tumorous, at least on my reading of the pathology report."

But in a later interview, she said she believed "CAL-3's" leg still would have required amputation. "They were going to have to take the leg off anyway because the knee was so badly shattered. It hadn't healed well."

In 1967, Durbin learned that at least one patient injected in the 1945–47 experiment had lived at least twenty years, and she began a concerted effort to find out what happened to the rest.

Two decades earlier, she was a young student washing beakers in the laboratory of Hamilton, one of the country's savviest scientists about the biological effects of plutonium.

Durbin, a plain-spoken scientist in her mid-60s, is a staunch defender of the project and says the data saved countless people from being overexposed in the workplace. She said the international community still uses the data to set limits for human exposure to plutonium.

"These things were not done to plague people or make them sick and miserable," she said. "They were not done to kill people. They were done to gain potentially valuable information.

"The fact that they were injected and provided this valuable data should almost be a sort of memorial rather than something to be ashamed of. It doesn't bother me to talk about the plutonium injectees because of the value of the information that they provided."

In late December 1972, Durbin turned the information she had gathered over to the now-defunct Center for Human Radiobiology at Argonne National Laboratory near Chicago. This was the organization that had followed the radium dial painters, the women who died of cancer after licking the radioactive brushes they used to paint watches.

It was decided that survivors' urine, blood and stools would be gathered on the metabolism unit of the University of Rochester's Strong Memorial Hospital. The Center for Human Radiobiology would do the chemical analyses.

Scientists also wanted to study the remains of deceased patients. Over the next five years, they exhumed three bodies and obtained the ashes of a fourth patient.

The MIT Radioactivity Center in Phoenix was in charge of getting permission for the exhumations from relatives. The staff there had done similar work in tracking down radium dial painters and other people exposed to radioactive elements.

The arrangement suited officials at Lawrence Berkeley Laboratory just fine. "The introduction of exhumed bodies into the politically charged Berkeley atmosphere might even result in picketing of the laboratory by students," a worried official is quoted as saying in the AEC report.

Los Alamos National Laboratory, which played a key role in the first phase, took a supporting role in the 1973 follow-up. Some samples from the 1973 studies were sent to Los Alamos, but Los Alamos scientists, particularly Langham, wanted to keep out of it the second time.

Langham, who performed the initial chemical analyses from eleven Rochester patients and an Oak Ridge accident victim, had grown weary of being identified with the experiment, Durbin wrote in a 1971 letter. He was distressed in particular that the Rochester patients had never been told they were the subjects of an experiment and resented the pervasive influence the project had on his entire professional life, Durbin wrote. "He said if such material were available, the Los Alamos group would be interested in participating, but that they did not want to be directly responsible nor in direct contact with whomever was actually obtaining samples," the letter states.

ELMER AND FREDNA'S TRIP to Chicago and Rochester began with a March 7, 1973, letter to their family doctor, A. O. Dykes, from Argonne National Laboratory.

"We are trying to locate a patient of yours by the name of Elmer Allen in order to do a follow-up study on treatment he received for a sarcoma in July 1947," wrote Austin Brues, medical director of Argonne's Center for Human Radiobiology.

"We are especially interested in cases of this sort, and his is of particular interest since he has this unusual malignant tumor and has shown such a long survival time," Brues wrote.

"Please assure him it would only be for observation and collection of excreta," he added. Nowhere in the letter is plutonium mentioned, a substance an AEC official later would point out dryly was not given for therapeutic reasons.

Elmerine, grown and with a family of her own at the time, remembers her parents' excitement. "It was like it was going to be an adventure. My mother called. She said, 'You know, I got this letter from this doctor that was one of your dad's doctors when he had his leg amputated in California. When she found out your father was still alive, she was just amazed and what they wanted to do, they wanted to see if we will come to the University of Rochester in New York to run some metabolism tests.'"

Scientist Rundo recalled seeing the patients. "I looked at them. I saw people who were in reasonably good states of health, considering their ages, considering one had lost a leg twenty-seven years earlier. These were normal people, nice people." The plutonium in Elmer was barely detectable. "His excretion rate was extremely low," Rundo said.

After the tests at Argonne, the Allens rested a day and then boarded a bus to Rochester, where another limousine took them to their hotel. Elmer spent fourteen days in the metabolic unit at Strong Memorial Hospital. Fredna kept several souvenirs of the trip, including a Polaroid snapshot of Elmer with a doctor she identified as Christine Waterhouse. A couple of the medical people even gave her their autographs. One was a scientist whose name appears in scientific papers describing the plutonium found in the hair and bones of exhumed corpses.

Fredna said she had no idea what the doctors were doing. "Every time I went to see him, he was in bed. They would study the food he would eat," she said.

For two weeks, Elmer ate the same kind of food. His urine and stool samples were gathered regularly. On the day he was to be discharged, he had a seizure. They stayed an extra day.

On April 17, 1974, more than a year after Elmer had been sent home, the AEC's Division of Inspection and the Biomedical and Environmental Research Division began an investigation. The reasons for the inquiry are not clear.

A detailed report of the findings later was prepared and classified "Official Use Only." The DOE now says it doesn't have the report, but *The Tribune* obtained a copy from a former Capitol Hill staffer. In the report, the DOE deleted the names of patients, doctors, scientists and investigators. The internal inquiry focused mostly on:

- Whether patients in the 1945–47 period had given their informed consent for the experiment.
- Whether the survivors in 1973 were properly informed of the true purpose of the follow-up studies and gave their informed consent.

- Whether the relatives of the deceased patients were properly informed about the exhumations.

The answers were no, no and no.

Investigators fanned out across fourteen cities, examining records and talking to scientists involved in both phases of the experiment. More than 250 documents were copied and brought back to AEC headquarters. The investigation uncovered a web of deceit that dated back fifty years. The investigators found:

- No written evidence that any of the patients were informed of the original plutonium injections or gave their consent. Witnesses claimed some patients were told orally they were going to receive a radioactive substance, but plutonium was a classified word at the time. Elmer was told only that he was to receive a radioactive substance.
- In 1973, survivors Elmer, Eda Schultz Charlton and John Mousso were not told the true reason scientists were interested in studying them. They also did not give their informed consent for the studies even though Argonne National Laboratory, as contractor with the AEC, had agreed to abide by regulations requiring such consent for human studies. Robert Loeb, spokesman for the University of Rochester Medical Center, said the hospital didn't require patients to sign informed consent forms because they were involved in excretion studies only.
- The relatives of the dead patients also were deceived or lied to about the true purpose of the exhumations.

One of the documents that illustrated the extent of the cover-up was the last paragraph of a December 21, 1972, memo written by Robert Rowland, a retired scientist who at that time was director for the Center for Human Radiobiology:

"Please note that outside of CHR we will never use the word plutonium in regard to these cases. 'These individuals are of interest to us because they may have received a radioactive material at some time' is the kind of statement to be made, if we need to say anything at all." (The words "never" and "plutonium" are underlined in the memo.)

Rowland, who still lives in the Chicago area, said in an interview that he was given those instructions "orally" by officials in Washington, D.C. "We were not in any way, shape or form to allude to plutonium," he recalled.

A. F. Stehney, another scientist from the Center for Human Radiobiology involved in the follow-up studies, said the plutonium patients weren't told the truth because everybody was "leery of getting these people all excited."

"We were told these people were pretty elderly and might get very upset if we started talking about radioactivity in their bodies."

While scientists were contacting living survivors about follow-up studies, others were trying to secure permission from relatives of deceased plutonium patients for exhumations. Here's what they agreed to tell relatives:

"An appropriate approach would be to say that the center was investigating the composition of radioactive materials that had been injected at an earlier date in an experimental type of treatment; and that since the composition of the mixture was not well known, there would be considerable scientific interest in investigating the nature of the isotope and the effects it may have had."

On September 24, 1973, the body of a twenty-year-old woman identified in official records as "HP-4" was exhumed. The patient's sister had given permission for the exhumation. "Since the sister did not inquire as to the reason for the injections, the issue was not broached," the AEC report revealed.

The relatives of seven deceased patients eventually were contacted. None was told the real reason, AEC investigators found. "Disclosure to all but one of the next of kin could be judged misleading in that the radioactive isotopes were represented as having been injected as an experimental treatment for the patient's disease," the report says.

AFTER THE INVESTIGATION, the AEC ordered that survivors be told the truth. Relatives of the deceased patients also were to be recontacted and told.

In May 1974, Brues, the medical director of the Center for Human Radiobiology, took a night flight to Dallas. There, he met another AEC official and the two of them drove to Milford, Texas, to tell Elmer's physician the truth behind the studies done a year earlier.

"I told him we found that the patient had received plutonium into the muscle of the sarcomatous leg three days before it was amputated, not enough in our belief to cause any trouble or to have any effect on the tumor, but that he should be carefully followed in any case because of the very small number of such cases that are living," Brues said.

Elmer's physician, Dr. Dewey H. Roberts, who was then eighty years old, thought the plutonium might have cured the cancer, Brues said. "Dr. Roberts was quick to form the belief that the injection may have cured the tumor: We tried to cool this but with questionable success. (I had given warning of this possibility before accepting the assignment.)," Brues wrote.

The Center for Human Radiobiology was "extremely anxious" to do an autopsy when Elmer died. It also wanted permission to check him again at intervals, Brues told Elmer's doctor.

Roberts assured the Chicago scientist he would be happy to cooperate and wanted advice on whom to call in case of serious illness or death. "He said these old fellows with hypertension, in his experience, are likely to go to sleep some night and not wake up," Brues said.

"We asked Roberts to tell the patient about the nature of the injection as he has a right to know. The records seems to indicate only that he gave voluntary consent to an injection of radioactive material," Brues said.

After the visit with Roberts, the two officials paid a "social visit" to Elmer. "Our visit was welcome; his wife was taking her grade-school class to the zoo in Dallas; he is moving into the new house, finest in the area, apparently somewhat financed by his two children who he visited when in the North," Brues said.

The two scientists didn't tell Elmer of the plutonium injection but advised him to talk with Roberts about a discussion they had had with him. Elmer told the two officials he would be happy to return for a "recheck" provided he didn't have to fly.

In a follow-up discussion, Elmer's doctor confirmed to AEC officials that Elmer had been told of the injection. "The patient was aware of the injection and wasn't much concerned although he did not know what it was that had been injected," the AEC report quotes Elmer's doctor as saying.

IN THE SPRING of 1974, James Liverman, a DOE official, met with Robert Berry, army general counsel, and Brig. Gen. R. W. Green, the deputy surgeon general of the army, to tell them they planned to inform the plutonium survivors of the long-ago injections.

"General Green was considerably concerned that no good was to be achieved in his view by surfacing a whole series of issues when nothing could in fact be done at this point in time with regard to changing those issues and that the patients or their relatives might in fact be worse off because of the public, social or psychological trauma," Liverman stated.

AEC officials also became worried in the mid-'70s about how to explain the experiment—should it ever become public.

But word eventually got out. In 1976, the experiment was reported in a Washington, D.C.-based newsletter called *Science Trends. The Washington Post* also reported the story on the front page on February 22, 1976.

In the *Post* story, an unnamed official said the department "had no plans to launch an investigation to try to learn more about the injection program." What the unnamed energy official didn't say was that an investigation had just been concluded two years earlier.

The DOE records dwindle after 1974. Unsigned, handwritten slips of paper kept score of how many patients were still alive as the years went by. The decision to discontinue the almost fifty-year-old experiment remains, in some ways, as mysterious as the decision to launch the project.

Stehney, one of the scientists involved in the later studies, said things just became too difficult. "There were things we didn't feel comfortable with. We thought we had done as much as could be done at that point."

Rundo, also involved in the follow-up studies, said it was his "vague" recollection that DOE told scientists to stop their investigation. "I think it was the lawyers who were concerned. They were afraid the families might sue," he said.

But Berkeley scientist Durbin tells a different story. "Someone went to talk with the one family and made misrepresentations.

"Those of us when we heard about that concluded the waters had been muddied, and we needed to let more time pass, let tempers cool. I was very angry that had happened," she said.

THE PLUTONIUM EXPERIMENT topped a litany of human experiments in a report issued in the late 1986 by the U.S. House of Representatives subcommittee on Energy, Conservation and Power. U.S. Rep. Edward J. Markey, a Massachusetts Democrat who chaired the subcommittee, compared the tests conducted by the DOE and its predecessors to the "kind of demented human experiments conducted by the Nazis."

"Documents provided by the Department of Energy reveal the frequent and systematic use of human subjects as guinea pigs for radiation experiments," the opening sentence of the report says.

Markey urged the DOE to make every effort to find the patients, follow up on radiation-associated diseases and to compensate "these unfortunate victims" for damages. The AEC, after its 1974 internal investigation, also recommended survivors be given medical surveillance, with the AEC or Department of Defense picking up the tab.

BUT THERE WAS NO POT of gold waiting for Elmer Allen, no government men who came to Italy in his waning years to try to make good.

Fighting his real and imagined ghosts, Elmer lived almost another five years after the subcommittee published its findings. Elmer died on June 30, 1991, of respiratory failure caused by pneumonia. He was eighty years old. On his death certificate, his occupation was listed as Pullman porter.

He spent some of his last days in silence at Italy's nursing home, a quiet place shaded by a large cottonwood tree. There, among the other aged residents, the cheerful nature of the amputee described by surgeons so many years ago was still evident.

"I knew he didn't want to be here, but he wasn't mean to us because he didn't want to be here. He tried to do quite a bit of stuff for himself," said Alithea Brown, a licensed vocational nurse at the Italy Convalescent Center.

"He wasn't a conversation starter. He would talk to you if you talked to him. I just never asked him how he lost his leg."

PART IV

Cold War Secrets

Introduction to
Aleksandr I. Solzhenitsyn's

The Gulag Archipelago

THE GULAG ARCHIPELAGO, one of the great books of the twentieth century, is a secret-history cathedral. At extreme risk, Solzhenitsyn thrust his "handful of truth" through the "gates of the abyss," the Soviet slave labor apparatus, revealing for the first time actual names, dates, and places of the system. Conceived by Solzhenitsyn as an "archipelago" or series of "islands"—camps, prison, detention centers—spread throughout the Soviet Union like a country within a country, the Gulag is an acronym for "Chief Administration of Corrective Labor Camps." Some forty to fifty million people served sentences in the Gulag from 1918 to 1953, mainly for "political" crimes such as commenting that Gorky was a bad writer, praying in church for the death of Stalin, or returning to the Soviet Union after having served as a prisoner of war of the Germans. On such pretexts people were arrested and confined as a way of keeping the population repressed and in constant fear of Stalin. "I must explain that *never once* did this whole book, in all its parts, lie on the same desk at the same time!" Solzhenitsyn wrote. "In September, 1965, when my work on the Archipelago was at its most intensive . . . my archive was raided and a novel impounded. At this point the parts of the Archipelago already written, and the materials for the other parts, were scattered, and never reassembled. . . . The jerkiness of the book, its imperfections, are the true mark of our persecuted literature."

Solzhenitsyn was born in 1918 in Kislovodsk in the northern Caucasus Mountains. He was an army captain during World War II. In 1945, he was arrested by Soviet counterintelligence agents who had discovered in his letters derogatory remarks about Stalin. He spent eight years in slave labor camps and three years in exile for his offense. In 1962, protected by Khrushchev's anti-Stalin campaign, Solzhenitsyn's first book, *One Day in the Life of Ivan Denisovich,* was published in the Soviet Union. In 1973, he authorized the Western publication of *The Gulag Archipelago.* This so angered the Soviet authorities that they exiled him from Russia in 1974. After living in Vermont, Solzhenitsyn returned to his homeland in 1994. In 1970, he was awarded the Nobel Prize in literature. As David Remnick, editor of *The New Yorker,* has written, "In terms of the effect he has had on history, Solzhenitsyn is the dominant writer of this century."

ADDITIONAL SOURCES

Scammel, Michael. *Solzhenitsyn.* New York: W. W. Norton and Company, 1984.

Solzhenitsyn, Aleksandr. *Cancer Ward.* New York: Farrar, Straus and Giroux, 1969.

———. *The First Circle.* New York: Harper and Row, 1968.

———. *The Gulag Archipelago 1918–1956: An Experiment in Literary Investigation.* vol. II, parts 3, 4, trans. Thomas Whitney. New York: Harper and Row, 1975.

———. *The Gulag Archipelago.* vol. III, parts 5, 6, 7, trans. Harry Willetts. New York: Harper and Row, 1978.

———. *One Day in the Life of Ivan Denisovich.* New York: Frederick A. Praeger, 1963.

Thomas, D. M. *Aleksandr Solzhenitsyn: A Century in His Life.* New York: St. Martin's Press, 1998.

Aleksandr I. Solzhenitsyn

Preface and Arrest

*THE GULAG ARCHIPELAGO 1918–1956: AN EXPERIMENT IN LITERARY
INVESTIGATION*, PARTS 1 AND 2, VOL. I, TRANSLATED FROM THE RUSSIAN
BY THOMAS P. WHITNEY, 1973

PREFACE

IN 1949 SOME FRIENDS and I came upon a noteworthy news item in *Nature*, a magazine of the Academy of Sciences. It reported in tiny type that in the course of excavations on the Kolyma River a subterranean ice lens had been discovered which was actually a frozen stream—and in it were found frozen specimens of prehistoric fauna some tens of thousands of years old. Whether fish or salamander, these were preserved in so fresh a state, the scientific correspondent reported, that those present immediately broke open the ice encasing the specimens and devoured them *with relish* on the spot.

The magazine no doubt astonished its small audience with the news of how successfully the flesh of fish could be kept fresh in a frozen state. But few, indeed, among its readers were able to decipher the genuine and heroic meaning of this incautious report.

As for us, however—we understood instantly. We could picture the entire scene right down to the smallest details: how those present broke up the ice in frenzied haste; how, flouting the higher claims of ichthyology and elbowing each other to be first, they tore off chunks of the prehistoric flesh and hauled them over to the bonfire to thaw them out and bolt them down.

We understood because we ourselves were the same kind of people as *those present* at that event. We, too, were from that powerful tribe of *zeks*, unique on the face of the earth, the only people who could devour prehistoric salamander *with relish*.

And the Kolyma was the greatest and most famous island, the pole of ferocity of that amazing country of *Gulag* which, though scattered in an Archipelago geographically, was, in the psychological sense, fused into a continent—an almost invisible, almost imperceptible country inhabited by the zek people.

And this Archipelago crisscrossed and patterned that other country within which it was located, like a gigantic patchwork, cutting into its cities, hovering over its streets. Yet there were many who did not even guess at its presence and many, many others who had heard something vague. And only those who had been there knew the whole truth.

But, as though stricken dumb on the islands of the Archipelago, they kept their silence.

By an unexpected turn of our history, a bit of the truth, an insignificant part of the whole, was allowed out in the open. But those same hands which once screwed tight our handcuffs now hold out their palms in reconciliation: "No, don't! Don't dig up the past! Dwell on the past and you'll lose an eye."

But the proverb goes on to say: "Forget the past and you'll lose both eyes."

Decades go by, and the scars and scores of the past are healing over for good. In the course of this period some of the islands of the Archipelago have shuddered and dissolved and the polar sea of oblivion rolls over them. And someday in the future, this Archipelago, its air, and the bones of its inhabitants, frozen in a lens of ice, will be discovered by our descendants like some improbable salamander.

I would not be so bold as to try to write the history of the Archipelago. I have never had the chance to read the documents. And, in fact, will anyone ever have the chance to read them? Those who do not wish to *recall* have already had enough time—and will have more—to destroy all the documents, down to the very last one.

I have absorbed into myself my own eleven years there not as something shameful nor as a nightmare to be cursed: I have come almost to love that monstrous world, and now, by a happy turn of events, I have also been entrusted with many recent reports and letters. So perhaps I shall be able to give some account of the bones and flesh of that salamander— which, incidentally, is still alive.

Arrest

How do people get to this clandestine Archipelago? Hour by hour planes fly there, ships steer their course there, and trains thunder off to it—but all with nary a mark on them to tell of their destination. And at ticket windows or at travel bureaus for Soviet or foreign tourists the employees would be astounded if you were to ask for a ticket to go there. They know nothing and they've never heard of the Archipelago as a whole or of any one of its innumerable islands.

Those who go to the Archipelago to administer it get there via the training schools of the Ministry of Internal Affairs.

Those who go there to be guards are conscripted via the military conscription centers.

And those who, like you and me, dear reader, go there to die, must get there solely and compulsorily via arrest.

Arrest! Need it be said that it is a breaking point in your life, a bolt of lightning which has scored a direct hit on you? That it is an unassimilable spiritual earthquake not every person can cope with, as a result of which people often slip into insanity?

The Universe has as many different centers as there are living beings in it. Each of us is a center of the Universe, and that Universe is shattered when they hiss at you: *"You are under arrest."*

If *you* are arrested, can anything else remain unshattered by this cataclysm?

But the darkened mind is incapable of embracing these displacements in our universe, and both the most sophisticated and the veriest simpleton among us, drawing on all life's experience, can gasp out only: "Me? What for?"

And this is a question which, though repeated millions and millions of times before, has yet to receive an answer.

Arrest is an instantaneous, shattering thrust, expulsion, somersault from one state into another.

We have been happily borne—or perhaps have unhappily dragged our weary way—down the long and crooked streets of our lives, past all kinds of walls and fences made of rotting wood, rammed earth, brick, concrete, iron railings. We have never given a thought to what lies behind them. We have never tried to penetrate them with our vision or our understanding. But there is where the *Gulag* country begins, right next to us, two yards away from us. In addition, we have failed to notice an enormous number of closely fitted, well-disguised doors and gates in these fences. All those gates were prepared for us, every last one! And all of a sudden the fateful gate swings quickly open, and four white male hands, unaccustomed to physical labor but nonetheless strong and tenacious, grab us by the leg, arm, collar, cap, ear, and drag us in like a sack, and the gate behind us, the gate to our past life, is slammed shut once and for all.

That's all there is to it! You are arrested!

And you'll find nothing better to respond with than a lamblike bleat: "Me? What for?"

That's what arrest is: it's a blinding flash and a blow which shifts the present instantly into the past and the impossible into omnipotent actuality.

That's all. And neither for the first hour nor for the first day will you be able to grasp anything else.

Except that in your desperation the fake circus moon will blink at you: "It's a mistake! They'll set things right!"

And everything which is by now comprised in the traditional, even literary, image of an arrest will pile up and take shape, not in your own disordered memory, but in what your family and your neighbors in your apartment remember: The sharp nighttime ring or the rude knock at the door. The insolent entrance of the unwiped jackboots of the unsleeping State Security operatives. The frightened and cowed civilian witness at their backs. (And what function does this civilian witness serve? The victim doesn't even dare think about it and the operatives don't remember, but that's what the regulations call for, and so he has to sit there all night long and sign in the morning.[1] For the witness, jerked from his bed, it is torture too—to go out night after night to help arrest his own neighbors and acquaintances.)

The traditional image of arrest is also trembling hands packing for the victim—a change of underwear, a piece of soap, something to eat; and no one knows what is needed, what is permitted, what clothes are best to wear; and the Security agents keep interrupting and hurrying you:

"You don't need anything. They'll feed you there. It's warm there." (It's all lies. They keep hurrying you to frighten you.)

The traditional image of arrest is also what happens afterward, when the poor victim has been taken away. It is an alien, brutal, and crushing force totally dominating the apartment for hours on end, a breaking, ripping open, pulling from the walls, emptying things from wardrobes and desks onto the floor, shaking, dumping out, and ripping apart—piling up mountains of litter on the floor—and the crunch of things being trampled beneath jackboots. And nothing is sacred in a search! During the arrest of the locomotive engineer Inoshin, a tiny coffin stood in his room containing the body of his newly dead child. The *"jurists"* dumped the child's body out of the coffin and searched it. They shake sick people out of their sickbeds, and they unwind bandages to search beneath them.[2]

Nothing is so stupid as to be inadmissible during a search! For example, they seized from the antiquarian Chetverukhin "a certain number of pages of Tsarist decrees"—to wit, the decree on ending the war with Napoleon, on the formation of the Holy Alliance, and a proclamation of public prayers against cholera during the epidemic of 1830. From our greatest expert on Tibet, Vostrikov, they confiscated ancient Tibetan manuscripts of great value; and it took the pupils of the deceased scholar thirty years to wrest them from the KGB! When the Orientalist Nevsky was arrested, they grabbed Tangut manuscripts—and twenty-five years later the deceased victim was posthumously awarded a Lenin Prize for deciphering them. From Karger they took his archive of the Yenisei Ostyaks and vetoed the alphabet and vocabulary he had developed for this people—and a small nationality was thereby left without any written language. It would take a long time to describe all this in educated speech, but there's a folk saying about the search which covers the subject: *They are looking for something which was never put there.* They carry off whatever they have seized, but sometimes they compel the arrested individual to carry it. Thus Nina Aleksandrovna Palchinskaya hauled over her shoulder a bag filled with the papers and letters of her eternally busy and active husband, the late great Russian engineer, carrying it into *their* maw—once and for all, forever.

For those left behind after the arrest there is the long tail end of a wrecked and devastated life. And the attempts to go and deliver food parcels. But from all the windows the answer comes in barking voices: "Nobody here by that name!" "Never heard of him!" Yes, and in the worst days in Leningrad it took five days of standing in crowded lines just to get to that window. And it may be only after half a year or a year that the arrested person responds at all. Or else the answer is tossed out: "Deprived of the right to correspond." And that means once and for all. "No right to correspondence"—and that almost for certain means: "Has been shot."[3]

That's how we picture arrest to ourselves.

The kind of night arrest described is, in fact, a favorite, because it has important advantages. Everyone living in the apartment is thrown into a state of terror by the first knock at the door. The arrested person is torn from the warmth of his bed. He is in a daze, half-asleep, helpless, and his judgment is befogged. In a night arrest the State Security men have a superiority in numbers; there are many of them, armed, against one person who hasn't even finished buttoning his trousers. During the arrest and search it is highly improbable that a crowd of potential supporters will gather at the entrance. The unhurried, step-by-step visits, first to one apartment, then to another, tomorrow to a third and a fourth, provide an opportunity for the Security operations personnel to be deployed with the maximum efficiency and to imprison many more citizens of a given town than the police force itself numbers.

In addition, there's an advantage to night arrests in that neither the people in neighboring apartment houses nor those on the city streets can see how many have been taken away. Arrests which frighten the closest neighbors are no event at all to those farther away. It's as if they had not taken place. Along that same asphalt ribbon on which the Black Marias scurry at night, a tribe of youngsters strides by day with banners, flowers, and gay, untroubled songs.

But those who *take,* whose work consists solely of arrests, for whom the horror is boringly repetitive, have a much broader understanding of how arrests operate. They operate according to a large body of theory, and innocence must not lead one to ignore this. The science of arrest is an important segment of the course on general penology and has been propped up with a substantial body of social theory. Arrests are classified according to various criteria: nighttime and daytime; at home, at work, during a journey; first-time arrests and repeats; individual and group arrests. Arrests are distinguished by the degree of surprise required, the amount of resistance expected (even though in tens of millions of cases no resistance was expected and in fact there was none). Arrests are also differentiated by the thoroughness of the required search;[4] by instructions either to make out or not to make out an inventory of confiscated property or seal a room or apartment; to arrest the wife after the husband and send the children to an orphanage, or to send the rest of the family into exile, or to send the old folks to a labor camp too.

No, no: arrests vary widely in form. In 1926 Irma Mendel, a Hungarian, obtained through the Comintern two front-row tickets to the Bolshoi Theatre. Interrogator Klegel was courting her at the time and she invited him to go with her. They sat through the show very affectionately, and when it was over he took her—straight to the Lubyanka. And if on a flowering June day in 1927 on Kuznetsky Most, the plump-cheeked, redheaded beauty Anna Skripnikova, who had just bought some navy-blue material for a dress, climbed into a hansom cab with a young man-about-town, you can be sure it wasn't a lovers' tryst at all, as the cabman understood very well and showed by his frown (he knew the *Organs* don't pay). It was an arrest. In just a moment they would turn on the Lubyanka and enter the black maw of the gates. And if, some twenty-two springs later, Navy Captain Second Rank Boris Burkovsky, wearing a white tunic and a trace of expensive eau de cologne, was buying a cake for a young lady, do not take an oath that the cake would ever reach the young lady and not be sliced up instead by the knives of the men searching the captain and then delivered to him in his first cell. No, one certainly cannot say that daylight arrest, arrest during a journey, or arrest in the middle of a crowd has ever been neglected in our country. However, it has always been clean-cut—and, most surprising of all, the victims, in cooperation with the Security men, have conducted themselves in the noblest conceivable manner, so as to spare the living from witnessing the death of the condemned.

Not everyone can be arrested at home, with a preliminary knock at the door (and if there is a knock, then it has to be the house manager or else the postman). And not everyone can be arrested at work either. If the person to be arrested is vicious, then it's better to seize him *outside* his ordinary milieu—away from his family and colleagues, from those who share his views, from any hiding places. It is essential that he have no chance to destroy, hide, or pass on anything to anyone. VIP's in the military or the Party were sometimes first given new assignments, ensconced in a private railway car, and then arrested en route. Some obscure, ordinary mortal, scared to death by epidemic arrests all around him and already depressed for a week by sinister glances from his chief, is suddenly summoned to the local Party committee, where he is beamingly presented with a vacation ticket to a Sochi sanatorium. The rabbit is overwhelmed and immediately concludes that his fears were groundless. After expressing his gratitude, he hurries home, triumphant, to pack his suitcase. It is only two hours till train time, and he scolds his wife for being too slow. He arrives at the station with time to spare. And there in the waiting room or at the bar he is hailed by an extraordinarily pleasant young man: "Don't you remember me, Pyotr Ivanich?" Pyotr Ivanich has difficulty remembering: "Well, not exactly, you see, although . . ." The young man, however, is overflowing with friendly concern: "Come now, how can that be? I'll have to remind you. . . ." And he bows respectfully to Pyotr Ivanich's wife: "You must forgive us. I'll keep him only *one minute*." The wife accedes, and trustingly the husband lets himself be led away by the arm—forever or for ten years!

The station is thronged—and no one notices anything. . . . Oh, you citizens who love to travel! Do not forget that in every station there are a GPU Branch and several prison cells.

This importunity of alleged acquaintances is so abrupt that only a person who has not had the wolfish preparation of camp life is likely to pull back from it. Do not suppose, for example, that if you are an employee of the American Embassy by the name of Alexander D. you cannot be arrested in broad daylight on Gorky Street, right by the Central Telegraph Office. Your unfamiliar friend dashes through the press of the crowd, and opens his plundering arms to embrace you: "Saaasha!" He simply shouts at you, with no effort to be inconspicuous. "Hey, pal! Long time no see! Come on over, let's get out of the way." At that moment a Pobeda sedan draws up to the curb. . . . And several days later TASS will issue an angry statement to all the papers alleging that informed circles of the Soviet government have no information on the disappearance of Alexander D. But what's so unusual about that? Our boys have carried out such arrests in Brussels—which was where Zhora Blednov was seized—not just in Moscow.

One has to give the *Organs* their due: in an age when public speeches, the plays in our theaters, and women's fashions all seem to have come off assembly lines, arrests can be of the most varied kind. They take you aside in a factory corridor after you have had your pass checked—and you're arrested. They take you from a military hospital with a temperature of 102, as they did with Ans Bernshtein, and the doctor will not raise a peep about your arrest—just let him try! They'll take you right off the operating table—as they took N. M. Vorobyev, a school inspector, in 1936, in the middle of an operation for stomach ulcer—and drag you off to a cell, as they did him, half-alive and all bloody (as Karpunich recollects). Or, like Nadya Levitskaya, you try to get information about your mother's sentence, and they give it to you, but it turns out to be a confrontation—and your own arrest! In the Gastronome—the fancy food store—you are invited to the special-order department and arrested there. You are arrested by a religious pilgrim whom you have put up for the night "for the sake of Christ." You are arrested by a meterman who has come to read your electric meter. You are arrested by a bicyclist who has run into you on the street, by a railway conductor, a taxi driver, a savings bank teller, the manager of a movie theater. Any one of them can arrest you, and you notice the concealed maroon-colored identification card only when it is too late.

Sometimes arrests even seem to be a game—there is so much super-fluous imagination, so much well-fed energy, invested in them. After all, the victim would not resist anyway. Is it that the Security agents want to justify their employment and their numbers? After all, it would seem enough to send notices to all the rabbits marked for arrest, and they would show up obediently at the designated hour and minute at the iron gates of State Security with a bundle in their hands—ready to occupy a piece of floor in the cell for which they were intended. And, in fact, that's the way collective farmers are arrested. Who wants to go all the way to a hut at night, with no roads to travel on? They are summoned to the village soviet—and arrested there. Manual workers are called into the office.

Of course, every machine has a point at which it is overloaded, beyond which it cannot function. In the strained and overloaded years of 1945 and 1946, when trainload after trainload poured in from Europe, to be swallowed up immediately and sent off to *Gulag,* all that excessive theatri-cality went out the window, and the whole theory suffered greatly. All the fuss and feathers of ritual went flying in every direction, and the arrest of tens of thousands took on the appearance of a squalid roll call: they stood there with lists, read off the names of those on one train, loaded them onto another, and that was the whole arrest.

For several decades political arrests were distinguished in our country precisely by the fact that people were arrested who were guilty of nothing and were therefore unprepared to put up any resistance whatsoever. There was a general feeling of being destined for destruction, a sense of having nowhere to escape from the GPU-NKVD (which, incidentally, given our internal passport system, was quite accurate). And even in the fever of epidemic arrests, when people leaving for work said farewell to their families every day, because they could not be certain they would re-turn at night, even then almost no one tried to run away and only in rare cases did people commit suicide. And that was exactly what was required. A submissive sheep is a find for a wolf.

This submissiveness was also due to ignorance of the mechanics of epidemic arrests. By and large, the *Organs* had no profound reasons for their choice of whom to arrest and whom not to arrest. They merely had overall assignments, quotas for a specific number of arrests. These quotas might be filled on an orderly basis or wholly arbitrarily. In 1937 a woman came to the reception room of the Novocherkassk NKVD to ask what she should do about the unfed unweaned infant of a neighbor who had been arrested. They said: "Sit down, we'll find out." She sat there for two hours—whereupon they took her and tossed her into a cell. They had a total plan which had to be fulfilled in a hurry, and there was no one available to send out into the city—and here was this woman already in their hands!

On the other hand, the NKVD did come to get the Latvian Andrei Pavel near Orsha. But he didn't open the door; he jumped out the window, escaped, and shot straight to Siberia. And even though he lived under his own name, and it was clear from his documents that he had come from Orsha, he was *never* arrested, nor summoned to the Organs, nor subjected to any suspicion whatsoever. After all, search for wanted persons falls into three categories: All-Union, republican, and provincial. And the pursuit of nearly half of those arrested in those epidemics would have been confined to the provinces. A person marked for arrest by virtue of chance circumstances, such as a neighbor's denunciation, could be easily replaced by another neighbor. Others, like Andrei Pavel, who found themselves in a trap or an ambushed apartment by accident, and who were bold enough to escape immediately, before they could be questioned, were never caught and never charged; while those who stayed behind to await justice got a term in prison. And the overwhelming majority—almost all—behaved just like that: without any spirit, helplessly, with a sense of doom.

It is true, of course, that the NKVD, in the absence of the person it wanted, would make his relatives guarantee not to leave the area. And, of course, it was easy enough *to cook up* a case against those who stayed behind to replace the one who had fled.

Universal innocence also gave rise to the universal failure to act. Maybe they *won't take* you? Maybe it will all blow over? A. I. Ladyzhensky was the chief teacher in a school in remote Kologriv. In 1937 a peasant approached him in an open market and passed him a message from a third person: "Aleksandr Ivanich, get out of town, *you are on the list!*" But he stayed: After all, the whole school rests on my shoulders, and *their own* children are pupils here. How can they arrest me? (Several days later he was arrested.) Not everyone was so fortunate as to understand at the age of fourteen, as did Vanya Levitsky: "Every honest man is sure to go to prison. Right now my papa is serving time, and when I grow up they'll put me in too." (They put him in when he was twenty-three years old.) The majority sit quietly and dare to hope. Since you aren't guilty, then how can they arrest you? *It's a mistake!* They are already dragging you along by the collar, and you still keep on exclaiming to yourself: "It's a mistake! *They'll set things straight and let me out!*" Others are being arrested en masse, and that's a bothersome fact, but in those other cases there is always some dark area: "Maybe *he* was guilty . . . ?" But as for you, you are obviously innocent! You still believe that the *Organs* are humanly logical institutions: they will set things straight and let you out.

Why, then, should you run away? And how can you resist right then? After all, you'll only make your situation worse; you'll make it more difficult for them to sort out the mistake. And it isn't just that you don't put up any resistance; you even walk down the stairs on tiptoe, as you are ordered to do, so your neighbors won't hear.[5]

At what exact point, then, should one resist? When one's belt is taken away? When one is ordered to face into a corner? When one crosses the threshold of one's home? An arrest consists of a series of incidental irrelevancies, of a multitude of things that do not matter, and there seems no point in arguing about any one of them individually—especially at a time when the thoughts of the person arrested are wrapped tightly about the big question: "What for?"—and yet all these incidental irrelevancies taken together implacably constitute the arrest.

Almost anything can occupy the thoughts of a person who has just been arrested! This alone would fill volumes. There can be feelings which we never suspected. When nineteen-year-old Yevgeniya Doyarenko was arrested in 1921 and three young Chekists were poking about her bed and through the underwear in her chest of drawers, she was not disturbed. There was nothing there, and they would find nothing. But all of a sudden they touched her personal diary, which she would not have shown even to her own mother. And these hostile young strangers reading the words she had written was more devastating to her than the whole Lubyanka with its bars and its cellars. It is true of many that the outrage inflicted by arrest on their personal feelings and attachments can be far, far stronger than their political beliefs or their fear of prison. A person who is not inwardly prepared for the use of violence against him is always weaker than the person committing the violence.

There are a few bright and daring individuals who understand instantly. Grigoryev, the Director of the Geological Institute of the Academy of Sciences, barricaded himself inside and spent two hours burning up his papers when they came to arrest him in 1948.

Sometimes the principal emotion of the person arrested is relief and even *happiness!* This is another aspect of human nature. It happened before the Revolution too: the Yekaterinodar schoolteacher Serdyukova, involved in the case of Aleksandr Ulyanov, felt only relief when she was arrested. But this feeling was a thousand times stronger during epidemics of arrests when all around you they were hauling in people like yourself and still had not come for you; for some reason they were taking their time. After all, that kind of exhaustion, that kind of suffering, is worse than any kind of arrest, and not only for a person of limited courage. Vasily Vlasov, a fearless Communist, whom we shall recall more than once later on, renounced the idea of escape proposed by his non-Party assistants, and pined away because the entire leadership of the Kady District was arrested in 1937, and they kept delaying and delaying his own arrest. He could only endure the blow head on. He did endure it, and then he relaxed, and during the first days after his arrest he felt marvelous. In 1934 the priest Father Irakly went to Alma-Ata to visit some believers in exile there. During his absence they came three times to his Moscow apartment to arrest him. When he returned, members of his flock met him at the station and refused to let him go home, and for eight years hid him in one apartment after another. The priest suffered so painfully from this harried life that when he was finally arrested in 1942 he sang hymns of praise to God.

In this chapter we are speaking only of the masses, the helpless rabbits arrested for no one knows what reason. But in this book we will also have to touch on those who in postrevolutionary times remained genuinely *political*. Vera Rybakova, a Social Democratic student, *dreamed* when she was in freedom of being in the detention center in Suzdal. Only there did she hope to encounter her old comrades—for there were none of them left in freedom. And only there could she work out her world outlook. The Socialist Revolutionary—the SR—Yekaterina Olitskaya didn't consider herself *worthy* of being imprisoned in 1924. After all, Russia's best people had served time and she was still young and had not yet done anything for Russia. But *freedom* itself was expelling her. And so both of them went to prison—with pride and happiness.

"Resistance! Why didn't you resist?" Today those who have continued to live on in comfort scold those who suffered.

Yes, resistance should have begun right there, at the moment of the arrest itself.

But it did not begin.

AND SO THEY ARE *leading* you. During a daylight arrest there is always that brief and unique moment when they are *leading* you, either inconspicuously, on the basis of a cowardly deal you have made, or else quite openly, their pistols unholstered, through a crowd of hundreds of just such doomed innocents as yourself. You aren't gagged. You really can and you really ought to *cry out*—to *cry out* that you are being arrested! That villains in disguise are trapping people! That arrests are being made on the strength of false denunciations! That millions are being subjected to silent reprisals! If many such outcries had been heard all over the city in the course of a day, would not our fellow citizens perhaps have begun to bristle? And would arrests perhaps no longer have been so easy?

In 1927, when submissiveness had not yet softened our brains to such a degree, two Chekists tried to arrest a woman on Serpukhov Square during the day. She grabbed hold of the stanchion of a street-lamp and began to scream, refusing to submit. A crowd gathered. (There had to have been that kind of woman; there had to have been that kind of crowd too! Passers-by didn't all just close their eyes and hurry by!) The quick young men immediately became flustered. They can't *work* in the public eye. They got into their car and fled. (Right then and there she should have gone to a railroad station and left! But she went home to spend the night. And during the night they took her off to the Lubyanka.)

Instead, not one sound comes from *your* parched lips, and that passing crowd naïvely believes that you and your executioners are friends out for a stroll.

I myself often had the chance to *cry out*.

On the eleventh day after my arrest, three SMERSH bums, more burdened by four suitcases full of war booty than by me (they had come to rely on me in the course of the long trip), brought me to the Byelorussian Station in Moscow. They were called a *Special Convoy*—in other words, a special escort guard—but in actual fact their automatic pistols only interfered with their dragging along the four terribly heavy bags of loot they and their chiefs in SMERSH counterintelligence on the Second Byelorussian Front had plundered in Germany and were now bringing to their families in the Fatherland under the pretext of convoying me. I myself lugged a fifth suitcase with no great joy since it contained my diaries and literary works, which were being used as evidence against me.

Not one of the three knew the city, and it was up to me to pick the shortest route to the prison. I had personally to conduct them to the Lubyanka, where they had never been before (and which, in fact, I confused with the Ministry of Foreign Affairs).

I had spent one day in the counterintelligence prison at army headquarters and three days in the counterintelligence prison at the headquarters of the front, where my cellmates had educated me in the deceptions practiced by the interrogators, their threats and beatings; in the fact that once a person was arrested he was never released; and in the inevitability of a *tenner*, a ten-year sentence; and then by a miracle I had suddenly burst out of there and for four days had traveled like a *free* person among *free* people, even though my flanks had already lain on rotten straw beside the latrine bucket, my eyes had already beheld beaten-up and sleepless men, my ears had heard the truth, and my mouth had tasted prison gruel. So why did I keep silent? Why, in my last minute out in the open, did I not attempt to enlighten the hoodwinked crowd?

I kept silent, too, in the Polish city of Brodnica—but maybe they didn't understand Russian there. I didn't call out one word on the streets of Bialystok—but maybe it wasn't a matter that concerned the Poles. I didn't utter a sound at the Volkovysk Station—but there were very few people there. I walked along the Minsk Station platform beside those same bandits as if nothing at all were amiss—but the station was still a ruin. And now I was leading the SMERSH men through the circular upper concourse of the Byelorussian-Radial subway station on the Moscow circle line, with its white-ceilinged dome and brilliant electric lights, and opposite us two parallel escalators, thickly packed with Muscovites, rising from below. It seemed as though they were all look-ing at me! They kept coming in an endless ribbon from down there, from the depths of ignorance—on and on beneath the gleaming dome, reaching toward me for at least one word of truth—so why did I keep silent?

Every man always has handy a dozen glib little reasons why he is right not to sacrifice himself.

Some still have hopes of a favorable outcome to their case and are afraid to ruin their chances by an outcry. (For, after all, we get no news from that other world, and we do not realize that from the very moment of arrest our fate has almost certainly been decided in the worst possible sense and that we cannot make it any worse.) Others have not yet attained the mature concepts on which a shout of protest to the crowd must be based. Indeed, only a revolutionary has slogans on his lips that are crying to be uttered aloud; and where would the uninvolved, peaceable average man come by such slogans? He simply *does not know what* to shout. And then, last of all, there is the person whose heart is too full of emotion, whose eyes have seen too much, for that whole ocean to pour forth in a few disconnected cries.

As for me, I kept silent for one further reason: because those Mus-covites thronging the steps of the escalators were too few for me, *too few!* Here my cry would be heard by 200 or twice 200, but what about the 200 million? Vaguely, unclearly, I had a vision that someday I would cry out to the 200 million.

But for the time being I did not open my mouth, and the escalator dragged me implacably down into the nether world.

And when I got to Okhotny Ryad, I continued to keep silent.

Nor did I utter a cry at the Metropole Hotel.

Nor wave my arms on the Golgotha of Lubyanka Square.

[Editor's Note: Solzhenitsyn placed a break in the chapter here. The remaining omitted six pages give further details of his arrest.]

NOTES

1. The regulation, purposeless in itself, derives, N.M. recalls, from that strange time when the citizenry not only was supposed to but actually dared to verify the actions of the police.

2. When in 1937 they wiped out Dr. Kazakov's institute, the "commission" broke up the jars containing the *lysates* developed by him, even though patients who had been cured and others still being treated rushed around them, begging them to preserve the miraculous medicines. (According to the official version, the lysates were supposed to be poisons; in that case, why should they not have been kept as material evidence?)

3. In other words, "We live in the cursed conditions in which a human being can disappear into the void and even his closest relatives, his mother and his wife . . . do not know for years what has become of him." Is that right or not? That is what Lenin wrote in 1910 in his obituary of Babushkin. But let's speak frankly: Babushkin was transporting arms for an uprising, and was caught with them when he was shot. He knew what he was doing. You couldn't say that about helpless rabbits like us.

4. And there is a separate Science of Searches too. I have had the chance to read a pamphlet on this subject for correspondence-school law students in Alma-Ata. Its author praises highly those police officials who in the course of their searches went so far as to turn over two tons of manure, eight cubic yards of firewood, or two loads of hay; cleaned the snow from an entire collective-farm vegetable plot, dismantled brick ovens, dug up cesspools, checked out toilet bowls, looked into doghouses, chicken coops, birdhouses, tore apart mattresses, ripped adhesive tape off people's bodies and even tore out metal teeth in the search for microfilm. Students were advised to begin and to end with a body search (during the course of the search the arrested person might have grabbed up something that had already been examined). They were also advised to return to the site of a search at a different time of day and carry out the search all over again.

5. And how we burned in the camps later, thinking: What would things have been like if every Security operative, when he went out at night to make an arrest, had been uncertain whether he would return alive and had to say good-bye to his family? Or if, during periods of mass arrests, as for example in Leningrad, when they arrested a quarter of the entire city, people had not simply sat there in their lairs, paling with terror at every bang of the downstairs door and at every step on the staircase, but had understood they had nothing left to lose and had boldly set up in the downstairs hall an ambush of half a dozen people with axes, hammers, pokers, or whatever else was at hand? After all, you knew ahead of time that those bluecaps were out at night for no good purpose. And you could be sure ahead of time that you'd be cracking the skull of a cutthroat. Or what about the Black Maria sitting out there on the street with one lonely chauffeur—what if it had been driven off or its tires spiked? The Organs would very quickly have suffered a short-

age of officers and transport and, notwithstanding all of Stalin's thirst, the cursed machine would have ground to a halt!

If . . . if . . . We didn't love freedom enough. And even more—we had no awareness of the real situation. We spent ourselves in one unrestrained outburst in 1917, and then we *hurried* to submit. We submitted *with pleasure!* (Arthur Ransome describes a workers' meeting in Yaroslavl in 1921. Delegates were sent to the workers from the Central Committee in Moscow to confer on the substance of the argument about trade unions. The representative of the opposition, Y. Larin, explained to the workers that their trade union must be their defense against the administration, that they possessed rights which they had won and upon which no one else had any right to infringe. The workers, however, were completely indifferent, simply *not comprehending* whom they still needed to be defended against and why they still needed any rights. When the spokesman for the Party line rebuked them for their laziness and for getting out of hand, and demanded sacrifices from them—overtime work without pay, reductions in food, military discipline in the factory administration—this aroused great elation and applause.) We purely and simply *deserved* everything that happened afterward.

Introduction to
Edward R. Murrow's

"A Report on Senator Joseph R. McCarthy"

E DWARD R. MURROW'S distinguished career in broadcast journalism
stretched from Hitler's 1938 arrival in Vienna, to London during the
Blitz, to the war in North Africa, Allied bombing raids over Berlin, and
the battlefields of Korea. Having heard his reports during the Blitz, who
can ever forget the poignant sound of his words: "This—is London."

But Murrow's finest hour was his television program broadcast on
March 9, 1954, at 10:30 P.M. from CBS *See It Now*'s Studio 41 in the Grand
Central Terminal Building in New York City. "No one man can terrorize a
whole nation unless we are all his accomplices," he told his staff while
preparing the report about Senator Joseph R. McCarthy, who used his
Senate committee to conduct a witch-hunt against people he accused of
being Communists. McCarthy's calumnies, half-truths, and false accusations were exposed in the broadcast. Murrow's closing statement is applicable to the present: "We proclaim ourselves, as indeed we are, the defenders
of freedom, what's left of it, but we cannot defend freedom abroad by
deserting it at home. The actions of the junior senator from Wisconsin
have caused alarm and dismay amongst our allies abroad and given considerable comfort to our enemies, and whose fault is that? Not really his,
he didn't create this situation of fear, he merely exploited it and rather
successfully. Cassius was right, 'The fault, dear Brutus, is not in our stars,
but in ourselves.'"

The day after the broadcast, CBS received the largest positive response
it had ever received to any program though Murrow did not believe the
program "was to any large degree responsible for McCarthy's downfall,"

wrote Alexander Kendrick in his biography of Murrow, *Prime Time*. Yet many Americans believed that McCarthy's censure months later by the Senate, effectively ending his career, was merely a ratification of the censure Murrow had delivered on television. His broadcast "marked the first time on American television that McCarthy's citations had ever been refuted by the recital of the true facts in each case," Kendrick observed.

As television became more inglorious and banal, as profits and entertainment became dominant, and as news divisions decreased in importance, Murrow's position at CBS weakened. He resigned in 1961, becoming director of the United States Information Agency (USIA) under President Kennedy. In 1964 he was awarded the Presidential Medal of Freedom, the highest civilian honor. He died less than a year later.

ADDITIONAL SOURCES

Bliss, Edward, Jr., ed. *In Search of Light: The Broadcasts of Edward R. Murrow, 1938–1961*. New York: Alfred A. Knopf, 1967.

Kendrick, Alexander. *Prime Time: The Life of Edward R. Murrow*. Boston, Toronto: Little, Brown and Co., 1969.

Museum of Television & Radio, internet site: www.mtr.org

Persico, Joseph E. *Edward R. Murrow: An American Original*. New York: McGraw-Hill, 1988.

Edward R. Murrow

"A Report on Senator Joseph R. McCarthy,"

SEE IT NOW, CBS, MARCH 9, 1954

Murrow: Good evening. Tonight *See It Now* devotes its entire half hour to a report on Senator Joseph R. McCarthy told mainly in his own words and pictures. But first ALCOA would like you to meet a man who has been with them for fifty years.

(COMMERCIAL)

Murrow: Because a report on Senator McCarthy is by definition controversial we want to say exactly what we mean to say and I request your permission to read from the script whatever remarks Murrow and Friendly *may* make. If the Senator believes we have done violence to his words or pictures and desires to speak, to answer himself, an opportunity will be afforded him on this program. Our working thesis tonight is this question.

"If this fight against Communism is made a fight against America's two great political parties the American people know that one of these parties will be destroyed and the Republic cannot endure very long as a one party system."

We applaud that statement and we think Senator McCarthy ought to. He said it, seventeen months ago in Milwaukee.

McCarthy: The American people realize this cannot be made a fight between America's two great political parties. If this fight against Communism is made a fight between America's two great political parties the American people know that one of those parties will be destroyed and the Republic cannot endure very long as a one party system.

Murrow: Thus on February 4th, 1954, Senator McCarthy spoke of one party's treason. This was at Charleston, West Virginia, where there were no cameras running. It was recorded on tape.

McCarthy: The issue between the Republicans and Democrats is clearly drawn. It has been deliberately drawn by those who have been in charge of twenty years of treason. The hard fact is—the hard fact is that those who wear the label, those who wear the label Democrat wear it with the stain of a historic betrayal.

Murrow: Seventeen months ago Candidate Eisenhower met Senator McCarthy in Green Bay, Wisconsin, and he laid down the ground rules on how he would meet Communism if elected.

Eisenhower: This is a pledge I make. If I am charged by you people to be the responsible head of the Executive Department it will be my initial responsibility to see that subversion, disloyalty, is kept out of the Executive Department. We will always appreciate and welcome Congressional investigation but the responsibility will rest squarely on the shoulders of the Executive and I hold that there are ample powers in the government to get rid of these people if the Executive Department is really concerned in doing it. We can do it with absolute assurance.

(APPLAUSE)

This is America's principle; trial by jury, of the innocent until proved guilty, and I expect to stand to do it.

Murrow: That same night in Milwaukee, Senator McCarthy stated what he would do if the general was elected.

McCarthy: I spent about a half hour with the general last night. While I can't—while I can't report that we agreed entirely on everything—I can report that when I left that meeting with the general, I had the same feeling as when I went in, and that is that he is a great American, and will make a great president, an outstanding president. But I want to tell you tonight, tell the American people as long as I represent you and the rest of the American people in the Senate, I shall continue to call them as I see them regardless of who happens to be president.

Murrow: November 24th, 1953.

McCarthy: A few days ago I read that President Eisenhower expressed the hope that by election time in 1954 the subject of Communism would be a dead and forgotten issue. The raw, harsh unpleasant fact is that Communism is an issue and will be an issue in 1954.

Murrow: On one thing the Senator has been consistent . . . Often operating as a one-man committee, he has traveled far, interviewed many, terrorized some, accused civilian and military leaders of the past administration of a great conspiracy to turn the country over to Communism, investigated and substantially demoralized the present State Department, made varying charges of espionage at Fort Monmouth. (The Army says it has been unable to find anything relating to espionage there.) He has interrogated a varied assortment of what he calls "Fifth Amendment Communists." Republican Senator Flanders of Vermont said of McCarthy today:

> *"He dons war paint; he goes into his war dance; he emits his war whoops; he goes forth to battle and proudly returns with the scalp of a pink army dentist."*

Other critics have accused the senator of using the bull whip and smear. There was a time two years ago when the senator and his friends said he had been smeared and bull whipped.

Mr. Keefe: You would sometimes think to hear the quartet that call themselves "Operation Truth" damning Joe McCarthy and resorting to the vilest smears I have ever heard. Well, this is the answer, and if I could express it in what is in my heart right now, I would do it in terms of the poet who once said:

> Ah 'tis but a dainty flower I bring you,
> Yes, 'tis but a violet, glistening with dew,
> But still in its heart there lies beauties concealed
> So in our heart our love for you lies unrevealed.

McCarthy: You know, I used to pride myself on the idea that I was a bit tough, especially over the past eighteen or nineteen months when we have been kicked around and bull whipped and damned. I didn't think that I could be touched very deeply. But tonight, frankly, my cup and my heart is so full I can't talk to you.

Murrow: But in Philadelphia, on Washington's Birthday, 1954, his heart was so full he could talk. He reviewed some of the General Zwicker testimony and proved he hadn't abused him.

McCarthy: Nothing is more serious than a traitor to this country in the Communist conspiracy. Question: "Do you think stealing $50 is more serious than being a traitor to the country and a part of the Communist conspiracy?" Answer: "That, sir, was not my decision."

Shall we go on to that for a while? I hate to impose on your time. I just got two pages. This is the abuse which is . . . the real meat of abuse, this is the Official reporter's record of the hearing. After he said he wouldn't remove that general from the army who cleared Communists, I said: "Then General, you should be removed from any command. Any man who has been given the honor of being promoted to general, and who says, 'I will protect another general who protectes Communists,' is not fit to wear that uniform, General."

(APPLAUSE)

"I think it is a tremendous disgrace to the Army to have to bring these facts before the public but I intend to give it to the public, General, I have a duty to do that. I intend to repeat to the press exactly what you said so that you can know that and be back here to hear it, General."

And wait 'til you hear the bleeding hearts scream and cry about our methods of trying to drag the truth from those who know, or should know, who covered up a Fifth Amendment Communist Major. But they say, "Oh, it's all right to uncover them but don't get rough doing it, McCarthy."

Murrow: But two days later, Secretary Stevens and the senator had lunch, agreed on a memorandum of understanding, disagreed on what the small type said.

Stevens: I shall never accede to the abuse of army personnel under any circumstance including committee hearings. I shall not accede to them being brow beaten or humiliated. In the light of those assurances although I did not propose cancellation of the hearing, I acceded to it. If it had not been for these assurances, I would never have entered into any agreement whatsoever.

Murrow: Then President Eisenhower issued a statement that his advisers thought censored the senator, but the senator saw it as another victory, called the entire Zwicker case "a tempest in a teapot."

McCarthy: If a stupid, arrogant or witless man in a position of power appears before our Committee and is found aiding the Communist Party, he will be exposed. The fact that he might be a general places him in no special class as far as I am concerned. Apparently—apparently, the president and I now agree on the necessity of getting rid of Communists. We apparently disagree only on how we should handle those who protect Communists. When the shouting and the tumult dies the American people and the president will realize that this unprecedented mud slinging against the committee by the extreme left-wing elements of press and radio were caused solely because another Fifth Amendment Communist was finally dug out of the dark recesses and exposed to the public view.

Murrow: Senator McCarthy claims that only the left-wing press criticized him on the Zwicker case. Of the fifty large circulation newspapers in the country, these are the left wing papers that criticized. These are the ones which supported him. The ratio is about three to one against the Senator. Now let us look at some of these left-wing papers that criticized the Senator.

> *The Chicago Tribune:* McCarthy will better serve his cause
> if he learns to distinguish the role of investigator from
> the role of avenging angel.
>
> *The New York Times:* The unwarranted interference of a
> demagogue—a domestic Munich.
>
> *The Times Herald,* Washington: Senator McCarthy's behav-
> ior toward Zwicker is not justified.
>
> *The Herald Tribune* of New York: McCarthyism involves as-
> sault on Republican assets.
>
> *Milwaukee Journal:* The line must be drawn and defended
> or McCarthy will become the government.
>
> *The Evening Star* of Washington: It was a bad day for every-
> one who resents and detests the bully boy tactics which
> Senator McCarthy often employs.

The New York World Telegram: Bamboozling, bludgeoning, distorting.

St. Louis Post-Dispatch: Unscroupulous bullying. What tragic irony—the president's advisers keep him from doing what ever decent instinct must command him to do.

That is the ratio from three to one of the left wing press.

There was one other interesting quote on the Zwicker controversy, and it came from the Senator himself.

McCarthy: May I say that I was extremely shocked when I heard that Secretary Stevens told two army officers they had to take part in the cover-up of those who promoted and coddled Communists. As I read his statement. I thought of that quotation "On what meat doth this, our Caesar, feed?"

Murrow: And upon what meat does Senator McCarthy feed? Two of the staples of his diet are the investigations (protected by immunity) and the half-truth. We herewith submit samples of both. First, the half-truth. This was an attack on Adlai Stevenson at the end of the '52 campaign. President Eisenhower, it must be said, had no prior knowledge of it.

McCarthy: I perform this unpleasant task because the American people are entitled to have the coldly documented history of this man who says he wants to be your president. But strangely, Alger—I mean Adlai . . . but let's move on to another part of the jigsaw puzzle. While you may think that there can be no connection between the debonair Democrat candidate and a dilapidated Massachusetts barn, I want to show you a picture of this barn and explain the connection. Here is the outside of the barn. Give me the picture of the inside of the barn. Here is the outside of the barn at Lee, Massachusetts. It looks as though it couldn't house a farmer's cow or goat. Here's the inside. (Showing picture) A beautiful, paneled conference room with maps of the Soviet Union. What way does Stevenson tie up with that?

My—my investigators went out and took pictures of the barn after we had been tipped off what was in it. Tipped off that there was in this barn all the missing documents from the Communist front—IPR. The

IPR which was named by the McCarran Committee—named before the McCarran Committee as a cover-up for Communist espionage. Let's take a look at the photostat of the document taken from the Massachusetts barn. One of those documents which was never supposed to see the light of day. Rather interesting it is. This is a document which shows that Alger Hiss and Frank Coe recommended Adlai Stevenson to the Mount Tremblant Conference which was called for the purpose of establishing foreign policy—postwar policy in Asia. As you know, Alger Hiss is a convicted traitor, Frank Coe is a man who has been named under oath before the Congressional Committee seven times as a member of the Communist Party. Why, why Hiss and Coe find that Adlai Stevenson is the man they want representing them at this conference? I don't know. Perhaps Adlai knows.

Murrow: But Senator McCarthy didn't permit his audience to hear the entire paragraph. This is the official record of the McCarran hearings and anyone could have bought it for two dollars. Quote: "Another possibility for the Mount Tremblant Conferences on Asia is someone from Knox's office or Stimson's office." (Frank Knox was our wartime Secretary of the Navy; Henry Stimson our Secretary of the Army, both distinguished Republicans) Coe and Hiss mentioned Adlai Stevenson, one of Knox's special assistants and Harvey Bundy, former assistant secretary of state under Hoover, and now assistant to Stimson because of their jobs.

We read from this documented record not in defense of Mr. Stevenson, but in defense of truth. Specifically, Mr. Stevenson's identification with that red barn was no more, no less than that of Knox, Stimson, or Bundy. It should be stated that Mr. Stevenson was once a member of the Institute of Pacific Relations. But so were such other loyal Americans as Senator Ferguson, John Foster Dulles, Paul Hoffman, Henry Luce, and Herbert F. Hoover. Their association carries with it no guilt, and that barn has nothing to do with any of them.

Now a sample investigation. The witness was Reed Harris, for many years a civil servant in the State Department directing the information service. Harris was accused of helping the Communistic cause by curtailing some broadcasts to Israel. Senator McCarthy summoned him and questioned him about a book he had written in 1932.

McCarthy: Mr. Reed Harris, your name is Reed Harris?

Answer: That's right.

McCarthy: You wrote a book in '32, is that correct?

Answer: Yes, I wrote a book and as I testified in executive session—

McCarthy: At the time you wrote the book—pardon me, go ahead, I'm sorry, proceed.

Answer: —at the time I wrote the book the atmosphere in the universities of the United States was greatly affected by the great depression then in existence, the attitudes of students, the attitudes of the general public were considerably different than they are at this moment, and for one thing there certainly was no awareness to the degree that there is today of the way the Communist Party works.

McCarthy: You attended Columbia University in the early thirties, is that right.

Answer: I did, Mr. Chairman.

McCarthy: Will you speak a little louder, sir?

Answer: I did, Mr. Chairman.

McCarthy: And you were expelled from Columbia?

Answer: I was suspended from classes on April 1, 1932. I was later reinstated and I resigned from the university.

McCarthy: You resigned from the university. Did the Civil Liberties Union provide you with an attorney at that time?

Answer: I had many offers of attorneys and one of those was from the American Civil Liberties Union, yes.

McCarthy: The question is did the Civil Liberties Union supply you with an attorney?

Answer: They did supply an attorney.

McCarthy: The answer is yes?

Answer: The answer is yes.

McCarthy: You know the Civil Liberties Union has been listed as a front for and doing the work of the Communist Party?

Answer: Mr. Chairman this was 1932.

McCarthy: I know it was 1932. Do you know they since have been listed as front for and doing the work of the Communist Party?

Answer: I do not know that they have been listed so, sir.

McCarthy: You don't know they have been listed?

Answer: I have heard that mentioned or read that mentioned.

McCarthy: You wrote a book in 1932. I'm going to ask you again at the time you wrote this book did you feel that professors should be given the right to teach sophomores that marriage "should be cast off of our civilization as antiquated and stupid religious phenomena?" Was that your feeling at that time?

Answer: My feeling was that professors should have the right to express their considered opinions on any subject whatever they were, sir.

McCarthy: I'm going to ask you this question again.

Answer: That includes that quotation, they should have the right to teach anything that came to their mind as being a proper thing to teach.

McCarthy: I'm going to make you answer this.

Answer: I'll answer yes, but you put an implication on it and you feature this particular point out of the book which of course is quite out of context, does not give a proper impression of the book as a whole. The American public doesn't get an honest impression of even that book bad as it is, from what you are quoting from it.

McCarthy: Then let's continue to read your own writings.

Answer: Twenty-one years ago again.

McCarthy: Yes, we shall try and bring you down to date if we can.

Answer: Mr. Chairman, two weeks ago Senator Taft took the position that I taught twenty-one years ago, that Communists and Socialists should be allowed to teach in the schools. It so happens nowadays I don't agree with Senator Taft as far as Communist teachers in the schools is concerned because I think Communists are in effect a plainclothes auxiliary of the Red Army, the Soviet Red Army, and I don't want to see them in any of our schools teaching.

McCarthy: I don't recall Senator Taft ever having any of the background that you have got.

Answer: I resent the tone of this inquiry very much, Mr. Chairman. I resent it not only because it is my neck, my public neck that you are I think very skillfully trying to wring, but I say it because there are thousands of able and loyal employees in the federal government of the United States who have been properly cleared according to the laws and the security practices of their agencies as I was, unless the new regime says no. I was before.

McCarthy: Do you think this book wrote then did considerable harm? Its publication might have had adverse influence on the public by an expression of views contained in it?

Answer: The sale of that book was so abysmally small, it was so unsuccessful that a question of its influence, really you can go back to the publisher, you'll see it was one of the most unsuccessful books he ever put out. He's still sorry about it just as I am.

McCarthy: Well I think that's a compliment to American intelligence I will say that.

Murrow: Senator McCarthy succeeded only in proving that Reed Harris had once written a bad book which the American people had proved twenty-two years ago by not buying it, which is what they eventually do with all bad ideas. As for Reed Harris, his resignation was accepted a month later with a letter of commendation. McCarthy claimed it was a victory. The Reed Harris hearing demonstrates one of the senator's techniques. Twice he said the American Civil Liberties Union was listed as a subversive front. The Attorney General's list does not and has never listed the ACLU as subversive nor does the FBI or any other government agency. And the American Civil Liberties Union holds in its files letters of commendation from President Eisenhower, President Truman, and General MacArthur.

Now let us try to bring the McCarthy story a little more up to date. Two years ago Senator Benton of Connecticut accused McCarthy of apparent perjury, unethical practice and perpetrating a hoax on the senate. McCarthy sued for two million dollars. Last week he dropped the case saying no one could be found who believed Benton's story. Several volunteers have come forward saying they believe it in its entirety.

Today Senator McCarthy says he's going to get a lawyer and force the networks to give him time to reply to Adlai Stevenson's speech. Earlier, the senator asked, "upon what meat does this our Caesar feed." Had he looked three lines earlier in Shakespeare's *Caesar* he would have found this line, which is not altogether inappropriate: "The fault, dear Brutus, is not in our stars, but in ourselves."

No one familiar with the history of this country can deny that congressional committees are useful. It is necessary to investigate before legislating, but the line between investigation and persecuting is a very fine one and the junior senator from Wisconsin had stepped over it repeatedly. His primary achievement has been in confusing the public mind as between internal and the external threat of Communism. We must not confuse dissent with disloyalty. We must remember always that accusation is not proof and that conviction depends upon evidence and due process of law. We will not walk in fear, one of another. We will not be driven by fear into an age of unreason if we dig deep in our history and our doctrine, and remember that we are not descended from fearful men, not from men who feared to write, to speak, to associate and to defend causes which were for the moment unpopular.

This is no time for men who oppose Senator McCarthy's methods to keep silent, or for those who approve. We can deny our heritage and our history but we cannot escape responsibility for the result. There is no way for a citizen of a republic to abdicate his responsibilities. As a nation we have come into our full inheritance at a tender age. We proclaim ourselves, as indeed we are, the defenders of freedom, what's left of it, but we cannot defend freedom abroad by deserting it at home. The actions of the junior senator from Wisconsin have caused alarm and dismay amongst our allies abroad and given considerable comfort to our enemies, and whose fault is that? Not really his, he didn't create this situation of fear, he merely exploited it and rather successfully. Cassius was right, "The fault, dear Brutus, is not in our stars, but in ourselves."

Good night, and good luck.

Introduction to
John Marks's

The Search for the "Manchurian Candidate"

"THE CIA PROBABLY PLAYED as big a role in the development and study of psychoactive drugs as the National Security Agency's codebreakers did in the development of computers," Thomas Powers writes in his introduction to *The Search for the "Manchurian Candidate."* The Agency's drug-testing program began in 1947, gained steam in 1949, and supposedly ended by the early 1970s. It was one of the Agency's most closely held secrets. In 1977, the CIA released 16,000 pages of documents under the Freedom of Information Act (FOIA). Marks was lucky. An FOIA window of opportunity at the CIA had opened briefly in the late 1970s in the wake of Watergate, the Rockefeller Commission's investigation of CIA covert activity against American citizens inside the United States, and the Church Committee's investigation of FBI and CIA abuses.

Marks began working in Washington, D.C., for the intelligence division of the State Department in 1968 but resigned after the secret American attacks on Cambodia. He later wrote with Victor Marchetti *The CIA and the Cult of Intelligence,* the first substantial work on the agency since David Wise and Thomas B. Ross's *The Invisible Government* exposed the inner workings of the organization in 1965.

"CIA officials started preliminary work on drugs and hypnosis shortly after the Agency's creation in 1947," Marks writes, "but the behavior-control program did not really get going until the Hungarian government put Josef Cardinal Mindszenty on trial in 1949." Cardinal Mindszenty, who had been a strong opponent of Communism when he was arrested on charges of treason, had "a glazed look in his eyes" as he "confessed to crimes of treason he apparently did not commit." The CIA wondered if hypnosis or drugs had played a role in his confession, and began to conduct its own mind-control experiments, including research on LSD.

The Search for the "Manchurian Candidate" was called by *New York Magazine* "the CIA exposé to end all CIA exposés." Senator Edward Kennedy said it "accomplished what two Senate committees could not." The book had a particularly strong impact in Canada, where some of the most harrowing research took place at the Allen Memorial Institute in Montreal. Revelations from Marks's book became the subject of at least three books by Canadian authors, and after some ten years of litigation, the U.S. government reached an out-of-court settlement of $750,000 with Canadian victims of the program. The Canadian government also paid compensation.

In the light of revelations about Guantanamo and Abu Ghraib, Marks's conclusions are particularly relevant. Sensory deprivation and behavioral modification, he wrote, "violate basic human rights just as much as physical abuse, even if they leave no marks on the body."

ADDITIONAL SOURCES

Cohen, Sidney. *The Beyond Within: The LSD Story.* New York: Atheneum, 1965.

Lee, Martin A. and Bruce Shlain. *Acid Dreams: The Complete Social History of LSD: The CIA, the Sixties, and Beyond.* New York: Grove/Atlantic, 1992.

Marchetti, Victor and John D. Marks. *The CIA and the Cult of Intelligence.* New York: Dell, 1989.

Powers, Thomas. *The Man Who Kept the Secrets: Richard Helms and the CIA.* New York: Pocket, 1983.

John Marks

LSD

THE SEARCH FOR THE "MANCHURIAN CANDIDATE," 1979

A LBERT HOFMANN'S DISCOVERY of LSD in 1943 may have begun a new age in the exploration of the human mind, but it took six years for word to reach America. Even after Hofmann and his coworkers in Switzerland published their work in a 1947 article, no one in the United States seemed to notice. Then in 1949, a famous Viennese doctor named Otto Kauders traveled to the United States in search of research funds. He gave a conference at Boston Psychopathic Hospital,[1] a pioneering mental-health institution affiliated with Harvard Medical School, and he spoke about a new experimental drug called d-lysergic acid diethylamide. Milton Greenblatt, the hospital's research director, vividly recalls Kauders' description of how an infinitesimally small dose had rendered Dr. Hofmann temporarily "crazy." "We were very interested in anything that could make someone schizophrenic," says Greenblatt. If the drug really did induce psychosis for a short time, the Boston doctors reasoned, an antidote—which they hoped to find—might cure schizophrenia. It would take many years of research to show that LSD did not, in fact, produce a "model psychosis," but to the Boston doctors in 1949, the drug showed incredible promise. Max Rinkel, a neuropsychiatrist and refugee from Hitler's Germany, was so intrigued by Kauders' presentation that he quickly contacted Sandoz, the huge Swiss pharmaceutical firm where Albert Hofmann worked. Sandoz officials arranged to ship some LSD across the Atlantic.

The first American trip followed. The subject was Robert Hyde, a Vermont-born psychiatrist who was Boston Psychopathic's number-two man. A bold, innovative sort, Hyde took it for granted that there would be no testing program until he tried the drug. With Rinkel and the hospital's senior physician, H. Jackson DeShon looking on, Hyde drank a glass of water with 100 micrograms of LSD in it—less than half Hofmann's dose, but still a hefty jolt. DeShon describes Hyde's reaction as "nothing very startling." The perpetually active Hyde insisted on making his normal hospital rounds while his colleagues tagged along. Rinkel later told a scientific conference that Hyde became "quite paranoiac, saying that we had not given him anything. He also berated us and said the company had cheated us, given us plain water. That was not Dr. Hyde's normal behavior; he is a very pleasant man." Hyde's first experience was hardly as dramatic as Albert Hofmann's, but then the Boston psychiatrist had not, like Hofmann, set off on a voyage into the complete unknown. For better or worse, LSD had come to America in 1949 and had embarked on a strange trip of its own. Academic researchers would study it in search of knowledge that would benefit all mankind. Intelligence agencies, particularly the CIA, would subsidize and shape the form of much of this work to learn how the drug could be used to break the will of enemy agents, unlock secrets in the minds of trained spies, and otherwise manipulate human behavior. These two strains—of helping people and of controlling them—would coexist rather comfortably through the 1950s. Then, in the 1960s, LSD would escape from the closed world of scholar and spy, and it would play a major role in causing a cultural upheaval that would have an impact both on global politics and on intimate personal beliefs. The trip would wind up—to borrow some hyperbole from the musical *Hair*— with "the youth of America on LSD."

THE COUNTERCULTURE GENERATION was not yet out of the nursery, however, when Bob Hyde went tripping: Hyde himself would not become a secret CIA consultant for several years. The CIA and the military intelligence agencies were just setting out on their quest for drugs and other exotic methods to take possession of people's minds. The ancient desire to control enemies through magical spells and potions had come alive again, and several offices within the CIA competed to become the head controllers. Men from the Office of Security's ARTICHOKE program

were struggling—as had OSS before them—to find a truth drug or hyp-
notic method that would aid in interrogation. Concurrently, the Technical
Services Staff (TSS) was investigating in much greater depth the whole
area of applying chemical and biological warfare (CBW) to covert operations. TSS was the lineal descendent of Stanley Lovell's Research and Development unit in OSS, and its officials kept alive much of the excitement
and urgency of the World War II days when Lovell had tried to bring out
the Peck's Bad Boy in American scientists. Specialists from TSS furnished
backup equipment for secret operations: false papers, bugs, taps, suicide
pills, explosive seashells, transmitters hidden in false teeth, cameras in tobacco pouches, invisible inks, and the like. In later years, these gadget wiz-
ards from TSS would become known for supplying some of history's
more ludicrous landmarks, such as Howard Hunt's ill-fitting red wig; but
in the early days of the CIA, they gave promise of transforming the spy
world.

Within TSS, there existed a Chemical Division with functions that few
others—even in TSS—knew about. These had to do with using chemicals
(and germs) against specific people. From 1951 to 1956, the years when
the CIA's interest in LSD peaked, Sidney Gottlieb, a native of the Bronx
with a Ph.D. in chemistry from Cal Tech, headed this division. (And for
most of the years until 1973, he would oversee TSS's behavioral programs
from one job or another.) Only thirty-three years old when he took over
the Chemical Division, Gottlieb had managed to overcome a pronounced
stammer and a clubfoot to rise through Agency ranks. Described by several acquaintances as a "compensator," Gottlieb prided himself on his
ability, despite his obvious handicaps, to pursue his cherished hobby, folk
dancing. On returning from secret missions overseas, he invariably
brought back a new step that he would dance with surprising grace. He
could call out instructions for the most complicated dances without a
break in his voice, infecting others with enthusiasm. A man of unortho-
dox tastes, Gottlieb lived in a former slave cabin that he had remodeled
himself—with his wife, the daughter of Presbyterian missionaries in In-
dia, and his four children. Each morning, he rose at 5:30 to milk the goats
he kept on his fifteen acres outside Washington. The Gottliebs drank only
goat's milk, and they made their own cheese. They also raised Christmas

trees which they sold to the outside world. Greatly respected by his former colleagues, Gottlieb, who refused to be interviewed for this book, is described as a humanist, a man of intellectual humility and strength, willing to carry out, as one ex-associate puts it, "the tough things that had to be done." This associate fondly recalls, "When you watched him, you gained more and more respect because he was willing to work so hard to get an idea across. He left himself totally exposed. It was more important for us to get the idea than for him not to stutter." One idea he got across was that the Agency should investigate the potential use of the obscure new drug, LSD, as a spy weapon.

At the top ranks of the Clandestine Services (officially called the Directorate of Operations but popularly known as the "dirty tricks department"), Sid Gottlieb had a champion who appreciated his qualities, Richard Helms. For two decades, Gottlieb would move into progressively higher positions in the wake of Helms' climb to the highest position in the Agency. Helms, the tall, smooth "preppie," apparently liked the way the Jewish chemist, who had started out at Manhattan's City College, could thread his way through complicated technical problems and make them understandable to nonscientists. Gottlieb was loyal and he followed orders. Although many people lay in the chain of command between the two men, Helms preferred to avoid bureaucratic niceties by dealing directly with Gottlieb.

On April 3, 1953, Helms proposed to Director Allen Dulles that the CIA set up a program under Gottlieb for "covert use of biological and chemical materials." Helms made clear that the Agency could use these methods in "present and future clandestine operations" and then added, "Aside from the offensive potential, the development of a comprehensive capability in this field . . . gives us a thorough knowledge of the enemy's theoretical potential, thus enabling us to defend ourselves against a foe who might not be as restrained in the use of these techniques as we are." Once again, as it would throughout the history of the behavioral programs, defense justified offense. Ray Cline, often a bureaucratic rival of Helms, notes the spirit in which the future director pushed this program: "Helms fancied himself a pretty tough cookie. It was fashionable among that group to fancy they were rather impersonal about dangers, risks, and human life. Helms would think it sentimental and foolish to be against something like this."

On April 13, 1953—the same day that the Pentagon announced that any U.S. prisoner refusing repatriation in Korea would be listed as a deserter and shot if caught—Allen Dulles approved the program, essentially as put forth by Helms. Dulles took note of the "ultra-sensitive work" involved and agreed that the project would be called MKULTRA.[2] He approved an initial budget of $300,000, exempted the program from normal CIA financial controls, and allowed TSS to start up research projects "without the signing of the usual contracts or other written agreements." Dulles ordered the Agency's bookkeepers to pay the costs blindly on the signatures of Sid Gottlieb and Willis Gibbons, a former U.S. Rubber executive who headed TSS.

As is so often the case in government, the activity that Allen Dulles approved with MKULTRA was already under way, even before he gave it a bureaucratic structure. Under the code name MKDELTA, the Clandestine Services had set up procedures the year before to govern the use of CBW products. (MKDELTA now became the operational side of MKULTRA.) Also in 1952, TSS had made an agreement with the Special Operations Division (SOD) of the army's biological research center at Fort Detrick, Maryland, whereby SOD would produce germ weapons for the CIA's use (with the program called MKNAOMI). Sid Gottlieb later testified that the purpose of these programs was "to investigate whether and how it was possible to modify an individual's behavior by covert means. The context in which this investigation was started was that of the height of the Cold War with the Korean War just winding down; with the CIA organizing its resources to liberate Eastern Europe by paramilitary means; and with the threat of Soviet aggression very real and tangible, as exemplified by the recent Berlin airlift" (which occurred in 1948).

In the early days of MKULTRA, the roughly six TSS professionals who worked on the program spent a good deal of their time considering the possibilities of LSD.[3] "The most fascinating thing about it," says one of them, "was that such minute quantities had such a terrific effect." Albert Hofmann had gone off into another world after swallowing less than 1/100,000 of an ounce. Scientists had known about the mind-altering qualities of drugs like mescaline since the late nineteenth century, but LSD was several thousand times more potent. Hashish had been around for millennia, but LSD was roughly a million times stronger (by weight). A two-suiter suitcase could hold enough LSD to turn on every man, woman, and child in the United States. "We thought about the possibility of putting some in a city water supply and having the citizens wander around in a more or less happy state, not terribly interested in defending themselves," recalls the TSS man. But incapacitating such large numbers of people fell to the Army Chemical Corps, which also tested LSD and even stronger hallucinogens. The CIA was concentrating on individuals. TSS officials understood that LSD distorted a person's sense of reality, and they felt compelled to learn whether it could alter someone's basic loyalties. Could the CIA make spies out of tripping Russians—or vice versa? In the early 1950s, when the Agency developed an almost desperate need to know more about LSD, almost no outside information existed on the subject. Sandoz had done some clinical studies, as had a few other places, including Boston Psychopathic, but the work generally had not moved much beyond the horse-and-buggy stage. The MKULTRA team had literally hundreds of questions about LSD's physiological, psychological, chemical, and social effects. Did it have any antidotes? What happened if it were combined with other drugs? Did it affect everyone the same way? What was the effect of doubling the dose? And so on.

TSS first sought answers from academic researchers, who, on the whole, gladly cooperated and let the Agency pick their brains. But CIA officials realized that no one would undertake a quick and systematic study of the drug unless the Agency itself paid the bill. Almost no government or private money was then available for what had been dubbed "experimental psychiatry." Sandoz wanted the drug tested, for its own commercial reasons, but beyond supplying it free to researchers, it would not assume the costs. The National Institutes of Mental Health had an interest in LSD's relationship to mental illness, but CIA officials wanted to know how the drug affected normal people, not sick ones. Only the military services, essentially for the same reasons as the CIA, were willing to sink much money into LSD, and the Agency men were not about to defer to them. They chose instead to take the lead—in effect to create a whole new field of research.

Suddenly there was a huge new market for grants in academia, as Sid Gottlieb and his aides began to fund LSD projects at prestigious institutions. The Agency's LSD pathfinders can be identified: Bob Hyde's group at Boston Psychopathic, Harold Abramson at Mt. Sinai Hospital and Columbia University in New York, Carl Pfeiffer at the University of Illinois Medical School, Harris Isbell of the NIMH-sponsored Addiction Research Center in Lexington, Kentucky, Louis Jolyon West at the University of Oklahoma, and Harold Hodge's group at the University of Rochester. The Agency disguised its involvement by passing the money through two conduits: the Josiah Macy, Jr., Foundation, a rich establishment institution which served as a cutout (intermediary) only for a year or two, and the Geschickter Fund for Medical Research, a Washington, D.C., family foundation, whose head, Dr. Charles Geschickter, provided the Agency with a variety of services for more than a decade. Reflexively, TSS officials felt they had to keep the CIA connection secret. They could only "assume," according to a 1955 study, that Soviet scientists understood the drug's "strategic importance" and were capable of making it themselves. They did not want to spur the Russians into starting their own LSD program or into devising countermeasures.

The CIA's secrecy was also clearly aimed at the folks back home. As a 1963 Inspector General's report stated, "Research in the manipulation of human behavior is considered by many authorities in medicine and related fields to be professionally unethical"; therefore, openness would put "in jeopardy" the reputations of the outside researchers. Moreover, the CIA Inspector General declared that disclosure of certain MKULTRA activities could result in "serious adverse reaction" among the American public.

At Boston Psychopathic, there were various levels of concealment. Only Bob Hyde and his boss, the hospital superintendant, knew officially that the CIA was funding the hospital's LSD program from 1952 on, to the tune of about $40,0)0 a year. Yet, according to another member of the Hyde group, Dr. DeShon, all senior staff understood where the money really came from. "We agreed not to discuss it," says DeShon. "I don't see any objection to this. We never gave it to anyone without his consent and without explaining it in detail." Hospital officials told the volunteer subjects something about the nature of the experiments but nothing about their origins or purpose. None of the subjects had any idea that the CIA was paying for the probing of their minds and would use the results for its own purposes; most of the staff was similarly ignorant.

Like Hyde, almost all the researchers tried LSD on themselves. Indeed, many believed they gained real insight into what it felt like to be mentally ill, useful knowledge for health professionals who spent their lives treating people supposedly sick in the head. Hyde set up a multidisciplinary program—virtually unheard of at the time—that brought together psychiatrists, psychologists, and physiologists. As subjects, they used each other, hospital patients, and volunteers—mostly students—from the Boston area. They worked through a long sequence of experiments that served to isolate variable after variable. Palming themselves off as foundation officials, the men from MKULTRA frequently visited to observe and suggest areas of future research. One Agency man, who himself tripped several times under Hyde's general supervision, remembers that he and his colleagues would pass on a nugget that another contractor like Harold Abramson had gleaned and ask Hyde to perform a follow-up test that might answer a question of interest to the Agency. Despite these tangents, the main body of research proceeded in a planned and orderly fashion. The researchers learned that while some subjects seemed to become schizophrenic, many others did not. Surprisingly, true schizophrenics showed little reaction at all to LSD, unless given massive doses. The Hyde group found out that the quality of a person's reaction was determined mainly by the person's basic personality structure (set) and the environment (setting) in which he or she took the drug. The subject's expectation of what would happen also played a major part. More than anything else, LSD tended to intensify the subject's existing characteristics—often to extremes. A little suspicion could grow into major paranoia, particularly in the company of people perceived as threatening.

Unbeknownst to his fellow researchers, the energetic Dr. Hyde also advised the CIA on using LSD in covert operations. A CIA officer who worked with him recalls: "The idea would be to give him the details of what had happened [with a case], and he would speculate. As a sharp M.D. in the old-school sense, he would look at things in ways that a lot of recent bright lights couldn't get.... He had a good sense of make-do." The Agency paid Hyde for his time as a consultant, and TSS officials eventually set aside a special MKULTRA subproject as Hyde's private funding mechanism. Hyde received funds from yet another MKULTRA subproject that TSS men created for him in 1954, so he could serve as a cutout for Agency purchases of rare chemicals. His first buy was to be $32,000 worth of corynanthine, a possible antidote to LSD, that would not be traced to the CIA.

Bob Hyde died in 1976 at the age of sixty-six widely hailed as a pacesetter in mental health. His medical and intelligence colleagues speak highly of him both personally and professionally. Like most of his generation, he apparently considered helping the CIA a patriotic duty. An Agency officer states that Hyde never raised doubts about his covert work. "He wouldn't moralize. He had a lot of trust in the people he was dealing with [from the CIA]. He had pretty well reached the conclusion that if they decided to do something [operationally], they had tried whatever else there was and were willing to risk it."

Most of the CIA's academic researchers published articles on their work in professional journals, but those long, scholarly reports often gave an incomplete picture of the research. In effect, the scientists would write openly about how LSD affects a patient's pulse rate, but they would tell only the CIA how the drug could be used to ruin that patient's marriage or memory. Those researchers who were aware of the Agency's sponsorship seldom published anything remotely connected to the instrumental and rather unpleasant questions the MKULTRA men posed for investigation. That was true of Hyde and of Harold Abramson, the New York allergist who became one of the first Johnny Appleseeds of LSD by giving it to a number of his distinguished colleagues. Abramson documented all sorts of experiments on topics like the effects of LSD on Siamese fighting fish and snails,[4] but he never wrote a word about one of his early LSD assignments from the Agency. In a 1953 document, Sid Gottlieb listed subjects he expected Abramson to investigate with the $85,000 the Agency was furnishing him. Gottlieb wanted "operationally pertinent materials along the following lines: a. Disturbance of Memory; b. Discrediting by Aberrant Behavior; c. Alteration of Sex Patterns; d. Eliciting of Information; e. Suggestibility; f. Creation of Dependence."

Dr. Harris Isbell, whose work the CIA funded through navy cover with the approval of the director of the National Institutes of Health, published his principal findings, but he did not mention how he obtained his subjects. As director of the Addiction Research Center at the huge federal drug hospital in Lexington, Kentucky, he had access to a literally captive population. Inmates heard on the grapevine that if they volunteered for Isbell's program, they would be rewarded either in the drug of their choice or in time off from their sentences. Most of the addicts chose drugs—usually heroin or morphine of a purity seldom seen on the street. The subjects signed an approval form, but they were not told the names of the experimental drugs or the probable effects. This mattered little, since the "volunteers" probably would have granted their informed consent to virtually anything to get hard drugs.

Given Isbell's almost unlimited supply of subjects, TSS officials used the Lexington facility as a place to make quick tests of promising but untried drugs and to perform specialized experiments they could not easily duplicate elsewhere. For instance, Isbell did one study for which it would have been impossible to attract student volunteers. He kept seven men on LSD for seventy-seven straight days.[5] Such an experiment is as chilling as it is astonishing—both to lovers and haters of LSD. Nearly twenty years after Dr. Isbell's early work, counterculture journalist Hunter S. Thompson delighted and frightened his readers with accounts of drug binges lasting a few days, during which Thompson felt his brain boiling away in the sun, his nerves wrapping around enormous barbed wire forts, and his remaining faculties reduced to their reptilian antecedents. Even Thompson would shudder at the thought of seventy-seven days straight on LSD, and it is doubtful he would joke about the idea. To Dr. Isbell, it was just another experiment. "I have had seven patients who have now been taking the drug for more than 42 days," he wrote in the middle of the test, which he called "the most amazing demonstration of drug tolerance I have ever seen." Isbell tried to "break through this tolerance" by giving triple and quadruple doses of LSD to the inmates.

Filled with intense curiosity, Isbell tried out a wide variety of unproven drugs on his subjects. Just as soon as a new batch of scopolamine, rivea seeds, or bufontenine arrived from the CIA or NIMH, he would start testing. His relish for the task occasionally shone through the dull scientific reports. "I will write you a letter as soon as I can get the stuff into a man or two," he informed his Agency contact.

No corresponding feeling shone through for the inmates, however. In his few recorded personal comments, he complained that his subjects tended to be afraid of the doctors and were not as open in describing their experiences as the experimenters would have wished. Although Isbell made an effort to "break through the barriers" with the subjects, who were nearly all black drug addicts, Isbell finally decided "in all probability, this type of behavior is to be expected with patients of this type." The subjects have long since scattered, and no one apparently has measured the aftereffects of the more extreme experiments on them.

One subject who could be found spent only a brief time with Dr. Isbell. Eddie Flowers was nineteen years old and had been in Lexington for about a year when he signed up for Isbell's program. He lied about his age to get in, claiming he was twenty-one. All he cared about was getting some drugs. He moved into the experimental wing of the hospital where the food was better and he could listen to music. He loved his heroin but knew nothing about drugs like LSD. One day he took something in a graham cracker. No one ever told him the name, but his description sounds like it made him trip—badly, to be sure. "It was the worst shit I ever had," he says. He hallucinated and suffered for sixteen or seventeen hours. "I was frightened. I wouldn't take it again." Still, Flowers earned enough "points" in the experiment to qualify for his "payoff " in heroin. All he had to do was knock on a little window down the hall. This was the drug bank. The man in charge kept a list of the amount of the hard drug each inmate had in his account. Flowers just had to say how much he wanted to withdraw and note the method of payment. "If you wanted it in the vein, you got it there," recalls Flowers who now works in a Washington, D.C., drug rehabilitation center.

Dr. Isbell refuses all request for interviews. He did tell a Senate subcommittee in 1975 that he inherited the drug payoff system when he came to Lexington and that "it was the custom in those days. . . . The ethical codes were not so highly developed, and there was a great need to know in order to protect the public in assessing the potential use of narcotics. . . . I personally think we did a very excellent job."

For every Isbell, Hyde, or Abramson who did TSS contract work, there were dozens of others who simply served as casual CIA informants, some witting and some not. Each TSS project officer had a skull session with dozens of recognized experts several times a year. "That was the only way a tiny staff like Sid Gottlieb's could possibly keep on top of the burgeoning behavioral sciences," says an ex-CIA official. "There would be no way you could do it by library research or the Ph.D. dissertation approach." The TSS men always asked their contacts for the names of others they could talk to, and the contacts would pass them on to other interesting scientists.

In LSD research, TSS officers benefited from the energetic intelligence gathering of their contractors, particularly Harold Abramson. Abramson talked regularly to virtually everyone interested in the drug, including the few early researchers not funded by the Agency or the military, and he reported his findings to TSS. In addition, he served as reporting secretary of two conference series sponsored by the Agency's sometime conduit, the Macy Foundation. These series each lasted over five-year periods in the 1950s; one dealt with "Problems of Consciousness" and the other with "Neuropharmacology." Held once a year in the genteel surroundings of the Princeton Inn, the Macy Foundation conferences brought together TSS's (and the military's) leading contractors, as part of a group of roughly twenty-five with the multidisciplinary background that TSS officials so loved. The participants came from all over the social sciences and included such luminaries as Margaret Mead and Jean Piaget. The topics discussed usually mirrored TSS's interests at the time, and the conferences served as a spawning ground for ideas that allowed researchers to engage in some healthy cross-fertilization.

Beyond the academic world, TSS looked to the pharmaceutical companies as another source on drugs—and for a continuing supply of new products to test. TSS's Ray Treichler handled the liaison function, and this secretive little man built up close relationships with many of the industry's key executives. He had a particular knack for convincing them he would not reveal their trade secrets. Sometimes claiming to be from the Army Chemical Corps and sometimes admitting his CIA connection, Treichler would ask for samples of drugs that were either highly poisonous, or, in the words of the onetime director of research of a large company, "caused hypertension, increased blood pressure, or led to other odd physiological activity."

Dealing with American drug companies posed no particular problems for TSS. Most cooperated in any way they could. But relations with Sandoz were more complicated. The giant Swiss firm had a monopoly on the Western world's production of LSD until 1953. Agency officials feared that Sandoz would somehow allow large quantities to reach the Russians. Since information on LSD's chemical structure and effects was publicly available from 1947 on, the Russians could have produced it any time they felt it worthwhile. Thus, the Agency's phobia about Sandoz seems rather irrational, but it unquestionably did exist.

On two occasions early in the Cold War, the entire CIA hierarchy went into a dither over reports that Sandoz might allow large amounts of LSD to reach communist countries. In 1951 reports came in through military channels that the Russians had obtained some 50 million doses from Sandoz. Horrendous visions of what the Russians might do with such a stockpile circulated in the CIA, where officials did not find out the intelligence was false for several years. There was an even greater uproar in 1953 when more reports came in, again through military intelligence, that Sandoz wanted to sell the astounding quantity of 10 kilos (22 pounds) of LSD— enough for about 100 million doses—on the open market.

A top-level coordinating committee which included CIA and Pentagon representatives unanimously recommended that the Agency put up $240,000 to buy it all. Allen Dulles gave his approval, and off went two CIA representatives to Switzerland, presumably with a black bag full of cash. They met with the president of Sandoz and other top executives. The Sandoz men stated that the company had never made anything approaching 10 kilos of LSD and that, in fact, since the discovery of the drug ten years before, its total production had been only 40 grams (about $1\frac{1}{2}$ ounces).[6] The manufacturing process moved quite slowly at that time because Sandoz used real ergot, which could not be grown in large quantities. Nevertheless, Sandoz executives, being good Swiss businessmen, offered to supply the U.S. Government with 100 grams weekly for an indefinite period, if the Americans would pay a fair price. Twice the Sandoz president thanked the CIA men for being willing to take the nonexistent 10 kilos off the market. While he said the company now regretted it had ever discovered LSD in the first place, he promised that Sandoz would not let the drug fall into communist hands. The Sandoz president mentioned that various Americans had in the past made "covert and sideways" approaches to Sandoz to find out about LSD, and he agreed to keep the U.S. Government informed of all future production and shipping of the drug. He also agreed to pass on any intelligence about Eastern European interest in LSD. The Sandoz executives asked only that their arrangement with the CIA be kept "in the very strictest confidence."

All around the world, the CIA tried to stay on top of the LSD supply. Back home in Indianapolis, Eli Lilly & Company was even then working on a process to synthesize LSD. Agency officials felt uncomfortable having to rely on a foreign company for their supply, and in 1953 they asked Lilly executives to make them up a batch, which the company subsequently donated to the government. Then, in 1954, Lilly scored a major breakthrough when its researchers worked out a complicated twelve- to fifteen-step process to manufacture first lysergic acid (the basic building block) and then LSD itself from chemicals available on the open market. Given a relatively sophisticated lab, a competent chemist could now make LSD without a supply of the hard-to-grow ergot fungus. Lilly officers confidentially informed the government of their triumph. They also held an unprecedented press conference to trumpet their synthesis of lysergic acid, but they did not publish for another five years their success with the closely related LSD.

TSS officials soon sent a memo to Allen Dulles, explaining that the Lilly discovery was important because the government henceforth could buy LSD in "tonnage quantities," which made it a potential chemical-warfare agent. The memo writer pointed out, however, that from the MKULTRA point of view, the discovery made no difference since TSS was working on ways to use the drug only in small-scale covert operations, and the Agency had no trouble getting the limited amounts it needed. But now the Army Chemical Corps and the Air Force could get their collective hands on enough LSD to turn on the world.

Sharing the drug with the army here, setting up research programs there, keeping track of it everywhere, the CIA generally presided over the LSD scene during the 1950s. To be sure, the military services played a part and funded their own research programs.[7] So did the National Institutes of Health, to a lesser extent. Yet both the military services and the NIH allowed themselves to be co-opted by the CIA—as funding conduits and intelligence sources. The Food and Drug Administration also supplied the Agency with confidential information on drug testing. Of the Western world's two LSD manufacturers, one—Eli Lilly—gave its entire (small) supply to the CIA and the military. The other—Sandoz—informed Agency representatives every time it shipped the drug. If somehow the CIA missed anything with all these sources, the Agency still had its own network of scholar-spies, the most active of whom was Harold Abramson who kept it informed of all new developments in the LSD field. While the CIA may not have totally cornered the LSD market in the 1950s, it certainly had a good measure of control—the very power it sought over human behavior.

SID GOTTLIEB and his colleagues at MKULTRA soaked up pools of information about LSD and other drugs from all outside sources, but they saved for themselves the research they really cared about: operational testing. Trained in both science and espionage, they believed they could bridge the huge gap between experimenting in the laboratory and using drugs to outsmart the enemy. Therefore the leaders of MKULTRA initiated their own series of drug experiments that paralleled and drew information from the external research. As practical men of action, unlimited by restrictive academic standards, they did not feel the need to keep their tests in strict scientific sequence. They wanted results now—not next year. If a drug showed promise, they felt no qualms about trying it out operationally before all the test results came in. As early as 1953, for instance, Sid Gottlieb went overseas with a supply of a hallucinogenic drug—almost certainly LSD. With unknown results, he arranged for it to be slipped to a speaker at a political rally, presumably to see if it would make a fool of him.

These were freewheeling days within the CIA—then a young agency whose bureaucratic arteries had not started to harden. The leaders of MKULTRA had high hopes for LSD. It appeared to be an awesome substance, whose advent, like the ancient discovery of fire, would bring out primitive responses of fear and worship in people. Only a speck of LSD could take a strong-willed man and turn his most basic perceptions into willowy shadows. Time, space, right, wrong, order, and the notion of what was possible all took on new faces. LSD was a frightening weapon, and it took a swashbuckling boldness for the leaders of MKULTRA to prepare for operational testing the way they first did: by taking it themselves. They tripped at the office. They tripped at safehouses, and sometimes they traveled to Boston to trip under Bob Hyde's penetrating gaze. Always they observed, questioned, and analyzed each other. LSD seemed to remove inhibitions, and they thought they could use it to find out what went on in the mind underneath all the outside acts and pretensions. If they could get at the inner self, they reasoned, they could better manipulate a person— or keep him from being manipulated.

The men from MKULTRA were trying LSD in the early 1950s—when Stalin lived and Joe McCarthy raged. It was a foreboding time, even for those not professionally responsible for doomsday poisons. Not surprisingly, Sid Gottlieb and colleagues who tried LSD did not think of the drug as something that might enhance creativity or cause transcendental experiences. Those notions would not come along for years. By and large, there was thought to be only one prevailing and hard-headed version of reality, which was "normal," and everything else was "crazy." An LSD trip made people temporarily crazy, which meant potentially vulnerable to the CIA men (and mentally ill, to the doctors). The CIA experimenters did not trip for the experience itself, or to get high, or to sample new realities. They were testing a weapon; for their purposes, they might as well have been in a ballistics lab.

Despite this prevailing attitude in the Agency, at least one MKULTRA pioneer recalls that his first trip expanded his conception of reality: "I was shaky at first, but then I just experienced it and had a high. I felt that everything was working right. I was like a locomotive going at top efficiency. Sure there was stress, but not in a debilitating way. It was like the stress of an engine pulling the longest train it's ever pulled." This CIA veteran describes seeing all the colors of the rainbow growing out of cracks in the sidewalk. He had always disliked cracks as signs of imperfection, but suddenly the cracks became natural stress lines that measured the vibrations of the universe. He saw people with blemished faces, which he had previously found slightly repulsive. "I had a change of values about faces," he says. "Hooked noses or crooked teeth would become beautiful for that person. Something had turned loose in me, and all I had done was shift my attitude. Reality hadn't changed, but I had. That was all the difference in the world between seeing something ugly and seeing truth and beauty."

At the end of this day of his first trip, the CIA man and his colleagues had an alcohol party to help come down. "I had a lump in my throat," he recalls wistfully. Although he had never done such a thing before, he wept in front of his coworkers. "I didn't want to leave it. I felt I would be going back to a place where I wouldn't be able to hold on to this kind of beauty. I felt very unhappy. The people who wrote the report on me said I had experienced depression, but they didn't understand why I felt so bad. They thought I had had a bad trip."

This CIA man says that others with his general personality tended to enjoy themselves on LSD, but that the stereotypical CIA operator (particularly the extreme counterintelligence type who mistrusts everyone and everything) usually had negative reactions. The drug simply exaggerated his paranoia. For these operators, the official notes, "dark evil things would begin to lurk around," and they would decide the experimenters were plotting against them.

The TSS team understood it would be next to impossible to allay the fears of this ever-vigilant, suspicious sort, although they might use LSD to disorient or generally confuse such a person. However, they toyed with the idea that LSD could be applied to better advantage on more trusting types. Could a clever foe "reeducate" such a person with a skillful application of LSD? Speculating on this question, the CIA official states that while under the influence of the drug, "you tend to have a more global view of things. I found it awfully hard when stoned to maintain the notion: I am a U.S. citizen—my country right or wrong. . . . You tend to have these good higher feelings. You are more open to the brotherhood-of-man idea and more susceptible to the seamy sides of your own society. . . . I think this is exactly what happened during the 1960s, but it didn't make people more communist. It just made them less inclined to identify with the U.S. They took a plague-on-both-your-houses position."

As to whether his former colleagues in TSS had the same perception of the LSD experience, the man replies, "I think everybody understood that if you had a good trip, you had a kind of above-it-all look into reality. What we subsequently found was that when you came down, you remembered the experience, but you didn't switch identities. You really didn't have that kind of feeling. You weren't as suspicious of people. You listened to them, but you also saw through them more easily and clearly. We decided that this wasn't the kind of thing that was going to make a guy into a turncoat to his own country. The more we worked with it, the less we became convinced this was what the communists were using for brainwashing."

The early LSD tests—both outside and inside the Agency—had gone well enough that the MKULTRA scientists moved forward to the next stage on the road to "field" use: They tried the drug out on people by surprise. This, after all, would be the way an operator would give—or get—the drug. First they decided to spring it on each other without warning. They agreed among themselves that a coworker might slip it to them at any time. (In what may be an apocryphal story, a TSS staff man says that one of his former colleagues always brought his own bottle of wine to office parties and carried it with him at all times.) Unwitting doses became an occupational hazard.

MKULTRA men usually took these unplanned trips in stride, but occasionally they turned nasty. Two TSS veterans tell the story of a coworker who drank some LSD-laced coffee during his morning break. Within an hour, states one veteran, "he sort of knew he had it, but he couldn't pull himself together. Sometimes you take it, and you start the process of maintaining your composure. But this grabbed him before he was aware, and it got away from him." Filled with fear, the CIA man fled the building that then housed TSS, located on the edge of the Mall near Washington's great monuments. Having lost sight of him, his colleagues searched frantically, but he managed to escape. The hallucinating Agency man worked his way across one of the Potomac bridges and apparently cut his last links with rationality. "He reported afterward that every automobile that came by was a terrible monster with fantastic eyes, out to get him personally," says the veteran. "Each time a car passed, he would huddle down against the parapet, terribly frightened. It was a real horror trip for him. I mean, it was hours of agony. It was like a dream that never stops—with someone chasing you."

After about an hour and a half, the victim's coworkers found him on the Virginia side of the Potomac, crouched under a fountain, trembling. "It was awfully hard to persuade him that his friends were his friends at that point," recalls the colleague. "He was alone in the world, and everyone was hostile. He'd become a full-blown paranoid. If it had lasted for two weeks, we'd have plunked him in a mental hospital." Fortunately for him, the CIA man came down by the end of the day. This was not the first, last, or most tragic bad trip in the Agency's testing program.[8]

By late 1953, only six months after Allen Dulles had formally created MKULTRA, TSS officials were already well into the last stage of their research: systematic use of LSD on "outsiders" who had no idea they had received the drug. These victims simply felt their moorings slip away in the midst of an ordinary day, for no apparent reason, and no one really knew how they would react.

Sid Gottlieb was ready for the operational experiments. He considered LSD to be such a secret substance that he gave it a private code name ("serunim") by which he and his colleagues often referred to the drug, even behind the CIA's heavily guarded doors. In retrospect, it seems more than bizarre that CIA officials—men responsible for the nation's intelligence and alertness when the hot and cold wars against the communists were at their peak—would be sneaking LSD into each other's coffee cups and thereby subjecting themselves to the unknown frontiers of experimental drugs. But these side trips did not seem to change the sense of reality of Gottlieb or of high CIA officials, who took LSD on several occasions. The drug did not transform Gottlieb out of the mind set of a master scientist-spy, a protégé of Richard Helms in the CIA's inner circle. He never stopped milking his goats at 5:30 every morning.

The CIA leaders' early achievements with LSD were impressive. They had not invented the drug, but they had gotten in on the American ground floor and done nearly everything else. They were years ahead of the scientific literature—let alone the public—and spies win by being ahead. They had monopolized the supply of LSD and dominated the research by creating much of it themselves. They had used money and other blandishments to build a network of scientists and doctors whose work they could direct and turn to their own use. All that remained between them and major espionage successes was the performance of the drug in the field.

That, however, turned out to be a considerable stumbling block. LSD had an incredibly powerful effect on people, but not in ways the CIA could predict or control.

NOTES

1. During the 1950s, Boston Psychopathic changed its name to Massachusetts Mental Health Center, the name it bears today.

2. Pronounced M-K-ULTRA. The MK digraph simply identified it as a TSS project. As for the ULTRA part, it may have had its etymological roots in the most closely guarded Anglo-American World War II intelligence secret, the ULTRA program, which handled the cracking of German military codes. While good espionage tradecraft called for cryptonyms to have no special meaning, wartime experiences were still very much on the minds of men like Allen Dulles.

3. By no means did TSS neglect other drugs. It looked at hundreds of others from cocaine to nicotine, with special emphasis on special-purpose substances. One 1952 memo talked about the urgent operational need for a chemical "producing general listlessness and lethargy." Another mentioned finding—as TSS later did—a potion to accelerate the effects of liquor, called an "alcohol extender."

4. As happened to Albert Hofmann the first time, Abramson once unknowingly ingested some LSD, probably by swallowing water from his spiked snail tank. He started to feel bad, but with his wife's help, he finally pinpointed the cause. According to brain and dolphin expert John Lilly, who heard the story from Mrs. Abramson, Harold was greatly relieved that his discomfort was not grave. "Oh, it's nothing serious," he said. "It's just an LSD psychosis. I'll just go to bed and sleep it off."

5. Army researchers, as usual running about five years behind the CIA, became interested in the sustained use of LSD as an interrogation device during 1961 field tests (called Operation THIRD CHANCE). The army men tested the drug in Europe on nine foreigners and one American, a black soldier named James Thornwell, accused of stealing classified documents. While Thornwell was reacting to the drug under extremely stressful conditions, his captors threatened "to extend the state indefinitely, even to a permanent condition of insanity," according to an army document. Thornwell is now suing the U.S. government for $30 million.

In one of those twists that Washington insiders take for granted and outsiders do not quite believe, Terry Lenzner, a partner of the same law firm seeking this huge sum for Thornwell, is the lawyer for Sid Gottlieb, the man who oversaw the seventy-seven-day trips at Lexington and even more dangerous LSD testing.

6. A 1975 CIA document clears up the mystery of how the Agency's military sources could have made such a huge error in estimating Sandoz's LSD supply (and probably also explains the earlier inaccurate report that the Russians had bought 50,000,000 doses). What happened, according to the document, was that the U.S. military attaché in Switzerland did not know the difference between a milligram (1/1,000 of a gram) and a kilogram (1,000 grams). This mix-up threw all his calculations off by a factor of 1,000,000.

7. Military security agencies supported the LSD work of such well-known researchers as Amedeo Marrazzi of the University of Minnesota and Missouri Institute of Psychiatry, Henry Beecher of Harvard and Massachusetts General Hospital, Charles Savage while he was at the Naval Medical Research Institute, James Dille of the University of Washington, Gerald Klee of the University of Maryland Medical School, Neil Burch of Baylor University (who performed later experiments for the CIA), and Paul Hoch and James Cattell of the New York State Psychiatric Institute, whose forced injections of a mescaline derivative led to the 1953 death of New York tennis professional Harold Blauer. (Dr. Cattell later told army investigators, "We didn't know whether it was dog piss or what it was we were giving him.")

8. TSS officials had long known that LSD could be quite dangerous. In 1952, Harvard Medical School's Henry Beecher, who regularly gave the Agency information on his talks with European colleagues, reported that a Swiss doctor had suffered severe depression after taking the drug and had killed herself three weeks later.

The description of Robert Hyde's first trip came from interviews with Dr. Milton Greenblatt, Dr. J. Herbert DeShon, and a talk by Max Rinkel at the 2nd Macy Conference on Neuropharmacology, pp. 235–36, edited by Harold A. Abramson, 1955; Madison Printing Company.

The descriptions of TSS and Sidney Gottlieb came from interviews with Ray Cline, John Stockwell, about 10 other ex-CIA officers, and other friends of Gottlieb.

Memos quoted on the early MKULTRA program include Memorandum from ADDP Helms to DCI Dulles, 4/3/53, Tab A, pp. 1–2 (quoted in Church Committee Report, Book I); APF A-1, April 13,1953, Memorandum for Deputy Director (Administration, Subject: Project MKULTRA—Extremely Sensitive Research and Development Program; #A/B, I, 64/6, 6 February 1952, Memorandum for the Record, Subject: Contract with [deleted] #A/B, I, 64/29, undated, Memorandum for Technical Services Staff, Subject: Alcohol Antagonists and Accelerators, Research and Development Project. The Gottlieb quote is from Hearing before the Subcommittee on Health and Scientific Research of the Senate Committee on Human Resources, September 21, 1977, p. 206.

The background data on LSD came particularly from The Beyond Within: The LSD Story by Sidney Cohen (New York: Atheneum, 1972). Other sources included Origins of Psychopharmacology: From CPZ to LSD by Anne E. Caldwell (Springfield, Ill.: Charles C. Thomas, 1970) and Document 352, "An OSI Study of the Strategic Medical Importance of LSD-25," 30 August 1955.

TSS's use of outside researchers came from interviews with four former TSSers. MKULTRA Subprojects 8, 10, 63, and 66 described Robert Hyde's work. Subprojects 7, 27, and 40 concerned Harold Abramson. Hodge's work was in subprojects 17 and 46. Carl Pfeiffer's Agency connection, along with Hyde's, Abramson's, and Isbell's, was laid out by Lyman B. Kirkpatrick, Memorandum for the Record, 1 December 1953, Subject: Conversation with Dr. Willis Gibbons of TSS re Olson Case (found at p. 1030, Kennedy Subcommittee 1975 Biomedical and Behavioral Research Hearings). Isbell's testing program was also described at those hearings, as it was in Document #14, 24 July, 1953, Memo For: Liaison & Security Officer/TSS, Subject #71 An Account of the Chemical Division's Contacts in the National Institute of Health; Document #37, 14 July 1954, subject [deleted]; and Document #41, 31 August, 1956, subject; trip to Lexington, Ky., 21–23 August 1956. Isbell's program was further described in a "Report on ADAMHA Involvement in LSD Research," found at p. 993 of 1975 Kennedy subcommittee hearings. The firsthand account of the actual testing came from an interview with Edward M. Flowers, Washington, D.C.

The section on TSS's noncontract informants came from interviews with TSS sources, reading the proceedings of the Macy Conferences on "Problems of Consciousness" and "Neuropharmacology," and interviews with several participants including Sidney Cohen, Humphrey Osmond, and Hudson Hoagland.

The material on CIA's relations with Sandoz and Eli Lilly came from Document #24, 16 November, 1953, Subject: ARTICHOKE Conference; Document #268, 23 October, 1953, Subject: Meeting in Director's Office at 1100 hours on 23 October with Mr. Wisner and [deleted]; Document #316, 6 January, 1954, Subject: Lysergic Acid Diethylamide (LSD-25); and Document #338, 26 October 1954, Subject: Potential Large Scale Availability of LSD through newly discovered synthesis by [deleted]; interviews with Sandoz and Lilly former executives; interviews with TSS sources; and Sidney Gottlieb's testimony before Kennedy subcommittee, 1977, p. 203.

Henry Beecher's US government connections were detailed in his private papers, in a report on the Swiss-LSD death to the CIA at p. 396, Church Committee Report, Book I, and in interviews with two of his former associates.

The description of TSS's internal testing progression comes from interviews with former staff members. The short reference to Sid Gottlieb's arranging for LSD to be given a speaker at a political rally comes from Document #A/B, II, 26/8, 9 June 1954, Subject: MKULTRA. Henry Beecher's report to the CIA on the Swiss suicide is found at p. 396, Church Committee Report, Book I.

PART V

Organized Crime, J. Edgar Hoover, and FBI Abuses

Introduction to
"The Kefauver Committee Report"

IN 1950 AND 1951, the Kefauver Committee, named after chairman Democratic Senator Estes Kefauver of Tennessee, and established to investigate the workings of organized crime, mesmerized the country. Though these were not the first congressional committee hearings to be televised, they were the first to reach a wide audience.

Although few families owned TVs at the time, people watched the proceedings in bars, restaurants, and businesses, riveted by the parade of colorful witnesses that included gangster Frank Costello and Virginia Hill, a reputed bag woman for the mob.

More important, the committee revealed to the public for the first time in detail the existence and modus operandi of an organized crime empire—the Mafia—that was revealed to be a highly secret, conspiratorial organization that had infiltrated state and local governments; a threat similar to that alleged at the same time about Communists on a national basis by Senator Joseph R. McCarthy.

A significant result of the hearings was the admission by J. Edgar Hoover that a nationwide crime syndicate existed—a fact he and the FBI had long denied. The hearings had significant results. Legalized gambling proposals were defeated in a number of states, and over seventy local crime commissions were established in cities across the country. Mobsters who had testified paid a price after the hearings: Frank Costello was forced to step down as boss of his family; Willie Moretti, who had supplied comic relief during his testimony, was executed by the mob, who feared he would be an informer; and Joey Adonis was deported to Italy.

As a result of the Kefauver Committee hearings, the Mafia became a lasting part of popular culture that has never tired of its real and imaginary history and exploits.

The hearings made Senator Kefauver into a national hero. He received the Democratic vice-presidential nomination in 1956 but the ticket with Adlai Stevenson was defeated by Dwight Eisenhower and Richard Nixon.

ADDITIONAL SOURCES

Abadinsky, Howard. *Organized Crime.* Belmont, C.A.: Wadsworth, 2002.

Bernstein, Lee. *The Greatest Menace: Organized Crime in Cold War America.* Amherst, Mass.: University of Massachusetts Press, 2002.

Kefauver, Estes. *Crime in America.* Garden City, N.Y.: Doubleday, 1951.

U.S. Congress. Senate. *Final Report of the Special Senate Committee to Investigate Organized Crime in Interstate Commerce.* 82nd Congress, 1st session, 1951, Report 307.

"The Kefauver Committee Report"

THIRD INTERIM REPORT OF THE SPECIAL SENATE COMMITTEE TO
INVESTIGATE ORGANIZED CRIME IN INTERSTATE COMMERCE, 1951

General Conclusions

1. Organized criminal gangs operating in interstate commerce are firmly entrenched in our large cities in the operation of many different gambling enterprises such as bookmaking, policy, slot machines, as well as in other rackets such as the sale and distribution of narcotics and commercialized prostitution. They are the survivors of the murderous underworld wars of the prohibition era. After the repeal of the prohibition laws, these groups and syndicates shifted their major criminal activities to gambling. However, many of the crime syndicates continued to take an interest in other rackets such as narcotics, prostitution, labor and business racketeering, black marketing, etc.

2. Criminal syndicates in this country make tremendous profits and are due primarily to the ability of such gangs and syndicates to secure monopolies in the illegal operations in which they are engaged. These monopolies are secured by persuasion, intimidation, violence, and murder. The committee found in some cities that law-enforcement officials aided and protected gangsters and racketeers to maintain their monopolistic position in particular rackets. Mobsters who attempted to compete with these entrenched criminal groups found that they and their followers were being subjected to arrest and prosecution while protected gang operations were left untouched.

3. Crime is on a syndicated basis to a substantial extent in many cities. The two major crime syndicates in this country are the Accardo-Guzik-Fischetti syndicate, whose headquarters are in Chicago; and the Costello-Adonis-Lansky syndicate based in New York. Evidence of the operations of the Accardo-Guzik-Fischetti syndicate was found by the committee in such places as Chicago, Kansas City, Dallas, Miami, Las Vegas, Nev., and the west coast. Evidence of the Costello-Adonis-Lansky operations was found in New York City, Saratoga, Bergen County, N. J., New Orleans, Miami, Las Vegas, the west coast, and Havana, Cuba. These syndicates, as well as other crimmal gangs throughout the country, enter profitable relationships with each other. There is also a close personal, financial, and social relationship between top-level mobsters in different areas of the country.

4. There is a sinister criminal organization known as the Mafia operating throughout the country with ties in other nations, in the opinion of the committee. The Mafia is the direct descendant of a criminal organization of the same name originating in the island of Sicily. In this country, the Mafia has also been known as the Black Hand and the Unione Siciliano. The membership of the Mafia today is not confined to persons of Sicilian origin. The Mafia is a loose-knit organization specializing in the sale and distribution of narcotics, the conduct of various gambling enterprises, prostitution, and other rackets based on extortion and violence. The Mafia is the binder which ties together the two major criminal syndicates as well as numerous other criminal groups throughout the country. The power of the Mafia is based on a ruthless enforcement of its edicts and its own law of vengeance, to which have been creditably attributed literally hundreds of murders throughout the country.

5. Despite known arrest records and well-documented criminal reputations, the leading hoodlums in the country remain, for the most part, immune from prosecution and punishment, although underlings of their gangs may, on occasion, be prosecuted and punished. This quasi-immunity of top-level mobsters can be as-

cribed to what is popularly known as the "fix." The fix is not always the direct payment of money to law-enforcement officials, although the committee has run across considerable evidence of such bribery. The fix may also come about through the acquisition of political power by contributions to political organizations or otherwise, by creating economic ties with apparently respectable and reputable businessmen and lawyers, and by buying public good will through charitable contributions and press relations.

Gambling Supports Big-Time Rackets

6. Gambling profits are the principal support of big-time racketeering and gangsterism. These profits provide the financial resources whereby ordinary criminals are converted into big-time racketeers, political bosses, pseudo businessmen, and alleged philanthropists. Thus, the $2 horse bettor and the 5-cent numbers player are not only suckers because they are gambling against hopeless odds, but they also provide the moneys which enable underworld characters to undermine our institutions.

   The legalization of gambling would not terminate the widespread predatory activities of criminal gangs and syndicates. The history of legalized gambling in Nevada and in other parts of the country gives no assurance that mobsters and racketeers can be converted into responsible businessmen through the simple process of obtaining State and local licenses for their gambling enterprises. Gambling moreover, historically has been associated with cheating and corruption.

   The committee has not seen any workable proposal for controlled gambling which would eliminate the gangsters or the corruption.

7. Rapid transmission of racing information and gambling information about other sporting events is indispensable to big-time bookmaking operations. This information is presently being pro-

vided by a monopoly operated by the Continental Press Service. The Continental Press Service, at critical times and in crucial places where the monopoly of bookmaking is at stake, yields to the domination and control of the Accardo-Guzik-Fischetti crime syndicate, to which it is beholden for its own monopoly in the wire-service field. The wire service is so vital to large bookmakers that they are compelled to pay what the traffic will bear to the Continental Press Service. This makes it possible for the Accardo-Guzik-Fischetti crime syndicate to participate in the profits of bookmaking operations throughout the country.

8. The backbone of the wire service which provides gambling information to bookmakers is the leased wires of the Western Union Telegraph Co. This company, in many parts of the country has not been fully cooperative with law-enforcement officials who have been trying to suppress organized criminal rackets which make use of telegraph facilities. By permitting its facilities to be used by bookmakers, Western Union has given aid and comfort to those engaged in violation of gambling laws. In some cases, Western Union officials and employees actually participated in bookmaking conspiracies by accepting bets and transmitting them to bookmakers. It should be noted that during the latter months of the committee's investigation, Western Union has taken steps to prevent this practice and has been more cooperative with the committee.

In many areas, of which New York is a notable example, the telephone companies have cooperated fully with law-enforcement officials. However, in still other areas, telephone companies have been much less cooperative. Local legislation is apparently necessary in many States to require telephone company officials to refuse facilities and remove existing facilities of suspected bookmakers and to call to the attention of local law-enforcement officials the use of telephone facilities by bookmakers.

9. Crime is largely a local problem. It must be attacked primarily at the local level, with supplementary aid, where appropriate,

from State and Federal authorities. The conduct of various forms of gambling enterprises, houses of prostitution, the distribution of narcotics, the use of intimidation, violence, and murder to achieve gang objectives are all violations of State laws. The public must insist upon local and State law-enforcement agencies meeting this challenge, and must not be deceived by the aura of romanticism and respectability, deliberately cultivated by the communities' top mobsters.

10. The Federal Government has the basic responsibility of helping the States and local governments in eliminating the interstate activities and interstate aspects of organized crime, and in facilitating exchange of information with appropriate safeguards between the Federal Government and local and State law-enforcement agencies as well as between law-enforcement agencies in the various States.

 The task of dealing with organized crime is so great that the public must insist upon the fullest measure of cooperation between law-enforcement agencies at all levels of Government without buck-passing. The committee feels that it has fully demonstrated the need for such cooperation. The time for action has arrived.

11. Wide-open gambling operations and racketeering conditions are supported by out-and-out corruption in many places. The wide-open conditions which were found in these localities can easily be cleaned up by vigorous law enforcement. This has been demonstrated in the past in many different communities and has received added demonstration during the life of our committee. The outstanding example is Saratoga, N. Y., which ran wide-open through the racing season of 1949 but was closed down tight in 1950.

12. Venal public officials have had the effrontery to testify before the committee that they were elected on "liberal" platforms calling for wide-open towns. The committee believes that these officials were put in office by gamblers and with gamblers' money, and that in the few cases where the public was

convinced that gambling is good for business, this myth was deliberately propagated by the paid publicists of the gambling interests. In many wide-open communities, so-called political leaders and law-enforcement officials have sabotaged efforts of civic-minded citizens to combat such wide-open conditions and the crime and corruption that they entailed.

13. The Treasury of the United States has been defrauded of huge sums of money in tax revenues by racketeers and gangsters engaged in organized criminal activities. Huge sums in cash handled by racketeers and gangsters are not reflected in their income tax returns. Income tax returns filed with the Federal Government have been inadequate since, as a rule, they contained no listing of the sources of income nor any itemization of the expenses. Gangsters and racketeers, moreover, do not keep books and records from which it might be possible to check tax returns.

14. Mobsters and racketeers have been assisted by some tax accountants and tax lawyers in defrauding the Government. These accountants and lawyers have prepared and defended income tax returns which they knew to be inadequate. At the very least, those who are guilty of such practices could be convicted of a misdemeanor and sent to jail for a year for every year in which they have failed to comply with the law.

The Bureau of Internal Revenue states that it has, to the best of its ability considering its limited manpower, been investigating these returns. It states further that when it pursues the case of one of these individuals, it prefers to set up against him a case of criminal tax evasion which is a felony, rather than the lesser offense of failing to keep proper books and records, which is a misdemeanor.

Despite this, the committee believes that the Bureau of Internal Revenue could, and should, make more frequent use of the sanctions provided for failure to keep proper books and records than it has heretofore. In any event, the Bureau of Internal Revenue should insist on adequate returns and proper books.

While the great majority of agents of the Bureau of Internal Revenue are honest and efficient, there have been relatively few instances in different parts of the country of lack of vigorous and effective action to collect income taxes from gangsters and racketeers.

15. A major question of legal ethics has arisen in that there are a number of lawyers in different parts of the country whose relations to organized criminal gangs and individual mobsters pass the line of reasonable representation. Such lawyers become true "mouthpieces" for the mob. In individual cases, they have become integral parts of the criminal conspiracy of their clients.

16. Evidence of the infiltration by organized criminals into legitimate business has been found, particularly in connection with the sale and distribution of liquor, real-estate operations, night clubs, hotels, automobile agencies, restaurants, taverns, cigarette-vending companies, juke-box concerns, laundries, the manufacture of clothing, and the transmission of racing and sport news. In some areas of legitimate activity, the committee has found evidence of the use by gangsters of the same methods of intimidation and violence as are used to secure monopolies in criminal enterprise. Gangster infiltration into business also aggravates the possibility of black markets during a period of national emergency such as we are now experiencing. Racketeers also have used labor unions as fronts to enable them to exploit legitimate businessmen.

17. In some instances legitimate businessmen have aided the interests of the underworld by awarding lucrative contracts to gangsters and mobsters in return for help in handling employees, defeating attempts at organization, and in breaking strikes. And the committee has had testimony showing that unions are used in the aid of racketeers and gangsters, particularly on the New York waterfront.

[Editor's Note: The selections follow the order in which they appear in the original report.]

Introduction

THE SPECIAL SENATE Committee to Investigate Organized Crime in Interstate Commerce had its genesis in Senate Resolution 202, which was submitted on January 5, 1950, by Senator Estes Kefauver, Democrat, Tennessee, who subsequently became chairman of the committee. The resolution was referred to the Committee on the Judiciary, and upon being reported by the chairman of that committee on February 27, 1950, was referred to the Committee on Rules and Administration.

It was reported out of the Rules Committee on March 23, 1950, and on May 3, 1950, was considered and agreed to by the Senate.

A week later, the President of the Senate appointed a committee consisting of the author of the resolution, Senator Kefauver, Senator Herbert R. O'Conor, Democrat, Maryland; Senator Lester C. Hunt, Democrat, Wyoming; Senator Alexander Wiley, Republican, Wisconsin, and Senator Charles W. Tobey, Republican, New Hampshire.

The function of the committee was to make a full and complete study and investigation to determine whether organized crime utilizes the facilities of interstate commerce or whether it operates otherwise through the avenues of interstate commerce to promote any transactions which violate Federal law or the law of the State in which such transactions might occur.

The committee was also charged with an investigation of the manner and extent of such criminal operations if it found them actually to be taking place and with the identification of the persons, firms, or corporations involved.

A third responsibility which was charged to the committee was the determination as to whether such interstate criminal operations were developing corrupting influences in violation of the Federal law or the laws of any State. For purposes of the resolution there was included in the area to be covered the District of Columbia, the respective Territories, and all possessions of the United States.

The committee was originally intended by resolution to submit a report to the Senate not later than February 28, 1951, as to its findings with such recommendations as might be deemed advisable. The authority conferred by the resolution was to have terminated on March 31, 1951, but both dates were extended, the date for the report to May 1, 1951, and the date for the committee's expiration to September 1, 1951.

The committee held hearings in pursuance of its charge in fourteen cities. They included Washington, D. C.; Tampa, Fla.; Miami, Fla.; New York City; Cleveland, Ohio; St. Louis, Mo.; Kansas City, Mo.; New Orleans, La.; Chicago, Ill.; Detroit, Mich.; Philadelphia, Pa.; Las Vegas, Nev.; Los Angeles, Calif., and San Francisco, Calif.

In all, it heard testimony from more than 600 witnesses. Many of these were high officials of the Federal, State, and city governments in various areas visited by the committee. The record of testimony covers thousands of pages of printed matter and constitutes one of the most valuable documents of its kind ever assembled. This record has for the most part been put into print and has been made available to law-enforcement officials and public authorities all over the country for their guidance and information. The balance of the record is being printed for publication, and with the extension of the life of the committee, will also be sent to parties in interest upon completion.

Chicago

CHICAGO, by virtue of its size and its location as a center of communications, transportation, and distribution of goods, has been and remains a focal point for the activities of organized criminals in the United
States. This does not mean that the law-enforcement officials of the city
have been uniformly lax in the performance of their duties, although
the committee has found evidence of deplorable laxity on the part of
individual officials. It does mean that because of the history of the city,
its physical location and its great size, the job of law enforcement in
Chicago remains a tremendous responsibility and challenge to the law-
enforcement agencies and to the citizens of Chicago and its surrounding
areas.

Gang Origins in 1920s

The roots of the criminal group operating in Chicago today go back
to the operations of the Torrio-Capone gang which terrorized Chicago
in the 1920's. Records seized by the police during that period indicated
that John Torrio, Al Capone, Jacob Guzik, Tony Accardo, Joseph Fusco,
Frank Nitti, John Patton, Murray Humphries, Paul (Ricca) DeLucia,
Alexander Greenberg, and others had built up an illegal empire netting
millions of dollars a year. In the late 1920s, Torrio abdicated his leadership and Al Capone took over. The activities of the Capone gang at this

time consisted largely of illegal liquor rackets, prostitution, gambling, and the control of horse-racing and dog-racing tracks. During this period the gang was particularly powerful in Burnham, Ill., a suburb of Chicago, whose mayor, John Patton, was closely associated with Torrio and Capone.

In 1924, the Torrio-Capone gang manned the polls during the mayoralty election in Cicero, another Chicago suburb, as part of a plan to take over the local government in Cicero. Following the 1924 election, Cicero became the headquarters for gang operations, and gang influence is still strong there today. In 1931, Al Capone was brought to trial and sentenced for Federal income-tax evasion after all attempts to establish his bootlegging operations had failed to put him in prison. Capone's place as leader of the gang was then taken by Frank Nitti, who, like Capone, was believed to have an interest in the Manhattan Brewery Co., and was an old-time member of the Torrio-Capone gang. At the time of Capone's conviction, the men who were believed to be important members of his underworld empire were, among others, Nitti, Louis Campagna, Paul Ricca, Jacob Guzik, Tony Accardo, Charles Fischetti, Edward Vogel, Hymie Levin, and Ralph Capone. Nitti committed suicide in 1943, while under indictment with a number of other Capone henchmen who were tried and convicted for a conspiracy to extort millions of dollars from the movie industry through their domination of the Motion Picture Operators Union. In 1943, Campagna, Ricca, Charles Gioe, Phil d'Andrea, Nick Circella, and John Rosselli, all of whom had been close to Capone, went to prison in connection with the movie extortion case. They have since been released from the Federal penitentiary.

Capone Gang Reactivated

Until the repeal of the eighteenth amendment in 1933, the manufacture and distribution of bootleg liquor constituted an important source of revenue for the Capone syndicate. After repeal, the Chicago underworld, like racketeers all over the country, concentrated its attention on the revenue possibilities of illegal gambling, extortion rackets, and infiltration of legitimate enterprises.

In Chicago, in many of the service industries, in the liquor industry, and in the unions, there has been a long history of activity by former Capone mobsters. Violence and bombings still occur. There is little doubt that members of the Capone syndicate use proceeds from their illegitimate activities to buy their way into hotels, restaurants, laundry services, dry-cleaning establishments, breweries, and wholesale and retail liquor businesses. In all such businesses their "contacts" give them a substantial advantage.

The extortion cases in the moving-picture industry, successfully prosecuted in New York, marked a milestone in governmental ability to cope with union infiltration by gangsters and the use of the powers of unions by gangsters in order to shake down business enterprises. The astonishing aftermath of the prosecution deserves detailed discussion. Paul Ricca, also known as Paul the Waiter and Paul DeLucia, undoubtedly one of the two or three leading figures in the Capone mob; Louis "Little New York" Campagna and Charlie "Cherry Nose" Gioe, who had been in partnership with Tony Accardo, were prominent in the mulcting of the movie industry. After their conviction and sentence, these three mobsters were visited in prison by Tony Accardo and Eugene Bernstein, the mouthpiece and tax lawyer for the mob. Bernstein and Accardo were indicted as a result of these visits because Accardo used the assumed name of another lawyer, Joseph Bulger. The trips to the prison from Kansas City to Fort Leavenworth were made in the automobile of Tony Gizzo, a prominent Kansas City mobster who has a history of close connections with the Capone syndicate.

The three mobsters were released on parole after serving a minimum period of imprisonment although they were known to be vicious gangsters. A prominent member of the Missouri bar presented their parole applications to the parole board, which granted the parole against the recommendations of the prosecuting attorney and of the judge who had presided at their trial. In the opinion of this committee, this early release from imprisonment of three dangerous mobsters is a shocking abuse of parole powers.

"You Don't Ask Questions"—
Bernstein

Another example of the efficiency of the underworld in releasing its leaders from the toils of the law is the story of the raising of funds for a tax settlement effected by the three above-mentioned mobsters, which they had to complete before they would be eligible for parole. Eugene Bernstein testified that he arranged this settlement. The Government's original claim against Campagna and DeLucia was about $470,000, including penalties. This liability was settled for $120,000 plus penalties of $70,000. Bernstein testified that $190,000 was delivered to his office in cash at various periods over a month by persons unknown to him. He had the almost inconceivable effrontery, as a member of the bar, to assert to the committee under oath that although he saw some of the persons who delivered the money he never asked them their names and that his office had no record whatsoever to indicate their identities. "You don't ask those fellows any questions," said Mr. Bernstein. He testified that he told Campagna and DeLucia that the money would have to be raised and that he also told this to Accardo. He testified that he visited Mrs. Campagna's home but did not remember what he told her. Neither DeLucia, Campagna, nor Mrs. Campagna had any idea of who might have been interested in providing funds or in how the funds were raised. Each had several hundred thousand dollars in cash hidden away in safety boxes in their homes. "It was a friend of mine," said DeLucia, "I would put up $190,000 for a friend of mine who needed it." The combined testimony of these witnesses represents a graphic demonstration of the willful, sullen, vicious contempt for the law still dominant in their hearts and minds. The connivance in this plot of a lawyer who obviously could provide the essential clues, if not the actual answers, brands the entire matter as even more shocking.

The most recent evidence of the intricacy of gangland's financial operations was provided in 1948 and 1949 when Ricca received loans totaling $80,000 from one Hugo Bennett, a salaried underling in the Sportsmen's Park Race Track and Florida dog tracks, formerly controlled by Edward O'Hare, John Patton, and the Capone syndicate. Bennett and his present boss, William H. Johnston, who figures prominently in our discussion of the Miami area, both worked at Sportsmen's Park under O'Hare. Patton, through his son, still has an important interest in the dog trades. Several prominent Capone mobsters worked at the dog tracks when this committee began its investigation.

The Mysterious $80,000 Loan

Ricca did not need the $80,000. By his own testimony, he had $300,000 in cash "stashed away." He owned a very valuable and pretentious farm of 700 acres and an elaborate home in a Chicago suburb. Bennett, on the other hand, had very meager assets and in order to make the loan to Ricca, borrowed $20,000 from Johnston and $15,000 from Max Silverberg, Johnston's restaurant concessionaire at the race tracks. Most of the remainder of the $80,000 was made available to Bennett by a highly questionable real-estate deal through which Johnston and a group of his own friends sold some land to the Miami Beach Kennel Club and made a huge profit. Bennett was cut in on this deal and the proceeds to him enabled him to complete the loan to Ricca.

Although Bennett went through the motions of obtaining mortgages, it was apparent to the lawyer who drew up these instruments that Bennett was determined to make the loans whether or not they could be properly secured. The evidence of the attorney and of Bennett, conflicting as it is on many points, clearly demonstrates that the mortgages were simply for the record. There is also ample reason to suspect that the $80,000 may have been a payoff for Ricca's approval of the wire service deal in which Accardo, Guzik, and Russell obtained an interest in the lucrative Miami Beach S. and G. gambling syndicate.

Several unions which were racketeer-infested and whose treasuries were raided by racketeers, had their headquarters in the same building where Tony Accardo operated his gambling enterprises and where he was in partnership with both Charlie Gioe and Harry Russell, whose Silver Bar tavern was also located there. The entire gang of union extortionists appear to be living in luxury in Florida, California, or Chicago and many of them have already acquired a thick veneer of respectability.

Bookmaking and the Race Wire

As the committee pointed out in its second interim report, the form of gambling which depends most on interstate commerce and interstate communications is off-track betting on horse racing and dog racing. The backbone of illegal bookmaking operations throughout the country is the up-to-the-minute information furnished by the Continental Press Service through its Nation-wide network of telephone and telegraph wires, and the intricate organization of distributors and subdistributors that gather and disseminate the news for Continental.

The heart of the racing news service centers in Chicago, where Continental has its main operating office, and from which most of its wires fan out to the rest of the country. While in Chicago, this committee focused its attention to a considerable degree on the operations of the Continental Press, its relations with the distributors through whom racing news flows, and the increasing domination of the wire service by the same racketeering elements who control the large-scale and lucrative handbook operations.

The headquarters of the race wire service have been established in Chicago since before John Torrio became the underworld king of the city in 1920. Interestingly enough, the building which was occupied by Monte Tennes and his General News Bureau racing service now houses the offices of the Continental Press Service, some thirty years later. But the story of the race wire service, while inextricably linked with Chicago's past and present, is not only a story of Chicago but of every city and town in the country into which the tentacles of the wire service reach. For this reason, the committee discusses the history and operations of the wire service in a separate section of this report.

The committee has described the workings of the Continental Press Service and exposed its facade of respectability and attempted insulation from the handbook operators who depend on it for information and on whom it depends for revenue. Just as the race wire service is essential to the success of large-scale betting operations, the substantial income which channels into Chicago from the wire service depends on the continuous operation of a flourishing handbook business. United Press and Associated Press pay a nominal fee of from $70 to $80 a month for the information that Continental distributes; the Illinois News Service, a single distributor, pays about $250,000 annually for the same service. The difference in these rates is the profit of the handbook operators which is passed on, in part, to the subdistributor and distributor for Continental, and ultimately to Continental.

Subdistributors Service Bookmakers

Since the last reorganization of the wire service in the Chicago area, the city of Chicago has been serviced by the R. and H. wire service, owned by the Capone mobsters, Ray Jones, Phil Katz, and Hymie Levin, and by Midwest News, now owned by John Scanlon, who participated in the Guzik-Accardo-Russell maneuver to take over the S and G, wire service in Florida. The list of wire service drops compiled by the Senate Committee on Interstate and Foreign Commerce indicates that R. and H. services over 100 individual drops in Chicago. The Midwest Service sends racing news to over 200 drops in Chicago, as well as to about 50 drops in the surrounding area in Illinois. The list does not designate the occupation of the subscribers or drops, but in the case of R. and H. and Midwest, both of which are themselves subdistributors, it is safe to assume that the listed drops are, almost without exception, handbook or lay-off establishments. Some idea of the magnitude of the operations involved can be obtained from a review of the income of a number of the members of the Capone syndicate who have been actively engaged in gambling. Louis Campagna told the committee that his bookmaking operations in Cicero netted about $80,000 to $90,000 a year before his conviction in the movie extortion case.

Harry Russell, who operated as a lay-off man for bookies in Kansas City, Omaha, and locations in Indiana and Michigan, was a partner with Accardo in the Owl Club, a bookie operation in Calumet City. In 1946, Russell reported an income of $26,000 from the club, and Accardo's share in the take has been as high as $45,000 in 1 year. In 1948, Joseph Corngold and Willie Heeney, members of the Cicero contingent of the Capone mob, grossed $51,000 on the handbook operation of the El Patio Club in Cicero.

The committee also heard testimony as to the extent of large bookie operations outside the immediate environs of Chicago. The income tax return of Charles Fischetti, who with his brother Rocco ran the lavish Vernon Country Club, showed a total net income of over $22,000 believed to be attributable to the gambling operations of the club. The Big House, a gambling place operated in nearby Indiana by William Gardner, Sonny Sheets, and Barry Hyams, who have close connections with the Chicago syndicate, took in $9,000,000 in 1948. William Spellisy, who operates on the Midwest wire service in Morris, Ill., testified that his handbook operations grossed $200,000 per annum, and Thomas Cawley, who operates on the Midwest wire service in La Salle County, showed a net profit of $68,000 from a half-interest in handbook and other large-scale gambling operations in La Salle and Streator.

Jack Doyle, gambling king of Gary, Ind., another subscriber to the wire service, conducts a large-scale handbook operation in that city along with other forms of gambling. Because of his political connections he is unmolested by law-enforcement officials. The profits from his illegal operations are enormous. Doyle told the committee nothing, but his detailed records on horse-race betting, poker roulette, craps, and slot-machine operations told much. From a mere $8,000 in 1943, his profits jumped to $120,000 in 1948.

Slot Machines Made in Chicago

Most of the coin machines in use throughout the country are manufactured in and around Chicago, and a large number of the machines have been purchased and operated inside the State of Illinois. The manufacture and distribution of slot machines has been a lucrative field of operation for a number of Capone mobsters. The Taylor Manufacturing Co. in Cicero, one of the largest manufacturers of gaming equipment in the country, is partially owned by Claude Maddox, a Capone mobster with a long criminal record, and Joseph Aiuppa, a close friend of Accardo and one of the leading members of the Capone syndicate. Over the past three years, the gross income of this operation has averaged between $200,000 and $300,000 a year.

Listed in its record of customers are some of the largest gambling establishments in the country. Total sales of gambling equipment by this company to one plush gambling establishment alone, the Hyde Park Club, were $75,000 for a period of three years.

The merchandising of coin machines and particularly slot machines is a business peculiarly adapted to the sales technique of the underworld, and a number of Chicago mobsters have been active in this field. Ed Vogel, old-time Capone henchman who evaded service of subpoena by the committee, is believed to control the distribution of slot machines in the North Side of Chicago and in the northwest suburbs. Vogel has a partnership interest in lucrative cigarette vending and juke box distributing business. Through arrangement with the owner of a privately operated golf club, Vogel has been collecting for years from the operation of the slot machines at the club on the basis of 60 percent for the club and 40 percent for Vogel. It is conservatively estimated that from this one source alone the revenue received by Vogel is $50,000 annually. Each week Vogel's representative and an employee of the club lock themselves in a room at the club and divide the take. The club was reimbursed by Vogel for the expense of new machines purchased by it. In the past year, the State police, on direction of Governor Stevenson and the State's attorney of Cook County, have made a concentrated effort to break up slot-machine operations in the State. State's Attorney Boyle testified that since November 1, 1949, his office had confiscated and destroyed 564 slot machines. Boyle testified that it was clear to him that a syndicate was behind the operations of the slot machines found in small taverns and gambling joints throughout the country because of the regularity with which slot machines reappeared in clubs that had been raided. During the period when the raids on slot machines were most intense, a number of hold-ups took place in private clubs that owned their own slot machines and the machines were removed from the premises. It seems apparent that the seizure of these slots was an effort by the syndicate to recoup their losses of machines seized by the law-enforcement agents.

Slot-Machine Profits Tempt Racketeers

The take on some of the slot machines operating in large gambling establishments, while not comparable to the sums taken in by some of the larger bookies, are tempting bait to the organized vultures operating in this field. Jack Doyle of Gary, Ind., reported ownership of 129 slot machines which brought in $60,000. Indicative of the size of Doyle's slot machine operation is the fact that in one year his expense for machines and parts totaled $24,000. The El Patio Club in Cicero grossed $23,000 on its slot-machine operations, and the Seven Gables, referred to before in connection with handbook operations, took in about $15,000 annually in the operation of its six slot machines. The 40-percent cut which Vogel, Francis Curry, and other members of the Capone syndicate are believed to take on the machines that they control constitutes a large-scale gambling racket, operating in the southern part of Illinois and across State lines into neighboring territories.

Policy—Big Business—Big Muscle

The large sums of money which annually pass into the hands of the Chicago bookmakers are the accumulations of large and small bets placed by occasional bettors and professional gamblers alike. The committee's investigations revealed that the city of Chicago harbors another huge gambling operation whose income in the millions is built upon a foundation of nickels, dimes, and quarters. It is estimated that the play on the policy wheels in Chicago's south side totaled for the past five years $150,000,000.

The densely populated South Side area of Chicago has for years been a fertile territory for the operation of policy wheels. Theodore Roe, a long-time policy operator estimated before the committee that 60 to 70 percent of the population of this area bet on the numbers to be drawn in the so-called policy wheel. There are approximately 15 to 20 wheels in operation in Chicago, 7 or 8 of which have a total play approximating 3 to 5 million dollars annually. The payoff on the wheels rarely goes above $50 to a bettor. In some instances when combinations are hit, the payoff may be 100 to 1. The placing of bets is handled by hundreds of low-paid employees and so-called commission writers who take and report the thousands of small wagers made each day. Bets are either made with a writer who goes from door to door with a book on which numbers can be played, or a would-be bettor can go to an established betting station and place a bet on the number to be drawn. In 1942 a number of the important policy racketeers, including Peter Tremont and Pat Manno (alias Manning), long-time associates of the Capone syndicate, were indicted by a Cook County grand jury for a conspiracy to operate a lottery. The subsequent trial resulted in a verdict of not guilty because of failure of the principal grand jury witness to testify. With the exception of this unsuccessful grand-jury action no major efforts have been made to break up Chicago's huge policy operation.

Theodore Roe could recall only one of his employees who had ever received a jail sentence in connection with his policy operations. Fines average from $25 up, and are absorbed by the wheel operator. Judging from sums taken out of the policy operations by the men who control them, these fines amount to no more than a reasonable expense of doing business.

Although for the most part the policy racket has operated in predominantly Negro sections of the city, the Capone syndicate has found the territory a fertile source of revenue. Peter Tremont and Pat Manno control the operations of the Rome-Silver Wheel and the Standard Golden Gate. From their gaudily named operations Tremont and Manno have averaged an annual take of from $80,000 to $100,000. The lesser partners in these two wheels, Fred, Tom, Jeff, and Sam Manno, brothers of Pat, have netted $50,000. The play on the wheels runs over $5,000,000 annually. In 1946,

Pat Manno was linked with others in an effort by Chicago racketeers to take over a $14,000,000 annual gambling policy and other racket activities in Dallas County, Tex. The committee heard testimony to the effect that a hoodlum known as Paul Jones came to Dallas in 1946 in an attempt to make arrangements with the Dallas police and sheriff-elect of Dallas County on behalf of the Chicago syndicate for undisturbed racket operations in Dallas. Lt. George Butler, one of the police officials approached, testified that Pat Manno had appeared in Dallas to convince the Dallas officials and local racketeers of the authenticity of Jones' scheme. A recording was made of Manno's conversation during this visit. On the record, Manno stated that he had been in the policy business for seventeen years in the city of Chicago.

Jones and others involved in the scheme to take over Dallas County were indicted and convicted of attempted bribery, but the Texas police never took any action against Manno in this connection.

The frankness of the recorded statement in the files of the committee is an interesting contrast to Manno's testimony, or lack thereof before this committee. He refused to answer most of the committee's questions on the grounds that he might incriminate himself, questions relating to his visit to Dallas, his acquaintance with Jones, his business associations with Peter Tremont or any aspects of his policy operations.

Gangster's Own Description of Operations

The records of Paul Jones' and Pat Manno's negotiations with the Dallas officials amply corroborates the existence and method of operation of organized criminals. Typical are the following recorded statements of Manno, whom his associate called the No. 5 man in the Chicago syndicate:

> *Sure. Once you get organized, you don't have to worry about money. Everything will roll in in a nice quiet manner, in a business-like way. You don't, he don't have to worry about it personally. Everybody will be happy I'm sure.* * * *

We're not going to come from Chicago down here * * * all local fellows. We're leaving that to him. He's representing us * * * and keep the, like calls, the muscle men, these petty * * *. These people can be called in too, you know * * *.

One thing I'm against, always was against. I don't like, like I was telling you last night, five or six joints in the radius of six blocks, a joint every block. That's one thing I've always talked against. I like one big spot and that's all. Out in the country, out of the city entirely. * * *

I don't run any of those places up there, gambling or anything like that. I got my own territory. I got certain business that I take care of for the last 16 or 17 years. I do very well, living comfortably, worry about nothing. As far as the set-up, these places like dice rooms or horse rooms and things like that, that's like another department I would call it. If I had a fellow sitting here with me that runs a certain game, he could give it to you in a minute. He could tell you what to expect and all that sort of stuff you see. But I have my own little concession, and that's the end. * * * Well, that's my business, policy. Policy is my business. That I could run. * * * I've been at it for 17 years.

The oldest, and probably the largest wheel now operating in Chicago is the Maine-Idaho-Ohio wheel, originally known as the Jones brothers wheel. Theodore Roe and the Jones brothers are partners in this wheel. The play on this wheel amounts to about $6,000,000 per year; the net income for 1949 was close to $700,000 and for 1948 it came to over $997,000. It is interesting to note that the gross for 1949 was about $1,000,000, and the gross for 1948 was about $1,300,000. In 1946, Edward Jones, one of the partners in the Jones brothers wheel, was kidnaped and held for ransom. The ransom demanded was $250,000. George Jones, a brother of the kidnaped Edward, negotiated with the unknown persons who were holding Edward. One hundred thousand dollars in ransom was paid, and Edward Jones was released. He left Chicago about a week later and has since resided in Mexico, although he continues to draw sums approximating $200,000 a year from the operations of the wheel. In his testimony before the committee, Jones stated that he had no idea who his kidnapers were, and that they had made no mention of the proceeds of the policy wheel. It may be noted, however, that Jacob Guzik recorded, simply as "from various sources," without explanation a single item of income in the amount of $100,000 for the year 1946.

The only large policy wheel operated by white persons other than the Rome-Silver and Standard-Golden Gate, which are owned by the Capone mobsters, Peter Tremont and Patrick Manno, is the Erie-Buffalo. This wheel, the gross play of which runs to $5,000,000 annually, was for years operated by the Benvenuti brothers. Because of favors done for Al Capone by the elder brother Julius, the mob laid off this wheel.

After the death of Capone and Julius, conditions changed rapidly. In 1947, Caesar and Leo owned the Erie-Buffalo wheel which netted them approximately $105,000 each from its operation. As a lucrative side line, the Benvenutis operated a paper company which supplied policy slips to wheels within and outside of the State of Illinois. This same year, Sam Pardy received as income $1,500 from the Benvenutis. His total income had never exceeded $5,000. In the same year, the homes of both Caesar and Leo were bombed. The muscle started.

In the year 1948, drastic changes took place in the internal organization of the Erie-Buffalo wheel. Suddenly Sam Pardy and Tom Manno, a brother of Pat and a junior partner in the Rome-Silver and Standard-Golden Gate wheels, appear as partners in Erie-Buffalo, each netting for 1948 from the operation of Erie-Buffalo $305,000 each. Tom Manno's income from the two Capone wheels in past years had been a mere $40,000. His vacancy was filled by his brother Sam Manno. Caesar and Leo Benvenuti contented themselves with receiving payments of $50,000 each from the wheel they previously owned.

In 1949, the new partners, Pardy and Manno, received $135,000 each from the Erie-Buffalo. Their "associates" Leo and Caesar Benvenuti were paid the same $50,000 each.

In the Erie-Buffalo records, a single significant item appeared in 1949 under the heading of "Special services." The amount covered under this item was $278,000, which was paid to the partnership of Anthony Accardo and Jacob Guzik. What the special services were bore no explanation. The result is self-evident. Three of the largest policy wheels in operation were under the dominance and control of the mob. In the middle of 1950, the Benvenutis left for an extended visit to Europe.

Legislators Oppose Anticrime Laws

Substantial testimony was adduced before the committee that certain members of the State legislature, particularly those living in districts most heavily infested by racketeers, vote against legislation designed to curb gangster activities and urged for passage by the vigorous Chicago Crime Commission and associate freely with their gangster constituents. Roland Libonati, Democratic State senator from the West Side, and a close associate of Capone's, spearheaded the opposition to the reform legislation proposed by the Chicago Crime Commission and Governor Stevenson and backed by the bar. Representative James J. Adducci, Republican member of the bipartisan coalition against reform, has represented Chicago's West Side for seventeen years. Adducci has been arrested a number of times in company with Capone mobsters and admitted to accepting campaign contributions from Lawrence Mangano, a well-known figure in the Capone hierarchy, explaining that in his district it was necessary to "accept finances from any kind of a business." Adducci has recently been indicted on the basis of his testimony before the committee that he received commissions amounting to $6,000 a year for securing orders from the State for printing and supplies.

It was perfectly obvious, as must be the case wherever large-scale law violations exist, that many of the law-enforcement officials have been corrupted, although in the time available to the committee, only a few cases could be found where direct payments to police could be established. On the other hand, the committee heard and saw shocking evidence of inefficient or nonexistent law enforcement; of unexplained wealth enjoyed by low-salaried police officials; of brazen neglect of duty on the part of local officials, and in some localities, of apathy amounting to approval on the part of the public.

Evidence of individual police payoffs is difficult to uncover, and it was neither possible nor desirable for this committee to engage in a prolonged search for specific instances of corruption. As John Rosselli, onetime Capone henchman, frankly stated before the committee, the wire service, the handbooks, the slot machines, and the other rackets which have thrived in the city of Chicago cannot operate without local corruption; if the handbooks are open, the conclusion is inescapable that the police are being paid off.

Punchboards

There are 30 to 40 punchboard manufacturers in the United States. The boards are shipped in interstate commerce. Their use in most of the States is contrary to local law. The Sax interests in Chicago are probably the largest makers of punchboards. There are about six or seven other leading producers. Total sales by all manufacturers is about $10,000,000 annually.

Of the total number of boards produced, 95 percent are so-called straight money or gambling boards. The remaining 5 percent are used for the merchandising of candy, cigars, cigarettes, etc. But even this type of board is often used for gambling.

Punchboards vary in price from $2 up, depending on the type and elaborateness of the board. A common type of board which sells for $2 will pay out $80 in prize money on a $120 total play, a $38 profit on a $2 investment. If, as sometimes happens, the board is destroyed, before the large money prizes are punched, the profit may be greater.

Some distributors and jobbers place the boards in locations on a commission basis, splitting the profits with the proprietor on a 50–50 basis.

Testimony was given to the committee that some concerns, for an additional cost over and above that of the board, will furnish a key to the board. In such circumstances, the probable profits to the proprietor and the chance of winning by the gullible gambler are obvious. The victimizing of the proprietor by a confederate of the jobber who has the key to the winning numbers is another method of operation.

The use of punchboards for gambling is on the increase. They provide a great incentive to gambling. A variation of the punchboard is the penny pushcards which have great attraction for children. Cease and desist orders of the Federal Trade Commission against the use of these boards have been upheld by the courts.

It is, of course, not possible to estimate with any great degree of exactitude the annual sum played on punchboards. In view of the number of boards manufactured, the committee believes that to estimate this figure to be $100,000,000 would be conservative.

Crime Conditions in Illinois

Cook County.—Law enforcement in the city of Chicago is primarily the responsibility of the mayor and the commissioner of police. Outside the city, but within the boundaries of Cook County, lie a number of incorporated villages each with its own mayor and its own chief of police. These areas are also under the jurisdiction of the State's attorney and the county sheriff, but the testimony before the committee revealed a pattern of continuing attempts to shift responsibility from one law enforcement agency to another.

As in other cities, the committee found that gambling operations were even more extensive and wide open just outside the city limits. The committee found evidence of lush gambling operations in Cicero, Burnham, Melrose Park, and other of the incorporated villages just outside Chicago.

Law enforcement in the areas outside the city has been particularly lax because of the ineffectiveness of the sheriff's office under former Sheriff Elmer M. Walsh, who did not stand for re-election, and his predecessors, and the indifference or outright dishonesty of the local chiefs of police. Sheriff Walsh's excuse for this laxity was lack of adequate personnel and lack of jurisdiction. The ward sponsorship system, which results in a complete turn-over of personnel in the sheriff's office with the election of each new sheriff, cannot possibly yield an effective enforcement agency.

In 1949, gambling conditions in the area outside Chicago had reached proportions which made it necessary for the State's attorney for the county to undertake gambling raids. Anthony A. Gherscovich, administrative assistant to the State's attorney, told the committee that prior to that time, the State's attorney's office had notified the sheriff and the chiefs of police of gambling operations within their jurisdiction but that nothing had been done to stop them. As a result of the raids conducted by the State's attorney, a number of chiefs of police were indicted. Henry Wlekinski, the chief of police of Calumet City, indicted for malfeasance in office, admitted to the jury that gambling was rampant in the city. He defended his action on the grounds that the license fees from illegal taverns were supporting the town and were responsible for the low tax rate enjoyed by its citizens. On the basis of this defense, he was acquitted of the charges and remains in office as chief of police. Gambling operations appeared to be unimpeded when this committee visited Calumet City.

A similar situation existed in Melrose Park where Rocco de Grazia, Capone mobster, has operated the famous Lumber Gardens and other wide-open establishments for years. The chief of police was notified of these operations by the State's attorney's office, but took no action to stop or curtail this wide-open gambling operation. He was indicted for nonfeasance but acquitted, and is still in office. The pattern is repeated in Cicero, which has had three chiefs of police in recent years, but which is still the seat of lucrative gambling operations by a number of members of the Capone syndicate. The records of the chiefs of police in these towns, where gambling joints could be identified merely by walking down the street, are records of neglect of official duty and shocking indifference to violations of law. Equally shocking is the acquiescence of the people of the towns, as evidenced by the acquittal of these men and their continuation in office.

A reason for lack of conscientious enforcement of gambling laws was disclosed by the testimony of Police Capt. Dan Gilbert, known as the world's richest cop and for many years chief investigator for the office of the State's attorney for Cook County. Gilbert, democratic candidate for sheriff of Cook County, testified before the committee that he placed bets himself with a well-known Chicago betting commissioner. He admitted this was not legal betting. In explanation, he testified, "I have been a gambler at heart." Although agreeing that raids could be initiated by his office on bookies in the city, Gilbert admitted it had not been done since 1939, despite the fact that practically every bookmaking establishment in the city of Chicago was listed is the recently published hearings before the

McFarland subcommittee of the Senate Interstate and Foreign Commerce Committee.

Grundy and La Salle Counties.—The story of local corruption and indifference which was repeated many times in testimony before the committee, is not confined to the locality of Cook County. In 1950, at the direction of Governor Stevenson, the State police made a number of raids on known gambling joints. Among the places raided was the Seven Gables Tavern in Grundy County, which contained a bookie operation with a play of about $200,000 a year, a crap table, a roulette wheel, and slot machines which were repaired by the father of the State's attorney for Grundy County. The gambling operations were apparently wide open, but William Spellisy, proprietor of the tavern, testified that he had never been bothered by the police before the 1950 raid.

The committee also heard testimony regarding large-scale bookie and slot machine operations in neighboring La Salle County.

Thomas Cawley admitted in his testimony that he had operated two books, roulette and a crap table for about 15 years in the towns of La Salle and Streator. Cawley testified that his large gambling operations were generally known, but that he had never been disturbed by the sheriff or the chief of police. Cawley denied that he had paid money for protection, but admitted making political contributions, and a close friendship with Mike Welter, ex-sheriff of La Salle County who was frequently visited by Francis Currie and Claude Maddox, old-time members of the Capone syndicate. Cawley testified before this committee that he received occasional orders to close operations, but that such orders were overlooked in a short time and operations resumed. When Mr. Cawley first testified before the committee in October 1950, he stated that operations in the county had been slowed down in the preceding three months, but by the time of his second appearance in December, gambling was proceeding as usual in La Salle County. Cawley told the committee that his operations were possible because 90 percent of the people in the county wanted it that way, and his point was proved by the election as sheriff of a man who openly supported gambling in La Salle County.

Madison and St. Clair Counties.—The committee heard from a number of citizens who stated that slot machines could be found "in such places as drug stores, confectioneries and even grocery stores" at all times since 1927 to the present. A notorious vice district known as the Valley ran without interference until closed by Federal military authorities. A grand jury in 1946, although plagued by lack of cooperation from prosecuting officials, found appalling vice and gambling conditions in St. Clair County. The committee heard testimony about similar wide-open conditions in Madison County.

Most shocking in Madison and St. Clair Counties was the utter blindness of law-enforcement officials and the evidence of their unexplained income. The testimony of John English, commissioner of public safety of East St. Louis, that he knew of no major law violations in his city seemed to the committee to verge on the incredible. He testified that he had never done anything to disturb the operations of Carroll and Mooney and did not know that they were among the biggest bookmakers in the country although this has been notorious on a nationwide basis for a long time. He stated that the first time he knew anything about Mooney's operations was when he read it in the papers. He also told the committee that it was his understanding that Carroll was violating no Federal or Illinois law. The committee asked him about a number of other well-known bookmakers whose operations were common knowledge in his area, but the commissioner asserted he knew nothing about them. He admitted having stated publicly that in his opinion "it was all right to bet any place else if they wanted to make a bet." With this kind of an attitude, it is no wonder that law was flagrantly disregarded in East St. Louis.

The committee had no better impression of the law-enforcement activities of Adolph Fisher who testified that he had been sheriff of St. Clair County from 1946 until 1950. Although the operations of C. J. Rich & Co. and of the Carroll-Mooney partnership were notorious throughout the United States, Sheriff Fisher, in whose county they were operating, told the committee he knew nothing about them. In fact, he testified that he first learned about Mooney and Carroll when this committee's investigation started. When it was pointed out to him that it had been a matter of public record as a result of Carroll's own testimony before the Senate Committee on Interstate and Foreign Commerce some months earlier, Sheriff Fisher corrected his testimony to say that at that time he sent a deputy down to the establishment but found nothing going on. He could not recall whether he sent the deputy in the daytime or nighttime or whether any efforts were made to follow up the investigation. This committee's investigators, however, had no difficulty whatever discovering the Carroll-Mooney operation going at full steam.

A similar picture was presented through the testimony of Mr. Dallas Harrell who had been sheriff of Madison County from 1946 to 1950. His very frank answer to a question of why he took no action in putting out of business large gambling establishments such as the 200 Club was that he left that up to the cities and "if the mayor and the chief of police and the citizens of Madison, the city of Madison, were satisfied with it, it suited me."

Although Sheriff Harrell testified that there were no commercial slot machines in Madison County while he was sheriff, the committee learned that the Bureau of Internal Revenue's list of persons who had paid the $100-per-annum tax on establishments in which slot machines were maintained had been published in the newspapers of St. Louis. Sheriff Harrell stated that he knew this; nevertheless no action was taken against slot machines.

There can be little doubt in the minds of the committee that "wide-open" conditions flourish in Madison and St. Clair Counties because of protection and "payoffs." Commissioner English, for example, never gave a satisfactory explanation of his large accumulation of assets since he became commissioner of public safety, nor the nature of the so-called "political contributions" which he reported as income. Chief of Police John Vickery, of Fairmont City, Ill., who had previously been a coal miner, first began to sport a Cadillac car and a $1,200 diamond ring when he became police chief. Perhaps his attitude toward bookmaking explains his sudden wealth. When asked why he permitted a bookmaking establishment to operate within a block of his police station, his answer was "I just never had had no complaint about it."

Syndication of Crime and the Mafia

Mafia Originally Had High Purpose

The Mafia was originally one of many secret societies organized in Sicily to free the island of foreign domination. The methods used for securing secrecy of operations, unity of command, intimidation and murder, and the silencing of informers, were adopted by a criminal group that became the Mafia after the Bourbons were driven from Sicily.

According to historians and the most authentic research material available, the following is the history of the Mafia:

The various secret organizations in Sicily were fused into a single group known as the Fratellanza or the "Brotherhood" which sometime later became known as the Mafia. Initiates and new members of this organization took solemn oaths never to reveal the secrets of the group under any circumstances and never to divulge the names of fellow members, even under torture. This secret association was organized in groups of ten members. Each group had a leader. The group leaders were known to each other but not to the members of the various groups. The group leaders reported to the provincial chief who in turn reported to the supreme chief in Palermo, a very wealthy and influential man.

This organization grew enormously in Sicily after 1860. Smuggling, cattle stealing, extortion, and shake-downs were its major criminal activities. The administration of justice was so openly defied by this organization that many attempts were made by law-enforcement agencies in Sicily to deal with it. Although many arrests were made, law-enforcement agencies found it extremely difficult to break the power of the Mafia. The arrested members of this organization would not talk. Witnesses of various crimes committed by members of the Mafia were intimidated and were afraid to testify. Political influence was used to protect Mafia members charged with crime. Good legal talent was always available for their defense. The various drives against the Mafia in Sicily which were made by Italian Governments from the 1870's down to Mussolini's time, were therefore largely ineffective in destroying the Mafia. However these drives had the effect of causing large numbers of Mafia members to migrate to the New World and many of them came to this country.

As early as the 1880's, New Orleans was the focal point of Mafia activity. According to Pasquale Corte, the Italian consul in New Orleans, large numbers of escaped Italian criminals settled there. These and other desperados grew rich and powerful upon the profits of robbery, extortion, assassination. Most of the victims were fellow countrymen who failed to pay the sums demanded by Mafia leaders.

The Mafia in New Orleans overreached itself when it ordered the murder of a popular police officer, David Hennessy. After he was murdered, a dozen Mafia leaders were arrested. None were convicted after a trial marred by the intimidation of witnesses and jury fixing. The defendants, however, who had been held in jail on other charges, were lynched by a mob of aroused New Orleans citizens. After these lynchings the power of the Mafia in New Orleans was temporarily broken.

The Mafia became established in other cities besides New Orleans. Moreover, like many other underworld organizations, it grew rich and powerful during prohibition in the sale and distribution of alcoholic beverages. In addition both during prohibition and since that time this organization has entered every racket promising easy money. Narcotics, pinball machines, slot machines, gambling in every form and description are some of its major activities at the present time.

Mafia Operates Behind
Legitimate Fronts

Many of the individuals suspected of connection with the Mafia operate behind legitimate fronts. The olive oil, cheese, and the export and import businesses are some of the favorite fronts for Mafia operations. They offer a cover, particularly, for narcotics operations. They also help explain interstate and international contacts between persons suspected of Mafia connections.

Mafia operations in this country have been described by the Narcotics Bureau as follows:

It is almost inevitable that the Mafia should take an important part in American criminal rackets. Here is a nationwide organization of outlaws in a sort of oath-bound, blood-cemented brotherhood dedicated to complete defiance of the law. Where personal advantage or interests are concerned, here is a more or less permanently established network, an organized maze of underground conduits, always ready and available when racket enterprise is to be furthered. The organization is such that a member in one part of the country can, with perfect confidence, engage in any sort of illicit business with members in any other section of the country. Most helpful to the Mafia has been the attitude on the part of many law-enforcement officers in connection with its murders. These are sometimes passed over lightly on the theory these cases are just hoodlums killing off one another and that it is not a matter on which to waste police time and energy.

The ruthless elimination of competitors from enterprises which Mafia leaders decide to take over, the ruthless elimination of persons who have weakened in their Mafia loyalties, failed to carry out Mafia orders, or who have informed against the Mafia, has left a trail of murder from Tampa to San Francisco. This is well illustrated by the following comments of the Narcotics Bureau:

Joseph Sica and Alfred Sica of California are satellites of Anthony Riz-zoti, alias Jack Dragna, and closely allied to members in New York and New Jersey from where they went to California several years ago. In 1949, a narcotics case was developed against the Sicas, principally upon the testimony of one Abraham Davidian who made purchases of narcotics from them, sometimes in lots costing more than $15,000. Early this year, while the case was pending for trial, Davidian was shot to death while asleep in his mother's home in Fresno.

Another west coast case of great importance was developed in 1944. This concerned a New York-California-Mexico smuggling ring in which Salvatore Maugeri and others were convicted. During the course of the investigation, a narcotics agent working undercover learned that one of the ring with whom he was negotiating, Charles "Big Nose" La-Gaipa, of Santa Cruz, Calif., was in bad odor with some of his criminal Mafia associates. LaGaipa disappeared. He never has been found. His car was recovered with blood on the seat and brain tissue on the dash-board.

One Nick DeJohn, active in the narcotics traffic in Chicago, and Thomas Buffa, active in the narcotics traffic in St. Louis, transferred their activities to California. A short time later, evidently for trying to muscle in, both were killed. Buffa died from shotgun fire. DeJohn's body was found in an automobile with wire twisted around the neck.

A member of this combine named Ignazio Antinori went to Ha-vana frequently to obtain narcotics for middle western members of this organization. The leader was Joseph DeLuca***. On one occasion, Antinori, in return for $25,000, delivered a poor grade of narcotic. The middle western group gave him 2 weeks in which to return the money. At the end of that period, having failed to make good, he was killed in Tampa by shotgun fire in 1940. Evidently the middle western group or-dered the Tampa leader to do this job. Thereafter his two sons contin-ued in the traffic. After considerable investigation, we arrested DeLuca, Antinori's two sons, Paul and Joseph, and many others involved in 1942. The testimony of one of the defendants, Carl Carramusa, served to assure conviction of all defendants. The sentences meted out to these vicious murderers were shockingly low. In the case of Joseph DeLuca,

who got three years, the court ordered that he not be deported on rec-
ommendation of the district attorney. After the leader, DeLuca, had
served one year, he was paroled. Carramusa had moved to Chicago to
escape vengeance by the combine. One morning, in 1945, as he was re-
pairing a fire in front of his home, he was killed by a shotgun blast be-
fore the eyes of his fifteen-year-old daughter. His murder remains
unsolved, but it unquestionably was the work of the Chicago members
of the combine on orders from the Kansas City group. The neighbors of
Carramusa who could have furnished information remained silent be-
cause of fear. This is the same pattern which follows all of their activi-
ties. Witnesses in narcotic cases against members of this combine refuse
to testify knowing that they will be marked for death.

Difficult To Obtain Reliable
Mafia Evidence

The committee found it difficult to obtain reliable data concerning the
extent of Mafia operation, the nature of the Mafia organization, and the
way it presently operates. One notable concrete piece of evidence is a
photograph of twenty-three alleged Mafia leaders from all over the
United States, arrested in a hotel in Cleveland in 1928. When arrested,
the group possessed numerous firearms. Among those arrested were
Joseph Profaci of New York, Vincent Mangano of New York, and "Red"
Italiano of Tampa. Profaci, who is considered by the experts to be one of
the top leaders of the Mafia, was questioned about this meeting at a
closed committee hearing. At first, he asserted that he was in Cleveland
in connection with his olive-oil business. Then after admitting that he
had no olive-oil business in Cleveland before 1935 or 1936, he was unable to give a satisfactory explanation of his presence at the Cleveland
convention.

Almost all the witnesses who appeared before the committee and who
were suspected of Mafia membership, either denied that they had ever
heard of the Mafia, which is patently absurd, or denied membership in the
Mafia. However, many of these witnesses readily admitted knowledge of

and associations and friendships with suspected Mafia characters in other parts of the country. A notable exception is Tony Gizzo, who testified in a closed hearing that he had heard that James Balestrere was the leader of the Mafia in Kansas City. Gizzo changed his testimony at the open hearing. Another notable exception is Philip D'Andrea who said that the Mafia was freely discussed in his home when he was a child, and that he understood it to be a widely feared extortion gang. On the basis of all the evidence before it, plus the off-the-record but convincing statements of certain informants who must remain anonymous, the committee is inclined to agree with the opinion of experienced police officers and narcotics agents who believe:

1. There is a nationwide crime syndicate known as the Mafia, whose tentacles are found in many large cities. It has international ramifications which appear most clearly in connection with the narcotics traffic.
2. Its leaders are usually found in control of the most lucrative rackets in their cities.
3. There are indications of a centralized direction and control of these rackets, but leadership appears to be in a group rather than in a single individual.
4. The Mafia is the cement that helps to bind the Costello-Adonis-Lansky syndicate of New York and the Accardo-Guzik-Fischetti syndicate of Chicago as well as smaller criminal gangs and individual criminals throughout the country. These groups have kept in touch with Luciano since his deportation from this country.
5. The domination of the Mafia is based fundamentally on "muscle" and "murder." The Mafia is a secret conspiracy against law and order which will ruthlessly eliminate anyone who stands in the way of its success in any criminal enterprise in which it is interested. It will destroy anyone who betrays its secrets. It will use any means available—political influence, bribery, intimidation, etc., to defeat any attempt off the part of law enforcement to touch its top figures or to interfere with its operations.

The Mafia today acts closely with many persons who are not of Sicilian descent. Moreover, it must be pointed out most strongly that the Mafia group comprises only a very small fraction of a percentage even of Sicilians. It would be most unfortunate if any inferences were erroneously drawn in any way derogatory to the vast majority of fine law-abiding citizens of Sicilian and Italian extraction.

Introduction To
Anthony Summers's

Official and Confidential

FOR YEARS, rumors of J. Edgar Hoover's homosexuality had floated around Washington. Those rumors appeared to be substantiated with the publication in 1993 of *Official and Confidential* by Anthony Summers, a biographer and former reporter for the BBC. Summers revealed that Hoover was a cross-dresser and that the mob had used proof of Hoover's homosexuality to blackmail him. The book shattered the myth of Hoover as an honest crime fighter, instead presenting a revisionist picture of the FBI director as, in the words of *The Washington Post*, a "Dorian Gray, melting into depravity."

Summers's book gained instant popular acceptance. But there was also harsh criticism. In his book, *J. Edgar Hoover, Sex, and Crime*, published two years later, historian Athan Theoharis charges Summers with "character assassination" and concludes, "Whether or not Hoover was homosexual—and I doubt that he was—the wily and cautious FBI director would never have put himself in a position that publicly compromised his sexuality." Theoharis summarily dismisses the accounts given by organized crime figures who were among Summers's main sources.

Which version is correct? The evidence in *Official and Confidential* is not beyond question. But airtight proof is rarely available about personal matters such as one's sexual behavior and the potential for blackmail that threatens to expose such behavior. Summers deserves credit for uncovering sources courageous enough to be quoted. Among his defenders was former Congressman Don Edwards, an authority on the FBI, who called the book "a serious work of scholarship." But critiques such as Theoharis's cannot be ignored. Neither can Summers's conclusions be easily dismissed.

His account demonstrates that not every work of secret history is conclusive.

ADDITIONAL SOURCES

Gentry, Curt. *J. Edgar Hoover: The Man and the Secrets.* New York: W. W. Norton, 1991.

Powers, Richard Gid. *Secrecy and Power: The Life of J. Edgar Hoover.* New York: Free Press, 1987.

Theoharis, Athan. *J. Edgar Hoover, Sex, and Crime.* Chicago: Ivan R. Dee, 1995.

Anthony Summers

Chapter Twenty-Two

OFFICIAL AND CONFIDENTIAL: THE SECRET LIFE

OF J. EDGAR HOOVER, 1993

**Intelligent gangsters from Al Capone to Moe Dalitz and
Meyer Lansky have always been fierce, voluble defenders
of the capitalist faith, and to that extent they were and
are J. Edgar Hoover's ideological kinsmen.**

—*Albert Fried, historian*

Edgar had a relationship with mob chieftain Frank Costello that lasted for years, and has never been satisfactorily explained. It started, apparently, with a seemingly innocuous meeting on a New York street.

Edgar recalled the occasion himself, in a private conversation with the veteran journalist Norma Abrams—a confidence she kept until shortly before her death in 1989.

"Hoover was an inveterate window-shopper," said Abrams. "Early one morning in the thirties, he told me, he was out walking on Fifth Avenue and somebody came up behind him and said, 'Good morning, Mr. Hoover.' He turned to see who it was, and it was Frank Costello. Costello said, 'I don't want to embarrass you,' and Hoover said, 'You won't embarrass me. We're not looking for you or anything.' They talked all the way to Fifty-seventh Street together, but God protected them, and there was no photographer around, or anyone. . . ."

The contact was renewed, as Edgar explained to Eduardo Disano, a Florida restaurateur who also knew Costello. "Hoover told me he and Costello both used apartments at the Waldorf," Disano recalled. "He said Costello asked him to come up and meet in his apartment. Hoover said he told him by all means he would meet him, but not in his room, downstairs. . . . I don't know what they talked about. Hoover was a very quiet man about business."

If Costello was trying to cultivate Edgar, it worked. Once they even took the risk of sitting together in the Stork Club. Costello was soon referring to Edgar as "John"—a habit he presumably picked up from Winchell. The mobster was to recall with a chuckle the day Edgar in turn took the lead and invited him for coffee. "I got to be careful about my associates," Costello told Edgar. "They'll accuse me of consorting with questionable characters. . . ."

In 1939, when Edgar was credited with the capture of racketeer Louis "Lepke" Buchalter, it was Costello who pulled strings to make it happen. This was the time the mob would remember as the Big Heat, when Thomas Dewey, then District Attorney, brought unprecedented pressure on organized crime. The heat was on, especially, for the capture of Lepke, the man they called the head of Murder, Inc.

Shortly before midnight on August 24, Edgar called in newsmen to hear a sensational announcement. He, personally, had just accepted Lepke's surrender on a New York street. It made a fine tale—Edgar, in dark glasses, waiting in a parked limousine for his encounter with one of the most dangerous criminals in America. Edgar said the FBI had "managed the surrender through its own sources," and it emerged that his friend Winchell had played a role as go-between. Edgar was covered in glory, to the rage of Dewey and the New York authorities, who said he had operated behind their backs.

He had indeed, thanks to a neat piece of manipulation by the mob. Lucky Luciano, issuing orders to Costello and Lansky from prison, had decided that to relieve law enforcement pressure on mob operations Lepke must be made to surrender. Word went to the gangster that he would be treated leniently if he surrendered to Edgar—a false promise, as it turned out, for he was to end up in the electric chair. Costello, meanwhile, met secretly with Edgar to hammer out the arrangements.

The beauty of it all, Luciano would recall, was that they achieved two things at once. They won relief from law enforcement pressure and simultaneously ensured that Edgar and Dewey—even the ego-obsessed Walter

Winchell—each got their "piece of the cake." For supreme practitioners of the Fix, the sacrifice of Lepke was a job well done.

William Hundley, the Justice Department attorney, had a glimpse of the way Costello handled Edgar. It happened by chance in 1961, when Hundley was staying at the apartment of his friend—and the mobster's attorney—Edward Bennett Williams. "At eight o'clock in the morning," Hundley recalled, "there was a knock at the door. There was a guy there with a big hat on, and this really hoarse voice. It was Frank Costello, and he came in, and we sat around eating breakfast. . . . Somehow the subject of Hoover came up, and Hoover liking to bet on horseracing. Costello mentioned that he knew Hoover, that they met for lunch. Then he started looking very leery of going on, but Ed told him he could trust me. Costello just said, 'Hoover will never know how many races I had to fix for those lousy ten-dollar bets.' He still looked leery, and I guess he didn't want to say much more."

In Costello, Edgar had one of the most powerful tipsters in gambling history. One of his primary mob functions was to control betting and fix races. Those who failed to cooperate got hurt, or worse. Edgar's relationship with him is corroborated by sources both inside and outside the mob. "Costello did give tips to Hoover," said Walter Winchell's colleague Herman Klurfeld. "He got them from [betting-parlor operator] Frank Erickson and passed them on through Winchell. , , , Sometimes Costello and Hoover met directly. Now and then, when Hoover was in the barbershop at the Waldorf, so was Frank Costello."

Chicago Mafia boss Sam Giancana reportedly had an inside track on the relationship. His half brother Chuck has claimed that Costello "worked the whole thing out. He knew Hoover was just like every other politician and copper, only meaner and smarter than most. Hoover didn't want an envelope each month . . . so we never gave him cash outright; we gave him something better: tips on fixed horse races. He could bet ten thousand dollars on a horse that showed twenty-to-one odds, if he wanted . . . and he has."

In 1990, aged eighty, New York mob boss Carmine Lombardozzi said Costello and Edgar "had contact on many occasions and over a long period. Hoover was very friendly toward the families. They took good care of him, especially at the races. . . . The families made sure he was looked after when he visited the tracks in California and on the East Coast. They had an understanding. He would lay off the families, turn a blind eye. It helped that he denied that we even existed. If there was anything they could do for him, information that did not hurt family business, they would provide it."

George Allen, Edgar's racecourse companion for forty years and a prominent public figure who had no connection to the mob, recalled a conversation between Edgar and Costello. "I heard Hoover in the Stork one night," he said, "tell Costello that as long as he stayed out of Hoover's bailiwick, he'd stay out of his."

Since Costello's principal business was gambling, and since gambling was not a federal offense, it could be said that Edgar's remark merely reflected the legal situation of the day. Other clues, however, suggest that his laissez-faire attitude went deeper. In the early fifties, when there were efforts to have Costello deported to Italy, there was no pressure from the FBI. According to Walter Winchell's friend Curly Harris, who knew both Edgar and the mobster, Edgar once went out of his way to protect Costello from his own agents.

"The doorman at Frank's apartment building," Harris remembered, "told him that there were a couple of FBI guys hanging around. So Frank got hold of Hoover on the phone and told him, 'What's the idea of these fellows being there? If you want to see me you can get to me with one phone call.' And Hoover looked into it, and he found out who the fellows were and why they were doing that. He said they weren't under any orders to do it, they'd taken it on themselves. He was very sore about it. And he had the agents transferred to Alaska or someplace the next day. . . . He and Costello had mutual friends."

To Costello, and to his associate Meyer Lansky, the ability to corrupt politicians, policemen and judges was fundamental to Mafia operations. It was Lansky's expertise in such corruption that made him the nearest there ever was to a true national godfather of organized crime.

Another Mafia boss, Joseph Bonanno, articulated the principles of the game. It was a strict underworld rule, he said, never to use violent means against a law enforcement officer. "Ways could be found," he said in his

memoirs, "so that he would not interfere with us and we wouldn't interfere with him." The way the Mafia found to deal with Edgar, according to
several mob sources, involved his homosexuality.

THE MOB BOSSES had been well placed to find out about Edgar's compro-
mising secret, and at a significant time and place. It was on New Year's Eve
1936, after dinner at the Stork Club, that Edgar was seen by two of Walter
Winchell's guests holding hands with his lover, Clyde. At the Stork, where
he was a regular, Edgar was immensely vulnerable to observation by mobsters. The heavyweight champion Jim Braddock, who also dined with
Edgar and Clyde that evening, was controlled by Costello's associate
Owney Madden. Winchell, as compulsive a gossip in private as he was in
his column, constantly cultivated Costello. Sherman Billingsley, the former bootlegger who ran the Stork, reportedly installed two-way mirrors
in the toilets and hidden microphones at tables used by celebrities.
Billingsley was a pawn of Costello's, and Costello was said to be the club's
real owner. He would have had no compunction about persecuting Edgar,
and he loathed homosexuals.

    Seymour Pollock, an associate of Meyer Lansky's, said in 1990 that
Edgar's homosexuality was "common knowledge" and that he had seen evidence of it for himself. "I used to meet him at the racetrack every once in a
while with lover boy Clyde, in the late forties and fifties. I was in the next
box once. And when you see two guys holding hands, well come on! . . .
They were surreptitious, but there was no question about it."

    Jimmy "The Weasel" Fratianno, the highest-ranking mobster ever to
have "turned" and testified against his former associates, was at the track
in 1948 when Frank Bompensiero, a notorious West Coast mafioso,
taunted Edgar to his face. "I pointed at this fella sitting in the box in
front," Fratianno recalled, "and said, 'Hey, Bomp, lookit there, it's J. Edgar
Hoover.' And Bomp says right out loud, so everyone can hear, 'Ah, that J.
Edgar's a punk, he's a fuckin' degenerate queer.' "

    Later, when Bompensiero ran into Edgar in the men's room, the FBI
Director was astonishingly meek. "Frank," he told the mobster, "that's not
a nice way to talk about me, especially when I have people with me." It was

clear to Fratianno that Bompensiero had met Edgar before and that he had absolutely no fear of Edgar.

Fratianno knew numerous other top mobsters, including Jack and Louis Dragna of Los Angeles and Johnny Roselli, the West Coast representative of the Chicago mob. All spoke of "proof " that Edgar was homosexual. Roselli spoke specifically of the occasion in the late twenties when Edgar had been arrested on charges of homosexuality in New Orleans. Edgar could hardly have chosen a worse city in which to be compromised. New Orleans police and city officials were notoriously corrupt, puppets of an organized crime network run by Mafia boss Carlos Marcello and heavily influenced by Meyer Lansky. If the homosexual arrest occurred, it is likely the local mobsters quickly learned of it.

Other information suggests Meyer Lansky obtained hard proof of Edgar's homosexuality and used it to neutralize the FBI as a threat to his own operations. The first hint came from Irving "Ash" Resnick, the Nevada representative of the Patriarcha family from New England, and an original owner-builder of Caesars Palace in Las Vegas. As a high-level mob courier, he traveled extensively. In Miami Beach, his Christmas destination in the fifties, he stayed at the Gulfstream, in a bungalow next to one used by Edgar and Clyde. "I'd sit with him on the beach every day," Resnick remembered. "We were friendly."

In 1971, Resnick and an associate talked with the writer Pete Hamill in the Galeria Bar at Caesars Palace. They spoke of Meyer Lansky as a genius, the man who "put everything together"—and as the man who "nailed J. Edgar Hoover." "When I asked what they meant," Hamill recalled, "they told me Lansky had some pictures—pictures of Hoover in some kind of gay situation with Clyde Tolson. Lansky was the guy who controlled the pictures, and he had made his deal with Hoover—to lay off. That was the reason, they said, that for a long time they had nothing to fear from the FBI."

Seymour Pollock, the criminal who saw Edgar and Clyde holding hands at the races, knew both Resnick and Lansky well. When Lansky's daughter had marital problems, it was Pollock who dealt with her husband. He and Lansky went back to the old days in prerevolutionary Cuba, when Havana was as important to the syndicate as Las Vegas. "Meyer," said Pollock in 1990, "was closemouthed. I don't think he even discussed the details of the Hoover thing with his brother. But Ash was absolutely right. Lansky had more than information on Hoover. He had page, chapter and verse. One night, when we were sitting around in his apartment at the Rosita de Hornedo, we were talking about Hoover, and Meyer laughed and said, 'I fixed that son of a bitch, didn't I?' " Lansky's fix, according to Pollock, also involved bribery—not of Edgar himself, but men close to him.

Lansky and Edgar frequented the same watering holes in Florida. Staff at Gatti's restaurant in Miami Beach recall that the mobster would sometimes be in the restaurant, at another table, at the same time as Edgar and Clyde. One evening in the late sixties, they were seated at adjoining tables. "But they just looked at one another," recalled Edidio Crolla, the captain at Gatti's. "They never talked, not here."

If Edgar's eyes met Lansky's, though, there was surely an involuntary flicker of fear. "The homosexual thing," said Pollock, "was Hoover's Achilles' heel. Meyer found it, and it was like he pulled strings with Hoover. He never bothered any of Meyer's people. . . . Let me go way back. The time Nevada opened up, Bugsy Siegel opened the Flamingo. I understand Hoover helped get the okay for him to do it. Meyer Lansky was one of the partners. Hoover knew who the guys were that whacked Bugsy Siegel, but nothing was done." (Siegel was killed, reportedly on Lansky's orders, in 1947.)

According to Pollock, Lansky and Edgar cooperated in the mid-fifties, when Las Vegas casino operator Wilbur Clark moved to Cuba. "Meyer brought Clark down to Havana," Pollock said. "I was against him coming. But I understand Hoover asked Meyer to bring Clark down. He owed Clark something. I don't know what. . . . There was no serious pressure on Meyer until the Kennedys came in. And even then Hoover never hurt Meyer's people, not for a long time."

Like Frank Costello, Lansky did seem to be untouchable—a phenomenon that triggered suspicions even within the Bureau. "In 1966," noted Hank Messick, one of Lansky's biographers, "a young G-Man assigned to go through the motions of watching Meyer Lansky began to take his job seriously and develop good informers. He was abruptly transferred to a rural area in Georgia. His successor on the Lansky assignment was an older man who knew the score. When he retired a few years later, he accepted a job with a Bahamian gambling casino originally developed by Lansky."

Also in the sixties a wiretap picked up a conversation between two mobsters in which, curiously, Lansky was referred to as "a stool pigeon for the FBI." The Royal Canadian Mounted Police, taping a conversation between a criminal in Canada and Lansky in the United States, were amazed to hear the mob chieftain reading from an FBI report that had been written the previous day.

There was no serious federal effort to indict Lansky until 1970, just two years before Edgar died. Then, it was the IRS rather than the FBI that spearheaded the investigation. Even the tax evasion charges collapsed, and Lansky lived on at liberty until his own death in 1983.

NOTES

Abrams: int. 1988; Disano: ints. Eduardo Disano, 1988; Stork: ints. Allan Witwer, Herman Klurfeld, 1988; "John": Earl Wilson, op. cit., p. 134, int. Earl Wilson, 1984; Lepke: *Collier's*, Apr. 12, 1947, *NYT*, Aug. 25, 26, 1939, *NY World-Telegram*, Mar. 6, 1944, NY *Daily Mirror*, Aug. 26, 1939, *Winchell Exclusive*, by Walter Winchell, Englewood Cliffs, NJ, Prentice-Hall, 1975, pp. 134ff, Martin Gosch, op. cit., pp. 240ff *Frank Costello: Prime Minister of the Underworld*, by George Wolf, with Joseph DiMona, NY, William Morrow, 1974, p. 121, ints. Herman Klurfeld, Joseph DiMona, Lyle Stuart, 1988, Klurfeld, op. cit., p. 83, *Treasury Agent*, by Andrew Tully, NY, Simon & Schuster, 1958, pp. 58ff; Hundley: reports of Mike Ewing, Nov. 29, 1978, from HSCA files, ints. William Hundley, 1988; Giancana: *Double Cross*, by Sam and Chuck Giancana, NY, Warner, 1992, pp. 132, 255ff, int. Sam Giancana (nephew), 1991; Lombardozzi: contact arranged by William Pepper, 1990; Allen: *D*, p. 25, int. Ovid Demaris, confirming that "Mafia boy" was Costello in orig. int.; deport?: memos re. Drew Pearson, Mar. 25, May 28, Sept. 17, 1951, Sept. 15, 1952, Jun. 1, 1954, FBI 94-8-350, London *Observer*, May 7, 1972; Harris: int. Curly Harris, 1988; Lansky expertise: ints. Hank Messick (Lansky biographer) and Richard Hammer (Luciano biographer), 1990; Bonanno: *Man of Honor*, by Joseph Bonanno, with Sergio Lalli, NY, Simon & Schuster, 1983, p. 156; Madden: Stephen Fox, op. cit., p. 226; Billingsley: *Collier's*, Nov. 23, 1958, *Gossip Wars*, by Milt Machlin, NY, Tower Books, 1981, pp. 189, 192ff; Costello loathed: Leonard Katz, op. cit., p. 221; Pollock: ints. Seymour Pollock, 1990, 1992, Hearings, House Select Committee on Crime, Dec. 7, 1971, p. 3, *NYT*, Dec. 9, 1971, *Brothers in Blood*, by David Chandler, NY, Dutton, 1975, p. 205; Fratianno: ints. Jimmy Fratianno, 1990, *Vengeance Is Mine*, by Michael Zuckerman, NY, Macmillan, 1987, p. 104, *Look*, Sept. 23, 1969, ints. Nicholas Lore, Jim Henderson, George Carr, 1990; Resnick: ints. Irving Resnick, Dana Resnick, Wm. Roemer, Jim Doyle, Pete Hamill, 1988, 1990, *Las Vegas Sun*, Jan. 19, 1989, *Miami Herald*, Jun. 22, 1983; watering holes: ints. Jesse and Grace Weiss, 1988; Gatti's: ints. Mike Gatti,

Edidio Crolla, 1988, 1989, *Miami Herald.* May 3, 1972; Messick: Hank Messick, *Hoover,* p. 209; stool pigeon: ibid., p. 200; RCMP: int. William Gallinaro, 1988; Lansky 1970: Hank Messick, *Lansky,* pp. 12ff, 255, int. Hank Messick, 1991; Weitz: int. John Weitz, 1988; Novel: ints. Gordon Novel, 1992, with research by Ed Tatro and Dennis Effle, and see *Coincidence or Conspiracy,* ed. Bernard Fensterwald and Michael Ewing, NY, Zebra, 1977, pp. 454ff; H checks of Donovan: Anthony Cave Brown, *Last Hero,* p. 222; "bastard": Leonard Mosley, op. cit., p. 124; Donovan probe of H: ibid., and Curt Gentry, op. cit., p. 295; Lansky/U.S. Intelligence: Rodney Campbell, op. cit., pp. 85, 98, 199ff, George Wolf, op. cit., p. 127, Bradley Smith, op. cit., p. 237, *Meyer Lansky: Mogul of the Mob,* by Dennis Eisenberg, Uri Dan, and Eli Landau, NY, Paddington Press, 1979, pp. 137ff, 145, 197ff, *Without Cloak or Dagger,* by Miles Copeland, NY, Simon & Schuster, 1974, p. 235.

Introduction to
"Dr. Martin Luther King, Jr., Case Study"

THE FOLLOWING SELECTION FROM the Church Committee's report on intelligence abuses describes FBI Director J. Edgar Hoover's vicious and illegal attempts to destroy Dr. Martin Luther King, Jr., as a leader of the civil rights movement. But the report glosses over many details and ignores the background and context of the FBI's campaign against King and his Southern Christian Leadership Conference (SCLC). In addition to Hoover's racism, two other strands emerge: the FBI's preoccupation with anti-Communism and with the Kennedys.

In 1962, Attorney General Robert Kennedy tried to reduce the FBI's domestic security apparatus, prompting Hoover to become concerned that his staff, budget, and power would be reduced. "The running battle between Hoover and Kennedy defined the larger political context for the escalation of activity against King," writes Taylor Branch in *Parting the Waters: America in the King Years 1954–1963*. For several years the FBI had conducted extensive surveillance of Stanley Levison, "King's closest white friend and the most reliable colleague of his life." Levison had helped the Communist Party and raised funds to defend its top officials, but the FBI found no proof of engagement in subversive activities. Nevertheless, Hoover continued to consider Levison a Communist agent and King a Communist sympathizer.

As the Civil Rights Movement gained momentum, Hoover put pressure on Robert Kennedy to permit the FBI to wiretap King. Afraid of charges that his brother, President Kennedy, was soft on Communism, and fearful that Hoover would reveal that one of his brother's recent mistresses came from *Communist* East Germany, Robert Kennedy allowed the FBI to begin electronic surveillance of King in October 1963. The next month, President Kennedy would be assassinated.

In 1964, the FBI sent King a tape that contained embarrassing revelations about his personal life, which Hoover thought would precipitate a break-up of King's marriage, and threatened to make the tape public. Accompanying the tape was an unsigned note implying that King should commit suicide: "King, there is only one thing left for you to do. You know what it is. . . . There is but one way out for you." The note and tape were received about a month before King was to receive the Nobel Peace Prize. King refused to back down. He accepted the prize and continued his activities.

ADDITIONAL SOURCES

Branch, Taylor. *Parting the Waters: America in the King Years 1954–1963.* New York: Simon and Schuster, 1988.

———. *Pillar of Fire: America in the King Years 1963–65.* New York: Simon and Schuster, 1998.

Garrow, David. *The FBI and Martin Luther King, Jr.* New York: W. W. Norton, 1981.

Navasky, Victor. *Kennedy Justice.* New York: Atheneum, 1977.

The Church Committee

"Dr. Martin Luther King, Jr., Case Study"

FINAL REPORT OF THE SELECT COMMITTEE TO STUDY
GOVERNMENTAL OPERATIONS WITH RESPECT TO INTELLIGENCE
ACTIVITIES, U.S. SENATE.

BOOK III, 1976

I. Introduction

From December 1963 until his death in 1968, Martin Luther King, Jr., was the target of an intensive campaign by the Federal Bureau of Investigation to "neutralize" him as an effective civil rights leader. In the words of the man in charge of the FBI's "war" against Dr. King:

No holds were barred. We have used [similar] techniques against Soviet agents. [The same methods were] brought home against any organization against which we were targeted. We did not differentiate. This is a rough, tough business.[1]

The FBI collected information about Dr. King's plans and activities through an extensive surveillance program, employing nearly every intelligence-gathering technique at the Bureau's disposal. Wiretaps, which were initially approved by Attorney General Robert F. Kennedy, were maintained on Dr. King's home telephone from October 1963 until mid-1965; the SCLC headquarter's telephones were covered by wiretaps for an even longer period. Phones in the homes and offices of some of Dr. King's close advisers were also wiretapped. The FBI has acknowledged sixteen occasions on which microphones were hidden in Dr. King's hotel and motel rooms in an "attempt" to obtain information about the "private activities of King and his advisers" for use to "completely discredit" them.[2]

FBI informants in the civil rights movement and reports from field offices kept the Bureau's headquarters informed of developments in the civil rights field. The FBI's presence was so intrusive that one major figure in the civil rights movement testified that his colleagues referred to themselves as members of "the FBI's golden record club."[3]

The FBI's formal program to discredit Dr. King with government officials began with the distribution of a "monograph" which the FBI realized could "be regarded as a personal attack on Martin Luther King,"[4] and which was subsequently described by a Justice Department official as "a personal diatribe . . . a personal attack without evidentiary support."[5]

Congressional leaders were warned "off the record" about alleged dangers posed by Reverend King. The FBI responded to Dr. King's receipt of the Nobel Peace Prize by attempting to undermine his reception by foreign heads of state and American ambassadors in the countries that he planned to visit. When Dr. King returned to the United States, steps were taken to reduce support for a huge banquet and a special "day" that were being planned in his honor.

The FBI's program to destroy Dr. King as the leader of the civil rights movement entailed attempts to discredit him with churches, universities, and the press. Steps were taken to attempt to convince the National Council of Churches, the Baptist World Alliance, and leading Protestant ministers to halt financial support of the Southern Christian Leadership Conference (SCLC), and to persuade them that "Negro leaders should completely isolate King and remove him from the role he is now occupying in civil rights activities."[6] When the FBI learned that Dr. King intended to visit the Pope, an agent was dispatched to persuade Francis Cardinal Spellman to warn the Pope about "the likely embarrassment that may result to the Pope should he grant King an audience."[7] The FBI sought to influence universities to withhold honorary degrees from Dr. King. Attempts were made to prevent the publication of articles favorable to Dr. King and to find "friendly" news sources that would print unfavorable articles. The FBI offered to play for reporters tape recordings allegedly made from microphone surveillance of Dr. King's hotel rooms.

The FBI mailed Dr. King a tape recording made from its microphone coverage. According to the chief of the FBI's Domestic Intelligence Division, the tape was intended to precipitate a separation between Dr. King and his wife in the belief that the separation would reduce Dr. King's stature.[7A] The tape recording was accompanied by a note which Dr. King and his advisers interpreted as a threat to release the tape recording unless Dr. King committed suicide. The FBI also made preparations to promote someone "to assume the role of leadership of the Negro people when King has been completely discredited."[8]

The campaign against Dr. King included attempts to destroy the Southern Christian Leadership Conference by cutting off its sources of funds. The FBI considered, and on some occasions executed, plans to cut off the support of some of the SCLC's major contributors, including religious organizations, a labor union, and donors of grants such as the Ford Foundation. One FBI field office recommended that the FBI send letters to the SCLC's donors over Dr. King's forged signature warning them that the SCLC was under investigation by the Internal Revenue Service. The IRS files on Dr. King and the SCLC were carefully scrutinized for financial irregularities. For over a year, the FBI unsuccessfully attempted to establish that Dr. King had a secret foreign bank account in which he was sequestering funds.

The FBI campaign to discredit and destroy Dr. King was marked by extreme personal vindictiveness. As early as 1962, Director Hoover penned on an FBI memorandum, "King is no good."[9] At the August 1963 March on Washington, Dr. King told the country of his dream that "all of God's children, black men and white men, Jews and Gentiles, Protestants and Catholics, will be able to join hands and sing in the words of the old Negro spiritual, 'Free at last, free at last. Thank God almighty, I'm free at last.' "[10] The FBI's Domestic Intelligence Division described this "demagogic speech" as yet more evidence that Dr. King was "the most dangerous and effective Negro leader in the country."[11] Shortly afterward, *Time* magazine chose Dr. King as the "Man of the Year," an honor which elicited Director Hoover's comment that "they had to dig deep in the garbage to come up with this one."[12] Hoover wrote "astounding" across the memorandum informing him that Dr. King had been granted an audience with the Pope despite the FBI's efforts to prevent such a meeting. The depth of Director Hoover's bitterness toward Dr. King, a bitterness which he had effectively communicated to his subordinates in the FBI, was apparent from the FBI's attempts to sully Dr. King's reputation long after his death.

Plans were made to "brief" congressional leaders in 1969 to prevent the passage of a "Martin Luther King Day." In 1970, Director Hoover told reporters that Dr. King was the "last one in the world who should ever have received" the Nobel Peace Prize.[13]

The extent to which Government officials outside of the FBI must bear responsibility for the FBI's campaign to discredit Dr. King is not clear. Government officials outside of the FBI were not aware of most of the specific FBI actions to discredit Dr. King. Officials in the Justice Department and White House were aware, however, that the FBI was conducting an intelligence investigation, not a criminal investigation, of Dr. King; that the FBI had written authorization from the Attorney General to wiretap Dr. King and the SCLC offices in New York and Washington; and that the FBI reports on Dr. King contained considerable information of a political and personal nature which was "irrelevant and spurious" to the stated reasons for the investigation.[14] Those high executive branch officials were also aware that the FBI was disseminating vicious characterizations of Dr. King within the government; that the FBI had tape recordings embarrassing to Dr. King which it had offered to play to a White House official and to reporters; and that the FBI had offered to "leak" to reporters highly damaging accusations that some of Dr. King's advisers were communists. Although some of those officials did ask top FBI officials about these charges, they did not inquire further after receiving false denials. In light of what those officials did know about the FBI's conduct toward Dr. King, they were remiss in failing to take appropriate steps to curb the Bureau's behavior. To the extent that their neglect permitted the Bureau's activities to go on unchecked, those officials must share responsibility for what occurred. The FBI now agrees that its efforts to discredit Dr. King were unjustified. The present Deputy Associate Director (Investigation) testified:

Mr. Adams: There were approximately twenty-five incidents of actions taken [to discredit Dr. King] . . . I see no statutory basis or no basis of justification for the activity.

The Chairman: Was Dr. King, in his advocacy of equal rights for black citizens, advocating a course of action that in the opinion of the FBI constituted a crime?

Mr. Adams: No, sir.

The Chairman: He was preaching non-violence was he not, as a method of achieving equal rights for black citizens?

Mr. Adams: That's right . . . Now as far as the activities which you are asking about, the discrediting, I know of no basis for that and I will not attempt to justify it.[15]

The FBI conducted its investigation of Dr. King and the SCLC under an FBI manual provision—called COMINFIL—permitting the investigation of legitimate noncommunist organizations, suspected by the FBI of having been infiltrated by communists, to determine the extent, if any, of communist influence. The FBI's investigation was based on its concern that Dr. King was being influenced by two persons—hereinafter referred to as Adviser A and Adviser B—that the Bureau believed were members of the Communist Party.

Officials in the Justice Department relied on the FBI's representations that both of these advisers were communists, that they were in a position to influence Dr. King, and that Adviser A in fact exercised some influence in preparing Dr. King's speeches and publications. Burke Marshall, assistant attorney general for civil rights from 1961–1965, testified that he "never had any reason to doubt [the FBI's] allegations concerning [Adviser A]." He recalled that the charges about Adviser A were "grave and serious," and said that he believed Attorney General Kennedy had permitted the investigation to proceed because:

> *Stopping the investigation in light of those circumstances would have run the risk that there would have been a lot of complaints that the Bureau had been blocked for political reasons from investigating serious charges about communist infiltration in the civil rights movement.*[17]

Edwin Guthman, press secretary for the Justice Department from 1961 through 1964, testified that Attorney General Robert Kennedy "viewed this as a serious matter," that he did not recall "that any of us doubted that the FBI knew what it was talking about," and that although the question of whether Adviser A was influencing Dr. King was never fully answered "we accepted pretty much what the FBI reported as being accurate."[18]

We have been unable to reach a conclusion concerning the accuracy of the FBI's charges that the two Advisers were members of the Communist Party, USA, or under the control of the party during the FBI's COMINFIL investigation. However, FBI files do contain information that Adviser A and Adviser B had been members of the Communist Party at some point prior to the opening of the COMINFIL investigation in October 1962. FBI documents provided to the Committee to support the Bureau's claim that both men were members of the Communist Party at the time the COMINFIL investigation was opened are inconclusive. Moreover, the FBI has stated that it cannot provide the Committee with the full factual basis for its charges on the grounds that to do so would Compromise informants of continuing use to the Bureau.

Without access to the factual evidence, we are unable to conclude whether either of those two Advisers was connected with the Communist Party when the "case" was opened in 1962, or at any time thereafter. We have seen no evidence establishing that either of those Advisers attempted to exploit the civil rights movement to carry out the plans of the Communist Party.

In any event, the FBI has stated that at no time did it have any evidence that Dr. King himself was a communist or connected with the Communist Party. Dr. King repeatedly criticized Marxist philosophies in his writing and speeches. The present deputy associate director of the FBI's Domestic Intelligence Division, when asked by the Committee if the FBI ever concluded that Dr. King was a communist, testified, "No, sir, we did not."[20]

The FBI's COMINFIL investigation appears to have centered almost entirely on discussions among Dr. King and his advisers about proposed civil rights activities rather than on whether those advisers were in fact agents of the Communist Party. Although the FBI conducted disruptive programs—COINTELPROs—against alleged communists whom it believed were attempting to influence civil rights organizations, the Bureau did not undertake to discredit the individual whom it considered Dr. King's most "dangerous" adviser until more than four years after opening the COMINFIL investigation.[21] Moreover, when a field office reported to FBI headquarters in 1964 that the Adviser was not then under the influence and control of the Communist Party, the FBI did not curtail either its investigations or discrediting program against Dr. King, and we have no indication that the Bureau informed the Justice Department of this finding.[22] Rather than trying to discredit the alleged communists it believed were attempting to influence Dr. King, the Bureau adopted the curious tactic of trying to discredit the supposed target of Communist Party interest—Dr. King himself.

Allegations of communist influence on Dr. King's organization must not divert attention from the fact that, as the FBI now states, its activities were unjustified and improper. In light of the Bureau's remarks about Dr. King, its reactions to his criticisms, the viciousness of its campaign to destroy him, and its failure to take comparable measures against the Advisers that it believed were communists, it is highly questionable whether the FBI's stated motivation was valid. It was certainly not justification for continuing the investigation of Dr. King for over six years, or for carrying out the attempts to destroy him.

Our investigation indicates that FBI officials believed that some of Dr. King's personal conduct was improper. Part of the FBI's efforts to undermine Dr. King's reputation involved attempts to persuade government officials that Dr. King's personal behavior would be an embarrassment to them. The Committee did not investigate Dr. King's personal life, since such a subject has no proper place in our investigation. Moreover, in order to preclude any further dissemination of information obtained during the electronic surveillances of Dr. King, the Committee requested the FBI to excise from all documents submitted to the Committee any information which was so obtained. We raise the issue of Dr. King's private life here only because it may have played a part in forming the attitudes of certain FBI and administration officials toward Dr. King.

Many documents which we examined contained allegations about the political affiliations and morality of numerous individuals. We have attempted to be sensitive to the privacy interests of those individuals, and have taken care not to advance the effort to discredit them. We have excised many of the Bureau's characterizations from the documents quoted in this report. In some cases, however, in order fully to explain the story, it was judged necessary to quote extensively from Bureau reports, even though they contain unsupported allegations. We caution the reader not to accept these allegations on their face, but rather to read them as part of a shameful chapter in the nation's history.

The reader is also reminded that we did not conduct an investigation into the assassination of Dr. King. In the course of investigating the FBI's attempts to discredit Dr. King, we came across no indication that the FBI was in any way involved in the assassination.

II. The COMINFIL Investigation

In October 1962 the FBI opened its investigation of the Southern Christian Leadership Conference and of its president, Dr. Martin Luther King, Jr. The investigation was conducted under an FBI manual provision captioned "COMINFIL"—an acronym for communist infiltration—which authorized investigations of legitimate noncommunist organizations which the FBI believed to be influenced by Communist Party members in order to determine the extent of the alleged communist influence.[23] These wide-ranging investigations were conducted with the knowledge of the attorney general and were predicated on vague executive directives and broad statutes.[24]

The FBI kept close watch on Dr. King and the SCLC long before opening its formal investigation. FBI Director J. Edgar Hoover reacted to the formation of the SCLC in 1957 by reminding agents in the field of the need for vigilance:

> In the absence of any indication that the Communist Party has attempted, or is attempting, to infiltrate this organization you should conduct no investigation in this matter. However, in view of the stated purpose of the organization, you should remain alert for public source information concerning it in connection with the racial situation.[25]

In May 1962 the FBI had included Dr. King on "Section A of the Reserve Index" as a person to be rounded up and detained in the event of a "national emergency."[26] During this same period the FBI ordered its field offices to review their files for "subversive" information about Dr. King and to submit that information to FBI headquarters in reports "suitable for dissemination."[27]

The Bureau had apparently also been engaged in an extensive surveillance of Dr. King's civil rights activities since the late 1950s under an FBI program called "Racial Matters." This program, which was unrelated to COMINFIL, required the collection of "all pertinent information" about the "proposed or actual activities" of individuals and organizations "in the racial field."[28] Surveillance of Dr. King's civil rights activities continued under the Racial Matters program after the COMINFIL case was opened. Indeed, the October 1962 memorandum which authorized the COMINFIL case specifically provided that "any information developed concerning the integration or racial activities of the SCLC must [also] be reported [under a] Racial Matters caption."[29]

The first FBI allegations that the Communist Party was attempting to infiltrate the SCLC appeared in a report from the FBI to Attorney General Robert F. Kennedy, dated January 8, 1962.[30] The report stated that one of Dr. King's advisers—hereinafter referred to as "Adviser A"—was a "member of the Communist Party USA."[31] Within a few months FBI reports were describing another of Dr. King's associates—hereinafter referred to as "Adviser B"—as a "member of the National Committee of the Communist Party.[32] The allegations concerning these two individuals formed the basis for opening the COMINFIL investigation in October 1962.

It is unclear why the FBI waited nine months to open the COMINFIL investigation.[33] The Bureau might have been hoping to acquire new information from microphone and wiretap surveillance of Adviser A's office, which was initiated in March 1962.[34] However, it does not appear that these surveillances collected any additional information bearing on the FBI's characterization of Adviser A as a "communist."

Despite the goals and procedures outlined in the COMINFIL section of the FBI Manual, the Bureau's investigation of Dr. King did not focus on whether any of his advisers were acting under Communist Party discipline and control or were working to enable the Communist Party to influence or control the SCLC. The microphone which had been installed in Adviser A's office in March 1962 was discontinued before the COMINFIL investigation began,[36] and, although wiretap coverage of Adviser A continued—and even intensified[37]—the information obtained appears to have related solely to his advice to Dr. King concerning the civil rights movement and not at all to the alleged Communist Party origins of that advice.[38] Two FBI reports prepared in succeeding years which summarize the FBI's information about Adviser A do not contain evidence substantiating his purported relationship with the Communist Party.[39]

Without full access to the Bureau's files, the Committee cannot determine whether the FBI's decision to initiate a COMINFIL investigation was motivated solely by sincere concerns about alleged communist infiltration, or whether it was in part influenced by Director Hoover's animosity toward Dr. King. The FBI director's sensitivity to criticism and his attitude toward Dr. King are documented in several events which occurred during the period when the FBI was considering initiating the COMINFIL investigation.

As early as February 1962, Director Hoover wrote on a memorandum that Dr. King was "no good."[40]

In January 1962, an organization called the Southern Regional Council issued a report criticizing the Bureau's inaction during civil rights demonstrations in Albany, Georgia.[41] An updated version of that report was released in November 1962. A section entitled "Where was the Federal Government" made the following observations about the FBI.

- There is a considerable amount of distrust among Albany Negroes for local members of the Federal Bureau of Investigation.
- With all the clear violations by local police of constitutional rights, with undisputed evidence of beatings by sheriffs and deputy sheriffs, the FBI has not made a single arrest on behalf of Negro citizens.
- The FBI has [taken] dozens of affidavits from Negro citizens complaining that their constitutional rights had been violated by city and county officials. But eight months later, there was no sign of action on these charges.
- The FBI is most effective in solving ordinary crimes, and perhaps it should stick to that.[42]

Newspaper coverage of the report's allegations were forwarded to Bureau headquarters by the Atlantic office. Although Bureau rules required prompt investigation of allegations such as those in the Southern Regional Council's Report, no investigation was undertaken.[43] Before even receiving the full report, Bureau officials were describing it as "slanted and biased," and were searching their files for information about the report's author.[44]

Shortly after the Report was issued, newspapers quoted Dr. King as saying that he agreed with the Report's conclusions that the FBI had not vigorously investigated civil rights violations in Albany. Dr. King reportedly stated:

> One of the great problems we face with the FBI in the South is that the agents are white Southerners who have been influenced by the mores of the community. To maintain their status, they have to be friendly with the local police and people who are promoting segregation.
>
> Every time I saw FBI men in Albany, they were with the local police force.[45]

FBI headquarters was immediately notified of Dr. King's remarks.[46] After noting that Dr. King's comments "would appear to dovetail with information . . . indicating that King's advisors are Communist Party (CP) members and he is under the domination of the CP,"[47] Bureau officials decided to contact Dr. King in an effort to "set him straight."[48]

The FBI's effort to contact Dr. King consisted of a, telephone, call to the SCLC office in Atlanta by Cartha D. DeLoach, head of the FBI's Crime Records Division, and one by the Atlanta Special Agent in Charge. Both calls were answered by secretaries who promised to ask Dr. King to return the calls. When Dr. King did not respond, DeLoach observed:

> It would appear obvious that Rev. King does not desire to be told the true facts. He obviously used deceit, lies, and treachery as propaganda to further his own causes . . . I see no further need to contacting Rev. King as he obviously does not desire to be given the truth. The fact that he is a vicious liar is amply demonstrated in the fact he constantly associate's with and takes instructions from [a] . . . member of the Communist Party.[49]

Two years later—in late 1964—the director was refusing to meet with Dr. King because "I gave him that opportunity once and he ignored it."[50]

William Sullivan, who was head of the Domestic Intelligence Division during the investigation of Dr. King, testified:

> [Director Hoover] was very upset about the criticism that King made publicly about our failure to protect the Negro in the South against violations of the Negro civil liberties, and King on a number of occasions soundly criticized the Director. . . . Mr. Hoover was very distraught over these criticisms and so that would figure in it. . . . I think behind it all was the racial bias, the dislike of Negroes, the dislike of the civil rights movement. . . . I do not think he could rise above that.[51]

The FBI sent frequent reports about Dr. King's plans and activities to officials in both the Justice Department and the White House from the initiation of the COMINFIL investigation until Dr. King's death in 1968. Despite the fact that the investigation of Dr. King failed to produce evidence that Dr. King was a communist, or that he was being influenced to act in a way inimical to American interests, no responsible government official ever asked the FBI to terminate the investigation. Their inaction appears to have stemmed from a belief that it was safer to permit the FBI to conduct the investigation than to stop the Bureau and run the risk of charges that the FBI was being muzzled for political reasons.

Burke Marshall testified that the "charges" made by the Bureau against Adviser A "were grave and serious." The Kennedy Administration had been outspoken in its support of Dr. King, and ordering the FBI to terminate its investigation would, in Marshall's opinion, "have run the risk" that there would have been a lot of complaints that the Bureau had been blocked for political reasons from investigating serious charges about communist infiltration in the civil rights, movement.[52]

Edwin O. Guthman, press chief for the Justice Department under Attorney General Kennedy, testified that Robert Kennedy viewed the charges about Adviser A:

*as a serious matter and not in the interest of the country and not in
the interest of the civil rights movement. . . . The question of whether
he was influencing King and his contacts with King, that was a matter
which was not fully decided, but in those days we accepted pretty much
what the FBI reported as being accurate.*[53]

Guthman testified that he was told by Kennedy in 1968 that Kennedy had
approved wiretap coverage of Dr. King's home and of two SCLC offices in
October 1963 because "he felt that if he did not do it, Mr. Hoover would
move to impede or block the passage of the Civil Rights Bill . . . and that
he felt that he might as well settle the matter as to whether [Adviser A] did
have the influence on King that the FBI contended. . . ."[54] Attorney General Kennedy's reasons for approving the wiretaps are discussed at length
in a subsequent chapter.[55] Of relevance here is the support which Guthman's observations lend to Marshall's recollection that Attorney General
Kennedy permitted the COMINFIL investigation to continue from concern about the truth of the FBI's charges and about the political consequences of terminating the investigation.

The Johnson Administration's willingness to permit the FBI to continue its investigation of Dr. King also appears to have involved political
considerations. Bill Moyers, President Johnson's assistant, testified that
sometime around the spring of 1965 President Johnson "seemed satisfied
that these allegations about Martin Luther King were not founded." Yet
President Johnson did not order the investigation terminated. When
asked the reason, Moyers explained that President Johnson:

*was very concerned that his embracing the civil rights movement and
Martin Luther King personally would not backfire politically. He
didn't want to have a Southern racist senator produce something that
would be politically embarassing to the president and to the civil rights
movement. We had lots of conversations about that . . . Johnson, as
everybody knows, bordered on paranoia about his enemies or about being trapped by other people's activities over which he had no responsibility.*[56]

Intelligence reports submitted by the Bureau to the White House and the Justice Department contained considerable intelligence of potential political value to the Kennedy and Johnson Administrations. The attorneys general were informed of meetings between Dr. King and his advisers, including the details of advice that Dr. King received, the strategies of the civil rights movement, and the attitude of civil rights leaders toward the administrations and their policies.[57] The implications of this inside knowledge were graphically described by one of Dr. King's legal advisers, Harry Wachtel:

> The easiest example I can give is that that if I'm an attorney representing one side, negotiating and trying to achieve something, and if the attorney on the other side had information about what my client was thinking and what we were talking about, it would become a devastatingly important impediment to our negotiation, our freedom of action.[58]

Burke Marshall, however, described the Bureau's reports about Dr. King and the SCLC as "of no use: it was stupid information." He elaborated:

> I was in touch with Martin King all the time about all kinds of information that went way beyond what was reported by the Bureau about what he was going to do, where he was going to be, the wisdom of what he was going to do, who he was going to do it with, what the political situation was. The Southern Christian Leadership Conference and Dr. King were in some sense close associates of mine. [Information of the type included in FBI reports] was all information that I would have had any way.[59]

[Editor's Note: Sections omitted include further details about FBI surveillance and attempts to discredit Dr. King.]

Conclusion

Although it is impossible to gauge the full extent to which the FBI's discrediting programs affected the civil rights movement, the fact that there was impact is unquestionable.

Rumors circulated by the FBI had a profound impact on the SCLO's ability to raise funds. According to Congressman Andrew Young, a personal friend and associate of Dr. King, the FBI's effort against Dr. King and the SCLC "chilled contributions. There were direct attempts at some of our larger contributors who told us that they had been told by agents that Martin had a Swiss bank account, or that Martin had confiscated some of the monies from the March on Washington for his personal use. None of that was true."[60] Harry Wachtel, one of Dr. King's legal counsels who handled many of the financial and fund raising activities of the SCLC, emphasized that the SCLC was always in need of funds. "Getting a grant or getting a contribution is a very fragile thing. A grant delayed has a very serious impact on an organization, whose financial condition was pretty rough."[61] Wachtel testified that the SCLC continually had to overcome rumors of poor financial management and communist connections.

> The material . . . stayed in the political bloodstream all the way through to the time of Dr. King's death, and even after. In our efforts to build a King Center, it was around. It was like a contamination.[62]

The SCLC leadership assumed that anything said in meetings or over the telephone would be intercepted by wiretaps, bugs, or informants. Ironically, the FBI memorandum reporting that a wiretap of the SCLC's Atlanta office was feasible stated:

> In the past when interviews have been conducted in the office of Southern Christian Leadership Conference certain employees when asked a question, in a half joking manner and a half serious manner replied, "You should know that already, don't you have our wires tapped?" It is noted in the past, State of Georgia has conducted investigations regarding subject and Southern Christian Leadership Conference.[63]

Harry Wachtel commented on the impact constant surveillance had on members of the SCLC:

When you live in a fishbowl, you act like you're in a fishbowl, whether you do it consciously or unconsciously. . . . I can't put specifics before you, except to say that it beggars the imagination not to believe that the SCLC, Dr. King, and all its leaders were not chilled or inhibited from all kinds of activities, political and even social.[64]

Wachtel also pointed out the ramifications stemming from the government's advance knowledge of what civil rights leaders were thinking:

It is like political intelligence. It did not chill us from saying it, but it affected the strategies and tactics because the people you were having strategies and tactics about were privy to what you were about. They knew your doubts. . . . Take events like strategies in Atlantic City. . . . Decision-making concerning which way to go, joining one challenge or not, supporting a particular situation, or not, had to be limited very strongly by the fact that information which was expressed by telephone, or which could even possibly be picked up by bugging, would be in the hands of the president.[65]

Perhaps most difficult to gauge is the personal impact of the Bureau's programs. Congressman Young told the Committee that while Dr. King was not deterred by the attacks which are now known to have been instigated in part by the FBI, there is "no question" but that he was personally affected:

It was a great burden to be attacked by people he respected, particularly when the attacks engendered by the FBI came from people like Ralph McGill. He sat down and cried at the New York Times editorial about his statement on Vietnam, but this just made him more determined. It was a great personal suffering, but since we don't really know all that they did, we have no way of knowing the ways that they affected us.[66]

[Editor's Note: Footnote numbers in the Conclusion have been updated to be in sequence.]

NOTES

INTRODUCTION

1. William Sullivan testimony, 11/1/75, p. 97.
2. Memorandum from Frederick Baumgardner to William Sullivan, 1/28/64.
3. Andrew Young testimony, 2/19/76, p. 55.
4. Memorandum from Alan Belmont to Clyde Tolson, 10/17/63.
5. Burke Marshall testimony, 3/3/76, p. 32.
6. Memorandum from William Sullivan to Alan Belmont, 12/16/64.
7. Memorandum from Frederick Baumgardner to William Sullivan, 8/31/64, p.1
7A. William Sullivan testimony, 11/1/75, pp. 104–105.
8. Memorandum from William Sullivan to Alan Belmont, 1/8/64.
9. Memorandum from James Bland to William Sullivan, 2/3/62.
10. Speech delivered by Dr. Martin Luther King during the March on Washington, 8/28/63.
11. Memorandum from William Sullivan to Alan Belmont, 8/30/63, p. 1.
12. Hoover note on United Press International release, 12/29/63.
13. *Time* magazine, 12/14/70.
14. Bill Moyers testimony, 3/2/76, pp. 17–18.
15. James Adams testimony, 11/19/75, Hearings, Vol. 6, p. 65.
16. omitted in original.
17. Marshall, 3/3/76, p. 55.
18. Edwin Guthman testimony, 3/16/76, p. 16.
19. Omitted in original.
20. Adams, 11/19/75, Hearings, Vol. 6, p. 66.
21. Airtel from FBI Director to New York Office, 3/18/66.
22. Memorandum from SAC, New York to Director, FBI, 4/14/64.

THE COMINFIL INVESTIGATION

23. FBI Manual Section 87e. The Section in effect at the time the FBI initiated its investigation of Dr. King and the SCLC was captioned, "Legitimate Noncommunist Organizations that are Communist Infiltrated," and provided in part: "(1) No investigation should be conducted without prior Bureau approval. (2) Investigations should be handled most discreetly by experienced agents. Advise Bureau promptly under caption 'COMINFIL (name of organization)' when one of the following exists and include your recommendation for instituting an investigation. (a) The Communist Party has specifically instructed its members to infiltrate the organization. (b) Communist Party members have infiltrated the organization in sufficient strength to influence or control the organization. (7) Data concerning following topics should be fully developed and reported on: (a) Basis for investigation and fact that our investigation is directed solely toward establishing extent of Communist Party infiltration, or that organization is specific target for infiltration, and that Bureau is not investigating legitimate activities of organization. (b) Address of organization. (c) Brief characterization of organization, including total membership. (d) Principal officers of organization. (e) Communist Party program to infiltrate this organization and influence its policy. (f) Results of this program, including Communist Party affiliations of officers and members." Clarence Kelley, the present director of the FBI, was asked by the Committee: "Taking the current manual and trying to understand its applicability laid against the facts in the Martin Luther King case, un-

der section 87 permission is granted to open investigations of the influence of non-subversive groups, and the first sentence reads: 'When information is received indicating that a subversive group is seeking to systematically infiltrate and control a nonsubversive group or organization, an investigation can be opened.' Now, I take it that is the same standard that was used in opening the investigation of the Southern Christian Leadership Conference in the 1960s, so that investigation could still be opened today under the current FBI manual?" Mr. KELLEY. "I think so."
(Clarence Kelley testimony, 12/10/75, Hearings, Vol. 6, p. 308.)

24. See Report, on the Development of FBI Domestic Investigations, p. 479.

25. Memorandum from Director, FBI to Special Agent in Charge, Atlanta, 9/20/57. The "stated purpose" of the SCLC was to organize a register-and-vote campaign among Negroes in the South. (Trezz Anderson, *Pittsburgh Courier*, 8/17/57.) Considerable "public source" information was recorded in FBI files both before and after this date.

26. The action memorandum stated that Dr. King's name "should be placed in Section A of the Reserve Index and tabbed communist." (Memorandum from Director, FBI, to SAC, Atlanta, 5/11/62.) Persons to be listed in Section A of the Reserve Index were described by the FBI as people "who in time of national emergency, are in a position to influence others against the national interest or are likely to furnish material financial aid to subversive elements due to their subversive associations and ideology." The types of persons to be listed in Section A included: "(a) Professors, teachers or leaders; (b) Labor union organizers or leaders; (c) Writers, lecturers, newsmen, entertainers, and others in the mass media field; (d) Lawyers, doctors, and scientists; (e) Other potentially influential persons on a local or national level; (f) Individuals who could potentially furnish material financial aid." See Committee staff report on Development of FBI Domestic Intelligence Investigations. Dr. King was placed on the Reserve Index despite the fact that as late as November 1961 the Atlanta Field Office had advised FBI Headquarters that there was "no information on which to base a security matter inquiry." (Airtel from SAC, Atlanta, to Director, FBI, 11/21/61.)

27. Memorandum from Director, FBI to SAC, Atlanta, 2/27/62. The instructions did not define what was meant by "subversive." Reports from field offices during the ensuing months considered as "subversive" such information as the fact that Dr. King had been one of 350 signers of a petition to abolish the House Committee on Un-American Activities. (FBI Report, New York, 4/13/62.) These instructions to the field were issued on the first day of Dr. King's trial in which he and seven hundred other civil rights demonstrators were charged in Albany, Georgia, with parading without a permit. (*Atlanta Constitution*, 2/28/62, p. 1.)

28. FBI Manual Section 122, p. 5. This policy was later interpreted as requiring "coverage" of demonstrations, meetings, "or any other pertinent information concerning racial activity." (Memorandum from Director, FBI to SAC, Atlanta, 6/27/63.)

29. Memorandum from Director, FBI, to SAC, Atlanta, 10/23/62, p. 2.

30. On the same day the Southern Regional Counsel—a respected civil rights study group—issued a report criticizing the Bureau's inaction during civil rights demonstration that were then occurring in Albany, Georgia. This report is discussed at pp. 89–90.

31. Memorandum from Director, FBI, to Attorney General, 1/5/62.

32. Memorandum from Frederick Baumgardner to William Sullivan, 10/22/62.

33. FBI headquarters first requested the field offices for recommendations concerning whether a COMINFIL investigation should be opened on July 20, 1962. This was the

same day on which officials in Albany, Georgia, sought a judicial ban against demonstrations led by Dr. King, alleging that Negroes had been endangering the lives of police officers "and agents of the Federal Bureau of Investigation." (*New York Times*, 7/22/62).

34. A microphone was installed in Adviser A's office on March 16, 1962 (Airtel from SAC. New York to Director, FBI, 3/16/62) and a wiretap was installed on his office telephone on, 3/20/62 (Airtel from SAO, New York to Director, FBI, 3/20/62). The wiretap was authorized by the Attorney General (Memorandum from Director, FBI to Attorney General, 3/6/62). The microphone was approved only at the FBI division level (Memorandum from James Bland to William Sullivan, 3/2/62).

35. FBI Manual Section 87, pp. 12–13, 83–85. Former Assistant Director Sullivan testified: "If a man is not under the discipline and control of the Communist Party, *ipso facto* he is not really a member of the Communist Party. The Party demands the man's complete discipline, the right of complete discipline over a Party member. That is why they have the graduations, you see, the fellow traveler, not a Party member, because he would not accept the entire discipline of the Party. The sympathizer, another graduation of it, what we call the dupe, the victim of Communist fronts and so forth. The key—I am glad you raised this question—the key to membership is does this man accept completely the Party discipline. If he does not, he is not regarded as a genuine member." (Sullivan, 11/1/75, p. 18.)

36. It was discontinued on August 16, 1962. See Airtels from SAC, New York to Director, FBI, 8/16/62 and 11/15/62, and Memorandum from Director, FBI to SAC, New York, 11/23/62.

37. The Attorney General authorized a wiretap on Adviser A's home telephone in November 1962 (memorandum from Director, FBI to Attorney General, 11/20/62).

38. E.g., Memorandum from Director, FBI, to Attorney General Kennedy.

39. Indeed, in April 1964 a field office reported that Adviser A was not under the influence of the Communist Party. Memorandum from SAC New York to Director, FBI, 4/14/64.

40. Memorandum from James Bland to William Sullivan, 2/3/62.

41. Special Report, Southern Regional Council, 1/8/62.

42. "Albany, A Study of Racial Responsibility," Southern Regional Council, 11/14/62.

43. Item #17, FBI Response to Senate Select Committee, 10/15/75. FBI rules provided that allegations about Bureau misconduct had to be investigated and that "every logical lead which will establish the true facts should be completely run out unless such action would embarrass the Bureau. . . ."

44. Memorandum from Alex Rosen to Alan Belmont, 11/15/62. The updated report was received at headquarters on December 5, 1962. (Memorandum from SAC, Atlanta to Director, FBI, 12/4/62.)

45. *Atlanta Constitution*, 11/19/62, p. 18. In 1961 a report issued by the U.S. Commission on Civil Rights, entitled "Justice," had addressed the problem of FBI agents investigating local law enforcement officials and reached a similar conclusion, including mistrust of the FBI by southern Blacks.

46. Memorandum from SAC, Atlanta, to Director, FBI, 11/19/62.

47. Memorandum from Alex Rosen to Alan Belmont, 11/20/62.

48. Memorandum from Alan Belmont to Clyde Tolson, 11/26/62. A decision was made that Dr. King should be contacted by both Assistant Director DeLoach and Assistant Director William Sullivan "in order that there will be a witness and there can be no charge of provincialism inasmuch as Cartha D. DeLoach comes from the South and Mr. Sullivan comes from the North." (Ibid.)

49. Memorandum from Cartha DeLoach to John Mohr, 1/15/63. FBI officials also "Interviewed" or otherwise contacted various newspaper publishers "to set [them] straight" about Dr. King's remarks. (Memorandum from Alex Rosen to Alan Belmont, 1/17/63.) One of the publishers contacted was described as "impressed with the Director" and as being on the "Special Correspondents List." (Letter from Cartha DeLoach to one of the publishers, 11/29/62, p. 3.) The FBI also took steps to "point out" the "evasive conduct of King" to the attorney general and Civil Rights Commission. (Letter, FBI Director to Attorney General, 1/18/63; Letter, FBI to Staff Director, Commission on Civil Rights, 1/18/63.)

50. Note on memorandum from Frederick Baumgardner to William Sullivan, 11/20/64.

51. William Sullivan testimony, 11/1/75, p. 62. Sullivan's assessment must be viewed in light of the feud that subsequently developed between Sullivan and Hoover and which ultimately led to Sullivan's dismissal from the FBI. That feud is discussed in the committee's final report.

52. Marshall, 3/3/76, p. 55.

53. Edwin Guthman testimony, 3/16/76, p. 16.

54. Guthman, 3/16/76, p. 5.

55. See pp. 115–116.

56. Bill Moyers testimony, 3/2/76, p. 22.

57. The FBI flies are replete with examples of politically valuable intelligence about Dr. King that was sent to the Justice Department and the White House. For instance, in May 1963, at a critical point in the Congressional debate over the public accommodations bill, Hoover informed the attorney general of a discussion between Dr. King and an adviser "concerning a conference which Reverend King reportedly has requested with you and the president." The discussion was reported to have centered on the Administration's sensitivity over its inability to control the racial situation and on the need to maintain the pace of civil rights activities "so that the president will have to look for an alternative." Dr. King was said to believe that the president would then be receptive to ideas from Dr. King which would provide a solution to "his problem, [his] fear of violence. . . ." Dr. King was said to have stated that if a conference with the president could not be worked out, then the movement would have to be "enlarged," and that "he would like to put so much pressure on the president that be would have to sign an Executive Order making segregation unconstitutional." (Memorandum from Director, FBI to Attorney General, 5/31/63.)

58. Harry Wachtel testimony, 2/27/76, p. 12.

59. Burke Marshall, 3/3/76, p. 54; 56–57.

CONCLUSION

60. Young, 2/19/76, pp. 25–26.

61. Wachtel, 2/27/769 pp. 31–32.

62. Wachtel, 2/27/76, p. 49.

63. Memorandum, Special Agent in Charge, Atlanta, to Director, FBI, 10/10/63.

64. Wachtel, 2/27/76, pp. 10, 19. 454

65. Wachtel, 2/27/76, p. 10.

66. Young, 2/19/76, p. 16.

Introduction to
"COINTELPRO: The FBI's Covert Action Programs Against American Citizens"

IN 1975, the Select Committee to Study Governmental Operations with Respect to Intelligence, chaired by Democratic Senator Frank Church of Idaho, was established to investigate longstanding abuses by the FBI and the CIA. When the committee issued its final report, a number of startling secrets were made public: illegal break-ins; CIA assassination plots, including a plan to use the Mafia to murder Fidel Castro; and the existence of COINTELPRO, an FBI acronym for its covert action programs. When the revelations became public, *The St. Louis Post-Dispatch* commented that it was "hard to imagine that there was any tactic too sordid for this federal agency to use."

COINTELPRO had been launched in 1956 following Supreme Court rulings that limited the government's power to act openly against so-called dissident groups. The program was allegedly suspended in 1971 after people, still unknown, broke into an FBI field office in Media, Pennsylvania, and stole a number of files. During the intervening fifteen years, the FBI had conducted a vigilante operation to undermine the civil rights movement, the Old Left, including the Communist and Socialist parties, and the New Left, including anti–Vietnam War protesters. COINTELPRO actions taken by the FBI included arson and criminal break-ins. Anonymous letters were sent to employers, urging them to fire FBI-targeted employees, and to spouses to destroy marriages. Disinformation campaigns were conducted and violent demonstrations provoked. In 1969, An FBI informant-provocateur, who was a bodyguard of Black Panther Party leader Mark Hampton, gave the bureau a detailed floor plan of

Hampton's apartment shortly before Chicago police killed Hampton in his bed. The list goes on.

The findings of the Church Committee and, at the same time, the House Select Committee on Intelligence, the so-called Pike Committee (chaired by New York Democratic Congressman Otis Pike), prevented an immediate resumption of COINTELPRO activities. But after 9/11 it is likely that the intelligence agencies resumed similar activities—only this time with different targets.

ADDITIONAL SOURCES

Blackstock, Nelson. *COINTELPRO: The FBI'S Secret War on Political Freedom.* New York: Vintage, 1986.

Churchill, Ward and Jim Vander Wall. *The COINTELPRO Papers: Documents from the FBI's Secret Wars Against Dissent in the United States.* Boston: South End Press, 2002.

Donner, Frank. *The Age of Surveillance: The Aims and Methods of America's Political Intelligence System.* New York: Alfred A. Knopf, 1980.

U.S. Congress. House. Select Committee on Intelligence. *Hearings on Domestic Intelligence Programs.* 94th Congress, 1st session, 1975.

The Church Committee

"COINTELPRO: The FBI's Covert Action Programs Against American Citizens"

FINAL REPORT OF THE SELECT COMMITTEE TO STUDY GOVERNMENTAL OPERATIONS WITH RESPECT TO INTELLIGENCE ACTIVITIES, U.S. SENATE.

BOOK III, 1976

II. The Five Domestic Programs

A. Origins

The origins of COINTELPRO are rooted in the Bureau's jurisdiction to investigate hostile foreign intelligence activities on American soil. Counterintelligence, of course, goes beyond investigation; it is affirmative action taken to neutralize hostile agents.

The Bureau believed its wartime counterattacks on foreign agents to be effective—and what works against one enemy will work against another. In the atmosphere of the Cold War, the American Communist Party (CPUSA) was viewed as a deadly threat to national security.

In 1956, the Bureau decided that a formal counterintelligence program, coordinated from headquarters, would be an effective weapon in the fight against Communism. The first COINTELPRO was therefore initiated.[63]

The CPUSA COINTELPRO accounted for more than half of all approved proposals.[64] The Bureau personnel involved believed that the success of the program—one action was described as "the most effective single blow ever dealt the organized communist movement—" made counterintelligence techniques the weapons of choice whenever the Bureau assessed a new and, in its view, equally serious threat to the country.

As noted earlier, law enforcement frustration also played a part in the origins of each COINTELPRO. In each case, Bureau witnesses testified

that the lack of adequate statutes, uncooperative or ineffective local police, or restrictive court rulings had made it impossible to use traditional
law enforcement methods against the targeted groups.

Additionally, a certain amount of empire building may have been at
work. Under William C. Sullivan, the Domestic Intelligence Division
greatly expanded its jurisdiction. Klan matters were transferred in 1964
to the Intelligence Division from the General Investigative Division; black
nationalist groups were added in 1967; and, just as the Old Left appeared
to be dying out,[65] the New Left was gradually added to the work of the Division's Internal Security Section in the late 1960s.

Finally, it is significant that the five domestic COINTELPROs were
started against the five groups which were the subject of intensified investigative programs. Of course, the fact that such intensive investigative programs were started at all reflects the Bureau's process of threat assessment:
the greater the threat, the more need to know about it (intelligence) and the
more impetus to counter it (covert action). More important, however, the
mere existence of the additional information gained through the investigative programs inevitably demonstrated those particular organizational
or personal weaknesses which were vulnerable to disruption. COINTEL-
PRO demonstrates the dangers inherent in the overbroad collection of
domestic intelligence; when information is available, it can be—and
was—improperly used.

B. The Programs

Before examining each program in detail, some general observations may
be useful. Each of the five domestic COINTELPROs had certain traits in
common. As noted above, each program used techniques learned from
the Bureau's wartime efforts against hostile foreign agents. Each sprang
from frustration with the perceived inability of law enforcement to deal
with what the Bureau believed to be a serious threat to the country. Each
program depended on an intensive intelligence effort to provide the information used to disrupt the target groups.

The programs also differ to some extent. The White Hate program, for
example, was very precisely targeted; each of the other programs spread

to a number of groups which do not appear to fall within any clear parameters.[67] In fact, with each subsequent COINTELPRO, the targeting became more diffuse.

The White Hate COINTELPRO also used comparatively few techniques which carried a risk of serious physical, emotional, or economic damage to the targets, while the Black Nationalist COINTELPRO used such techniques extensively. The New Left COINTELPRO, on the other hand, had the highest proportion of proposals aimed at preventing the exercise of free speech. Like the progression in targeting, the use of dangerous, degrading, or blatantly unconstitutional techniques also appears to have become less restrained with each subsequent program.

1. CPUSA.—The first official COINTELPRO program, against the Communist Party, USA, was started in August 1956 with Director Hoover's approval. Although the formal program was instituted in 1956, COINTELPRO-type activities had gone on for years. The memorandum recommending the program refers to prior actions, constituting "harassment," which were generated by the field during the course of the Bureau's investigation of the Communist Party." These prior actions were instituted on all ad hoc basis as the opportunity arose. As Sullivan testified, "[Before 1956] we were engaged in COINTELPRO tactics, divide, confuse, weaken in diverse ways, all organization. . . . [Before 1956] it, was more sporadic. It depended on a given office. . . ."[69]

In 1956, a series of field conferences was held to discuss the development of new security informants. The Smith Act trials and related proceedings had exposed over 100 informants, leaving the Bureau's intelligence apparatus in some disarray. During the field conferences, a formal counterintelligence program was recommended, partly because of the gaps in the informant ranks.[70]

Since the Bureau had evidence that until the late 1940s the CPUSA had been "blatantly" involved in Soviet espionage, and believed that the Soviets were continuing to use the Party for "political and intelligence purposes,"[71] there was no clear line of demarcation in the Bureau's switch from foreign to domestic counterintelligence. The initial areas of concentration were the use of informants to capitalize on the conflicts within the Party over Nikita

Khrushchev's denunciation of Stalin; to prevent the CP's efforts to take over (via a merger) a broad-based socialist group; to encourage the Socialist Workers Party in its attacks on the CP; and to use the IRS to investigate underground CP members who either failed to file, or filed under false names.

As the program proceeded, other targets and techniques were developed, but until 1960 the CPUSA targets were Party members, and the techniques were aimed at the Party organization (factionalism, public exposure, etc.)

2. THE 1960 EXPANSION.—In March 1960, CPUSA COINTELPRO field offices received a directive to intensify counterintelligence efforts to prevent Communist infiltration ("COMINFIL") of mass organizations, ranging from the NAACP[72] to a local scout troop.[73] The usual technique would be to tell a leader of the organization about the alleged Communist in its midst, the target, of course, being the alleged Communist rather than the organization. In an increasing number of cases, however, both the alleged Communist and the organization were targeted, usually by planting a news article about Communists active in the organization. For example, a newsman was given information about Communist participation in a SANE march, with the express purpose being to discredit SANE as well as the participants, and another newspaper was alerted to plans of Bettina Aptheker to join a United Farm Workers picket line.[74] The 1960 "COMINFIL" memorandum marks the beginning of the slide from targeting CP members to those allegedly under CP "influence" (such civil right's leaders as Martin Luther King, Jr.) to "fellow travelers" (those, taking positions supported by the Communists, such as school integration, increased minority hiring, and opposition to HUAC.)[75]

3. SOCIALIST WORKERS PARTY.—The Socialist Workers Party ("SWP") COINTELPRO program was initiated on October 12, 1961, by the headquarters supervisor handling the SWP desk (but with Hoover's concurrence) apparently on a theory of even-handed treatment: if the Bureau has a program against the CP, it was only fair to have one against the Trotskyites. (The COINTELPRO unit chief, in response to a question about why the Bureau targeted the SWP in view of the fact that the SWP's

hostility to the Communist Party had been useful in disrupting the CPUSA, answered, "I do not think that the Bureau discriminates against subversive organizations."[76]

The program was not given high priority—only forty-five actions were approved—and was discontinued in 1969, two years before the other four programs ended. (The SWP program was then subsumed in the New Left COINTELPRO.) Nevertheless, it marks an important departure from the CPUSA COINTELPRO: although the SWP had contacts with foreign Trotskyite groups, there was no evidence that the SWP was involved in espionage. These were, in C. D. Brennan's phrase, "home grown tomatoes."[77] The Bureau has conceded that the SWP has never been engaged in organizational violence, not has it taken any criminal steps toward overthrowing the country.[78]

Nor does the Bureau claim the SWP was engaged in revolutionary acts. The party was targeted for its rhetoric; significantly, the originating letter points to the SWPs "open" espousal of its line, "through running candidates for public office" and its direction and/or support of "such causes as Castro's Cuba and integration problems arising in the South." Further, the American people had to be alerted to the fact that "the SWP is not just another socialist group but follows the revolutionary principles of Marx, Lenin, and Engles as interpreted by Leon Trotsky."[79]

Like the CPUSA COINTELPRO, non-party members were also targeted, particularly when the SWP and the Young Socialist Alliance (the SWP's youth group) started to cosponsor antiwar marches.[80]

4. WHITE HATE.—The Klan COINTELPRO began on July 30, 1964, with the transfer of the "responsibility for development of informants and gathering of intelligence on the KKK and other hate groups" from the General Investigative Division to the Domestic Intelligence Division. The memorandum recommending the reorganization also suggested that, "counterintelligence and disruption tactics be given further study by DID and appropriate recommendations made."[81]

Accordingly, on September 2, 1964, a directive was sent to seventeen field offices instituting a COINTELPRO against Klan-type and hate organizations "to expose, disrupt, and otherwise neutralize the activities of the various Klans and hate organizations, their leadership, and adherents."[82] Seventeen Klan organizations and nine "hate" organizations (e.g., American Nazi Party, National States Rights Party, etc.) were listed as targets. The field offices were also instructed specifically to consider "Action Groups"—"the relatively few individuals in each organization who use strong arm tactics and violent actions to achieve their ends."[83] However, counterintelligence proposals were not to be limited to these few, but were to include any influential member if the opportunity arose. As the unit chief stated:

> The emphasis was on determining the identity and exposing and neutralizing the violence prone activities of "Action Groups," but also it was important to expose the unlawful activities of other Klan organizations. We also made an effort to deter or counteract the propaganda and to deter violence and to deter recruitment where we could. This was done with the view that if we could curb the organization, we could curb the action or the violence within the organization.[84]

The White Hate COINTELPRO appears to have been limited, with few exceptions,[85] to the original named targets. No "legitimate" right wing organizations were drawn into the program, in contrast with the earlier spread of the CPUSA and SWP programs to nonmembers. This precision has been attributed by the Bureau to the superior intelligence on "hate" groups received by excellent informant penetration.

Bureau witnesses believe the Klan program to have been highly effective. The unit chief stated:

> I think the Bureau got the job done . . . I think that one reason we were able to get the job done was that we were able to use counterintelligence techniques. It is possible that we eventually could have done the job without counterintelligence techniques. I am not sure we could have done it as well or as quickly.[86]

This view was shared by George C. Moore, section chief of the Racial Intelligence Section, which had responsibility for the White Hate and Black Nationalist COINTELPROs:

I think from what I have seen and what I have read, as far as the coun-
terintelligence program, on the Klan is concerned, that it was effective.
I think it was one of the most effective programs I have ever seen the
Bureau handle as far as any group is concerned.[87]

5. BLACK NATIONALIST–HATE GROUPS.[88]—In marked contrast to
prior COINTELPROs, which grew out of years of intensive intelligence
investigation, the Black Nationalist COINTELPRO and the Racial Intelligence Investigative Section were set up at about the same time in 1967.

Prior to that time, the Division's investigation of "Negro matters" was
limited to instances of alleged Communist infiltration of civil rights
groups and to monitoring civil rights protest activity. However, the long,
hot summer of 1967 led to intense pressure on the Bureau to do something to contain the problem, and once again, the Bureau heeded the call.

The originating letter was sent out to twenty-three field offices on August 25, 1967, describing the program's purpose as

> . . . *to expose, disrupt, misdirect, discredit, or otherwise neutralize the*
> *activities of black nationalist, hate-type organizations and groupings,*
> *their leadership, spokesmen, membership, and supporters, and to*
> *counter their propensity for violence and civil disorder. . . . Efforts of*
> *the various groups to consolidate their forces or to recruit new or youth-*
> *ful adherents must be frustrated.*[89]

Initial group targets for "intensified attention" were the Southern Christian Leadership Conference, the Student Nonviolent Coordinating Committee, Revolutionary Action Movement, Deacons for Defense and Justice,
Congress of Racial Equality, and the Nation of Islam. Individuals named
as targets were Stokely Carmichael, H. "Rap" Brown, Elijah Muhammed,
and Maxwell Stanford. The targets were chosen by conferring with Headquarters personnel supervising the racial cases; the list was not intended
to exclude other groups known to the field.

According to the Black Nationalist supervisor, individuals and organizations were targeted because of their propensity for violence or their
"radical or revolutionary rhetoric [and] actions":

Revolutionary would be [defined as] advocacy of the overthrow of the
Government. . . . Radical [is] a loose term that might cover, for exam-
ple, the separatist view of the Nation of Islam, the influence of a group
called U.S. Incorporated. . . . Generally, they wanted a separate black
nation. . . . They [the NOI] advocated formation of a separate black
nation on the territory of five Southern states.[90]

The letter went on to direct field offices to exploit conflicts within and between groups; to use news media contacts to disrupt, ridicule, or discredit
groups; to preclude "violence-prone" or "rabble rouser" leaders of these
groups from spreading their philosophy publicly; and to gather information on the "unsavory backgrounds"—immorality, subversive activity,
and criminal activity—of group members.[91]

According to George C. Moore, the Southern Christian Leadership
Conference was included because

. . . at that time it was still under investigation because of the commu-
nist infiltration. As far as I know, there were not any violent propensi-
ties, except that I note . . . in the cover memo [expanding the program]
or somewhere, that they mentioned that if Martin Luther King decided
to go a certain way, he could cause some trouble. . . . I cannot explain it
satisfactorily . . . this is something the section inherited.[92]

On March 4, 1968, the program was expanded from twenty-three to
forty-one field offices.[93] The letter expanding the program lists five long-
range goals for the program:

(1) to prevent the "coalition of militant black nationalist groups,"
    which might be the first step toward a real "Mau Mau" in
    America;
(2) to prevent the rise of a "messiah" who could "unify, and elec-
    trify," the movement, naming specifically Martin Luther King,
    Stokely Carmichael, and Elijah Muhammed;
(3) to prevent violence on the part of black nationalist groups, by

pinpointing "potential troublemakers" and neutralizing them "before they exercise their potential for violence";

(4) to prevent groups and leaders from gaining "respectability" by discrediting them to the "responsible" Negro community, to the white community (both the responsible community and the "liberals"—the distinction is the Bureau's, and to Negro radicals; and

(5) to prevent the long range growth of these organizations, especially among youth, by developing specific tactics to "prevent these groups from recruiting young people."[94]

6. THE PANTHER DIRECTIVES.—The Black Panther Party ("BPP") was not included in the first two lists of primary targets (August 1967 and March 1968) because it had not attained national importance. By November 1968, apparently the BPP had become sufficiently active to be considered a primary target. A letter to certain field offices with BPP activity dated November 25, 1968, ordered recipient offices to submit "imaginative and hard-hitting counterintelligence measures aimed at crippling the BPP." Proposals were to be received every two weeks. Particular attention was to be given to capitalizing upon the differences between the BPP and U.S., Inc. (Ron Karenga's group), which had reached such proportions that "it is taking on the aura of gang warfare with attendant threats of murder and reprisals."[95]

On January 30, 1969, this program against the BPP was expanded to additional offices, noting that the BPP was attempting to create a better image. In line with this effort, Bobby Seale was conducting a "purge"[96] of the party, including expelling police informants. Recipient offices were instructed to take advantage of the opportunity to further plant the seeds of suspicion concerning disloyalty among ranking officials.[97]

Bureau witnesses are not certain whether the Black Nationalist program was effective. Mr. Moore stated:

I know that the . . . overall results of the Klan [COINTELPRO] was much more effective from what I have been told than the Black

Extremism [COINTELPRO] because of the number of informants in the Klan who could take action which would be more effective. In the Black Extremism Group . . . we got a late start because we did not have extremist activity [until] '67 and '68. Then we had to play catch-up. . . . It is not easy to measure effectiveness. . . . There were police-men killed in those days. There were bombs thrown. There were establishments burned with molotov cocktails. . . . We can measure that damage. You cannot measure over on the other side, what lives were saved because somebody did not leave the organization or suspi-cion was sown on his leadership and this organization gradually de-clined and [there was] suspicion within it, or this organization did not join with [that] organization as a result of a black power conference which was aimed toward consolidation efforts. All we know, either through their own ineptitude, maybe it emerged through counterintelli-gence, maybe, I think we like to think that that helped to do it, that there was not this development. . . . What part did counterintelligence [play?] We hope that it did play a part. Maybe we just gave it a nudge.[98]

7. NEW LEFT.—The Internal Security Section had undergone a slow transition from concentrating on the "Old Left"—the CPUSA and SWP—to focusing primarily on the activities of the "New Left"—a term which had no precise definition within the Bureau.[99] Some agents defined "New Left" functionally, by connection with protests. Others defined it by phi-losophy, particularly antiwar philosophy.

On October 28, 1968, the fifth and final COINTELPRO was started against this undefined group. The program was triggered in part by the Columbia campus disturbance. Once again, law enforcement methods had broken down, largely (in the Bureau's opinion) because college ad-ministrators refused to call the police on campus to deal with student demonstrations. The atmosphere at the time was described by the Head-quarters agent who supervised the New Left COINTELPRO:

During that particular time, there was considerable public, Adminis-tration—I mean governmental Administration [and] news media in-terest in the protest movement to the extent that some groups, I don't recall any specifics, but some groups were calling for something to be done to blunt or reduce the protest movements that were disrupting campuses. I can't classify it as exactly an hysteria, but there was considerable interest [and concern]. That was the framework that we were working with. . . . It would be my impression that as a result of this hysteria, some governmental leaders were looking to the Bureau.[100]

And, once again, the combination of perceived threat, public outcry, and law enforcement frustration produced a COINTELPRO.

According to the initiating letter, the counterintelligence program's purpose was to "expose, disrupt, and otherwise neutralize," the activities of the various New Left organizations, their leadership, and adherents, with particular attention to Key Activists, "the moving forces behind the New Left." The final paragraph contains an exhortation to a "forward look, enthusiasm, and interest" because of the Bureau's concern that "the anarchist activities of a few can paralyze institutions of learning, induction centers, cripple traffic, and tie the arms of law enforcement officials all to the detriment of our society." The internal memorandum recommending the program further sets forth the Bureau's concerns:

> *Our Nation is undergoing an era of disruption and violence caused to a large extent by various individuals generally connected with the New Left. Some of these activists urge revolution in America and call for the defeat of the United States in Vietnam. They continually and falsely allege police brutality and do not hesitate to utilize unlawful acts to further their so-called causes.*

The document continues:

> *The New Left has on many occasions viciously and scurrilously attacked the director and the Bureau in an attempt to hamper our investigation of it and to drive us off the college campuses.*[101]

Based on those factors, the Bureau decided to institute a new COINTELPRO.

8. New Left Directives.—The Bureau's concern with "tying the hands of law enforcement officers," and with the perceived weakness of college administrators in refusing to call police onto the campus, led to a May 23, 1968, directive to all participating field offices to gather information on three categories of New Left activities:

(1) false allegations of police brutality, to "counter the widespread charges of police brutality that invariably arise following student-police encounters";

(2) immorality, depicting the "scurrilous and depraved nature of many of the characters, activities, habits, and living conditions representative of New Left adherents"; and

(3) action by college administrators, "to show the value of college administrators and school officials taking a firm stand," and pointing out "whether and to what extent faculty members rendered aid and encouragement."

The letter continues, "Every avenue of possible embarrassment must be vigorously and enthusiastically explored. It cannot be expected that information of this type will be easily obtained, and an imaginative approach by your personnel is imperative to its success."[103]

The order to furnish information on "immorality" was not carried out with sufficient enthusiasm. On October 9, 1968, headquarters sent another letter to all offices, taking them to task for their failure to "remain alert for and to seek specific data depicting the depraved nature and moral looseness of the New Left" and to "use this material in a vigorous and enthusiastic approach to neutralizing them."[104] Recipient offices were again instructed to be "particularly alert for this type of data"[105] and told:

As the current school year commences, it can be expected that the New Left with its antiwar and anti-draft entourage will make every effort to confront college authorities, stifle military recruiting, and frustrate the Selective Service System. Each office will be expected, therefore, to afford this program continuous effective attention in order that no opportunity will be missed to destroy this insidious movement.[106]

As to the police brutality and "college administrator" categories, the Bureau's belief that getting tough with students and demonstrators would solve the problem, and that any injuries which resulted were deserved, is reflected in the Bureau's reaction to allegations of police brutality following the Chicago Democratic Convention.

On August 28, 1968, a letter was sent to the Chicago field office instructing it to "obtain all possible evidence that would disprove these charges" [that the Chicago police used undue force] and to "consider measures by which cooperative news media may be used to counteract these allegations." The administrative "note" (for the file) states:

> Once again, the liberal press and the bleeding hearts and the forces on the left are taking advantage of the situation in Chicago surrounding the Democratic National Convention to attack the police and organized law enforcement agencies. . . . We should be mindful of this situation and develop all possible evidence to expose this activity and to refute these false allegations.[107]

In the same vein, on September 9, 1968, an instruction was sent to all offices which had sent informants to the Chicago convention demonstrations, ordering them to debrief the informants for information "indicating incidents were staged to show police reacted with undue force and any information that authorities were baited by militants into using force."[108] The offices were also to obtain evidence of possible violations of anti-riot laws.[109]

The originating New Left letter had asked all recipient offices to respond with suggestions for counterintelligence action. Those responses were analyzed and a letter sent to all offices on July 6, 1968, setting forth twelve suggestions for counterintelligence action which could be utilized by all offices. Briefly the techniques are:

(1) preparing leaflets designed to discredit student demonstrators, using photographs of New Left leadership at the respective universities. "Naturally, the most obnoxious pictures should be used";

(2) instigating "personal conflicts or animosities" between New Left leaders;

(3) creating the impression that leaders are "informants for the Bureau or other law enforcement agencies";

(4) sending articles from student newspapers or the "underground press" which show the depravity of the New Left to university officials, donors, legislators, and parents. "Articles showing advocation of the use of narcotics and free sex are ideal";

(5) having members arrested on marijuana charges;

(6) sending anonymous letters about a student's activities to parents, neighbors, and the parents' employers. "This could have the effect of forcing the parents to take action";

(7) sending anonymous letters or leaflets describing the "activities and associations" of New Left faculty members and graduate assistants to university officials, legislators, Boards of Regents, and the press. "These letters should be signed 'A Concerned Alumni,' or 'A Concerned Taxpayer'";

(8) "using cooperative press contacts" to emphasize that the "disruptive elements" constitute a "minority" of the students. "The press should demand an immediate referendum on the issue in question";

(9) exploiting the "hostility" among the SDS and other New Left groups toward the SWP, YSA, and Progressive Labor Party;

(10) using "friendly news media" and law enforcement officials to disrupt New Left coffeehouses near military bases which are attempting to "influence members of the Armed Forces";

(11) using cartoons, photographs, and anonymous letters to "ridicule" the New Left; and

(12) using "misinformation" to "confuse and disrupt" New Left activities, such as by notifying members that events have been cancelled.[110]

As noted earlier, the lack of any Bureau definition of "New Left" resulted in targeting almost every antiwar group,[111] and spread to students demonstrating against anything. One notable example is a proposal targeting a student who carried an "obscene" sign in a demonstration protesting administration censorship of the school newspaper, and another student who sent a letter to that paper defending the demonstration.[112] In another article regarding "free love" on a university campus was anonymously mailed to college administrators and state officials since free love allows "an atmosphere to build up on campus that will be a fertile field for the New Left."[113]

None of the Bureau witnesses deposed believes the New Left COINTELPRO was generally effective, in part because of the imprecise targeting.

III. The Goals of COINTELPRO: Preventing or Disrupting the Exercise of First Amendment Rights

The origins of COINTELPRO demonstrate that the Bureau adopted extralegal methods to counter perceived threats to national security and public order because the ordinary legal processes were believed to be insufficient to do the job. In essence, the Bureau took the law into its own hands, conducting a sophisticated vigilante operation against domestic enemies.

The risks inherent in setting aside the laws, even though the purpose seems compelling at the time, were described by Tom Charles Huston in his testimony before the Committee[114]:

> The risk was that you would get people who would be susceptible to political considerations as opposed to national security considerations, or would construe political considerations to be national security considerations, to move from the kid with a bomb to the kid with a picket sign, and from the kid with the picket sign to the kid with the bumper sticker of the opposing candidate. And you just keep going down the line.[115]

The description is apt. Certainly, COINTELPRO took in a staggering range of targets. As noted earlier, the choice of individuals and organizations to be neutralized and disrupted ranged from the violent elements of the Black Panther Party to Martin Luther King, Jr., who the Bureau concedes was an advocate of nonviolence; from the Communist Party to the Ku Klux Klan; and from the advocates of violent revolution such as the Weathermen, to the supporters of peaceful social change, including the Southern Christian Leadership Conference and the Inter-University Committee for Debate on Foreign Policy.

The breadth of targeting springs partly from a lack of definition for the categories involved, and partly from the Bureau's belief that dissident speech and association should be prevented because they were incipient steps toward the possible ultimate commission of an act which might be criminal. Thus, the Bureau's self-imposed role as protector of the existing political and social order blurred the line between targeting criminal activity and constitutionally protected acts and advocacy.

The clearest example of actions directly aimed at the exercise of constitutional rights are those targeting speakers, teachers, writers or publications, and meetings or peaceful demonstrations.[116] Approximately 18 percent of all approved COINTELPRO proposals fell into these categories.[117]

The cases include attempts (sometimes successful) to get university and high school teachers fired; to prevent targets from speaking on campus; to stop chapters of target groups from being formed; to prevent the distribution of books, newspapers, or periodicals; to disrupt news conferences; to disrupt peaceful demonstrations, including the SCLCs Washington Spring Project and Poor People's Campaign, and most of the large antiwar marches; and to deny facilities for meetings or conferences.

A. Efforts to Prevent Speaking

An illustrative example of attacks on speaking concerns the plans of a dissident stockholders' group to protest a large corporation's war production at the annual stockholders meeting.[118] The field office was authorized to furnish information about the group's plans (obtained from paid informants in the group) to a confidential source in the company's management. The

Bureau's purpose was not only to "circumvent efforts to disrupt the corporate meeting," but also to prevent any attempt to "obtain publicity or embarrass" corporate officials.[119]

In another case,[120] anonymous telephone calls were made to the editorial desks of three newspapers in a Midwestern city, advising them that a lecture to be given on a university campus was actually being sponsored by a Communist-front organization. The university had recently lifted its ban on Communist speakers on campus and was experiencing some political difficulty over this decision. The express purpose of the phone calls was to prevent a Communist-sponsored speaker from appearing on campus and, for a time, it appeared to have worked. One of the newspapers contacted the director of the university's conference center. He in turn discussed the meeting with the president of the university who decided to cancel the meeting.[121] The sponsoring organization, supported by the ACLU, took the case to court, and won a ruling that the university could not bar the speaker. (Bureau headquarters then ordered the field office to furnish information on the judge.) Although the lecture went ahead as scheduled, headquarters commended the field office for the affirmative results of its suggestion: the sponsoring organization had been forced to incur additional expense and attorneys' fees, and had received newspaper exposure of its "true communist character."

B. Efforts to Prevent Teaching

Teachers were targeted because the Bureau believed that they were in a unique position to "plant the seeds of communism [or whatever ideology was under attack] in the minds of unsuspecting youth." Further, as noted earlier, it was believed that a teacher's position gave respectability to whatever cause he supported. In one case, a high school teacher was targeted for inviting two poets to attend a class at his school. The poets were noted for their efforts in the draft resistance movement. This invitation led to an investigation by the local police, which in turn provoked sharp criticism from the ACLU. The field office was authorized to send anonymous letters to two local newspapers, to the city Board of Education, and to the high school administration, suggesting that the ACLU should not criticize the police for probing into high school activities, "but should rather have focused attention on [the teacher] who has been a convicted draft dodger." The letter continued, "[the teacher] is the assault on academic freedom and not the local police." The purpose of the letter, according to Bureau documents, was "to highlight [the teacher's] anti-draft activities at the local high school" and to "discourage any efforts" he may make there. The letter was also intended to "show support for the local police against obvious attempts by the New Left to agitate in the high schools."[122] No results were reported.

In another case,[123] a university professor who was "an active participant in New Left demonstrations" had publicly surrendered his draft card and had been arrested twice, (but not convicted) in antiwar demonstrations. The Bureau decided that the professor should be "removed from his position" at the university. The field office was authorized to contact a "confidential source" at a foundation which contributed substantial funds to the university, and "discreetly suggest that the [foundation] may desire to call to the attention of the University administration questions concerning the advisability of [the professor's] continuing his position there." The foundation official was told by the university that the professor's contract would not be renewed, but in fact the professor did continue to teach. The following academic year, therefore, the field office was authorized to furnish additional information to the foundation official on the professor's arrest and conviction (with a suspended sentence) in another demonstration. No results were reported.

In a third instance, the Bureau attempted to "discredit and neutralize" a university professor and the Inter-University Committee for Debate on Foreign Policy, in which he was active. The field office was authorized to send a fictitious name letter to influential state political figures, the mass media, university administrators, and the Board of Regents, accusing the professor and "his protesting cohorts" of "giving aid and comfort to the enemy," and wondering "if the strategy is to bleed the United States white by prolonging the war in Vietnam and pave the way for a takeover by Russia." No results were reported.[124]

C. Efforts to Prevent Writing and Publishing

The Bureau's purpose in targeting attempts to speak was explicitly to prevent the "propagation" of a target's philosophy and to deter "recruitment" of new members. Publications and writers appear to have been targeted for the same reasons. In one example,[125] two university instructors were targeted solely because they were influential in the publication of and contributed financial support to a student "underground" newspaper whose editorial policy was described as "left-of-center, antiestablishment, and opposed [to] the University administration." The Bureau believed that if the two instructors were forced to withdraw their support of the newspaper, it would "fold and cease publication. . . . This would eliminate what voice the New Left has in the area." Accordingly, the field office was authorized to send an anonymous letter to a university official furnishing information concerning the instructors' association with the newspaper, with a warning that if the university did not persuade the instructors to cease their support, the letter's author would be forced to expose their activities publicly. The field office reported that as a result of this technique, both teachers were placed on probation by the university president, which would prevent them from getting any raises.

Newspapers were a common target. The Black Panther Party paper was the subject of a number of actions, both because of its contents and because it was a source of income for the Party.[126] Other examples include contacting the landlord of premises rented by two "New Left" newspapers in an attempt to get them evicted;[127] an anonymous letter to a state legislator protesting the distribution on campus of an underground newspaper "representative of the type of mentality that is following the New Left theory of immorality on certain college campuses";[128] a letter signed "Disgusted Taxpayer and Patron" to advertisers in a student newspaper intended to "increase pressure on the student newspaper to discontinue the type of journalism that had been employed" (an article had quoted a demonstrator's "vulgar language");[129] and proposals (which, according to the Bureau's response to a staff inquiry, were never carried out) to physically disrupt printing plants.[130]

D. Efforts to Prevent Meeting

The Bureau also attempted to prevent target groups from meeting. Frequently used techniques include contacting the, owner of meeting facilities in order to have him refuse to rent to the group;[131] trying to have a group's charter revoked;[132] using the press to disrupt a "closed" meeting by arriving unannounced;[133] and attempting to persuade sponsors to withdraw funds.[134] The most striking examples of attacks meeting, however, involve the use of "disinformation."[135]

In one "disinformation" case, the Chicago Field Office duplicated blank forms prepared by the National Mobilization Committee to End the War in Vietnam ("NMC") soliciting housing for demonstators coming to Chicago for the Democratic National Convention. Chicago filled out 217 of these forms with fictitious names and addresses and sent them to the NMC, which provided them to demonstrators who made "long and useless journeys to locate these addresses." The NMC then decided to discard all replies received on the housing forms rather than have out-of-town demonstrators try to locate nonexistent addresses.[136] (The same program was carried out when the Washington Mobilization Committee distributed housing forms for demonstrators coming to Washington for the 1969 Presidential inaugural ceremonies.)[137]

In another case, during the demonstrations accompanying inauguration ceremonies, the Washington Field Office discovered that NMC marshals were using walkie-talkies to coordinate their movements and activities. WFO used the same citizen band to supply the marshals with misinformation and, pretending to be an NMC unit, countermanded NMC orders.[138]

In a third case[139] a midwest field office disrupted arrangements for state university students to attend the 1969 inaugural demonstrations by making a series of anonymous telephone calls to the transportation company. The calls were designed to confuse both the transportation company and the SDS leaders as to the cost of transportation and the time and place for leaving and returning. This office also placed confusing leaflets around the campus to show different times and places for demonstration-planning meetings, as well as conflicting times and dates for traveling to Washington.

In a fourth instance, the "East Village Other" planned to bomb the

Pentagon with flowers during the 1967 NMC rally in Washington. The New York office answered the ad for a pilot, and kept up the pretense right to the point at which the publisher showed up at the airport with 200 pounds of flowers, with no one to fly the plane. Thus, the Bureau was able to prevent this "agitational-propaganda activity as relates to dropping flowers over Washington."[140]

The cases discussed above are just a few examples of the Bureau's direct attack on speaking, teaching, writing, and meeting. Other instances include targeting the New Mexico Free University for teaching, among other things, "confrontation politics" and "draft counseling training." [141] In another case, an editorial cartoonist for a northeast newspaper was asked to prepare a cartoon which would "ridicule and discredit" a group of antiwar activists who traveled to North Vietnam to inspect conditions there; the cartoon was intended to "depict [the individuals] as traitors to their country for traveling to North Vietnam and making utterances against the foreign policy of the United States."[142] A professor was targeted for being the faculty advisor to a college group which circulated "The Student As Nigger" on campus." A professor conducting a study on the effect and social costs of McCarthyism was targeted because he sought information and help from the American Institute of Marxist Studies.[144] Contacts were made with three separate law schools in an attempt to keep a teaching candidate from being hired, or once hired, from getting his contract renewed.[145]

The attacks on speaking, teaching, writing, and meeting have been examined in some detail because they present, in their purist form, the consequences of acting outside the legal process. Perhaps the Bureau was correct in its assumption that words lead to deeds, and that larger group membership produces a greater risk of violence. Nevertheless, the law draws the line between criminal acts and constitutionally protected activity, and that line must be kept.[146] As Justice Brandeis declared in a different context fifty years ago:

> Our government is the potent, the omnipresent teacher. For good or for ill, it teaches the whole people, by its example. Crime is contagious. If the Government becomes a lawbreaker, it breeds contempt for law: it invites everyman to become a law unto himself. To declare that in the

administration of the criminal law the end justifies the means—to de-
clare that the Government may commit crimes in order to secure the
conviction of the private criminal—would bring terrible retribution.
Against the pernicious doctrine this Court shoud resolutely set its face.
Olmstead v. U.S., *277 U.S. 439,485 (1927)*

NOTES

63. Memorandum from Alan Belmont to L. V. Boardman, 8/28/56, Hearings, vol. 6, exhibit 12.
64. 1,388 of a total of 2,370.
65. Excerpt from materials prepared for the FBI Director's briefing of the House Appropriations Subcommittee, FY 1966, p. 2.
66. [Number missing in original text.] According to Sullivan, membership in the Communist Party declined steadily through the '60s. When the CPUSA membership dropped below a certain figure, Director Hoover ordered that the membership figures be classified. Sullivan believes that this was done to protect the Bureau's appropriations. (Sullivan, 11/1/75, pp. 33–34.)
67. For instance, the Southern Christian Leadership Conference was targeted as a "Black Nationalist–Hate Group." (memorandum from FBI headquarters to all SAC's, 3/4/68, p. 4.)
68. [Number missing in original text.] Memorandum from Alan Belmont to L. V. Beardman, 8/28/56, Hearings, Vol. 6. exhibit 12.
69. Sullivan testimony, 11/1/75, pp. 42–43.
70. As noted earlier, Bureau personnel also trace the decision to adopt counterintelligence methods to the Supreme Court decisions overturning the Smith Act convictions. As the unit chief put it, "The Supreme Court rulings had rendered the Smith Act technically unenforceable ... it made it ineffective to prosecute Communist Party members, made it impossible to prosecute Communist Party members at the time." (Unit chief, 10/16/75, p. 14).
71. Unit chief, 10/16/75, p. 10.
72. Memorandum from New Haven Field Office to FBI Headquarters, 5/24/60.
73. Memorandum from Milwaukee Field Office to FBI Headquarters, 7/13/60, pp. 1–2.
74. Memorandum from FBI Headquarters to San Francisco Field Office, 9/13/68.
75. Sullivan, 11/1/75, p. 29.
76. Unit chief, 10/16/75, p. 40.
77. Charles D. Brennan testimony, Senate Select Committee on Campaign Activities, 6/13/73, p. 10.
78. Robert Shackleford testimony, 2/6/76, pp. 88–89.
79. Memorandum from FBI Headquarters.
80. For example, anonymous letters were sent to the parents of two nonmember students participating in a hunger strike against the war at a midwest college, because the fast was sponsored by the Young Socialist Alliance. The letters warned that the students' participation "could lead to injury to [their] health and damage [their] academic standing," and alerted them to their sons', "involvement in left wing activities." It was hoped that

the parents would "protest to the college that the fast is being allowed" and that the Young Socialist Alliance was permitted on campus. (Memorandum from FBI headquarters to Cleveland Field Office, 11/29/68.)

81. Memorandum from J. H. Gale to Charles Tolsen, 7/30/64, p. 5. Opinion within the Division had been sharply divided on the merits of this transfer. Some saw it as an attempt to bring the Intelligence Division's expertise in penetrating secret organizations to bear on a problem—Klan involvement in the murder of civil rights workers—creating tremendous pressures on the Bureau to solve. Traditional law enforcement methods were insufficient because of a lack of Federal statutes, and the noncooperation of local law enforcement. Others thought that the Klan's activities were essentially a law enforcement problem, and that the transfer would dilute the Division's major internal security responsibility. Those who opposed the transfer lost, and trace many of the Division's subsequent difficulties to this "substantial enlargement" of the Division's responsibilities. (Unit chief, 10/16/75, pp. 45–47.)

82. Memorandum from FBI Headquarters to Atlanta Field Office, 9/2/64, p. 1.

83. FBI Headquarters memorandum, 9/2/64, p. 3.

84. Unit Chief, 10/14/75, p. 54.

85. A few actions were approved against the "Minutemen," when it became known that members were stockpiling weapons.

86. Unit Chief, 10/16/75, p. 48.

87. Moore, 11/3/75, p. 31.

88. Note that this characterization had no substantive meaning within the Bureau. See p. 4.

89. Memorandum from FBI Headquarters to all SAC's, 8/25/67.

90. Black Nationalist supervisor, 10/17/75, pp. 66–67. The supervisor stated that individual NOI members were involved with sporadic violence against police, but the organization was not itself involved in violence. (Black National supervisor, 10/17/75, p. 67.) Moore agreed that the NOI was not involved in organizational violence, adding that the Nation of Islam had been unjustly blamed for violence in the ghetto riots of 1967 and 1968: "We had a good informant coverage of the Nation of Islam. . . . We were able to take a very positive stand and tell the Department of Justice and tell everybody else who accused the Nation of Islam . . . [that they] were not involved in any of the riots or disturbances. Elijah Muhammed kept them under control, and he did not have them on the streets at all during any of the riots." (Moore, 11/3/75, p. 36.)

When asked why, therefore, the NOI was included as a target, Mr. Moore answered: "Because of the potential, they did represent a potential . . . they were a paramilitary type. They had drills, the Fruit of Islam, they had the capability because they were a force to be reckoned with, with the snap of his finger Elijah Muhammed could bring them into any situation. So that there was a very definite potential, very definite potential." (Moore, 11/3/75, p. 37.)

91. The unit chief, who wrote the letter on instructions from his superiors, concedes that the letter directed field offices to gather personal life information on targets, not for "scandalous reasons," but "to deter violence or neutralize the activities of violence-prone groups." (Unit chief, 10/16/75, p. 66.)

92. Moore, 11/3/75, pp. 37, 39, 40.

93. Primary targets listed in this second letter are the Southern Christian Leadership Conference, the Student Nonviolent Coordinating Committee, Revolutionary Action

Movement, Nation of Islam, Stokely Carmichael, H. "Rap" Brown, Martin Luther King, Maxwell Stanford, and Elijah Muhammed. CORE was dropped for reasons no witness was able to reconstruct. The agent who prepared the second letter disagreed with the inclusion of the SCLC, but lost. (Black Nationalist supervisor, 10/17/75, p. 14.)

94. Memorandum from FBI headquarters to all SAC's, 3/4/68, pp. 3–4.

95. Memorandum from FBI Headquarters to Baltimore Field Office, 11/25/68.

96. Memorandum from FBI Headquarters to all SAC's, 1/30/69.

97. This technique, the "snitch jacket," was used in all COINTELPRO programs.

98. Moore, 11/3/75, pp. 34, 50–52.

99. As the New Left supervisor put it, "I cannot recall any document that was written defining New Left as such. It is my impression that the characterization of New Left groups rather than being defined at any specific time by document, it more or less grew. . . ." Agreeing it was a very amorphous term, he added: "It has never been strictly defined, as far as I know. . . . It is more or less an attitude I would think." (New Left supervisor, 10/28/75, pp. 7–8.)

100. New Left supervisor, 10/28/75, pp. 21–22.

101. Memorandum from Charles D. Brennan to William C. Sullivan, 5/9/68.

102. [Number and note missing in original text.]

103. Memorandum from FBI headquarters to all SAC's, 5/23/68. Memorandum from FBI headquarters to all SACs, 10/9/68. This time the field offices got the message. One example of information furnished under the "Immorality" caption comes from the Boston field office:

"[Informant] who has provided reliable information in the past concerning the activities of the New Left in the Metropolitan Boston area has advised that numerous meetings concerning anti-Vietnam and/or draft activity are conducted by members sitting around the table or a living room completely in the nude. These same individuals, both male and female, live and sleep together regularly and it is not unusual to have these people take up residence with a different partner after a six or seven month period.

"According to the informant, the living conditions and habits of some of the New Left adherents are appalling in that certain individuals have been known to wear the same clothes for an estimated period of weeks and in some instances for months. Personal hygiene and eating habits are equally neglected by these people, the informant said."

"The informant has noted that those individuals who most recently joined the movement are in most instances the worst offenders as far as moral and personal habits are concerned. However, if these individuals remain in the movement for any length of time, their appearance and personal habits appear to improve somewhat." (Memorandum from Boston Field Office to FBI Headquarters, 6/13/68.)

106. Memorandum from FBI Headquarters to all SACs, 10/9/68.

107. Memorandum from FBI Headquarters to Chicago Field Office, 8/28/68.

108. Memorandum from FBI Headquarters to all SAC's, 9/9/68.

109. Note that there was no attempt to determine whether the allegations were true. Ramsey Clark, Attorney General at the time, testified that he did not know that either directive had been issued and that "they are highly improper." He also noted that the Bureau's close working relationship with state and local police forces had made it necessary to "preempt the FBI" in cases involving the investigation of police misconduct "we found it necessary to use the Civil Rights Division, and that is basically what we did." (Clark, 12/3/75, Hearings vol. 6. pp. 254–255.)

110. Memorandum from FBI Headquarters to all SAC's, 7/6/68.

111. The New Left supervisor confirmed what the documents reveal: "legitimate" (nonviolent) antiwar groups were targeted because they were "lending aid and comfort" to more disruptive groups. According to the New Left supervisor:

> This [nonviolent groups protesting against the war] was the type of thing that the New Left, the violent portion, would seize upon. They could use the legitimacy of an accepted college group or outside group to further their interests." (New Left supervisor, 10/28/75, p. 39.)
>
> Nonviolent groups were thus disrupted so there would be less opportunity for a violent group to make use of them and their respectability. Professors active in "New Left matters," whether involved in violence or just in general protest, were targeted for "using [their] good offices to lend aid and comfort to the entire protest movement or to help disrupt the school through [their] programs." (New Left supervisor, 10/28/75, p. 69.)

112. Memorandum from FBI Headquarters, Minneapolis Field Office, 11/4/68.

113. Memorandum from FBI Headquarters to San Antonio Field Office, 8/27/68.

114. Huston was the Presidential assistant who coordinated the 1970 recommendations by an interagency committee for expanded domestic intelligence, including concededly illegal activity. The so-called "Huston Plan" is the subject of a separate report.

115. Tom Charles Huston testimony, 9/23/75, Hearings, Vol. 2, p. 45.

116. The usual constitutional inquiry is whether the government is "chilling" First Amendment rights by indirectly discouraging a protected activity while pursuing an otherwise legitimate purpose. In the case of COINTELPRO, the Bureau was not attempting indirectly to chill free speech or association; it was squarely attacking their exercise.

117. The percentage is derived from a cross-indexed tabulation of the Petersen Committee summaries. Interestingly, these categories account for 39 percent of the approved "New Left" proposals, which reflects both the close connection between antiwar activities and the campuses, and the "aid and comfort" theory of targeting, in which teachers were targeted for advocating an end to the war through nonviolent means.

118. The group was composed largely of university teachers and clergymen who had bought shares in order to attend the meeting. (Memorandum from Minneapolis Field Office to FBI headquarters, 4/1/70.)

119. Memorandum from FBI Headquarters to Minneapolis Field Office, 4/23/70; memorandum from Minneapolis Field Office to FBI Headquarters, 4/1/70.

120. Memorandum from Detroit Field Office to FBI Headquarters, 10/26/60; memoranda from FBI Headquarters to Detroit Field Office, 10/27/60, 10/28/60, 10/31/60; memorandum from F. J. Baumgardner to Alan H. Belmont, 10/26/60.

121. It is interesting to note that after the anonymous calls to the newspapers giving information on the "communist nature" of the sponsor, the conference center director called the local FBI office to ask for information on the speaker. He was informed that Bureau records are confidential and that the Bureau could not make any comment.

122. Memorandum from FBI Headquarters to Pittsburgh Field Office, 6/19/69.

123. Memorandum from FBI Headquarters to Pittsburgh Field Office, 5/1/70.

124. Memorandum from Detroit Field Office to FBI Headquarters, 10/11/66, memorandum from FBI Headquarters to Detroit Field Office, 10/26/66.

125. Memorandum from Mobile Field Office to FBI Headquarters, 12/9/70; memorandum from FBI Headquarters to Mobile Field Office, 12/31/70; memorandum from Mobile Field Office to FBI Headquarters, 2/3/71.

126. In one example, a letter signed "A Black Parent" was sent to the mayor, the Superintendent of Schools, the Commander of the American Legion, and two newspapers in a northeastern city protesting a high school's subscription to the BPP newspaper. The letter was also intended to focus attention on the teacher who entered the subscription "so as to deter him from implementing black extremist literature and philosophy into the Black History curriculum" of the school system. (Memorandum from Buffalo Field Office to FBI Headquarters, 2/5/70.)

127. Memorandum from Los Angeles Field Office to FBI Headquarters, 9/9/68; memorandum from FBI Headquarters to SAC, Los Angeles Field Office, 9/23/68.

128. Memorandum from Newark Field Office to FBI Headquarters, 5/23/69; memorandum from FBI Headquarters to Newark Field Office, 6/4/69.

129. Memorandum from Detroit Field Office to FBI Headquarters, 2/28/69; memorandum from FBI Headquarters to Detroit Field Office, 3/27/69.

130. For example, one proposal requested that the FBI Lab prepare a quart of solution "capable of duplicating a scent of the most foul smelling feces available," along with a dispenser capable of squirting a narrow stream for a distance of approximately three feet. The proposed targets were the physical plant of a New Left publisher and BPP publications prior to their distribution. Headquarters instructed the field office to furnish more information about the purpose for the material's use and the manner and security with which it would be used. The idea was then apparently dropped. (Memorandum from Detroit Meld Office to FBI Headquarters, 10/13/70; memorandum from FBI Headquarters to Detroit Field Office, 10/23/70.)

131. Memorandum from FBI Headquarters to Los Angeles Field Office, 9/23/68.

132. Memorandum from FBI Headquarters to San Antonio Field Office, 5/13/69.

133. Memorandum from FBI Headquarters to Indianapolis Field Office, 6/17/68.

134. Memorandum from FBI Headquarters to all SAC's, 12/30/68.

135. One of the 12 standard techniques referred to in the New Left memorandum discussed at pp. 25–26, disinformation bridges the line between "counterintelligence" and sabotage.

136. Memorandum from Chicago Field Office to FBI Headquarters, 9/9/68; memorandum from Charles Brennan to William C. Sullivan, 8/15/68.

137. Memorandum from Washington Field Office to FBI Headquarters, 1/21/69.

138. Egil Krogh has stated to the Committee staff that he was in charge of coordinating D.C. law enforcement efforts during demonstrations, and gained the cooperation of NMC marshals to ensure an orderly demonstration. This law enforcement/NMC coordination was effected through the same walkie-talkie system the Bureau was disrupting. (Memorandum from FBI Headquarters to Washington Field Office, 1/10/69; staff summary of Egil Krogh interview, 5/23/75.)

139. Memorandum from Cincinnati Field Office to FBI Headquarters, 12/20/68; memorandum from FBI Headquarters to Cinncinnati Field Office, 12/29/68.

140. Memoranda from New York Field Office to FBI Headquarters, 9/15/67, 9/26/67, and 10/17/67; memorandum from FBI Headquarters to New York Field Office, 9/29/67. By letter of January 14, 1976, the Bureau submitted specific instances of "action, other than arrest and prosecution, to prevent any stage of [a] crime or violent acts from be-

Introduction to
Jon Wiener's

Gimme Some Truth

ON FEBRUARY 4, 1972, Senator Strom Thurmond sent a memo to the White House and Attorney General John Mitchell informing them that John Lennon and so-called radical friends were planning a national concert tour to coincide with the 1972 election campaign. Arguing that Lennon's appearances would "pour tremendous amounts of money into the coffers of the New Left" and lead to confrontations between protesters and police, Thurmond suggested that the government deport Lennon, a British citizen. Within a few weeks, the Immigration and Naturalization Service (INS) told Lennon that he had to leave the country.

While government surveillance of prominent entertainers and artists was not new, Lennon's deportation order was one of the unusual instances when the government publicly took hostile action against a prominent figure. Lennon fought back. He sued the INS and former attorney generals Mitchell and Richard Kleindienst, arguing he was a victim of a political vendetta. After Lennon turned to the courts to prevent his deportation, government harassment continued on another front. A 1972 FBI memo reported that the New York City Police Department was trying to obtain evidence to arrest Lennon and Yoko Ono for narcotics use.

It took Jon Wiener, a professor of history at the University of California, Irvine, and a contributing editor of *The Nation*, fourteen years of litigation to force the government to release pages it had withheld under the Freedom of Information Act from Lennon's FBI file. Finally, in 1997, the ACLU, acting on behalf of Wiener, and the FBI agreed to settle.

Much of the information that was released was trivial. For example,

ing initiated" which had been taken. The examples were intended to aid in developing "preventive action" guidelines.

One of the examples was the prevention of the publisher's plan to drop flowers over the Pentagon: "A plan was thus thwarted which could well have resulted in tragedy had another pilot accepted such a dangerous flying mission and violated Federal or local regulations in flying low over the Pentagon which is also in the heavy traffic pattern of the Washington National Airport." The letter does not explain why it was necessary to act covertly in this case. If flying over the Pentagon violates Federal regulations, the Bureau could have arrested those involved when they arrived at the airport. No informant was involved; the newspaper had advertised openly for a pilot.

141. Memorandum from FBI Headquarters to Albuquerque Field Office, 3/19/69.
142. Memorandum from Boston Field Office to FBI Headquarters, 1/22/66.
143. [Number is missing in original text.] Memorandum from FBI Headquarters to El Paso Field Office, 12/6/68.
144. Memorandum from FBI Headquarters to New York Field Office, 3/19/65.
145. Memorandum from FBI Headquarters to Cleveland and Boston Field Offices, 5/6/64.
146. Mr. Huston learned that lesson as well:

"We went from this kind of sincere intention, honest intention, to develop a series of justifications and rationalizations based upon this . . . distorted view of inherent executive power and from that, whether it was direct . . . or was indirect or inevitable, as I tend to think it is, you went down the road to where you ended up, with these people going into the Watergate.

"And so that has convinced me that you have just got to draw the line at the top of the totem pole, and that we would then have to take the risk—it is not a risk-free choice, but it is one that, I am afraid, in my judgment, that we do not have any alternative but to take." (Huston, 9/23/75, p. 45.)

[Editor's Note: Introduction and Summary sections not reprinted. Notes reflect original numbering.]

one report written by an informer in 1972 described a trip to New York by antiwar activists to meet with movement leaders, including "a girl there named Linda" who had a parrot that "interjects 'Right On' whenever the conversation gets rousing." The FBI refused to release this report for twenty-five years, going all the way to the Supreme Court to prevent the public from learning about the voluble parrot.

The Lennon files contained no evidence that "Lennon committed any criminal acts: no bombings, no terrorism, no conspiracies. His activities were precisely the kind protected by the First Amendment, which is not limited to U.S. citizens," Wiener writes. What the Lennon story reveals is "the culture of secrecy that undermines democracy."

"The John Lennon files," he concludes, "constitute a small but significant chapter in the history of the sixties, and of the Watergate era, and also in the history of bureaucratic secrecy and government abuse of power. They confirm Richard Nixon's place in the annals of rock 'n' roll as the man who tried to deport John Lennon, and thus they support the claim that rock in the sixties had some kind of political significance."

ADDITIONAL SOURCES

Coleman, Ray. *Lennon.* New York, St. Louis, San Francisco, Toronto: McGraw-Hill Book Company, 1984.

Mitgang, Herbert. *Dangerous Dossiers: Exposing the Secret War Against America's Greatest Authors.* New York: Ballantine, 1988.

Wiener, Jon. *Come Together: John Lennon and His Time.* New York: Random House, 1984.

Jon Wiener

Introduction and Getting Started

GIMME SOME TRUTH: THE JOHN LENNON FBI FILES, 1999

Introduction

When FBI director J. Edgar Hoover reported to the Nixon White House in 1972 about the bureau's surveillance of John Lennon, he began by explaining that Lennon was a "former member of the Beatles singing group." Apparently Hoover wanted to show that although he was no rock fan, at least he knew who Lennon was. When a copy of this letter arrived in response to my 1981 Freedom of Information Act (FOIA) request, the entire text was withheld, as were almost 200 other pages, on the grounds that releasing it would endanger the national security. That seemed unlikely. So, with the help of the American Civil Liberties Union (ACLU) of Southern California, I filed a lawsuit under the FOIA in 1983, asking the court to order the release of the withheld pages. Fourteen years later, after the case went to the Supreme Court, the FBI finally agreed to settle almost all the outstanding issues of the case, to release all but ten of the documents, and to pay $204,000 to the ACLU for court costs and attorney fees. The most significant 100 pages of the Lennon file are reproduced in this volume.

The Lennon FBI files document an era when rock music seemed to have real political force, when youth culture, for perhaps the first time in American history, was mounting a serious challenge to the status quo in Washington, when President Nixon responded by mobilizing the FBI and the Immigration and Naturalization Service (INS) to silence the man from England who was singing "Give Peace a Chance" at his first live concert in the United States since 1966. Lennon's file dates from 1971, a year when the war in Vietnam was killing hundreds of thousands, when Nixon was facing reelection, and when the "clever Beatle" was living in New York and joining up with the antiwar movement. The Nixon administration learned that he and some radical friends were talking about organizing a national concert tour to coincide with the 1972 election campaign, a tour that would combine rock music and radical politics, during which Lennon would urge young people to register to vote, and vote against the war, which meant, of course, against Nixon.

The administration learned about Lennon's idea from an unlikely source: Senator Strom Thurmond. Early in 1972 he sent a secret memo to Attorney General John Mitchell and the White House reporting on Lennon's plans and suggesting that deportation "would be a strategy counter-measure."

That was exactly the sort of thing John Dean, the counsel to the president, had suggested in his famous 1971 memo: "We can use the available political machinery to screw our political enemies." The word was passed to the INS, which began deportation proceedings a month later.[1] The Nixon administration's efforts to "neutralize" Lennon—their term—to silence him as a spokesman for the peace movement, are the central subject of Lennon's FBI file.

Throughout fourteen years of FOIA litigation over the files, which began in 1983, the FBI maintained that its surveillance of Lennon was not an abuse of power but rather a legitimate law enforcement activity. It's true that in 1972 Lennon associated with antiwar activists who had been convicted of conspiring to disrupt the Democratic National Convention four years earlier. It's true that he spoke out against the war at rallies and demonstrations. But the files contain no evidence that Lennon committed any criminal acts: no bombings, no terrorism, no conspiracies. His activities were precisely the kind protected by the First Amendment, which is not limited to U.S. citizens.

The story of the Lennon files is also the story of the fourteen-year legal battle to win release of the withheld pages, a story about the ways the Reagan, Bush, and Clinton administrations resisted the requirements of the FOIA. The basic issue here was not simply John Lennon. The basic issue was that government officials everywhere like secrecy. By keeping the public from learning what they have done, they hope to avoid criticism, hinder the opposition, and maintain power over citizens and their elected representatives. Classified files and official secrets lie at the heart of the modern governmental bureaucracy and permit the undemocratic use of power to go unrecognized and unchallenged by citizens.

Democracy, however, is not powerless before this practice. In the fight against government secrecy, America has led the world. In 1966 Congress passed the FOIA, which requires that officials make public the information in their files to "any person" who requests it, unless it falls into a small number of exempted categories, including "national security." The Act was substantially expanded in 1974 in the wake of revelations of White House abuse of power during the Watergate scandal. The FOIA, in effect, created a notable challenge to the history of government secrecy; it provided a set of rules and procedures, officials and offices dedicated not to the collection and maintenance of secrets but rather to their release to the public. Journalists, scholars, and activists have used the FOIA to scrutinize the operations of government agencies and expose official misconduct and lying, including the FBI's illegal efforts to harass, intimidate, disrupt, and otherwise interfere with lawful political actions. The John Lennon FBI files provide an example.

Before considering that history, it's important to acknowledge that the FOIA in many respects has been a spectacular success, as Americans have demonstrated an impressive appetite for government information. In 1990, for example, federal agencies received 491,000 FOIA requests and spent $83 million responding to them. The Defense Department received the most, 118,000 requests, while the FBI received 11,000, and the CIA, 4,000. The FOIA further requires that agencies report the extent of their denials of such requests: the agency with the highest denial rate in 1990, strangely enough, was the Office of Ethics, which refused to release 75 percent of requested documents. In contrast, the Department of Health and Human Services denied only 2 percent of the requests it received. The staff at the FBI's Freedom of Information Section processing FOIA requests consists of eight agents and 245 support employees, sixty-five of whom work on national security declassification. In 1990, 421,000 previously classified pages were released; requesters filed 993 administrative appeals of decisions to withhold documents; 263 requests that had been denied were in litigation.[2]

The most fundamental justification for governmental secrecy is "national security." Thus the FOIA exempts from disclosure any material "which reasonably could be expected to cause damage to the national security."[3] What constitutes a "reasonable expectation" is obviously the issue. Because of the long-standing belief in the legitimacy of keeping secret diplomatic and military information, the claim that releasing any particular document could reasonably be expected to damage "national security" has been difficult to refute, which opens the FOIA to abuse by officials with something to hide. How federal officials have interpreted the national security exemption to the FOIA provides the most important test of government practice, and lies at the heart of the John Lennon FBI files litigation.

The original FOIA of 1966 had no provision for judicial review of "national security" information. The Act exempted material "specifically required by Executive Order to be kept secret in the interest of national defense or foreign policy." The law, however, contained no provisions authorizing courts to consider government decisions to withhold documents under the "national security" claim. In a 1973 Supreme Court ruling, Justice Potter Stewart pointed out this flaw: the FOIA provided "no means to question any Executive decision to stamp a document 'secret,' however cynical, myopic, or even corrupt that decision might have been."[4] The Court went on to note that Congress could establish procedures to permit courts to review such decisions.

This use of the "national security" exemption to conceal government misconduct came to the fore in 1974, in the wake of the Watergate revelations of White House abuses of power. At that time the issue was framed in an apolitical way as a problem of "overclassification of national security information." Congress held extensive hearings documenting the problem and accepted the Supreme Court's suggestion, passing a series of amendments that significantly strengthened the FOIA, especially in relation to "national security" claims. The 1974 amendments instructed courts to determine *de novo* whether the national security exemption was being properly applied in particular cases. Courts were authorized to conduct *in camera* reviews of documents for which the government claimed the national security exemption. Most important, courts were empowered to overrule executive officials' decisions classifying documents under the "national security" claim. For the first time, courts could order the release of improperly classified documents. President Ford vetoed the legislation, objecting specifically to the provision empowering the courts to overrule executive branch classification decisions. This provision, he declared, was an unconstitutional infringement on executive power. Congress overrode Ford's veto, and the amendments became part of the FOIA. Nine years later, the ACLU of California asked the court to overrule the Reagan administration's claims that parts of the Lennon FBI file had to be withheld to protect "national security."

Secret government files like Lennon's have a history. The Cold War provided a great impetus to government secrecy, which was justified as a necessary response to Soviet efforts to "destroy our free and democratic system" at a time when their "preferred technique is to subvert by infiltration and intimidation," as the government explained in 1950 in the policy statement "NSC 68." Cold War presidents secretly authorized the FBI to monitor radical activists, who included not just potential spies or saboteurs but "writers, lecturers, newsmen, entertainers, and others in the mass media field" who "might influence others against the national interest," as the Senate's Church Committee explained after Watergate.[5]

But the federal government began spying on Americans long before the Cold War, as Daniel Patrick Moynihan observes in his book *Secrecy*. Most of the structure of secrecy now in place, he argues, has its origin in the World War I Espionage Act, passed into law in 1917 at the urging of President Woodrow Wilson. The former Princeton history professor declared in his 1915 State of the Union message that recent immigrants had "poured the poison of disloyalty into the very arteries of our national life," and he urged Congress to "save the honor and self respect of the nation. Such creatures of passion, disloyalty, and anarchy must be crushed out." Congress responded with the Espionage Act and, in 1918, the Sedition Act, which made it a crime to "utter, print, write, or publish any disloyal, profane, scurrilous, or abusive language about the form of government of the United States." It also made it a crime to "advocate any curtailment of production in this country of any thing . . . necessary or essential to the prosecution of the war."[6]

In fact the first FBI files on people suspected of disloyalty date from before World War I. The bureau was created in 1908; it opened a file on Ezra Pound in 1911, after he published in the first issue of *The Masses*, a socialist magazine. It opened a file on Max Eastman in 1912 on the grounds that he was editor of *The Masses* and "a true believer in free love." It opened a file on Walter Lippmann the same year, noting that the recent Harvard graduate was secretary to the socialist mayor of Schenectady. Herbert Mitgang and Natalie Robins have shown that the FBI kept files on at least 150 of the country's leading writers, from Sinclair Lewis to William Faulkner to Ernest Hemingway to Norman Mailer and James Baldwin.[7] Thus the insatiable appetite of Hoover's FBI for derogatory gossip and malicious trivia, evident in the Lennon file, was nothing new. But unlike other writers and artists the FBI watched, Lennon wasn't persecuted simply because of what he thought or wrote. The Nixon administration was after him because of what he did—and what he planned to do.

The Lennon files constitute a small but significant chapter in the history of the sixties, and of the Watergate era, and also in the history of bureaucratic secrecy and government abuse of power. They confirm Richard Nixon's place in the annals of rock 'n' roll as the man who tried to deport John Lennon, and thus they support the claim that rock in the sixties had some kind of political significance. Of course some have seen Nixon's pursuit of Lennon as a simple case of paranoia, in which the president and the New Left shared the same delusion. But the record shows there was a rationale behind Nixon's campaign to silence Lennon that was not simply nutty. Lennon's plan to mobilize young voters against the war may not have affected the outcome of the 1972 election, but it had a clear and reasonable logic behind it.

The Lennon FBI files include some comic and hilarious moments. The FBI at points looks more like the Keystone Cops than the Gestapo. But the campaign to "neutralize" Lennon wasn't a joke; it was a crime.

The experiences of exaltation and anger that rock music provided in the late sixties were not in themselves political experiences. Lennon knew that. He also knew that rock could become a potent political force when it was linked to real political organizing, when, for example, it brought young people together to protest the Vietnam War. The Lennon FBI files chronicle Lennon's commitment to test the political potential of rock music. They also document the government's commitment to stop him. The investigation of Lennon was an abuse of power, a kind of rock 'n' roll Watergate.

Getting Started

Early in 1981, shortly after John Lennon's murder on December 8, 1980, I filed a Freedom of Information Act (FOIA) request for any files the FBI had kept on Lennon. The FBI released some documents in May. But of the 281 pages staff said they had reviewed, they withheld 199 (more than 70 percent) in their entirety. The documents were withheld mostly under three different FOIA exemptions: protection of the privacy of others named in a document, protection of the identities of confidential sources, and "national security."[1]

The documents that were released included one page that had Lennon's name at the top but was otherwise blacked out under the national security exemption; a variety of documents discussing the Nixon administration's effort in 1972 to deport Lennon, including a letter suggesting that Lennon be "arrested if at all possible on possession of narcotics charge," which would make him "immediately deportable"; and several pages, completely blacked out, from the Detroit FBI reporting on Lennon's appearance at the "John Sinclair Freedom Rally" in Ann Arbor in December 1971. Most interesting was a letter from J. Edgar Hoover to H. R. Haldeman, assistant to the president, dated April 25, 1972, that had been withheld in its entirety under the national security exemption. Since Haldeman was the closest official to Nixon, this document provided crucial evidence that the Lennon investigation was a political one, significant at the highest levels of the Nixon White House.

When these documents began arriving in my mailbox in the spring of 1981, American politics was beginning a shift of historic proportions toward the right. Ronald Reagan had been elected in November 1980, bringing to power the Republican right wing that had failed to elect Barry Goldwater sixteen years earlier. The "Reagan Revolution" rested on an ideological commitment to "law and order," which Lennon had challenged, and a passionate hostility to "the sixties," which Lennon personified. The fight for the Lennon files would be a battle with the Reagan administration.

When the FBI informed me it was withholding 70 percent of the Lennon files, the letter also said, "You may appeal to the associate attorney general." I did. My appeal argued that information about Lennon's plans to demonstrate against Nixon should not have been withheld under the "national security" exemption, a decision I called "arbitrary and capricious." I argued that the other withheld material was "not properly covered by the exemptions claimed."

Reagan's assistant attorney general for legal policy, Jonathan C. Rose, responded six weeks later: "After careful consideration of your appeal, I have decided to affirm the initial action in this case." The national security material, he wrote, was "being referred to the Department Review Committee for review," but the rest had been "properly withheld."

Six months after that, the assistant attorney general informed me that the review committee had completed its work and concluded that eight of the national security pages could be declassified. But the FBI still wasn't going to release them. While those pages were no longer being withheld on national security grounds, the bureau now claimed they fell under other exemptions: personal privacy and confidential source information. So my administrative appeal produced little of significance. The assistant attorney general's letter denying my appeal concluded, "Judicial review of my action on this appeal is available to you in the United States District Court for the judicial district in which you reside." It was time to find a lawyer.

The FOIA gives federal courts the power "to order the production of any agency records improperly withheld from the complainant." That's what I wanted the courts to do. I asked a variety of organizations and attorneys for help in bringing an FOIA lawsuit against the FBI. Victor Navasky, editor of *The Nation* magazine, suggested four criteria for picking a lawyer: find one you trust; who understands the case; who cares about it; and who will do it for no money except an award of fees at the end. Courts had awarded attorney fees in some successful FOIA appeals, recently in an appeal for documents about Vietnam Veterans against the War (VVAW), so money at the end remained a possibility.

In search of a lawyer, I talked to the Reporters Committee for Freedom of the Press, the Fund for Investigative Journalism, and the Fund for Open Information and Accountability ("FOIA, Inc."). I talked to the Media Alliance in San Francisco and the Center for Investigative Reporting in Oakland. I talked to the American Historical Association's Committee on Access to Documents. I talked to the Playboy Foundation, well known for its defense of the First Amendment. I talked to Frank Wilkinson, who had sued the FBI for his file, the largest on any individual, and who headed an organization called the National Coalition against Repressive Legislation originally established to fight HUAC. I talked to the San Francisco attorney who had been awarded fees in the VVAW case. I talked to prominent radical attorneys including Leonard Weinglass. I talked to Leon Friedman, who Victor Navasky called "the best FOIA attorney in the country."

All the attorneys told me the same thing that Leon Friedman did: "I took a couple of these, hoping to win, and got burned. I'm not in a position to do this kind of thing. You can't win on national security any more. Try the ACLU."

So I talked to Ramona Ripston and Fred Okrand of the ACLU of Southern California. Okrand, who was legal director, told me, "I don't know of anyone who'd be interested, but I'll ask around and if I come up with anyone, I'll have them call you." That was in January 1983, and it didn't sound promising. But shortly thereafter, Okrand's successor, Paul Hoffman, called to schedule a meeting at which I would present my case to him and Mark Rosenbaum, the ACLU general counsel.

At the meeting, I presented my documents and arguments, anxious that this was my last best hope. Nervously, I showed that I had followed the ACLU's model letters requesting material under the FOIA and that I had exhausted my administrative appeals. It turned out that their biggest concern was not about the case but about their potential client, the possible plaintiff: was I some kind of obsessed fan? or perhaps a burned-out hippie, living in the past? or a conspiracy buff, eager to prove Reagan had ordered Lennon's assassination? They brightened noticeably when they learned I had been granted tenure six years earlier at the University of California, Irvine; that I had published not just in *Radical America, Dissent,* and *Socialist Review* but also in the *American Historical Review* and the *Journal of Modern History,* and the distinguished British scholarly journal *Past and Present.* They saw they would be able to argue that the plaintiff was a respected historian who sought the Lennon files as part of his research on the American past. Convinced that their potential client was a mild-mannered professor and not some kind of nut, the two of them decided the ACLU of Southern California would take the case. Rosenbaum, who eventually succeeded Hoffman as ACLU legal director, served as the colead attorney throughout the next fifteen years of litigation.

In a 1998 interview, he discussed the ACLU's considerations in taking the case: "It was simple to decide. The timing was coincident with a national frustration with the administration of the FOIA, particularly in the areas of national security and informants. Agencies were coming forward with boilerplate refusals. The law's presumption in favor of disclosure had, for all intents and purposes, been dissolved, and the FBI in particular was choosing what they wanted to disclose. If any case could take us back to legislative objective favoring disclosure, this would be the one." So the ACLU's first goal was not just to get the documents, but to challenge "systemic problems in implementing the FOIA."[2]

The ACLU had a second goal: to publicize the value of the FOIA and expose the ways in which it was being subverted by the FBI. The files on Lennon provided an excellent example that could win media attention.

Mark Rosenbaum is a remarkable figure. Known as both a brilliant legal strategist and a passionate and effective courtroom advocate, he graduated from the University of Michigan in 1970 and went on to Harvard Law School. In 1973, on the verge of dropping out because the classes seemed so uninteresting, Rosenbaum went to work as a clerk in the law office of Leonard Boudin and Leonard Weinglass. At that moment, they, along with Ramsey Clark, happened to be representing Daniel Ellsberg, the government researcher who was being prosecuted by the Nixon administration for leaking the Pentagon Papers to the *New York Times.* Rosenbaum describes the experience of working on the Ellsberg defense as "the turning point of my life."

JOHN C. STENNIS, MISS., CHAIRMAN

STUART SYMINGTON, MO.   MARGARET CHASE SMITH, MAINE
HENRY M. JACKSON, WASH.   STROM THURMOND, S.C.
SAM J. ERVIN, JR., N.C.   JOHN G. TOWER, TEX.
HOWARD W. CANNON, NEV.   PETER H. DOMINICK, COLO.
THOMAS J. McINTYRE, N.H.   BARRY GOLDWATER, ARIZ.
HARRY F. BYRD, JR., VA.   RICHARD S. SCHWEIKER, PA.
HAROLD E. HUGHES, IOWA   WILLIAM B. SAXBE, OHIO
LLOYD BENTSEN, TEX.

T. EDWARD BRASWELL, JR., CHIEF COUNSEL AND STAFF DIRECTOR

United States Senate

COMMITTEE ON ARMED SERVICES
WASHINGTON, D.C. 20510

February 4, 1972

FEB 7 1972

Honorable William Timmons
The White House
Washington, D. C.

Dear Bill:

Find attached a memorandum to me from the staff of the
Internal Security Subcommittee of the Judiciary Committee.
I am a member of the subcommittee as well as the full
Judiciary Committee.

This appears to me to be an important matter, and I think
it would be well for it to be considered at the highest
level.

As I can see, many headaches might be avoided if appropriate action be taken in time.

With kindest regards and best wishes,

Very truly,

Strom Thurmond

Strom Thurmond

ST:x

Enclosure

P.S. Also find attached a memorandum entitled "John
M. Thomas" concerning the Vice President about which
I also talked with you. I sent the Vice President a
copy of this.

The Thurmond letter.

JOHN LENNON

John Lennon, presently visiting in the United States, is a British citizen. He was a member of the former musical group known as "The Beatles." He has claimed a date of birth of September 10, 1940, and he is presently married to a Japanese citizen, one Yoko Ono.

The December 12, 1971, issue of the New York Times shows that Lennon and his wife appeared for about 10 minutes at about 3:00 a.m. on December 11, 1971, at a rally held in Ann Arbor, Michigan, to protest the continuing imprisonment of John Sinclair, a radical poet.

Radical New Left leaders Rennie Davis, Jerry Rubin, Leslie Bacon, Stu Albert, Jay Craven, and others have recently gone to the New York City area. This group has been strong advocates of the program to "dump Nixon." They have devised a plan to hold rock concerts in various primary election states for the following purposes: to obtain access to college campuses; to stimulate 18-year old registration; to press for legislation legalizing marihuana; to finance their activities; and to recruit persons to come to San Diego during the Republican National Convention in August 1972. These individuals are the same persons who were instrumental in disrupting the Democratic National Convention in Chicago in 1968.

According to a confidential source, whose information has proved reliable in the past, the activities of Davis and his group will follow the pattern of the rally mentioned above with reference to John Sinclair. David Sinclair, the brother of John, will be the road manager for these rock festivals.

Davis and his cohorts intend to use John Lennon as a drawing card to promote the success of the rock festivals and rallies. The source feels that this will pour tremendous amounts of money into the coffers of the New Left and can only inevitably lead to a clash between a controlled mob organized by this group and law enforcement officials in San Diego.

The source felt that if Lennon's visa is terminated it would be a strategy counter-measure. The source also noted the caution which must be taken with regard to the possible alienation of the so-called 18-year old vote if Lennon is expelled from the country.

Memo from Senate Internal Security Subcommittee staff accompanying the Thurmond letter.

March 6, 1972

Dear Strom:

In connection with your previous inquiry
concerning the former member of the Beatles,
John Lennon, I thought you would be interested
in learning that the Immigration and Naturalization Service has served notice on him that
he is to leave this country no later than
March 15. You may be assured the information
you previously furnished has been appropriately
noted.

With warm regards,

Sincerely,

William E. Timmons
Assistant to the President

Honorable Strom Thurmond
United States Senate
Washington, D. C. 20510

bcc: Mr. Harlington Wood, Department of Justice - for your information
bcc: Tom Korologos - for your information

WET:VO:jlh

The White House response.

After the Ellsberg case, Rosenbaum went back to Harvard Law School and graduated in 1974. He then joined the ACLU of Southern California as a staff counsel—hired by the new executive director, Ramona Ripston. Stanley Sheinbaum, then head of the ACLU Board of Directors, personally put up the $10,000 required to pay Rosenbaum's salary for the first year. The year before taking on the Lennon FBI files case, he had gone to the Supreme Court, along with Harvard law professor Laurence Tribe, to challenge school segregation in Los Angeles.[3]

In subsequent years Rosenbaum would serve as colead counsel in the ACLU lawsuit seeking to overturn California's Proposition 187, the anti-immigrant initiative, and as the point man in the ACLU fight to maintain affirmative action programs. He also successfully defended the constitutionality of the "Motor Voter" registration act, challenged by California governor Pete Wilson before the Ninth Circuit Court of Appeals. And in 1995 he argued before the Supreme Court a case in which the Court held that residency requirements for Aid to Families with Dependent Children program recipients were unconstitutional.[4]

When the ACLU decided in 1983 to take the Lennon files case, Rosenbaum called Dan Marmalefsky, a Los Angeles attorney with the firm Hufstedler, Miller, Carlson & Beardsley (which later merged with Morrison & Foerster). Another brilliant young lawyer, Marmalefsky had graduated from the University of California, Berkeley in 1976 and from Yale Law School in 1980, where he received an award for his work in legal services. He went on to specialize in complex civil and criminal business litigation. In 1982 he had served as co-counsel for a group of Salvadorean refugees seeking political asylum, assisting with an appeal to the Ninth Circuit. He also had experience with FOIA litigation, primarily from using it for discovery in criminal cases, starting with the defense of John DeLorean in 1982, and had worked with Rosenbaum pro bono on several other ACLU cases. Marmalefsky accepted Rosenbaum's offer to work on this one, and the two served as co-lead counsel for the next fifteen years.

Marmalefsky told me that the decision to take a pro bono case was his alone and didn't require permission from anyone at his firm. "The basic question concerns time, balancing pro bono work against the amount of fee-generating work I do," he explained. "Because when I take pro bono cases, I don't do it halfway. I treat them the same as any other matters and devote the necessary time—whatever it takes."[5]

The two had just won a case before the Supreme Court in 1983, an ACLU challenge to the California Penal Code section making it a crime for a person to refuse to provide identification when asked by a police officer. The Court accepted their argument that the law violated the First Amendment and voided the statute for vagueness and overbreadth.[6]

In 1985 he and Rosenbaum would bring to the Supreme Court a case challenging the constitutionality of the enforcement of draft registration.[7] He also litigated prosecutors' duty to present exculpatory testimony before a grand jury and the right of public access to juvenile court proceedings. But Marmalefsky's practice wasn't all pro bono; in other cases he helped successfully defend Kirk Kerkorian in a $1 billion damage suit over the sale of MGM to Giancarlo Parretti in 1990, and as co-counsel, he won an $11 million verdict for an investor defrauded in commodities trading.

WHEN ROSENBAUM and Marmalefsky went to work on the case, 69 pages out of 281 in the Lennon FBI file were being withheld in their entirety under various claims, and portions of dozens of others were also withheld. The FOIA not only allows judges to order agencies to release withheld documents but also requires that if a requester brings a case before a judge, "the court shall determine the matter *de novo,* and may examine the contents of such agency records *in camera* to determine whether such records or any part thereof shall be withheld . . . and the burden is on the agency to sustain its action."[8] Equally important was the section of President Reagan's executive order on classification, which declared that "in no case shall information be classified in order to conceal violations of law . . . [or] to prevent embarrassment to a person, organization, or agency."[9]

Because the FBI cited three different exemptions under the FOIA for withholding most of the information, challenging the withholding required litigating each exemption separately, and each had a separate body of case law to be studied and invoked.

When Rosenbaum and Marmalefsky sat down to discuss strategy, they conceded that the law was clear that we would never get some of the withheld information; the names of confidential informants, for instance, were clearly protected. So we decided at the outset to notify the FBI that we were not seeking those names, the names of FBI or nonfederal law enforcement officers, or technical source symbol numbers. We were challenging the claims made for withholding only some of the information: particularly the material claimed under "national security" and the information provided by confidential sources. We were not seeking the names of the informers, but we were seeking the information they provided.

The "national security" information provided the most obvious target—how could release of twelve-year-old information about a dead rock star possibly endanger the national security?—but was also the most difficult to obtain. Mark Rosenbaum told me that the biggest problem in the case was that "courts fear divulging national security documents. They believe that courts should tread lightly in this area. They pay enormous deference to executive branch claims concerning national security."[10]

Still, Rosenbaum and Marmalefsky had at least one significant avenue of attack. The FOIA exemption covers any material "which reasonably could be expected to cause damage to the national security," but the task of determining what constitutes "damage" is assigned by the Act to the president, who issues executive orders on classification of documents. At the time my FOIA request was filed in 1981, the relevant executive order required federal agencies considering FOIA requests to consider the public interest. The benefit to the public was to be balanced against the possible harm that could result from release of documents. If the public interest outweighed the possible harm, the documents had to be released. That policy, the "public interest balancing act," had been established by President Carter.[11] Since the public benefit from release of the Lennon files would be considerable, and the possible harm to the national security was small or nonexistent, the argument for releasing those pages was a strong one.

Disaster struck almost immediately. Between the submission of the original FOIA request in 1981 and the filing of the lawsuit in 1983, President Reagan issued a new executive order on classification that eliminated the public interest balancing act. Under the new Reagan policy, the FBI was required to withhold all documents "the unauthorized disclosure of which reasonably could be expected to cause damage to the national security," period. The FBI was now permitted to withhold any information that might possibly result in damage to the national security, no matter how great the public interest that would be served by its release, and no matter how insignificant or unlikely the damage, as long as the "expectation" of damage was "reasonable." The ACLU team had lost its strongest argument for release of the national security documents in the Lennon file. Until a Democratic president could be elected, who would presumably restore the Carter-era public interest balancing act, we would face a serious obstacle to the release of that material. Nevertheless, a judge could find that the expectation of damage was not reasonable or that the files were being withheld improperly to conceal information that would embarrass the FBI—and then order their release.

Wiener v. FBI was filed by Rosenbaum and Marmalefsky on March 22, 1983, in U.S. district court in Los Angeles. The lawsuit sought three things: an injunction ordering the FBI to release the documents, a written finding stating that the FBI "acted arbitrarily or capriciously" in withholding the documents, and last but not least, an award of costs and attorney fees.[12] Rosenbaum and Marmalefsky pointed out that under the law the burden of justifying the withholding of documents rested on the FBI. But the ACLU team's strategy in the case was not to start by asking the judge to order the prompt release of the withheld documents; it was necessary to go through several preliminary procedural steps. The first was to ask the court to order the FBI to provide an index of every document at issue along with "a detailed justification covering each refusal to release agency records." Once the FBI had stated its justifications document by document, each justification could be challenged and shown to be inadequate, and on that basis the judge could then order the bureau to release the documents.

This was the established procedure: the bureau provided the plaintiffs with an affidavit known as a "Vaughn index"—the court's term for the document itemizing the government's justifications for refusing to disclose documents.[13] The purpose of the index was to provide the FOIA requester with a meaningful opportunity to contest the FBI's arguments in court. When the D.C. Circuit Court of Appeals established the Vaughn index procedure in 1973, it addressed the basic dilemma facing FOIA plaintiffs, a dilemma we faced: how to challenge a government decision to

withhold a document when the contents of the document remained unknown to the challenger? The plaintiff's lack of knowledge about the contents of the withheld document "seriously distorts the traditional
adversary nature of our legal system's form of dispute resolution," the circuit court explained. "Ordinarily, the facts relevant to a dispute are more
or less equally available to adverse parties." An index was necessary, the
court argued, to "assure that a party's right to information is not submerged beneath governmental obfuscation and mischaracterization."
Preserving the adversary nature of the proceedings would turn out to be
the key to the Ninth Circuit Court of Appeals ruling against the FBI nine
years after the case was first field.

WIENER V. FBI was assigned to Judge Robert M. Takasugi in Los Angeles
district court. Born in Tacoma, Washington, in 1930, Takasugi at age
twelve was interned in a wartime "relocation camp" for three years, along
with the entire Japanese American population of the West Coast, for the
duration of World War II. After the war he went to UCLA as an under-
graduate in the mid-fifties, then served in the army for two years, and
graduated from University of Southern California Law School in 1959. He
worked in a variety of judicial positions and was appointed to the federal
bench in 1976.

We thought that his wartime experience might make him more sensitive to the issue of government abuse of power—especially after Judge
Takasugi called his wartime internment experience "an education to be
fair" in May 1995 at a gathering sponsored by the Japanese American National Museum and the Los Angeles Jewish Federation. Along with four
other Japanese American judges—including Lance Ito, who at the time was
presiding over the O. J. Simpson criminal trial, Takasugi recalled indignities
like sleeping on straw mattresses, sharing toilets with hundreds of other
people, and using tin cans to cover knotholes in the thin walls of the
wooden barracks to keep out the dust. Along with the others, he described
how the experience of internment had led him toward a career in law and
how it sensitized him to civil liberties issues. "It has certainly affected me
twenty-six hours a day," Judge Takasugi told the audience. All the judges at

the event warned of the dangers of anti-immigrant hysteria; Judge Takasugi "spoke caustically of the stereotypic singsong impersonation of Judge Ito by Senator Alphonse M. D'Amato, Republican of New York, in a recent radio interview, calling it 'a disgrace.'" Judge Takasugi also told about how his father lost his home and property as a result of the wartime "relocation" program and died at age fifty-seven of a stroke, brought on, the judge said, by "feelings of helplessness" at the Tule Lake internment camp.[14]

The gathering coincided with the opening of an exhibit about the internment program, which included a reconstructed barracks moved to the museum from the Heart Mountain internment camp site in Wyoming. Reporters asked Judge Takasugi whether it resembled the place where he had lived. "Yeah, exactly," he replied, "but the floors were tar, so on a hot day we started sinking." A photographer asked him if he was willing to step inside. "I don't want to go back in, really," Judge Takasugi said. "I'll take the loyalty oath."[15]

While the Lennon files were being debated in Judge Takasugi's courtroom, a movement for "redress and reparations" for Japanese Americans interned during World War II was gaining strength in national politics. In 1988 Congress officially apologized and authorized reparation payments to victims of the internment program. It seemed as if Judge Takasugi's youthful experience of government abuse of power might make him more sensitive to the issues in the Lennon FBI files case.

The FBI's Argument

The FBI was represented in the case by Peter Osinoff, an assistant U.S. attorney. He was a thirty-one-year-old New York native who had graduated magna cum laude from Yale in 1973 and then from Stanford Law School.

The FBI in due time produced its Vaughn index to the Lennon files. But instead of providing specific arguments justifying each deletion from the FBI file, the bureau submitted a master list of justifications for withholding material—a codebook. The blacked-out passages on file pages were marked with marginal notations referring to particular justifications in the codebook. Obviously the codebook justifications were generic. It turned out that the FBI submitted the same master list of justifications in all FOIA litigation. Mark Rosenbaum wrote in a letter to the FBI attorneys in September 1983 that the explanation in the codebook "is really not more than a generalized elaboration of the exemption asserted: it is mainly just wordier." Despite the vagueness and generality of the codebook, the courts had been sympathetic to the FBI's use of boilerplate justifications. Rosenbaum and Marmalefsky decided that challenging the codebook would be the first element in their strategy to win release of the Lennon FBI files.

The FBI's Vaughn index of the Lennon file was accompanied in June 1983 by the "Declaration of Robert J. Chester," supervisor of the FBI's FOIA Section, which defended the FBI's procedures for all exemptions, except national security—for that the FBI submitted a separate statement by another official. Agent Chester explained that the names of FBI agents were being withheld because targets of FBI investigations "carry grudges which last for years and [these people] seek any excuse to harass the responsible Agent." Recognizing that the target of the investigation in this case was dead and the plaintiff was a mild-mannered history professor, Chester conceded that "in the instant case, there is no apparent evidence that plaintiff constitutes a threat to law enforcement personnel." That was deeply gratifying. Nevertheless, he added, "in light of the highly publicized nature of this particular case, it is important that Agents' identities be protected even absent evidence of potential physical harm to their persons."

Chester provided an equally rich justification for withholding information provided by confidential sources: "Informant identification has become a paramount consideration to members of the criminal and subversive elements." Again, he had no evidence that the plaintiff in this case belonged to those elements. But that did not prevent him from continuing to argue: "Members of the criminal and subversive elements do not require proof beyond a reasonable doubt when they seek to ferret out the individual who has cooperated with law enforcement authorities."

The FOIA permits the FBI to withhold confidential source material only if it had been gathered as part of a legitimate law enforcement purpose; thus it was necessary for the FBI to state the law enforcement purpose of the investigation of Lennon. The Chester declaration did that: the

FBI had investigated Lennon in 1972, Chester told the court, "to determine if John Lennon was in violation of Federal law," namely, "the National Security Act of 1947."

This was a strange claim, one that would turn out to be helpful for our case. The National Security Act of 1947 created the Central Intelligence Agency. Congress was concerned at the time about whether the proposed CIA would serve the president as "a Gestapo of his own if he wants it," in the words of a Republican congressman from Ohio. So the security act made it clear that the CIA would be prohibited from "investigations inside the continental limits of the United States" and would not have "police, law enforcement, or internal security functions."[16] To claim that law as one Lennon was suspected of violating was strange not only because it wasn't a criminal statute but also because eventually it would be revealed that the CIA had indeed compiled files on Lennon's domestic political activities, in violation of the very same National Security Act of 1947.

The FBI codebook for the Lennon file divided "national security" material into eleven subcategories, starting with "identity of a foreign government . . . engaged in a cooperative, confidential relationship with the United States" and ending with "intelligence information gathered by the United States about or from a foreign country, group or individual." The FBI's arguments regarding national security deletions from the Lennon files were presented in a court declaration by Special Agent Robert F. Peterson, supervisor of the National Security Affidavits Unit at FBI headquarters, who reported that he had been "designated by the Attorney General of the United States as an original Top Secret classification authority."

Information provided by a national security confidential source had to be withheld, Peterson declared, because disclosure could permit "hostile entities" to assess "areas and targets which may have been compromised." But who were the "hostile entities" in this case? Surely not the ACLU. Release of the information could also lead to exposure of the people who provided it, threatening them with "loss of life, jobs, friends, status, etc." This was the problem with the codebook approach—none of this boilerplate argument had anything to do with the Lennon file.

The most significant part of Peterson's declaration concerned the category "foreign government information," which the FBI claimed as the basis for withholding numerous documents. These had to be withheld, Peterson argued, "due to the delicate nature of international diplomacy." Release of the foreign government information in the Lennon file could lead to "political or economic instability, or to civil disorder or unrest" in the foreign country that supplied the information, he declared. It could "jeopardize the lives, liberty or property" of U.S. tourists visiting the country. It could "endanger United States Government personnel there." Then came the most remarkable claim made in fourteen years of Lennon file litigation: release of foreign government information in the Lennon file, Agent Peterson declared, could "lead to foreign . . . military retalia- tion against the United States."

Britain was obviously the source of the "foreign government informa- tion," but it seemed unlikely that British citizens would attack visiting American tourists or government personnel in retaliation for the release of information gathered by British authorities. British economic instability might be a problem, but it was unlikely to be exacerbated by the release of information about Lennon. Most important, we felt confident that the Thatcher government would not engage in military retaliation against the United States if our government released British information on Lennon.

What could the John Lennon FBI file contain that had been provided by the British government? The Nixon administration had begun depor- tation proceedings against Lennon in 1972 after learning of his antiwar and anti-Nixon activities in an election year. This is the point at which "information gathered by the United States . . . from a foreign country" enters the story. The Nixon administration claimed as the legal basis for its effort to deport Lennon his 1969 conviction on misdemeanor charges of cannabis possession in Britain. Presumably the FBI's Lennon file con- tained information from the British government regarding that event.

Thus in response to an FOIA request for the FBI's Lennon file, the classification officer—the man with the magic marker—blacked-out pas- sages that originated with the British government and marked them with the code referring to "foreign relations or foreign activities of the U.S."; the reader then looked up the code in the codebook and found the official description of "damage to the national security reasonably expected to re- sult from unauthorized disclosure"; among the boilerplate list of possible damages, the FBI included "foreign military retaliation against the U.S." To add insult to injury, Special Agent Peterson also declared that he had made "every effort" to be "reasonable" and provide "sufficient detail" so that the court could "rationally determine" that the FBI was right.

The Lennon file also contained five documents originating with the CIA. These were part of the FBI's file on Lennon because the FBI had received them from the CIA. Confronted by an FOIA request, the FBI sent these documents back to the CIA so that the agency could decide whether to release or withhold them. The official CIA justification for withholding this material was prepared by Louis J. Dube, the information review officer for the Directorate of Operations of the CIA. In his affidavit, submitted in December 1983, he declared that he was acting on "advice of the CIA Office of General Counsel." "As a senior CIA official," he wrote, in a chain of command "running from the President of the United States to the Director of Central Intelligence . . . to me, I hold original classification authority at the TOP SECRET level." Dube declared that, in document HQ-1, a "one word CIA cryptonym" was being withheld under both the (b)(1) national security exemption as well as the (b)(3) intelligence sources and methods exemption.

A cryptonym, Agent Dube explained, is a code word "used to conceal the true nature or identity of some intelligence activity." The use of cryptonyms "provide[s] an additional measure of security in the event a document comes into the possession of a hostile foreign power." If the cryptonym used in the Lennon files were disclosed, "the intelligence service of a hostile foreign power" would be able to "divine the nature and purpose of the CIA activity" in question. But it was obvious to any power, hostile or not, that the purpose of the CIA activity in question had been to gather information about John Lennon's political activities. (In 1987, the cryptonym would be released.)

The CIA released one of its Lennon documents in September 1984—a teletype dated February 8, 1972, reporting on Lennon's plan for a "caravan of entertainers who will follow U.S. primaries and raise funds for local radical groups along the way." About half of it was blacked out under the national security exemption, but one word in the heading was released: "MHCHAOS."

Rosenbaum and Marmalefsky agreed that the word rang a bell, and since I was the historian, I was dispatched to the UCLA Research Library reference room. The news indices there were clear: "MHCHAOS" was a secret, illegal CIA program of surveillance of domestic political dissent, a violation of the CIA charter that had been revealed in 1976. "MH" was a CIA code indicating worldwide area of operations. The CHAOS program had been launched in August 1967, under Director Richard Helms, by James Jesus Angleton, the CIA's chief of counterintelligence, and headed by Richard Ober, a counterintelligence specialist in the Directorate of Plans, Harvard '43. Ober's tasks had already included developing CIA strategy to respond to the revelation by *Ramparts* magazine in February 1967 that the CIA had been secretly funding the National Student Association for fifteen years. Under the CHAOS operation, the investigation of *Ramparts* was expanded to cover the entire underground press and given "highest priority." To keep the illegal activity from being leaked by CIA employees, the operation was housed in the basement of CIA headquarters in Langley, Virginia, in specially shielded vaults that blocked electronic eavesdropping.

The CIA sent Operation CHAOS domestic intelligence reports on political dissent first to President Johnson and later to Nixon, as well as to Henry Kissinger and John Dean, counsel to the president. Under Nixon, the CHAOS program was expanded to sixty agents, who, according to Angus MacKenzie, "became the Nixon administration's primary source of intelligence about the antiwar leadership."[17]

CIA Operation CHAOS was revealed in 1976 by Representative Bella Abzug's House Subcommittee on Government Information and Individual Rights. The CIA director at the time was George Bush, who conceded in congressional testimony that "the operation in practice resulted in some improper accumulation of material on legitimate domestic activities." He defended the agency, declaring that "only a very small fraction of reporting on the activities of American citizens in the US was done by the CIA." Abzug proposed that individuals who had been targets of Operation CHAOS be notified by the CIA and given a chance to review their dossiers. Bush replied that notification was unworkable and proposed instead that the CIA "destroy . . . all the information which was improperly collected under the so-called CHAOS program." Because of congressional insistence, Bush agreed that the FOIA would make Operation CHAOS files available under the Act.[18] Thus the appearance of the CHAOS memo here.

Just eight months after the ACLU suit was filed, the government changed attorneys. Peter Osinoff, who had represented the FBI, left the U.S. Attorney's Office for private practice, and the Justice Department reassigned the case in November 1983 to Stephen D. Petersen, a forty-year-old graduate of the University of Iowa and Iowa Law School. Dan Marmalefsky promptly wrote Petersen, expressing "concerns with the delays in the FBI response to this lawsuit," protesting that two months had passed since he had requested a more specific Vaughn index. Fourteen years later Rosenbaum and Marmalefsky would still be arguing many of the same issues.

THE FBI ACCOUNTING of file pages in their Vaughn index included two unexpected and previously unknown sets of materials: Lennon files from the FBI field office in Washington, D.C., (as opposed to headquarters) and in Houston. When filing FOIA requests, it is vital for requesters to contact not only FBI headquarters in Washington, D.C., but also FBI field offices in cities where investigations were conducted. The field office files contain the raw material from investigations, while headquarters files contain mostly summaries. I had requested Lennon files from field offices in New York, Detroit, and Los Angeles but not from Houston or Washington, D.C.; nevertheless the FBI provided copies of those documents.

A careful examination of the released pages in Lennon's New York file indicated that a Lennon file had also been opened in Miami, yet no Miami file had been produced along with those from Houston and Washington, D.C. So in 1983 I filed a new FOIA request for Lennon files in the Miami field office, providing the Miami file number for Lennon that appeared on New York FBI memos. In May 1983 I received a reply: "A search of the index to the central records system of the Miami Office reveals no information identifiable with your request." As for the file whose number I requested, it "was destroyed in connection with the routine file destruction program during September of 1977."

The Miami file could have been an important one; it may have contained evidence of the government's efforts to set up Lennon for a drug bust. A memo from the New York FBI dated July 1972, released in the first batch of pages, suggested that "Miami should note that LENNON is reportedly a 'heavy user of narcotics.' . . . This information should be emphasized to local Law Enforcement Agencies covering MIREP, with regards to subject being arrested if at all possible on possession of narcotics charges." ("MIREP" was FBI newspeak for the 1972 Miami Republican National Convention.) The Miami Lennon file that the FBI said it had destroyed might have contained further information about that element of the FBI's harassment of Lennon.

The ACLU team raised the issue of the Miami file with FBI attorneys. Petersen replied in November 1983 that the statement provided by the Miami FBI "was a statutorily sufficient response." He added, "I hope this information is responsive to your letter."

The *Miami Herald* picked up the story and quoted local FBI spokesman Joe Del Campo confirming that "there once was a Lennon file in Miami, but there is no way to know what was in it." He explained that "the local office has a carefully regulated file destruction program, in which outdated closed files are destroyed at specified intervals."[19] Yet none of the other offices with Lennon files had destroyed theirs.

The ACLU's Argument

In an effort to provide the courts with a sense of the historical significance of the Lennon files, and of the broader context in which they had been created, the ACLU team submitted a document in October 1987 modestly titled "The Declaration of Jonathan M. Wiener." In it the plaintiff argued that FBI files released under FOIA requests had become a major research tool for historians of the 1960s; that Lennon was widely regarded as a significant historical figure; that the lawsuit was seeking only information of genuine historical significance; and that the Lennon FBI files contained evidence of Nixon administration abuses of power.

The declaration sketched out some recent history: for Nixon and

Hoover, another historian had written, "The world was a battlefield filled with active or potential enemies." Lennon became identified as one of those enemies because he publicly opposed Nixon's reelection. In Nixon's mind, "he was a victim forced forever to defend himself against unrelenting and unscrupulous enemies." Hoover supported Nixon's beliefs: he told Nixon at a private meeting in October 1971, "More than anything else, I want to see you reelected in 1972."[20]

Hoover's rhetoric about antiwar activists like Lennon "was even more violent than Nixon's," according to his biographer. Hoover characterized the antiwar activist of the sixties as " 'new . . . different . . . a paradox because he is difficult to judge by the normal standards of civilized life. . . . His main reason for being is to destroy, blindly and indiscriminately, to tear down and provoke chaos. . . . They conceive of themselves as the catalyst of destruction—bringing to death a society they so bitterly hate.' "[21] This attitude helped shape the FBI's conduct in its investigations of Lennon.

The declaration reminded the court that the bureau acknowledged it had engaged in illegal and unconstitutional activities in investigating antiwar activists during the sixties. The man who headed the FBI's Intelligence Division during the sixties, who was deeply involved in the FBI's investigations of the antiwar movement, William Sullivan, testified before a congressional committee in 1975: "Never once did I hear anybody, including myself, raise the question: 'Is this course of action which we have agreed upon lawful, is it legal, is it ethical or moral.' We never gave any thought to this line of reasoning, because we were just naturally pragmatic."[22]

The declaration quoted John Ehrlichman, who served as J. Edgar Hoover's contact with the Nixon White House and received Hoover's reports. "The Bureau dealt excessively in rumor, gossip and conjecture," he wrote in his memoir of this period. "Sometimes a report was based on 'a confidential source'—the Bureau euphemism for wiretapping or bugging. Even then the information was often hearsay." The FBI had repeatedly refused to release documents from the Lennon file it described as based on "confidential sources." But the FOIA does not permit the bureau to withhold information gathered by improper law enforcement techniques. The 1976 report of the Senate Select Committee on Intelligence, chaired by Frank Church, concluded that the FBI during this period engaged in a "pattern of reckless disregard of activities that threatened our constitution."[23]

The declaration argued that the Nixon campaign against Lennon was related to the Watergate abuses of power. Lennon was not the only one of Nixon's "enemies" to feel the power of the White House early in 1972. Gordon Liddy and E. Howard Hunt proposed in January that the Committee to Re-Elect the President spend $1 million on covert operations, including mugging demonstrators at the Republican National Convention and abducting the leaders to Mexico. Jerry Rubin and Abbie Hoffman were selected for abduction; Lennon was not. When the plan was presented to Attorney General Mitchell, he said it was "not quite what I had in mind" and cost too much.[24] Liddy came back with a plan to break into Democratic National Committee headquarters in Washington to plant bugs and photograph documents. Mitchell liked that better. The operation was carried out on June 17 at the Watergate offices of the Democratic National Committee; Washington police caught the perpetrators in the act. A cover-up directed by H. R. Haldeman and John Ehrlichman successfully kept the press from developing the story until after Nixon's reelection.

The declaration concluded that the Nixon administration's persecution of Lennon was one small part of a massive, illegal effort to ensure Nixon's reelection, one example of an abuse of power that eventually led Congress to move toward Nixon's impeachment, and that Lennon's FBI file contained the best and in some cases the only documentation of some Nixon-era abuses of presidential power. Release of these documents therefore would contribute to establishing a complete record of those historically significant events.

JUDGE TAKASUGI held a hearing February 6, 1984, in which both sides presented their arguments. In the courtroom, Rosenbaum and Marmalefsky looked splendid in their dark blue suits, although it was not hard to tell the ACLU team from the FBI attorneys: Rosenbaum and Marmalefsky were the ones with beards. Rosenbaum was also wearing cowboy boots.

The ACLU team had four specific objections to the FBI's codebook approach. First, Marmalefsky rose to challenge the bureau regarding confidential source material: the FOIA distinguished between information provided under a guarantee of confidentiality that was explicit and one that was not. If an FBI source had received an explicit promise that his or her identity would not be revealed, the information in question was absolutely protected from release under the FOIA. That was not the case for information provided by sources who had only an implied promise of confidentiality. Marmalefsky argued that the FBI had failed to distinguish between guarantees that were explicit and those that were only implied. That issue was called "expressed versus implied confidentiality." Second, the FBI had failed to explain how the information provided by confidential sources was gathered as part of a legitimate law enforcement investigation. What was missing was the "rational nexus."

Then Rosenbaum addressed the issue of national security information. The FBI's claims regarding the damage that would be caused by the release of foreign government information were too broad, he argued—they had a "lack of specificity." Finally, he told the court that the withholding of numerous entire pages was unacceptable; the courts required the segregation of all nonexempt portions of particular pages and the release of the rest of each page. This issue was called "segregability."

The ACLU team cited some important precedents in support of its argument. The closest parallel FOIA case had been brought in 1976 by a Berkeley graduate student, David Dunaway, who was writing a Ph.D. dissertation on Pete Seeger. That suit concerned the FBI file on the Weavers and other folk music groups and organizations. In 1981 Judge Peckham of the Northern District of California wrote that "we cannot blindly accept" the vague generalities in the codebook. The documents in that case "concern the comings and goings of U.S. citizens 20 to 30 years ago. . . . [V]irtually all of the information is of the most mundane character, information which has no apparent relationship to the security of this nation today, if it ever had." He ordered the documents to be released in their entirety.[25]

Another key case was that of Frank Wilkinson, executive director of the National Coalition against Repressive Legislation, founded to organize opposition to the McCarthy hearings and to the House Committee on Un-American Activities. In that case, Wilkinson argued that in the early 1960s the FBI targeted his organization as part of the illegal COINTELPRO

operation, that the FBI investigation was intended "not to uncover potential criminal activity, but instead to monitor and disrupt plaintiff's lawful
activities through the use of various illegal techniques such as warrantless
electronic surveillance, 'black bag jobs,' and *agents provacateur* [sic]." In
that case 12,000 documents were at issue. Judge Tashima of the Central
District of California ruled that the FBI coding system consisted of vague
generalities that "do not enable this Court meaningfully to assess the validity of the agency's claims."[26] Because the government had not met its burden, he ordered the FBI to release the documents. By citing these cases,
Rosenbaum and Marmalefsky were providing Judge Takasugi with precedents he could rely on if he were to rule that the FBI's Vaughn index was inadequate.

The government attorneys replied that the FBI had done what was
legally required and that if the judge wanted they would submit the
original uncensored FBI file pages for *in camera* review by the judge. In
response to the ACLU team's arguments that confidential source information could not be withheld if the government lacked a legitimate law enforcement purpose in the investigation, FBI attorney Petersen replied that
the prevailing law in three federal circuits held that FBI records "are *in-
herently* records compiled for 'law enforcement purposes.' " That was a
chilling argument. The standard in the Ninth Circuit, where the case was
being tried, required a "rational nexus" between the documents and a legitimate law enforcement purpose.

The government had already responded briefly to the "Declaration of
Jonathan M. Wiener": "While interesting reading," the FBI told the court
in its reply, the declaration was "mostly composed of hearsay, improper
opinion, and irrelevant matter." It urged the court to ignore it.

Petersen reminded Judge Takasugi that the FBI brief had provided an
explanation of "The Origination of the FBI Investigation Concerning
John Lennon." He cited the 1968 Civil Obedience Act and the Anti-Riot
Act, which made it a felony to travel interstate with the intent to encourage, incite, or participate in a riot. Congress had passed this law in response to the demonstrations at the Democratic National Convention
in 1968, in the hope of preventing a recurrence in 1972. Lennon had
been associating in 1971–72 with Jerry Rubin and Rennie Davis, who had

been convicted of similar crimes in Chicago in 1968 and who had formed a group "apparently dedicated to creating disruptions," Petersen told the judge, at the 1972 Republican convention. Therefore, Petersen continued, the FBI's investigation of Lennon had a legitimate law enforcement purpose, and the withholding of confidential source information was required under the FOIA. That had a certain logic; however, the government had earlier given a different basis for the investigation of Lennon, the National Security Act of 1947. Rosenbaum and Marmalefsky would highlight this contradiction in subsequent litigation.

On the "national security" material, Petersen argued that Judge Takasugi should defer to executive branch decisions. Judges were unqualified to overrule decisions made by career officials whose responsibility was national security classification. Thus, he argued, the assignment of a "national security" classification to any FBI document was "absolute." The judicial review process provided for in the FOIA, he argued, was "limited to a determination that the procedures set forth by the applicable Executive Order have been followed and that the classification decision was made in good faith"; in other words, Petersen told Takasugi, "the court may not review or second-guess the substantive decision to classify." He cited the D.C. Circuit making precisely that argument.

The brief Petersen had submitted pointed out that another court went beyond the "reasonable basis" standard for withholding documents. "In view of the knowledge, experience and positions held by the three affiants regarding military secrets, military planning and national security," a D.C. Circuit judge declared, "their affidavits were to be treated by the courts with 'utmost deference.'"[27] The implication was clear: if "utmost deference" were to become the prevailing standard, the judicial review provisions of the FOIA would become virtually useless, and the withheld Lennon files would never be released.

JUDGE TAKASUGI responded five weeks later, in March 1984, to the ACLU motion to compel a new and more adequate Vaughn index. He agreed that the FBI's index to the Lennon documents lacked the required specificity. But instead of ordering the bureau to provide the plaintiff with a new and detailed Vaughn index, he ordered the FBI to submit more specific affidavits to him *in camera*—affidavits Rosenbaum and Marmalefsky would not be allowed to see. The FBI promptly filed two *in camera* affidavits by Agents Peterson and Chester, which presumably made new arguments, and gave the judge a copy of the uncensored Lennon FBI file. Apparently they were confident he would conclude that the files indeed did contain national security information.

The ACLU team objected to the FBI's submission of documents to the judge *in camera,* pointing out that the Vaughn decision that governed this kind of case criticized *in camera* inspection of documents because "it is necessarily conducted without benefit of criticism and illumination by a party with the actual interest in forcing disclosure." In August 1984, Rosenbaum and Marmalefsky filed a motion asking the judge either to release the *in camera* affidavits or order the FBI to prepare a more adequate Vaughn index. Without such rulings, "the litigation will essentially have lost its adversary character," the ACLU team concluded.

Media Watch 1983–84

The first steps in the ACLU's project of publicizing the value of the FOIA and its subversion by the FBI came when the lawsuit was first announced and my book *Come Together: John Lennon in His Time* was published, drawing on files that had been released. The publisher, Random House, organized a ten-city author tour in 1983, which featured the story of the withheld files and the historian who had sued the FBI to win their release. As the ACLU had hoped, the story was covered by Dan Rather, *ABC 20/20,* the *CBS Morning News, People* magazine, and most of the country's newspapers. CNN's Dave Rinn was energetic enough to ask Haldeman and Nixon for comment; both refused.[28]

The *Today* show producers didn't want to have me on alone. They invited the White House to send a spokesman to respond to my account of the Reagan administration's fight to prevent release of the Lennon files. Senator Orrin Hatch, one of the smartest and most articulate spokesmen of the Right, was chosen to provide the administration response. For anyone who thought the Reagan White House didn't care about the Lennon files, the selection of Senator Hatch must have been illuminating. (He canceled at the last minute.)

The ACLU was delighted to get the story on TV, but often the context undermined the seriousness of the issues. In Chicago on a live morning TV show, the other guests were Soupy Sales, Miss USA—a J. C. Penney promotion—and a drug-sniffing dog that was sent out into the studio audience. Another live morning TV show, in Detroit, had a smaller budget for their dog segment: "Coming up, John Lennon and the FBI—but first, Name That Breed!" A picture of a dog went up on the screen, and viewers were invited to phone the station and "name that breed. We'll be back with the correct answer—and the John Lennon FBI files—right after this message." Cut to commercial.

Some treated the story seriously but got it wrong: instead of "FBI refuses to release files on Lennon," dozens of newspapers ran stories in June 1984 headed "Senator Thurmond Tried to Deport Lennon," attributing that information to documents released in *Wiener v. FBI.* But that story had been told almost a decade earlier, in 1975, by Chet Flippo in *Rolling Stone.*[29]

And occasionally the story provided a platform for diatribes against "the sixties." Ronald Radosh, a former sixties leftist who had joined the right, reviewed *Come Together* in the *Washington Post,* where he wrote that the book shared J. Edgar Hoover's delusions about Lennon's political significance.[30] The *Princeton Alumni Weekly* ran a report on the Princeton graduate, class of '66, who had sued the FBI for the Lennon files, which prompted Bill Black Jr., class of '67, to write a letter to the editor declaring that another Princeton alumnus of the same era had "bombed a computer center at the University of Wisconsin in 1970, killing a graduate student and wounding four other persons. I do not understand how Wiener could have forgotten so prominent a member of his small group, who graduated to terrorism and murder." That claim was completely untrue and indeed libelous, as editor Charles Creesy '65 was informed. The next issue bore an abject apology from Black, who conceded that his statement was "without basis and completely in error. I regret this error and any harm it may have caused." That ran next to a box from the editors headed "An Apology and Retraction."[31]

NOTES

INTRODUCTION

1. The story is told in Jon Wiener, *Come Together: John Lennon in His Time* (New York: Random House, 1984). The John Dean "enemies list" memo was revealed in the *New York Times*, June 29, 1973. For Dean's account of the relationship between the Nixon White House and the FBI, see John Dean, *Blind Ambition: The White House Years* (New York: Simon & Schuster, 1976). For other examples of presidents' political use of the FBI, see Athan Theoharis, *From the Secret Files of J. Edgar Hoover* (Chicago: Ivan R. Dee, 1991), ch. 12.

2. *Access Reports* 17 (October 30, 1991), 5; Marvin Lewis (assistant chief, FBI, FOIA/PA Section), interview with author, April 16, 1992.

3. 5 U.S.C. § 552(b)(1).

4. *EPA v. Mink*, 410 U.S. 73, 95.

5. Quoted in introduction to Athan Theoharis, ed., *A Culture of Secrecy: The Government Versus the People's Right to Know* (Lawrence: University of Kansas Press, 1998), 2–3.

6. Quoted in Daniel Patrick Moynihan, *Secrecy: The American Experience* (New Haven: Yale University Press, 1998), 89, 97.

7. Natalie Robins, *Alien Ink: The FBI's War on Freedom of Expression* (New York: William Morrow, 1992), 32–37; Herbert Mitgang, *Dangerous Dossiers: Exposing the Secret War against America's Greatest Authors* (New York: Ballantine, 1988).

CHAPTER 1: GETTING STARTED

1. A few documents were withheld under the 5 U.S.C. § 552(b)(3) exemption, "information withheld pursuant to statute." Two statutes were cited: visa records and tax returns. Privacy and confidential sources were both subsections of the same exemption—(b)(7), law enforcement records. The official categories were (b)(7)(C), "unwarranted invasion of personal privacy," and (b)(7)(E), "confidential source material." For subsections of the exemption categories, see glossary.

2. Mark Rosenbaum, interview with author, Los Angeles, February 28, 1998.

3. *Crawford v. Board of Education*, 102 S.Ct. 3211 (1982).

4. *Green v. Anderson*, 115 S.Ct. 1398 (1995).

5. Dan Marmalefsky, interview with author, Los Angeles, February 28, 1998.

6. *Kolender v. Lawson*, 103 S.Ct. 1855 (1983).

7. *Wayte v. U.S.*, 105 S.Ct. 1524 (1985).

8. 5 U.S.C. § 552(a)(4)(B).

9. Executive Order 12356 (April 2, 1982), sec. 1.6(a).

10. Rosenbaum interview.

11. Executive Order 12065 (December 1, 1978).

12. This and all other quotations from plaintiff's and defendant's attorneys are from legal briefs and other court papers, of various titles and dates, in author's possession—unless otherwise cited.

13. The term "Vaughn index" comes from *Vaughn v. Rosen,* 484 F.2d 820 (D.C. Cir. 1973), cert. denied, 415 U.S. 977 (1974).

14. David Margolick, "Japanese-American Judges Reflect on Internment," *New York Times,* May 19, 1995.

15. Ibid.

16. Angus MacKenzie, *Secrets: The CIA's War at Home* (Berkeley: University of California Press, 1997), 9–11.

17. Ibid., 30; see also ibid., 20, 26–29.

18. Ibid., 68–71.

19. Stephen K. Doig, "FBI Ordered to Explain Why Lennon Files Shredded," *Miami Herald,* August 10, 1994.

20. Richard Gid Powers, *Secrecy and Power: The Life of J. Edgar Hoover* (New York: Free Press, 1987), 440, 474.

21. Ibid., 449.

22. William Sullivan testimony, November 1, 1975, quoted in Senate Select Committee to Study Government Operations with Respect to Intelligence Activities, *Final Report,* book 2, 94th Cong., 2d sess., 1976, 14.

23. John Ehrlichman, *Witness to Power* (New York: Simon & Schuster, 1982), 159; *Wilkinson v. FBI,* 633 F. Supp. 336, 349 (C.D. Cal. 1986); *Powers, Secrecy and Power,* 487.

24. Quoted in Jeb Stuart Magruder, *An American Life: One Man's Road to Watergate* (New York: Atheneum, 1974), 89.

25. *Dunaway v. Webster,* 519 F.Supp. 1058, 1065–66, 1070 (N.D. Cal. 1981).

26. *Wilkinson v. FBI,* 99 F.R.D. 148 (C.D. Cal. 1983).

27. *Taylor v. Dept. of the Army,* 684 F.2d 99 (D.C. Cir. 1982).

28. Haldeman described the relationship between the Nixon White House and the FBI in H.R. Haldeman and Joseph DiMona, *The Ends of Power* (New York: Times Books, 1978).

29. Chet Flippo, "Lennon's Lawsuit: Memo from Thurmond," *Rolling Stone,* July 31, 1975, 16. For examples of the 1984 Thurmond story, see *New York Post,* June 30, 1984; *Miami Herald,* June 30, 1984; *Cleveland Plain Dealer,* June 30, 1984; *Detroit Free Press,* June 30, 1984.

30. Ronald Radosh, "John Lennon's Separate Peace," *Washington Post,* July 31, 1984.

31. *Princeton Alumni Weekly,* November 21, 1984, December 19, 1984.

PART VI

Hidden Sides of the Vietnam War

Introduction to
Morley Safer's

"Report on the 1964 Gulf of Tonkin Incident"

I N 1964, although American military advisors had been in Vietnam for at least three years, popular and political sentiment had resisted a large-scale commitment of troops on a war footing. But the 1964 Gulf of Tonkin resolution gave the Congressional seal of approval to President Lyndon Johnson to wage war "as the President shall determine" in Vietnam. The resolution passed unanimously in the House. In the Senate, only Democratic senators Ernest Gruening of Alaska and Wayne Morse of Oregon voted against it. Convincing Congress that two American destroyers had been attacked by North Vietnamese PT boats on August 4, 1964, in the Gulf of Tonkin, Johnson immediately escalated the war by ordering air strikes against North Vietnam. The war shifted into high gear, leading to almost 500,000 American troops in Vietnam and eventually to 50,000 American deaths and millions of Vietnamese casualties.

But as the details of the Gulf of Tonkin incident became known, questions were raised as to whether there had, in fact, been any attack. Even after Congress voted to repeal the resolution in 1970 the details remained murky. Morley Safer's *60 Minutes* program, based in part on previously undisclosed cable traffic, provided new information and undermined claims that a second attack had occurred. The program helped push public opinion against the war, which eventually ended with the signing of the Paris Peace Accords in January 1973, and the withdrawal of all American soldiers two months later.

Safer had only been a coeditor at *60 Minutes* for a few months when his program on the Gulf of Tonkin Resolution aired. He went on to receive a Lifetime Achievement Emmy from the National Academy of Television Arts and Sciences and the George Polk Memorial Career Achievement Award.

ADDITIONAL SOURCES

Safer, Morley. *Flashbacks: On Returning to Vietnam*. New York: Random House, 1990.

U.S. Congress. Senate. Senate Committee on Foreign Relations. [The Gulf of Tonkin, the 1964 Incidents]. 90th Congress, 2nd Session, Washington, D.C.: GPO, 1968.

Wells, Tom. *The War Within: America's Battle Over Vietnam*. Berkeley, Calif.: University of California Press, 1994.

Morley Safer

"Report on the 1964 Gulf of Tonkin Incident"

60 MINUTES, CBS, MARCH 16, 1971

Safer: The date: August 4, 1964. For most people it triggers no particular emotion. It is no December 7, 1941. But August 4 is important whether you remember the date or not. It was on that date in the Gulf of Tonkin, off the coast of North Vietnam, that the American war in Vietnam really began. And the incident that began it has become as controversial as the war itself. The U.S. destroyers *Maddox* and *Turner Joy* were attacked by Communist torpedo boats. Or were they?

It is now six years and seven months since the Tonkin incident and the Tonkin Resolution. The incident produced the resolution, and the resolution was quite simple. It gave the president the right to protect American troops in Vietnam with whatever means he felt necessary, the power to prevent further aggression by North Vietnam and to prevent South Vietnam from falling to the Communists. Few people at the time thought it would take more than six years and almost 45,000 dead Americans—and more—to achieve those ends. Boys who were twelve years old that August died last week in Vietnam.

Let's go back to August 4 and the U.S. Destroyer *Maddox* and try to find out what happened that night in the Gulf of Tonkin.

In July of 1964, units of the Seventh Fleet were patrolling the South China Sea off the coast of Vietnam. The United States was not at war with North Vietnam, but it was helping South Vietnam with massive economic and military aid. Then this is what happened, according to the Pentagon's official reenactment narrated by Chet Huntley.

Huntley: On August 2, the United States Navy Destroyer *Maddox*, on patrol in international waters in the Gulf of Tonkin, begins to track three unknown craft approaching from the northwest. They are identified as North Vietnamese PT boats, armed with torpedoes and .37 millimeter guns. When warnings from the *Maddox* failed to stop the oncoming PT boats she opened fire.

The *Maddox,* joined by the Destroyer C. *Turner Joy,* resumes its routine patrol, but the next night the men on watch in the two destroyers once again detect unidentified contacts on radar. The attack by the North Vietnamese boats is renewed. After a three-hour running battle in which two of the PT boats are sunk, the attackers break contact.

Safer: There was no argument about the first fight. Sunday afternoon, August 2nd. It happened. The *Maddox* against three North Vietnamese PT boats. Something like this painting that hangs in the *Maddox* wardroom. The North Vietnamese said the *Maddox* invaded their waters and they chased her out. The United States says that the *Maddox* was in neutral waters, that although the *Maddox* fired first, it was in self-defense when the North Vietnamese PT boats were about to attack. We're fairly sure all three PT boats were hit and none of the torpedoes hit the *Maddox.* But the *Maddox* very likely was hit. There was a bullet hole up there in the aft gun director. It was repaired later and painted over, no sign of it today.

But two nights later, the night of the controversial battle, the *Maddox* did not take any damage or suffer any losses, which is but one of many reasons why Senate investigators now believe there never was any battle that night. The *Maddox* and the *Turner Joy* reported that they were ambushed at the beginning of the evening by perhaps five or six torpedo boats. But that wound down by midnight to perhaps one boat with two torpedoes. And yet, the destroyers reported a total of twenty-two torpedoes fired at them. They were doing a lot of firing themselves. Some people say they were firing at phantoms. The North Vietnamese always said that they were never there, that it simply was an excuse to get into the war.

The officer in charge of the destroyer division which included the *Maddox* and the *Turner Joy* was on board the *Maddox* that night. He's Captain John Herrick, Annapolis 1943, still on active duty. We asked him to return to the *Maddox,* now a training ship, and recall the confusing events of August 4, 1964.

Herrick: Well, I think the uncertainty is due to the fact that it was night, it was dark, and we didn't really eyeball these boats. We did have witnesses, eyeball witnesses, on the *Turner Joy.* I considered them dependable witnesses. However, there are people who still doubt that what they saw was boats. I do not. We had sensors who sighted the boats on radar. We had sonar that picked up noise (indistinct) in the water. We had visual sightings. I think the preponderance of evidence, any judge in a courtroom would have to accept our witness evidence and our sensor evidence, radar and sonar, and the only conclusion a logical man could reach was that we were attacked.

Safer: Just above the bridge of the *Maddox* where Captain Herrick was is the main gun director. And inside the director was a sailor who was in charge of firing those powerful five-inch guns. His job was to open fire once the enemy targets were spotted on radar or sonar. Those are the main methods for detecting targets you can't see directly. The man in charge of the main gun director, August 4, 1964, was a four-year veteran, he was also an expert sonar man, Patrick Park. Park is now a businessman in Los Angeles.

Tell me, do you think that night, August 4, in the pitch black, in a heavy swell, rain storms, was there anything to shoot at out there?

Park: No, I don't—I'm certain that there was not anything to shoot at, right from the beginning. The Captain asked me immediately after the attack, to go down and evaluate all the recordings that had been made of noise that was—that sonar was recording. And I kept myself pretty busy for the next three days really, trying to evaluate these things and determine if we had anything that might have been even a question mark, that might have been a torpedo or anything else in the water not related to the two ships or noise of either one of them.

Safer: And what was your evaluation?

Park: Absolutely nothing.

Herrick: Well, Park has a right to his own opinions of course, and I do not concur with him, but he has a right to those opinions.

Safer: Three decks below the main deck and locked under the waterline is

the *Maddox* sonar room. Here on the night of August 4, as the noise of
the big guns roared around them overhead, the *Maddox* sonar men listen for underwater sounds of approaching torpedoes, trying to separate
torpedo noises from their own ship's noise. Captain Herrick would later
describe a sonar man's reports as "overeager." The sailor on the sonar
console that night was David Mallow of Jal', New Mexico. Dave Mallow
is still in the navy. Still a sonarman at the Fleet School in Key West,
Florida.

Mallow: What happened? We were attacked. Torpedoes were in the water,
what I presumed were torpedoes, and I don't know how they can say
that there wasn't a torpedo, when I heard it, the *Turner Joy* saw it, and
then they're going to turn around and say that there wasn't one. Now
I'm certain in my mind that there was an attack.

Safer: Below Patrick Park in the main gun director, below Captain Herrick on the bridge, below them both is the Combat Information Center
and radar room. Here the job was to find enemy targets coming back by
way of radar signals, ending up as blips on this television screen. One of
the men running radar the night of August 4, 1964, was James Stankevitz, a four-year veteran. He's a civilian now and lives in Stevens Point,
Wisconsin.

Stankevitz: The only doubt I have is not to whether there was an attack or
not, I know there was, but as to where the attack came from. In other
words, we were steaming in a southerly direction and we picked up contacts off of our port side which would be on the east side of us. North
Vietnam was on the west side of us. Which meant that those ships that
were out there, torpedo boats or whatever, and they definitely were
there, were coming from either lying in wait for us out there, or coming
from an island which is a possession of Red China. And they proceeded
to close us. Then we started having difficulty with radar, where radar
would pick up intermittently and where we even had a hard time of
keeping track of the *Turner Joy*.

Safer: Just how hard a time the *Maddox* had spotting its sister ship, the
Turner Joy, that night is a memory that Patrick Park will never lose.
Park, in charge of the five-inch guns up in the main gun director, had
been getting target calls from the radar room throughout the night. But

he wouldn't fire because he could not see the targets on his own radar. Then around midnight he got the fattest target of the evening.

Park: So we get the word to open fire and at the same time I realized that that's the other ship and—

Safer: The *Turner Joy*.

Park: That's correct. And the radar operator also realized this and both of us said simultaneously, "That's the *Turner Joy*." So instead of opening fire as the word came down, all three of them about the same time: "That's the *Turner Joy*." "Open fire."

Safer: Just let's go down to these two models here.

Park: We had a good broadside shot of the *Turner Joy*, right like this, as far away, well, let's say fifteen hundred yards distance here. But—and, of course, all of our five-inch guns were pointed and ready to be fired at her. So we radio requested information from the *Turner Joy* and they lost contact on us quite a while back also, it seems, so then the Captain asked the *Turner Joy* to turn on their running lights and in doing so, I looked in the gunsight there, or the sight that I have and there she was right in the crosshairs. Right on her. The best contact we had all night.

Safer: What would have happened had you obeyed that order to fire?

Park: Well, we wouldn't have missed. That's about all I can say for it. We would have got her.

Safer: If confusion abounded during combat, mystery surrounded the black box. It had been brought aboard along with sixteen electronic specialists when the *Maddox* stopped at Taiwan a few days before the battle of Tonkin. The box was actually gray in color, but the men called it "the black box." It was placed between the smoke stacks on the *Maddox* and was removed after the battle. There's been an unending argument about what the black box was for, but it did contain sophisticated electronic instruments. Captain Herrick confirmed to us what had long been surmised: One of the things that the black box was for was to intercept North Vietnamese messages and those intercepts were proof enough that the North Vietnamese had attacked.

One of the controversial things in this whole affair are those intercepts.

Herrick: The intercepts were made by a—on a black box, which I was not acquainted with inside. I did not feel that I had the need to know what they were doing. I merely used the product of what they produced. And they did produce messages that warned me that we were being attacked.

Safer: The North Vietnamese, who openly admit the events of August 2, in fact would probably concur with your description of it, they say nothing happened the night of August 4.

Herrick: But I had messages presented to me which were their reports of damage to the boats that attacked us that night.

Safer: On the night of the fourth?

Herrick: On the night of the fourth.

Safer: As a result of your fire?

Herrick: As a result of our fire.

Safer: Tell me more about that.

Herrick: That's all I know. We had intercepted reports that told us that they had suffered damage that night.

Safer: Senator Fulbright and his Committee, however, were not persuaded by the black box intercepts. They were more interested in what Secretary McNamara told them four years later, that the black box had been used, in his words, to "stimulate" North Vietnamese and Chinese Communist radar by means of pinpointing their radar installations. But Captain Herrick says that this was not so.

Herrick: I would say that we had no way of stimulating North Vietnamese radar. This was not electronically feasible. We had no equipment to do any such thing.

Morse: The Johnson Administration concealed from the American people the truth about what the *Maddox* was doing in the Gulf of Tonkin. The *Maddox* was a spy ship.

Safer: Former Senator Wayne Morse of Oregon. Morse and former Senator Ernest Gruening were the only two men in the entire Congress of the United States who voted against the Tonkin Gulf Resolution.

Morse: She lost all her characteristic as a naval destroyer as far as international law was concerned. She had the appearance of a destroyer, if you didn't check her spy equipment. But she was a spy ship.

Herrick: Intelligence mission. I wouldn't call it a spy mission. This was a ship equipped with the normal equipment that a destroyer normally carries and was equipped also with the black box, as it has been called since then. But not a spy mission in that sense; I don't like the word spy mission. It was an intelligence mission, an information-gathering mission.

Safer: Would it be accurate to compare the *Maddox*'s mission in the Gulf of Tonkin with the *Pueblo*'s mission off North Korea?

Herrick: I'm not aware of the equipment on the *Pueblo* or how she was equipped, but I would say that she was much better equipped for this type of thing than the *Maddox* which is a ship of the line, not designed for that sort of thing.

Morse: She'd been taken weeks before the Gulf of Tonkin incident to Taiwan and fitted out as one of the top spy ships of the United States Navy. And the Administration never let that important fact out in their testimony before the Foreign Relations Committee. Had they let even that much out, the Resolution would never have come out of the Committee.

Safer: What was the specific mission that night?

Morse: Her specific mission was to stimulate the electronic instruments of North Vietnam so that the United States could find out what the North Vietnamese military plans were. And that's what she did. And she went into the national waters of North Vietnam. Oh, the Administration said she didn't because she never went into the three-mile limit. But we knew that North Vietnam claimed a twelve-mile limit and we recognize the twelve-mile limit for China and North Korea. And if we wanted to dispute whether or not they were entitled to the three-mile limit, you know where we should have been? Before the Security Council of the United Nations, not acting unilaterally, as an aggressor nation. You know why we didn't go before the Security Council? We'd have lost. And the Administration knew it. We weren't looking for a peaceful out, but we intended to make war.

Safer: The doubts about what happened August 4, 1964, have weighed heavily on the senator who was President Johnson's principal ally in steering the Tonkin Gulf Resolution through the Senate, J. William Fulbright, chairman of the Foreign Relations Committee. He spent many of the next six years trying to repeal the Resolution.

Fulbright: I am personally convinced in my own mind that no attack took place on the fourth. But of course, it's impossible really in a way for me to prove it negative. I'll put it this way. They most certainly did not prove the affirmative case, that there was an attack.

Safer: But on the night of August 4, 1964, hardly anyone doubted Defense Secretary Robert McNamara's official version. McNamara, now president of the World Bank, declined an invitation to recall the events of Tonkin Gulf on this broadcast. But he left office in March 1968, unshaken in his contention that two U.S. destroyers had been illegally and deliberately attacked while on normal routine patrol somewhere near the middle of Tonkin Gulf. Senator Fulbright disagrees.

Fulbright: If one telegram, which we later found from Commander Herrick of the *Maddox*, had been made available to the Committee at that time, I'm quite sure they would have had long hearings, gone into it thoroughly. And if they had been able to discover the facts as they actually were, I don't think they would have passed the Resolution, because it was based on absolutely false, erroneous information. The events that they related then of August 4, 1964, were not true. Our ships—it was not an unprovoked, deliberate attack; in fact, there was no attack at all.

Safer: Secretary McNamara, in his briefing to the nation and the Congress, never mentioned that message from Captain Herrick, which came in right after the night battle of August 4. "Review of action makes many recorded contacts and torpedoes fired appear doubtful. Freak weather effects and overeager sonar man may have accounted for many reports. No actual visual sightings by *Maddox*. Suggest complete evaluation before any further action."

Other things McNamara left out or didn't know or touched on too lightly were warnings from various commanders in the Pacific. They warned that North Vietnam regarded the *Maddox* as an enemy who was helping the South Vietnamese patrol boats shell the North. The shelling had occurred just before the *Maddox* reached Tonkin Gulf. On July 31, the South Vietnamese used four patrol boats like these, which the U.S. Navy had just given them, to hit these two North Vietnamese islands, Han Mi, three miles from the North Vietnam mainland, and Han Nu, four miles from the mainland. It was the first shelling of North Vietnam of its kind and they held the United States as responsible as the South

Vietnamese. And this was known to the Naval Command because the black box, whatever else it was doing, was intercepting North Vietnamese communications.

Early Sunday morning, August 2, Captain John Herrick, division commander aboard the *Maddox,* sent his first warning to the Seventh Fleet. Herrick to Seventh Fleet: "Consider continuance of patrol presents an unacceptable risk." Seventh Fleet to Maddox: "When considered prudent resume itinerary." In other words, take care of yourself, but stay there.

You were concerned even though you hadn't sighted a torpedo boat yet?

Herrick: Well, we were threatened that night by concentrations of junks, which made us believe we were unwelcome in that area. We did avoid them and proceeded to the east until we avoided the concentration of junks and continued with our patrol.

Safer: That afternoon, Sunday, August 2, 1964, the first battle of Tonkin Gulf. The *Maddox* fired first. Warning shots, the Pentagon said, and from the nearby carrier *Ticonderoga,* navy planes attacked the PT boats. North Vietnam said they had chased the *Maddox* out of their waters, and warned America to stay away. In Washington, the president went to church with Mrs. Johnson and set a soothing tone for the nation. The next day the president ordered the *Turner Joy* to join the *Maddox* and, if attacked, to destroy the attacking force.

From Fleet Commander: "In view of *Maddox* incident, consider it our best interest that we assert right of freedom of the seas and resume Gulf of Tonkin patrol earliest." That same message to Captain Herrick told him that his CPA, his closest point of approach to the coastline of North Vietnam, would be eight nautical miles. And his closest point of approach to the North Vietnamese islands would be four nautical miles.

And from Task Force 77 steaming in the South China Sea, a most somber warning: "It is apparent that DRV," North Vietnam, "has thrown down the gauntlet and now considers itself at war with the United States. It is felt they will attack U.S. forces on sight with no regard to cost. U.S. ships in Gulf of Tonkin can no longer assume that they will be considered neutrals exercising the right of free transit."

CINCPAC, Commander in Chief Pacific, to *Maddox*: "Patrol will A) Clearly demonstrate our determination to continue these operations. B) Possibly draw North Vietnamese Navy patrol boats northward away from area of 34A opps."

What were we really doing there that night?

Morse: Well, we were protecting operation 34A. Operation 34A was an operation, that's the code name, whereby South Vietnamese patrol boats bombarded two North Vietnamese islands and two security posts on the mainland of North Vietnam on two different nights. My suspicion was that the *Maddox* was a decoy ship. And that's exactly what she was. This is what the Secretary of Defense said: "Our navy played absolutely no part in, was not associated with, was not aware of any South Vietnam actions." Now let me point out how he concealed the facts. He didn't even tell us about the message that the Joint Chief's of Staff had sent out of the Pentagon to the commander of the Pacific about operation 34A. You mean to tell me that the Secretary of Defense didn't know about that?

Safer: Early in the morning of August 4, the black box on the *Maddox* intercepts a North Vietnamese message and the warning goes out from Captain Herrick to the Fleet. Maddox to Fleet: "Evaluation of information from various sources indicates North Vietnam considers patrol directly involved with 34A opps. North Vietnam considers the United States ships present as enemies because of these operations."

Was it also your function in Tonkin to possibly withdraw enemy resistance from South Vietnamese commando hit-and-run raids that were happening that night off the coast—coastal islands of North Vietnam?

Herrick: Not to my knowledge, Morley, we have no—this was not included in our briefing and if it happened, it happened, but this was not the mission we were sent up there to do.

Safer: Could it be, indeed, that you were part of operation 34A of the South Vietnamese commando raids that were happening in the South without even knowing it?

Herrick: No possibility, no. No connection. This was entirely separate operation, and would have been conducted regardless of whether there were 34 Alpha Opps as they were called.

Safer: Whether Herrick knew it or not, on the night of August 3, the night before, the South Vietnamese Navy, again using American supplied patrol boats, raided the mainland of North Vietnam. Operation 34A. It was the first time the mainland had been shelled and the North Vietnamese blamed the Americans. The battle of Tonkin Gulf took place the night of August 4 Tonkin time. It was twelve hours earlier in Washington. President Johnson talked to his aides many times during the day. One of them was McGeorge Bundy, the president's adviser on national security. Bundy, now president of the Ford Foundation, declined an invitation by *60 Minutes* to recall that day in the White House.

The president reached his decision early. He would bomb North Vietnam. The president was assured an attack had taken place, even though Captain Herrick on board the *Maddox* still had his doubts. Herrick cabled: "Entire action leaves many doubts except for apparent attempted ambush at beginning. Suggest thorough reconnaissance in daylight by aircraft."

And at 1:30 A.M. the message we have already seen, the message that Senator Fulbright later said could have changed history. It showed Captain Herrick even more doubtful. "Review of action makes many recorded contacts and torpedoes fired appeared doubtful. Freak weather effects, and overeager sonar man may have accounted for many reports. No actual visual sightings by *Maddox.* Suggest complete evaluation before any further actions."

But the White House and the Pentagon and Pacific Headquarters kept pressing Captain Herrick for absolute certainly immediately. At 2:45 A.M. Tonkin time, Herrick to headquarters: "Details of action present a confusing picture although certain original ambush was bonafide."

Your original messages to the Pentagon in Washington did leave some doubt, is that correct?

Herrick: They were intended to. I wanted to have a little time to interview the CO of the *Maddox* and the *Turner Joy* and to accumulate the information necessary to arrive at a logical conclusion of what happened that night. And after that information was in, then I verified my previous reports and stated that I definitely felt that we had been attacked that night.

Safer: It's also been suggested that Washington was putting a great deal of pressure on you to come up with some positive answers to what happened that night. A positive answer being, "Yes, we were attacked."

Herrick: Well, I'm sure they needed one. And that's what we were trying to obtain for them and we did and sent it in.

Safer: By 6:00 o'clock that evening in Washington, President Johnson had given the final go ahead for the bombing of North Vietnam. After that, the president called the leaders of Congress to the White House to tell them. They were unanimously behind him. The president asked them for a resolution of support. But a resolution had already been drafted weeks before at the State Department to give the president power to take any action to repel aggression and save South Vietnam. Again 100 percent backing from the leaders of both parties. And yet while Seventh Fleet pilots were preparing to attack, the Pentagon was still pressing the commander in chief of the Pacific, Admiral Sharp, to press Captain Herrick on the *Maddox* to, in McNamara's words, "make damn sure there had been an attack."

Admiral Sharp to Herrick: "1) Can you confirm absolutely that you were attacked? 2) Can you confirm sinking of PT boats? 3) Desire reply directly with supporting evidence."

Captain Herrick's final report shortly after 8:00 P.M., Washington time. He still had doubts. "*Maddox* scored no known hits and never positively identified a boat. No known damage or personnel casualties to either ship. *Turner Joy* claims sinking one boat and damaging another. The first boat to close *Maddox* probably fired torpedo at *Maddox,* which was heard but not seen. All subsequent *Maddox* torpedo reports were doubtful in that it is supposed that sonar man was hearing ship's own propeller beat."

But by now it's all academic. President Johnson goes on television shortly before midnight to announce the bombing of North Vietnam. The next day at the United Nations, Ambassador Adlai Stevenson explains American action and calls for world support. Two days later, Congress passes the Tonkin Resolution. It gives the president authority to take America deep into Vietnam and open war, without a declaration of war. The president would later refer to the Tonkin Gulf Resolution as his authority for the actions he took in Vietnam. He told Walter Cronkite last winter that there were unknown risks in an actual declaration of war on North Vietnam.

Johnson: I didn't ask for a declaration of war because I didn't know what treaty China might have with North Vietnam, or Russia might have with North Vietnam. The Communists have these agreements among themselves. And if we'd declared war against North Vietnam that might automatically declare war against China and bring them in, trigger the thing. Or the Soviet Union.

Fulbright: The president, you remember, was in the midst of a campaign for the presidency. His platform was, "I'm against a widening of the war." He used to say in his speeches, "I am not about to send American boys to Asia to fight the battles that Asian boys should fight," and similar statements. Barry Goldwater was supposed to be the warmonger and the hawk. And this was one reason I was taken in. I was supporting the idea of Johnson. So—a declaration of war is just the opposite of what this was represented to be. This was a resolution to prevent a war. Now I think if he'd come in for a war the country would have been shocked, I don't think they had any idea of going to war in this way.

Johnson: But I didn't want any doubt about the American Congress. Anyone serving in Congress twenty-five years as I had served in Congress wasn't about to undertake the responsibilities and the dangers I had in South Vietnam without the Congress being with me. And the Congress was with me before that resolution went up. Every single man in that room recommended it and advocated it. But when the going got hard, when the road got longer and dustier, when the casualties started coming in, why certain folks started looking for the cellar. And they—a good many of them have. And I don't question their right to do so. I don't even criticize them for taking that position if that's what their conscience dictates. But I just wish their conscience had been operating when they were making these other decisions because Congress gave us this authority in August 1964, to do whatever may be necessary; that's pretty far-reaching. That's the sky's the limit.

Morse: At the time I referred to it as another sinking of the *Maine.*

Safer: Suggesting?

Morse: Well, you know what the best historical advice is in regard to the sinking of the *Maine*. It was a deliberate act on the part of the United States to have an excuse to go to war against Spain. The Gulf of Tonkin was a deliberate aggressive act on the part of the Johnson Administration to justify making war against North Vietnam.

Safer: Three weeks after the Tonkin incident, the *Maddox* put into Subic Bay in the Philippines. Investigators from the Pentagon came aboard and interrogated most of the crew. Testimony only of those who thought they had seen enemy action was later presented to the Fulbright Committee. No testimony from those who thought nothing was there.

Morse: Well, don't pay any attention to what the military says after the fact to make a case before the fact. If you rely upon the American military for credibility, then you're easy prey.

Safer: Another Pentagon report investigated how the top military commanders handled the Tonkin incident. The Fulbright Committee asked to see that report but was refused. The report is still secret, but a former assistant defense secretary remembers what it said.

Warnke: As far as the facts are concerned, I think it's pretty clear that there was an attack on the American destroyers. Now the attack was nothing as dramatic as blowing up the battleship *Maine,* but nonetheless, the proof indicated that an attack occurred. So what people are questioning now is really the validity of our entire Vietnamese involvement.

Safer: Were we waiting for an incident at the time?

Warnke: Oh, I would say, trying to reconstruct history, that probably we were on the alert for the kind of provocation that would lead us to react, yes. And the Tonkin Gulf incident just provided the trigger for an American response that would have occurred in any event at some point in history. American involvement, it seems to me, was not precipitated by the Tonkin Gulf incident. It has just come to characterize a policy which many of us have concluded since was mistaken judgment.

Safer: In January, Congress finally repealed the Tonkin Gulf Resolution. Senator Fulbright's argument was: "The Resolution, like any other contract based on misrepresentation, was null and void."

Was the Resolution based on misrepresentation? We may never

know. The Fulbright Committee dropped its investigation in 1968 and never came up with a final, definitive report. Some have questioned: Is that the way to run an investigation? But more important about the Tonkin incident: Is that the way a great nation goes to war?

Unfortunately—yes. History is studded with debatable, even trifling incidents that triggered great wars. And now again, the Tonkin Gulf incident and the Indochina war.

It is a question that the Congress and the country is debating today— six and a half years later, at least a million Indochinese dead, 300,000 American wounded, 44,631 American dead. And more to come.

Introduction to
Seymour M. Hersh's

"The Massacre at My Lai"

On the morning of March 16, 1968, a platoon of American soldiers under the command of Lieutenant William Calley killed hundreds of civilians—primarily old men, women, children, and babies—in My Lai, a hamlet in Vietnam. Many were herded into a ditch and executed with automatic weapons. The massacre stopped only after an American helicopter crew landed near the remaining Vietnamese hiding in a bunker and threatened to fire on the American soldiers if they continued their attack. A military investigation, begun after a soldier reported details of routine brutality against civilians, was conducted by Colin Powell, then a young U.S. army major, who refuted claims that a massacre had occurred.

Seymour Hersh's exposure of the extent of the massacre is a centerpiece of American secret history. A young, freelance journalist, Hersh first heard of the carnage from Ron Ridenhour, a soldier who had learned of the events at My Lai secondhand. Ridenhour had sent letters about the massacre to President Nixon, the Pentagon, the State Department, the Joint Chiefs of Staff, and members of Congress. Hersh published his articles in November 1969 through a small news agency, The Dispatch News Service, providing details of the massacre as well as the army's efforts to hide the truth. His revelations released a firestorm of attention. *Life* magazine obtained photos of the carnage. Major news outlets including *Time, Newsweek,* and CBS all followed with stories of their own, turning My Lai into one of the seminal events of the war.

Under increasing pressure, Calley was convicted in 1971 of premeditated murder and initially sentenced to life in prison. Of the twenty-six soldiers initially charged, Calley was the only one found guilty. He eventually served only about three years under house arrest at Fort Benning, Georgia. In his defense, Calley claimed that he was "following orders" from his superior, Captain Ernest Medina, who denied giving the orders and was acquitted.

Hersh went on to become the preeminent American investigative journalist. He received a Pulitzer Prize in 1970 for his My Lai articles and more than a dozen major journalism prizes including George Polk awards and a National Book Critics Circle Award for *The Price of Power: Kissinger in the Nixon White House*. In 2004, he wrote about abuses at the Abu Ghraib prison in Iraq (see below)—an eerie echo of what happens when soldiers "follow orders."

ADDITIONAL SOURCES

Hersh, Seymour M. *My Lai 4: A Report on the Massacre and Its Aftermath.* New York: Random House, 1970.

———. *Cover-up: The Army's Secret Investigation of the Massacre at My Lai 4.* New York: Random House, 1972.

Olson, James and Randy Roberts. *My Lai: A Brief History with Documents.* New York: Bedford/St. Martin's, 1998.

Seymour M. Hersh

The Massacre at My Lai

"Lieutenant Accused of
Murdering 109 Civilians"

FORT BENNING, GA., Nov. 13—Lt. William L. Calley Jr., twenty-six years old, is a mild-mannered, boyish-looking Vietnam combat veteran with the nickname "Rusty." The Army is completing an investigation of charges that he deliberately murdered at least 109 Vietnamese civilians in a search-and-destroy mission in March 1968 in a Viet Cong stronghold known as "Pinkville."

Calley has formally been charged with six specifications of mass murder. Each specification cites a number of dead, adding up to the 109 total, and charges that Calley did "with premeditation murder . . . Oriental human beings, whose names and sex are unknown, by shooting them with a rifle."

The army calls it murder; Calley, his counsel and others associated with the incident describe it as a case of carrying out orders.

"Pinkville" has become a widely known code word among the military in a case that many officers and some Congressmen believe will become far more controversial than the recent murder charges against eight Green Berets.

ARMY INVESTIGATION TEAMS spent nearly one year studying the incident before filing charges against Calley, a platoon leader of the Eleventh Brigade of the Americal Division at the time of the killings.

Calley was formally charged on or about Sept. 6, 1969, in the multiple deaths, just a few days before he was due to be released from active service.

Calley has since hired a prominent civilian attorney, former Judge George W. Latimer of the U.S. Court of Military Appeals, and is now awaiting a military determination of whether the evidence justifies a general court-martial. Pentagon officials describe the present stage of the case as the equivalent of a civilian grand jury proceeding.

Calley, meanwhile, is being detained at Fort Benning, where his movements are sharply restricted. Even his exact location on the base is a secret; neither the provost marshal, nor the Army's Criminal Investigation Division knows where he is being held.

The Army has refused to comment on the case, "in order not to prejudice the continuing investigation and rights of the accused." Similarly, Calley—although agreeing to an interview—refused to discuss in detail what happened on March 16, 1968.

However, many other officers and civilian officials, some angered by Calley's action and others angry that charges of murder were filed in the case, talked freely in interviews at Fort Benning and Washington.

THESE FACTORS are not in dispute:

The Pinkville area, about six miles northeast of Quang Ngai, had been a Viet Cong fortress since the Vietnam war began. In early February 1968, a company of the Eleventh Brigade, as part of Task Force Barker, pushed through the area and was severely shot up.

Calley's platoon suffered casualties. After the Communist Tet offensive in February 1968, a larger assault was mounted, again with high casualties and little success. A third attack was quickly mounted and it was successful.

The Army claimed 128 Viet Cong were killed. Many civilians also were killed in the operation. The area was a free fire zone from which all non-Viet Cong residents had been urged, by leaflet, to flee. Such zones are common throughout Vietnam.

One man who took part in the mission with Calley said that in the earlier two attacks "we were really shot up."

"Every time we got hit it was from the rear," he said. "So the third time in there the order came down to go in and make sure no one was behind.

"We were told to just clear the area. It was a typical combat assault formation. We came in hot, with a cover of artillery in front of us, came down the line and destroyed the village.

"There are always some civilian casualties in a combat operation. He isn't guilty of murder."

The order to clear the area was relayed from the battalion commander to the company commander to Calley, the source said.

Calley's attorney said in an interview: "This is one case that should never have been brought. Whatever killing there was was in a firefight in connection with the operation."

"You can't afford to guess whether a civilian is a Viet Cong or not. Either they shoot you or you shoot them.

"This case is going to be important—to what standard do you hold a combat officer in carrying out a mission?

"There are two instances where murder is acceptable to anybody: where it is excusable and where it is justified. If Calley did shoot anybody because of the tactical situation or while in a firefight, it was either excusable or justifiable."

Adding to the complexity of the case is the fact that investigators from the army inspector general's office, which conducted the bulk of the investigation, considered filing charges against at least six other men involved in the action March 16.

A Fort Benning infantry officer has found that the facts of the case justify Calley's trial by general court-martial on charges of premeditated murder.

Pentagon officials said that the next steps are for the case to go to Calley's brigade commander and finally to the Fort Benning post commander for findings on whether there should be a court-martial. If they so hold, final charges and specifications will be drawn up and made public at that time, the officials said.

Calley's friends in the officer corps at Fort Benning, many of them West Point graduates, are indignant. However, knowing the high stakes of the case, they express their outrage in private.

"They're using this as a Goddamned example," one officer complained. "He's a good soldier. He followed orders.

"There weren't any friendlies in the village. The orders were to shoot anything that moved."

Another officer said "It could happen to any of us. He has killed and has seen a lot of killing . . . Killing becomes nothing in Vietnam. He knew that there were civilians there, but he also knew that there were VC among them."

A third officer, also familiar with the case, said: "There's this question—I think anyone who goes to (Viet) Nam asks it. What's a civilian? Someone who works for us at day and puts on Viet Cong pajamas at night?"

There is another side of the Calley case—one that the army cannot yet disclose. Interviews have brought out the fact that the investigation into the Pinkville affair was initiated six months after the incident, only after some of the men who served under Calley complained.

The army has photographs purported to be of the incident, although these have not been introduced as evidence in the case, and may not be.

"They simply shot up this village and (Calley) was the leader of it," said one Washington source. "When one guy refused to do it, Calley took the rifle away and did the shooting himself."

Asked about this, Calley refused to comment.

One Pentagon officer discussing the case tapped his knee with his hand and remarked, "Some of those kids he shot were this high. I don't think they were Viet Cong. Do you?"

None of the men interviewed about the incident denied that women and children were shot.

A source of amazement among all those interviewed was that the story had yet to reach the press.

"Pinkville has been a word among GIs for a year," one official said. "I'll never cease to be amazed that it hasn't been written about before."

A high-ranking officer commented that he first heard talk of the Pinkville incident soon after it happened; the officer was on duty in Saigon at the time.

Why did the army choose to prosecute this case? On what is it basing the charge that Calley acted with premeditation before killing? The court-martial should supply the answers to these questions, but some of the men already have their opinions.

"The army knew it was going to get clobbered on this at some point," one military source commented. "If they don't prosecute somebody, if this stuff comes out without the army taking some action, it could be even worse."

ANOTHER VIEW that many held was that the top level of the military was concerned about possible war crime tribunals after the Vietnam war.

As for Calley—he is smoking four packs of cigarettes daily and getting out of shape. He is 5-foot-3, slender, with expressionless gray eyes and thinning brown hair. He seems slightly bewildered and hurt by the charges against him. He says he wants nothing more than to be cleared and return to the army.

"I know this sounds funny," he said in an interview, "but I like the army . . . and I don't want to do anything to hurt it."

Friends described Calley as a "gung-ho army man . . . army all the way." Ironically, even his staunchest supporters admit, his enthusiasm may be somewhat to blame.

"Maybe he did take some order to clear out the village a little bit too literally," one friend said, "but he's a fine boy."

CALLEY HAD BEEN SHIPPED home early from Vietnam, after the army refused his request to extend his tour of duty. Until the incident at Pinkville, he had received nothing but high ratings from his superior officers. He was scheduled to be awarded the Bronze and Silver Stars for his combat efforts, he said. He has heard nothing about the medals since arriving at Fort Benning.

Calley was born in Miami, Fla., and flunked out of the Palm Beach Junior College before enlisting in the army. He became a second lieutenant in September 1967, shortly after going to Vietnam. The army lists his home of record as Waynesville, N.C.

An information sheet put out by the public affairs officer of the Americal Division the day after the March 16 engagement contained this terse mention of the incident: "The swiftness with which the units moved into the area surprised the enemy. After the battle the Eleventh Brigade moved into the village searching each hut and tunnel."

"Hamlet Attack Called 'Point-Blank Murder' "

Washington, Nov. 20—Three American soldiers who participated in the March 1968 attack on a Vietnam village called Pinkville said in interviews made public today that their army combat unit perpetrated, in the words of one, "point-blank murder" on the residents.

"The whole thing was so deliberate. It was point-blank murder and I was standing there watching it," said Sgt. Michael Bernhardt, Franklin Square, N.Y., now completing his army tour at Fort Dix, N.J.

Bernhardt was a member of one of three platoons of an Eleventh Infantry Brigade company under the command of Capt. Ernest Medina. The company entered the Viet Cong–dominated area on March 16, 1968, when on a search-and-destroy mission. Pinkville, known to Vietnamese as Song My village, is about six miles northeast of Quang Ngai.

The army has charged Lt. William L. Calley Jr., Miami, one of Medina's platoon leaders, with the murder of 109 South Vietnamese civilians in the attack. A squad leader in Calley's platoon, Sgt. David Mitchell, St. Francisvilie, La., is under investigation for assault with intent to murder.

At least four other men, including Medina, are under investigation in connection with the incident. Calley and his attorney, George W. Latimer, Salt Lake City, have said that the unit was under orders to clear the area.

Bernhardt, interviewed at Fort Dix, said he had been delayed on the operation and fell slightly behind the company, then led by Calley's platoon, as it entered the village. This is his version of what took place:

"They (Calley's men) were doing a whole lot of shooting up there, but none of it was incoming—I'd been around enough to tell that. I figured they were advancing on the village with fire power.

"I walked up and saw these guys doing strange things. They were doing it three ways. One: They were setting fire to the hootches and huts and waiting for people to come out and then shooting them up. Two: They were going into the hootches and shooting them up. Three: They were gathering people in groups and shooting them.

"As I walked in, you could see piles of people all through the village . . . all over. They were gathered up into large groups.

"I saw them shoot an M-79 (grenade launcher) into a group of people who were still alive. But it (the shooting) was mostly done with a machine gun. They were shooting women and children just like anybody else.

"We met no resistance and I only saw three captured weapons. We had no casualties. It was just like any other Vietnamese village—old Papa-san, women and kids. As a matter of fact, I don't remember seeing one military-age male in the entire place, dead or alive. The only prisoner I saw was about fifty."

An Army communique reporting on the operation said that Medina's company recovered two M-1 rifles, a carbine, a shortwave radio and enemy documents in the assault. The Viet Cong body count was listed as 128 and there was no mention of civilian casualties.

Bernhardt, short and intense, told his story in staccato fashion, with an obvious sense of relief at finally talking about it. At one point he said to his interviewer: "You're surprised? I wouldn't be surprised at anything these dudes (the men who did the shooting) did."

Bernhardt said he had no idea precisely how many villagers were shot. He said that he had heard death counts ranging from 170 to more than 700.

Bernhardt also said he had no idea whether Calley personally shot 109 civilians, as the army has charged. However, he said, "I know myself that he killed a whole lot of people." Residents of the Pinkville areas have told newspapermen that 567 villagers were killed in the operation.

Why did the men run amuck?

"It's my belief," the sergeant said, "that the company was conditioned to do this. The treatment was lousy . . . We were always out in the bushes. I think they were expecting us to run into resistance at Pinkville and also expecting them (the Viet Cong) to use the people as hostages."

A few days before the mission, he said, the men's general contempt for Vietnamese civilians intensified when some GIs walked into a landmine, injuring nearly twenty and killing at least one member of the company.

Why didn't he report the incident at the time?

"After it was all over, some colonel came down to the fire-base where we were stationed and asked about it, but we heard no further. Later they (Medina and some other officers) called me over to the command post and asked me not to write my Congressman."

(The army subsequently substantiated Bernhardt's accusation. In a private letter dated Aug. 6, 1969, Col. John G. Hill, Jr., a deputy for staff action control in the office of Army Chief of Staff William C. Westmoreland, wrote that Medina acknowledged that he had requested Bernhardt to wait until a brigade investigation of the incident was completed. Nothing came of the investigation.)

Bernhardt said that about 90 percent of the sixty to seventy men in the short-handed company were involved in the shootings. He took no part, he said. "I only shoot at people who shoot at me," was his explanation.

"The army ordered me not to talk," Bernhardt told the interviewer. "But there are some orders that I have to personally decide whether to obey; I have my own conscience to consider.

"The whole thing has kind of made me wonder if I could trust people any more."

His opinion, he said, is that a higher ranking officer must have ordered the destruction of Pinkville. "Calley's just a small fry," he said.

Bernhardt said the army must have known at high levels just what did happen at Pinkville.

"They've got pictures. Some dude went along on the mission and shot pictures," he said.

Bernhardt said the photographs were shown to him in the Article 32 proceeding, which concluded that the charges against Calley were justified.

"They showed a mass of people . . . this pile-up of people. I don't see how anybody could say it was artillery or crossfire that killed those people," he said.

(*The Cleveland Plain Dealer* printed today photographs showing

South Vietnamese civilians allegedly killed in the incident. It said the photographs came from a former army combat photographer, Ronald L. Haeberle, Cleveland.)

(Haeberle said in a copyright story that he joined the company just before it entered the village and heard from the men that the villagers were suspected of being Viet Cong sympathizers. He said he saw men, women and children killed.)

Another witness to the shootings was Michael Terry, Orem, Utah, then a member of the C Platoon of Medina's company and now a sophomore at nearby Brigham Young University. Interviewed at his home, Terry said he, too, came on the scene moments after the killings began.

"They just marched through shooting everybody," he said. "Seems like no one said anything . . . They just started pulling people out and shooting them."

At one point, he said, more than twenty villagers were lined up in front of a ditch and shot.

"They had them in a group standing over a ditch—just like a Nazi-type thing . . . One officer ordered a kid to machine-gun everybody down, but the kid just couldn't do it. He threw the machine gun down and the officer picked it up . . ." Terry said.

"I don't remember seeing any men in the ditch. Mostly women and kids."

Later, he and the platoon team he headed were taking a lunch break near the ditch when, Terry said, he noticed "some of them were still breathing . . . They were pretty badly shot up. They weren't going to get any medical help, and so we shot them. Shot maybe five of them . . ."

Why did it happen?

"I think that probably the officers didn't really know if they were ordered to kill the villagers or not . . . A lot of guys feel that they (the South Vietnamese civilians) aren't human beings; we just treated them like animals."

Apparently one officer, who was not from Medina's company, attempted to halt the shootings. Terry and Bernhardt both reported that a helicopter pilot from an aviation support unit landed in the midst of the incident and attempted to quell it.

The officer warned that he would report the shootings. On the next day, the pilot was killed in action and the subsequent investigation started by officials of the Eleventh Brigade was dropped after one and a half days because of insufficient evidence.

Terry said he first learned of the present investigation when he was interviewed last spring by a colonel from the Army Inspector General's office. Bernhardt was not questioned until a team from the army's Criminal Investigation Division visited him two months ago.

The third witness to the Pinkville shootings cannot be identified. He is still on active duty with the army on the West Coast. But he corroborated in detail the Bernhardt and Terry descriptions of that day in March 1968.

"I was shooting pigs and a chicken while the others were shooting people," he said. "It isn't just a nightmare; I'm completely aware of how real this was.

"It's something I don't think a person would understand—the reality of it just didn't hit me until recently, when I read about it again in the newspapers."

All three GIs were read key excerpts from a three-page letter sent in March by a former GI, Ronald Ridenhour, to the army and thirty other officials, including some senators. The letter outlined the Pinkville incident as he understood it. It was Ridenhour's persistence that prompted the army to begin its high-level investigation in April.

Ridenhour, now a student at Claremont (Calif.) Men's College, was not in Medina's company and did not participate in the shootings. He relied on information from Terry and Bernhardt, among many others, to draft his letter.

Calley's attorney refused to comment on the new charges brought out in the interviews. But another source, discussing Calley's position, said, "Nobody's put the finger yet on the man who started it."

The source said also that he understood that Calley and other officers in the company initially resisted the orders but eventually did their job. Calley's platoon led the attack on the village, with the other units forming a horseshoe-shaped cordon around the area, to prevent enemy troops from fleeing.

"I don't care whether Calley used the best judgment or not—he was faced with a tough decision," the source said.

"Ex-GI Tells of Killing Civilians
at Pinkville"

Terre Haute, Ind., Nov. 25—A former GI told in interviews yesterday how he executed, under orders, dozens of South Vietnamese civilians during the United States Army attack on the village of Song My in March 1968. He estimated that he and his fellow soldiers shot 370 villagers during the operation in what has become known as Pinkville.

Paul Meadlo, twenty-two years old, West Terre Haute, Ind., a farm community near the Illinois border, gave an eyewitness account—the first made available thus far—of what happened when a platoon led by Lt. William L. Calley, Jr., entered Pinkville on a search-and-destroy mission. The army has acknowledged that at least 100 civilians were killed by the men; Vietnamese survivors had told reporters that the death total was 567.

Meadlo, who was wounded in a mine accident the day after Pinkville, disclosed that the company captain, Ernest Medina, was in the area at the time of the shootings and made no attempt to stop them.

Calley, twenty-six, Waynesville, N.C., has been accused of the premeditated murder of 109 civilians in the incident. Medina, as commander of the Eleventh Infantry Brigade unit, is under investigation for his role in the shootings. Last week the army said that at least twenty-four other men were under investigation, including Calley's chief noncommissioned officer, Sgt. David Mitchell, twenty-nine, St. Francisville, La., who is being investigated for assault with intent to commit murder. Calley was ordered yesterday to stand general court-martial.

Here is Meadlo's story as given in interviews at his mother's home near Terre Haute:

"There was supposed to have been some Viet Cong in Pinkville and we began to make a sweep through it. Once we got there we began gathering up the people . . . started putting them in big mobs. There must have been about forty or forty-five civilians standing in one big circle in the middle of the village . . . Calley told me and a couple of other guys to watch them.

" 'You know what I want you to do with them' he said," Meadlo related. He and the others continued to guard the group. "About ten minutes later Calley came back. 'Get with it,' he said. 'I want them dead.'

"So we stood about ten or fifteen feet away from them, then he (Calley) started shooting them. Then he told me to start shooting them. . . . I started to shoot them, but the other guys (who had been assigned to guard the civilians) wouldn't do it.

"So we (Meadlo and Calley) went ahead and killed them. I used more than a whole clip—actually I used four or five clips," Meadlo said. (There are 17 M-16 shells in a clip.) He estimated that he killed at least 15 civilians—or nearly half of those in the circle.

Asked what he thought at the time, Meadlo said, "I just thought we were supposed to do it." Later, he said that the shooting "did take a load off my conscience for the buddies we'd lost. It was just revenge, that's all it was."

The company had been in the field for forty days without relief before the Pinkville incident on March 16, and had lost a number of men in mine accidents. Hostility to the Vietnamese was high in the company, Meadlo said.

The killings continued.

"We had about seven or eight civilians gathered in a hootch, and I was going to throw a hand grenade in. But someone told us to take them to the ditch (a drainage ditch in the village into which many civilians were herded—and shot).

"Calley was there and said to me, 'Meadlo, we've got another job to do.' So we pushed our seven to eight people in with the big bunch of them. And so I began shooting them all. So did Mitchell, Calley . . . (At this point Meadlo could not remember any more men involved). I guess I shot maybe twenty-five or twenty people in the ditch."

His role in the killings had not yet ended.

"After the ditch, there were just some people in hootches. I knew there were some people down in one hootch, maybe two or three, so I just threw a hand grenade in."

Meadlo is a tall, clean-cut son of an Indiana coal mine worker. He married his high-school sweetheart in suburban Terre Haute, began rearing a family (he has two children) and was drafted. He had been in Vietnam four months at the time of Pinkville. On the next day, March 17, his foot was blown off, when, while following Calley on an operation, a land mine was set off.

As Meadlo was waiting to be evacuated, other men in the company had reported that he told Calley that "this was his (Meadlo's) punishment for what he had done the day before." He warned, according to onlookers, that Calley would have his day of judgment too. Asked about this, Meadlo said he could not remember.

Meadlo is back at a factory job now in Terre Haute, fighting to keep a full disability payment from the Veterans' Administration. The loss of his right foot seems to bother him less than the loss of his self-respect.

Like other members of his company, he had been called just days before the interview by an officer at Fort Benning, Ga., where Calley is being held, and advised that he should not discuss the case with reporters. But, like other members of his company, he seemed eager to talk.

"This has made him awful nervous," explained his mother, Mrs. Myrtle Meadlo, fifty-seven, New Goshen, Ind. "He seems like he just can't get over it.

"I sent them a good boy and they made him a murderer."

Why did he do it?

"We all were under orders," Meadlo said. "We all thought we were doing the right thing. . . . At the time it didn't bother me."

He began having serious doubts that night about what he had done at Pinkville. He says he still has them.

"The kids and the women—they didn't have any right to die."

"In the beginning," Meadlo said, "I just thought we were going to be murdering the Viet Cong." He, like other members of his company, had attended a squad meeting the night before, at which time Company Commander Medina promised the boys a good firefight.

Calley and his platoon were assigned the key role of entering the Pinkville area first.

"When we came in we thought we were getting fired on," Meadlo said, although the company suffered no casualties, apparently because the Viet Cong had fled from the area during the night.

"We came in from this open field, and somebody spotted this one gook out there. He was down in a shelter, scared and huddling. . . . Someone said, 'There's a gook over here,' and asked what to do with him. Mitchell said, 'Shoot him,' and he did. The gook was standing up and shaking and waving his arms when he got it.

"Then we came onto this hootch, and one door was hard to open."

Meadlo said he crashed through the door and "found an old man in there shaking.

"I told them, 'I got one,' and it was Mitchell who told me to shoot him. That was the first man I shot. He was hiding in a dugout, shaking his head and waving his arms, trying to tell me not to shoot him."

After the carnage, Meadlo said, "I heard that all we were supposed to do was kill the VC. Mitchell said we were just supposed to shoot the men."

Women and children also were shot. Meadlo estimated that at least 310 persons were shot to death by the Americans that day.

"I know it was far more than 100 as the U.S. Army now says. I'm absolutely sure of that. There were bodies all around."

He has some haunting memories, he says. "They didn't put up a fight or anything. The women huddled against their children and took it. They brought their kids real close to their stomachs and hugged them, and put their bodies over them trying to save them. It didn't do much good," Meadlo said.

Two things puzzled him. He vigorously disputes the repeated reports of an artillery barrage before the village was approached.

"There wasn't any artillery barrage whatsoever in the village. Only some gunships firing from above," he said.

The South Vietnamese government said Saturday that twenty civilians were killed in the Pinkville attack, most of them victims of tactical air strikes or an artillery barrage laid down before the U.S. troops moved in. The government denied reports of a massacre.

Meadlo is curious also about the role of Capt. Medina in the incident.

"I don't know if the C.O. (Company Commander) gave the order to kill or not, but he was right there when it happened. Why didn't he stop it? He and Calley passed each other quite a few times that morning, but didn't say anything. Medina just kept marching around. He could've put a stop to it anytime he wanted."

The whole operation took about thirty minutes, Meadlo said.

As for Calley, Meadlo told of an incident a few weeks before Pinkville.

"We saw this woman walking across this rice paddy and Calley said, 'Shoot her,' so we did. When we got there the girl was alive, had this hole in her side. Calley tried to get someone to shoot her again; I don't know if he did."

In addition, Calley and Medina had told the men before Pinkville, Meadlo said, "that if we ever shoot any civilians, we should go ahead and plant a hand grenade on them."

Meadlo is not sure, but he thinks the feel of death came quickly to the company once it got to Vietnam.

"We were cautious at first, but as soon as the first man was killed, a new feeling came through the company . . . almost as if we all knew there was going to be a lot more killing."

Introduction to Neil Sheehan's "Vietnam Archive" from *"The Pentagon Papers"*

I N 1967, secretary of Defense Robert McNamara commissioned a top-secret history of the U.S. role in Indochina that eventually covered the period from the end of World War II to May 1968, the month peace talks began in Paris after President Johnson had limited further military involvement in Vietnam and announced his intention not to run for office again. Only some fifteen copies of the classified history, about 7,000 pages of narrative and supporting documents, were distributed. But Daniel Ellsberg, an analyst at the Rand Corporation, a research institute with close ties to the government, leaked the report to *The New York Times,* which on June 13, 1971, began publishing articles based on the information contained in the history, which became known as "The Pentagon Papers." After three installments appeared, the Department of Justice, under President Nixon, obtained a temporary restraining order against further publication, claiming that national security would be harmed. The issue was fought in the courts as the *Times, The Washington Post,* and other newspapers that had begun publishing the study argued against the order. In a landmark decision, on June 30th, the Supreme Court ruled that the newspapers could continue publication.

"The Pentagon Papers" provide a rare glimpse into the workings of the executive branch, and make clear "the deep-felt need of the government insider for secrecy," lead reporter Neil Sheehan wrote. "And even within the inner world, only a small number of men at the top know what is really happening." The papers also revealed a deep cynicism toward the public and a disregard for the loss of life.

As Sheehan noted, rarely has a collection of documents such as "The Pentagon Papers" come to light in modern history. He cited as other examples: the release of the secret Czarist archives after the Russian Revolution in 1917, the publication by the Weimar Republic after World War I of the records of imperial Germany, and the capture of the Nazi archives by the Allies after World War II.

ADDITIONAL SOURCES

Ellsberg, Daniel. *Secrets: A Memoir of Vietnam and the Pentagon Papers.* New York: Viking, 2002.

McNamara, Robert S. with Brian VanDeMark. *In Retrospect: The Tragedy and Lessons of Vietnam.* New York: Vintage, 1996.

Morris, Errol, director. *The Fog of War.* Sony Pictures Classics, 2003.

Rudenstine, David. *The Day the Presses Stopped: A History of the Pentagon Papers Case.* Berkeley, Calif.: University of California Press, 1998.

Sheehan, Neil, Hedrick Smith, E. W. Kenworthy, and Fox Butterfield. *The Pentagon Papers as Published by The New York Times.* Toronto, New York, London: Bantam Books, 1971.

Neil Sheehan

"Vietnam Archive: Study Tells How Johnson Secretly Opened Way to Ground Combat"

THE NEW YORK TIMES, JUNE 15, 1971

PRESIDENT JOHNSON decided on April 1, 1965, to use American ground troops for offensive action in South Vietnam because the Administration had discovered that its long-planned bombing of North Vietnam—which had just begun—was not going to stave off collapse in the South, the Pentagon's study of the Vietnam war discloses. He ordered that the decision be kept secret.

"The fact that this departure from a long-held policy had momentous implications was well recognized by the Administration leadership," the Pentagon analyst writes, alluding to the policy axiom since the Korean conflict that another land war in Asia should be avoided.

Although the President's decision was a "pivotal" change, the study declares, "Mr. Johnson was greatly concerned that the step be given as little prominence as possible."

The decision was embodied in National Security Action Memorandum 328, on April 6, which included the following paragraphs:

"5. The President approved an 18–20,000 man increase in U.S. military support forces to fill out existing units and supply needed logistic personnel.

"6. The President approved the deployment of two additional Marine Battalions and one Marine Air Squadron and associated headquarters and support elements.

"7. The President approved a change of mission for all Marine Battalions deployed to Vietnam to permit their more active use under conditions to be established and approved by the Secretary of Defense in consultation with the Secretary of State."

The paragraph stating the President's concern about publicity gave stringent orders in writing to members of the National Security Council:

"11. The President desires that with respect to the actions in paragraphs 5 through 7, premature publicity be avoided by all possible precautions. The actions themselves should be taken as rapidly as practicable, but in ways that should minimize any appearance of sudden changes in policy, and official statements on these troop movements will be made only with the direct approval of the Secretary of Defense, in consultation with the Secretary of State. The President's desire is that these movements and changes should be understood as being gradual and wholly consistent with existing policy."

The period of increasing ground-combat involvement is shown in the Pentagon papers to be the third major phase of President Johnson's commitment to South Vietnam. This period forms another section of the presentation of those papers by *The New York Times*.

The papers, prepared by a large team of authors in 1967–68 as an official study of how the United States went to war in Indochina, consist of 3,000 pages of analysis and 4,000 pages of supporting documents. The study covers nearly three decades of American policy toward Southeast Asia. Thus far *The Times*'s reports on the study, with presentation of key documents, have covered the period of clandestine warfare before the Tonkin Gulf incidents in 1964 and the planning for sustained bombing of North Vietnam to begin early the next year.

In the spring of 1965, the study discloses, the Johnson Administration pinned its hopes on air assaults against the North to break the enemy's will and persuade Hanoi to stop the Vietcong insurgency in the South. The air assaults began on a sustained basis on March 2.

"Once set in motion, however, the bombing effort seemed to stiffen rather than soften Hanoi's backbone, as well as the willingness of Hanoi's allies, particularly the Soviet Union, to work toward compromise," the study continues.

"Official hopes were high that the Rolling Thunder program . . . would rapidly convince Hanoi that it should agree to negotiate a settlement to the war in the South. After a month of bombing with no response from the North Vietnamese, optimism began to wane," the study remarks.

"The U.S. was presented essentially with two options: (1) to withdraw unilaterally from Vietnam leaving the South Vietnamese to fend for themselves, or (2) to commit ground forces in pursuit of its objectives. A third option, that of drastically increasing the scope and scale of the bombing, was rejected because of the concomitant high risk of inviting Chinese intervention."

And so within a month, the account continues, with the Administration recognizing that the bombing would not work quickly enough, the crucial decision was made to put the two Marine battalions already in South Vietnam on the offensive. The 3,500 marines had landed at Danang on March 8—bringing the total United States force in South Vietnam to 27,000—with their mission restricted to the static defense of the Danang airfield.

Orders Put in Writing

As a result of the President's wish to keep the shift of mission from defense to offense imperceptible to the public, the April 1 decision received no publicity "until it crept out almost by accident in a State Department release on 8 June," in the words of the Pentagon study.

The day before, the hastily improvised static security and enclave strategies of the spring were overtaken by a request from Gen. William C. Westmoreland, the American commander in Saigon, for nearly 200,000 troops. He wanted these forces, the Pentagon study relates, to hold off defeat long enough to make possible a further build-up of American troops.

"Swiftly and in an atmosphere of crisis," the study says, President Johnson gave his approval to General Westmoreland's request a little more than a month later, in mid-July. And once again, the study adds, Mr. Johnson concealed his decision.

But the President, the narrative continues, was now heeding the counsel of General Westmoreland to embark on a full-scale ground war. The study for this period concludes that Mr. Johnson and most of his Administration were in no mood for compromise on Vietnam.

As an indication of the Administration's mood during this period, the study cites "a marathon public-information campaign" conducted by Secretary of State Dean Rusk late in February and early in March as sustained bombing was getting under way.

Mr. Rusk, the study says, sought "to signal a seemingly reasonable but in fact quite tough U.S. position on negotiations, demanding that Hanoi 'stop doing what it is doing against its neighbors' before any negotiations could prove fruitful.

"Rusk's disinterest in negotiations at this time was in concert with the view of virtually all of the President's key advisers, that the path to peace was not then open," the Pentagon account continues. "Hanoi held sway over more than half of South Vietnam and could see the Saigon Government crumbling before her very eyes. The balance of power at this time simply did not furnish the U.S. with a basis for bargaining and Hanoi had no reason to accede to the hard terms that the U.S. had in mind. Until military pressures on North Vietnam could tilt the balance of forces the other way, talk of negotiation could be little more than a hollow exercise."

A Position of Compromise

The study also says that two of the President's major moves involving the bombing campaign in the spring of 1965 were designed, among other aims, to quiet critics and obtain public support for the air war by striking a position of compromise. But in fact, the account goes on, the moves masked publicly unstated conditions for peace that "were not 'compromise' terms, but more akin to a 'cease and desist' order that, from the D.R.V./VC point of view, was tantamount to a demand for their surrender." "D.R.V." denotes the Democratic Republic of Vietnam; "VC" the Vietcong.

In Mr. Johnson's first action, his speech at the Johns Hopkins University in Baltimore on April 7, he offered to negotiate "without posing any preconditions" and also held out what the study calls a "billion-dollar carrot" in the form of an economic-development program for the Mekong River Basin financed, by the United States, in which North Vietnam might participate.

The second action was the unannounced five-day pause in bombing in May, during which the President called upon Hanoi to accept a "political solution" in the South. This "seemed to be aimed more at clearing the decks for a subsequent intensified resumption than it was at evoking a reciprocal act of deescalation by Hanoi," the study says. Admiral Raborn, in his May 6 memorandum, had suggested a pause for this purpose and as an opportunity for Hanoi "to make concessions with some grace."

The air attacks had begun Feb. 8 and Feb. 11 with reprisal raids, codenamed Operations Flaming Dart I and II, announced as retaliation for Vietcong attacks on American installations at Pleiku and Quinhon.

In public Administration statements on the air assaults, the study goes on, President Johnson broadened "the reprisal concept as gradually and imperceptibly as possible" into sustained air raids against the North, in the same fashion that the analyst describes him blurring the shift from defensive to offensive action on the ground during the spring and summer of 1965.

The study declares that the two February strikes—unlike the Tonkin Gulf reprisals in August, 1964, which were tied directly to a North Vietnamese attack on American ships—were publicly associated with a "larger pattern of aggression" by North Vietnam. Flaming Dart II, for example, was characterized as "a generalized response to 'continued acts of aggression,'" the account notes.

"Although discussed publicly in very muted tones," it goes on, "the second Flaming Dart operation constituted a sharp break with past U.S. policy and set the stage for the continuing bombing program that was now to be launched in earnest."

In another section of the study, a Pentagon analyst remarks that "the change in ground rules . . . posed serious public-information and stage-managing problems for the President."

It was on Feb. 13, two days after this second reprisal, that Mr. Johnson ordered Operation Rolling Thunder. An important influence on his unpublicized decision was a memorandum from his special assistant for national security affairs, McGeorge Bundy, who was heading a fact-finding mission in Vietnam when the Vietcong attack at Pleiku occurred on Feb. 7. With Mr. Bundy were Assistant Secretary of Defense John T. McNaughton and Deputy Assistant Secretary of State Leonard Unger.

"A policy of sustained reprisal against North Vietnam" was the strategy advocated by Mr. Bundy in his memorandum, drafted on the President's personal Boeing 707, Air Force One, while returning from Saigon the same day."

The memorandum explained that the justification for the air attacks against the North, and their intensity, would be keyed to the level of Vietcong activity in the South.

"Sustained Pressure" Sought

"We are convinced that the political values of reprisal require a continuous operation," Mr. Bundy wrote. "Episodic responses geared on a one-for-one basis to 'spectacular' outrages would lack the persuasive force of sustained pressure. More important still, they would leave it open to the Communists to avoid reprisals entirely by giving up only a small element of their own program. . . . It is the great merit of the proposed scheme that to stop it the Communists would have to stop enough of their activity in the South to permit the probable success of a determined pacification effort."

The analyst notes, however, that Mr. Bundy's memorandum was a "unique articulation of a rationale for the Rolling Thunder policy" because Mr. Bundy held out as the immediate benefit an opportunity to rally the anti-Communist elements in the South and achieve some political stability and progress in pacification. "Once such a policy is put in force," Mr. Bundy wrote, in summary conclusions to his memorandum, "we shall be able to speak in Vietnam on many topics and in many ways, with growing force and effectiveness."

It was also plausible, he said, that bombing in the North, "even in a low key, would have a substantial depressing effect upon the morale of Vietcong cadres in South Vietnam."

Mr. Bundy, the study remarks, thus differed from most other proponents of bombing. These included Ambassador Maxwell D. Taylor, who despaired of improving the Saigon Government's effectiveness and who wanted bombing primarily as a will-breaking device "to inflict such pain or threat of pain upon the D.R.V. that it would be compelled to order a stand-down of Vietcong violence," in the study's words.

As several chapters of the Pentagon study show, a number of Administration strategists—particularly Walt W. Rostow, chairman of the State Department's Policy Planning Council—had assumed for years that "calculated doses" of American air power would accomplish this end.

Mr. Bundy, while not underrating the bombing's "impact on Hanoi" and its use "as a means of affecting the will of Hanoi," saw this as a "longer-range purpose."

"This Program Seems Cheap"

The bombing might not work. Mr. Bundy acknowledged. "Yet measured against the costs of defeat in Vietnam," he wrote, "this program seems cheap. And even if it fails to turn the tide—as it may—the value of the effort seems to us to exceed its cost."

President Johnson informed Ambassdor Taylor of his Rolling Thunder decision in a cablegram drafted in the White House and transmitted to Saigon late in the afternoon of Sunday, Feb. 13.

The cable told the Ambassador that "we will execute a program of measured and limited air action jointly with the GVN [the Government of Vietnam] against selected military targets in D.R.V., remaining south of the 19th Parallel until further notice."

"Our current expectation," the message added, "is that these attacks might come about once or twice a week and involve two or three targets on each day of operation."

Mr. Johnson said he hoped "to have appropriate GVN concurrence by Monday if possible. . . ."

The study recounts that "Ambassador Taylor received the news of the President's new program with enthusiasm. In his response, however, he explained the difficulties he faced in obtaining authentic GVN concurrence 'in the condition of virtual nongovernment' which existed in Saigon at that moment."

Gen. Nguyen Khanh, the nominal commander of the South Vietnamese armed forces, had ousted the civilian cabinet of Premier Tran Van Huong on Jan. 27. Led by Air Vice Marshal Nguyen Cao Ky, a group of young generals—the so-called Young Turks—were in turn intriguing against General Khanh.

(A footnote in the account of the first reprisal strikes, on Feb. 8, says that Marshal Ky, who led the South Vietnamese planes participating in the raid, caused "consternation" among American target controllers by dropping his bombs on the wrong targets. "In a last minute switch," the footnote says, Marshal Ky "dumped his flight's bomb loads on an unassigned target in the Vinhlinh area, in order, as he later explained, to avoid colliding with U.S.A.F. aircraft which, he claimed, were striking his originally assigned target when his flight arrived over the target area." Adm. U.S. Grant Sharp, commander of United States forces in the Pacific, reported the incident to the Joint Chiefs.)

Cables to the Embassies

Referring to the political situation in Saigon, the account says: "This Alice-in-Wonderland atmosphere notwithstanding, Taylor was undaunted."

"It will be interesting to observe the effect of our proposal on the internal political situation here," the Ambassador cabled back to Mr. Johnson in Washington about the bombing. "I will use the occasion to emphasize that a dramatic change is occurring in U.S. policy, one highly favorable to GVN interests but demanding a parallel dramatic change of attitude on the part of the GVN. Now is the time to install the best possible Government as we are clearly approaching a climax in the next few months."

Ambassador Taylor apparently obtained what concurrence was possible and on Feb. 8 another cable went out from the State Department to London and eight United States Embassies in the Far East besides the one in Saigon. The message told the ambassadors of the forthcoming bombing campaign and instructed them to "inform head of government or State (as appropriate) of above in strictest confidence and report reactions."

Both McGeorge Bundy and Ambassador Taylor had recommended playing down publicity on the details of the raids. "Careful public statements of U.S.G. [United States Government], combined with fact of continuing air actions, are expected to make it clear that military action will continue while aggression continues," the cable said. "But focus of public attention will be kept as far as possible on D.R.V. aggression; not on joint GVN/US military operations."

The President had scheduled the first of the sustained raids, Rolling Thunder I, for Feb. 20. Five hours after the State Department transmitted that cable, a perennial Saigon plotter, Col. Pham Ngoc Thao, staged an unsuccessful "semi-coup" against General Khanh and "pandemonium reigned in Saigon," the study recounts. "Ambassador Taylor promptly recommended cancellation of the Feb. 20 air strikes and his recommendation was equally promptly accepted" by Washington, the Pentagon study says.

The State Department sent a cablegram to the various embassies rescinding the instructions to notify heads of government or state of the planned air war until further notice "in view of the disturbed situation in Saigon."

The situation there, the study says, remained "disturbed" for nearly a week while the Young Turks also sought to get rid of General Khanh.

"The latter made frantic but unsuccessful efforts to rally his supporters," the study says, and finally took off in his plane to avoid having to resign as commander in chief. "Literally running out of gas in Nhatrang shortly before dawn on Feb. 21 he submitted his resignation, claiming that a 'foreign hand' was behind the coup. No one, however, could be quite certain that Khanh might not 're-coup' once again, unless he were physically removed from the scene."

This took three more days to accomplish, and on Feb. 25 General Khanh finally went into permanent exile as an ambassador at large, with Ambassador Taylor seeing him off at the airport, "glassily polite," in the study's words.

"It was only then that Taylor was able to issue, and Washington could accept, clearance for the long-postponed and frequently rescheduled first Rolling Thunder strike."

Less than three weeks earlier, in his memorandum to the President predicting that "a policy of sustained reprisal" might bring a better government in Saigon, McGeorge Bundy had said he did not agree with Ambassador Taylor that General Khanh "must somehow be removed from the . . . scene."

"We see no one else in sight with anything like his ability to combine military authority with some sense of politics," the account quotes Mr. Bundy as having written.

In the meantime two more Rolling Thunder strikes—II and III—had also been scheduled and then canceled because, the study says, the South Vietnamese Air Force was on "coup alert," in Saigon.

During part of this period, air strikes against North Vietnam were also inhibited by a diplomatic initiative from the Soviet Union and Britain. They moved to reactivate their co-chairmanship of the 1954 Geneva conference on Indochina to consider the current Vietnam crisis. Secretary Rusk cabled Ambassador Taylor that the diplomatic initiative would not affect Washington's decision to begin the air war, merely its timing.

According to the Pentagon study, the Administration regarded the possibility of reviving the Geneva conference of 1954, which had ended the French Indochina War, "not as a potential negotiating opportunity, but as a convenient vehicle for public expression of a tough U.S. position."

But, the account adds, this "diplomatic gambit" had "languished" by the time General Khanh left Saigon, and the day of his departure Mr. Johnson scheduled a strike, Rolling Thunder IV, for Feb. 26.

The pilots had been standing by, for nearly a week, with the orders to execute a strike being canceled every 24 hours.

But the order to begin the raid was again canceled, a last time, by monsoon weather for four more days.

Rolling Thunder finally rolled on March 2, 1965, when F-100 Super Sabre and F-105 Thunderchief jets of the United States Air Force bombed an ammunition depot at Xombang while 19 propeller-driven A-1H fighter-bombers of South Vietnam struck the Quangkhe naval base.

The various arguments in the Administration over how the raids ought to be conducted, which had developed during the planning stages, were now revived in sharper form by the opening blow in the actual air war.

Secretary McNamara, whose attention to management of resources and cost-effectiveness is cited repeatedly by the study, was concerned about improving the military efficacy of the bombing even before the sustained air war got under way.

He had received bomb damage assessments on the two reprisal strikes in February, reporting that of 491 buildings attacked, only 47 had been destroyed and 22 damaged. The information "caused McNamara to fire off a rather blunt memorandum" to Gen. Earle G. Wheeler, Chairman of the Joint Chiefs of Staff, on Feb. 17, the account says.

"I Am Quite Satisfied"

"Although the four missions [flown during the two raids] left the operations at the targets relatively unimpaired, I am quite satisfied with the results," Mr. McNamara began. "Our primary objective, of course, was to communicate our political resolve. This I believe we did. Future communications or resolve, however, will carry a hollow ring unless we accomplish more military damage than we have to date. . . . Surely we cannot continue for months accomplishing no more with 267 sorties than we did on these four missions." A sortie is a flight by a single plane.

General Wheeler replied that measures were being taken to heighten the destructiveness of the strikes and said that one way to accomplish this was to give the operational commander on the scene "adequate latitude" to attack the target as he saw fit, rather than seeking to control the details from Washington.

One measure approved by the President on March 9 was the use of napalm in North Vietnam.

And the day before, the day that 3,500 marines came ashore at Danang to protect the airfield there, Ambassador Taylor had already expressed, in two cables to Washington, what the historian describes as "sharp annoyance" with the "unnecessarily timid and ambivalent" way in which the air war was being conducted.

No air strikes had been authorized by the President beyond the initial Rolling Thunder raids that began on March 2, and, according to the study, the Ambassador was irritated at "the long delays between strikes, the marginal weight of the attacks and the great ado about behind-the-scenes diplomatic feelers."

General Westmoreland Concurs

With the concurrence of General Westmoreland, Ambassador Taylor proposed "a more dynamic schedule of strikes, a several week program relentlessly marching north" beyond the 19th Parallel, which President Johnson had so far set as a limit, "to break the will of the D.R.V."

Ambassador Taylor cabled: "Current feverish diplomatic activity particularly by French and British" was interfering with the ability of the United States to "progressively turn the screws on D.R.V."

"It appears to me evident that to date D.R.V. leaders believe air strikes at present levels on their territory are meaningless and that we are more susceptible to international pressure for negotiations than they are," the Ambassador said. He cited as evidence a report from J. Blair Seaborn, the Canadian member of the International Control Commission, who, in Hanoi earlier that month, had performed one of a series of secret diplomatic missions for the United States.

Mr. Seaborn had been sent back to convey directly to the Hanoi leaders an American policy statement on Vietnam that had been delivered to China on Feb. 24 through its embassy in Warsaw.

"No Designs" on the D.R.V.

In essence, the Pentagon study reports, the policy statement said that while the United States was determined to take whatever measures were necessary to maintain South Vietnam, it "had no designs on the territory of North Vietnam, nor any desire to destroy the D.R.V."

The delivery of the message to the Chinese was apparently aimed at helping to stave off any Chinese intervention as a result of the forthcoming bombing campaign.

But the purpose in sending Mr. Seaborn back, the study makes clear, was to convey the obvious threat that Hanoi now faced "extensive future destruction of . . . military and economic investments" if it did not call off the Vietcong guerrillas and accept a separate, non-Communist South.

Premier Pham Van Dong of North Vietnam, who had seen Mr. Seaborn on two earlier visits, declined this time, and the Canadian had to settle for the chief North Vietnamese liaison officer for the commission, to whom he read Washington's statement.

The North Vietnamese officer, the account says, commented that the message "contained nothing new and that the North Vietnamese had already received a briefing on the Warsaw meeting" from the Chinese Communists.

This treatment led the Canadian to sense "a mood of confidence" among the Hanoi leaders, Ambassador Taylor told Washington in a cablegram, and Mr. Seaborn felt "that Hanoi has the impression that our air strikes are a limited attempt to improve our bargaining position and hence are no great cause for immediate concern."

"Our objective should be to induce in D.R.V. leadership an attitude favorable to U.S. objectives in as short a time as possible in order to avoid a build-up of international pressure to negotiate," the Ambassador said.

To Dispel Any Illusions

Therefore, he went on, it was necessary to "begin at once a progression of U.S. strikes north of 19th Parallel in a slow but steadily ascending movement" to dispel any illusions in Hanoi.

"If we tarry too long in the south [below the 19th Parallel], we will give Hanoi a weak and misleading signal which will work against our ultimate purpose," he said.

The next Rolling Thunder strikes, on March 14 and 15, were the heaviest of the air war so far, involving 100 American and 24 South Vietnamese planes against barracks and depots on Tiger Island off the North Vietnamese coast and the ammunition dump near Phuqui, 100 miles southwest of Hanoi.

For the first time, the planes used napalm against the North, a measure approved by Mr. Johnson on March 9 to achieve the more efficient destruction of the targets that Mr. McNamara was seeking and to give the pilots protection from antiaircraft batteries.

But the Ambassador regarded these, too, as an "isolated, stage-managed joint U.S./GVN operation," the Pentagon study says. He sent Washington another cable, saying that "through repeated delays we are failing to give the mounting crescendo to Rolling Thunder which is necessary to get the desired results."

Meanwhile, Admiral Sharp in Honolulu and the Joint Chiefs in Washington were quickly devising a number of other programs to broaden and intensify the air war now that it had begun.

On March 21, Admiral Sharp proposed a "radar busting day" to knock out the North Vietnamese early-warning system, and a program "to attrite harass and interdict the D.R.V. south" of the 20th Parallel by cutting lines of communication, "LOC" in official terminology.

The "LOC cut program" would choke off traffic along all roads and rail lines through southern North Vietnam by bombing strikes and would thus squeeze the flow of supplies into the South.

"All targets selected are extremely difficult or impossible to bypass," the admiral said in a cable to the Joint Chiefs. "LOC network cutting in this depth will degrade tonnage arrivals at the main 'funnels' and will develop a broad series of new targets such as backed-up convoys, offloaded material dumps and personnel staging areas at one or both sides of cuts."

These probable effects might in turn "force major D.R.V. log flow to sea-carry and into surveillance and attack by our SVN [South Vietnamese] coastal sanitization forces," the admiral added.

In Washington at this time, the narrative goes on, the Joint Chiefs were engaged in an "interservice division" over potential ground-troop deployments to Vietnam and over the air war itself.

Gen. John P. McConnell, Chief of Staff of the Air Force adopted a "maverick position" and was arguing for a short and violent 28-day bombing campaign. All of the targets on the original 94-target list drawn up in May 1964, from bridges to industries, would be progressively destroyed.

"He proposed beginning the air strikes in the southern part of North Vietnam and continuing at two- to six-day intervals until Hanoi was attacked," the study continues.

The raids would be along the lines of the mighty strikes, including the use of B-52 bombers, that the Joint Chiefs had proposed in retaliation for the Vietcong mortar attack in Beinhoa airfield on Nov. 1, 1964, the narrative says. General McConnell contended that his plan was consistent with previous bombing proposals by the Joint Chiefs.

The general abandoned his proposal, however, when the other members of the Joint Chiefs decided to incorporate Admiral Sharp's "LOC cut program" and some of General McConnell's individual target concepts into a bombing program of several weeks. They proposed this to Mr. McNamara on March 27.

This plan proposed an intense bombing campaign that would start on road and rail lines south of the 20th Parallel and then "march north" week by week to isolate North Vietnam from China gradually by cutting road and rail lines above Hanoi. In later phases upon which the Joint Chiefs had not yet fully decided, the port facilities were to be destroyed to isolate North Vietnam from the sea. Then industries outside populated areas would be attacked "leading up to a situation where the enemy will realize that the Hanoi and Haiphong areas will be the next logical targets in our continued air campaign."

But the President and Mr. McNamará declined to approve any multi-week program, the study relates. "They clearly preferred to retain continual personal control over attack concepts and individual target selection."

Alternate Targets Approved

In mid-March, after a Presidential fact-finding trip to Vietnam by Gen. Harold K. Johnson, the Army Chief of Staff, the President did regularize the bombing campaign and relaxed some of the restrictions. Among the innovations was the selection of the targets in weekly packages with the precise timing of the individual attacks left to the commanders on the scene. Also, "the strikes were no longer to be specifically related to VC atrocities" and "publicity on the strikes was to be progressively reduced," the study says.

The President did not accept two recommendations from General Johnson relating to a possible ground war. They were to dispatch a division of American troops to South Vietnam to hold coastal enclaves or defend the Central Highlands in order to free Saigon Government forces for offensive action against the Vietcong. The second proposal was to create a four-division force of American and Southeast Asia Treaty Organization troops, who, to interdict infiltration, would patrol both the demilitarized zone along the border separating North and South Vietnam and the Laotian border region.

Better organization for the air war meant that concepts such as Admiral Sharp's "LOC cut program" and his "radar busting" were now incorporated into the weekly target packages. But President Johnson and Secretary McNamara continued to select the targets and to communicate them to the Joint Chiefs—and thus, eventually, to the operating strike forces—in weekly Rolling Thunder planning messages issued by the Secretary of Defense.

Hopes Were Waning

Operation Rolling Thunder was thus being shifted from an exercise in air power "dominated by political and psychological considerations" to a "militarily more significant, sustained bombing program" aimed at destroying the capabilities of North Vietnam to support a war in the South.

But the shift also meant that "early hopes that Rolling Thunder could succeed by itself " in persuading Hanoi to call off the Vietcong were also waning.

"The underlying question that was being posed for the Administration at this time was well formulated," the study says, by Mr. McNaughton in a memorandum drafted on March 24 for Secretary McNamara in preparation for the April 1–2 National Security Council meetings.

"Can the situation inside SVN be bottomed out (a) without extreme measures against the DRV and/or (b) without deployment of large numbers of U.S. (and other) combat troops inside SVN?"

Mr. McNaughton's answer was "perhaps, but probably no."

General Westmoreland stated his conclusions in a half-inch-thick report labeled "Commander's Estimate of the situation in SVN." The document, "a classic Leavenworth-style analysis," the analyst remarks, referring to the Command and General Staff College, was completed in Saigon on March 26 and delivered to Washington in time for the April 1–2 strategy meeting.

The Saigon military commander and his staff had begun working on this voluminous report on March 13, the day after General Johnson left Vietnam with his ground war proposals of an American division to hold enclaves and a four-division American and SEATO force along the borders, the study notes.

General Westmoreland predicted that the bombing campaign against the North would not show tangible results until June at the earliest, and that in the meantime the South Vietnamese Army needed American reinforcements to hold the line against growing Vietcong strength and to carry out an "orderly" expansion of its own ranks.

And, paraphrasing the report, the study says that the general warned that the Saigon troops, "although at the moment performing fairly well, would not be able in the face of a VC summer offensive to hold in the South long enough for the bombing to become effective."

General Westmoreland asked for reinforcements equivalent to two American divisions, a total of about 70,000 troops, counting those already in Vietnam.

They included 17 maneuver battalions. The general proposed adding two more Marine battalion landing teams to the two battalions already at Danang in order to establish another base at the airfield at Phubai to the north; putting an Army brigade into the Bienhoa-Vungtau area near Saigon, and using two more Army battalions to garrison the central coastal ports of Quinhon and Nhatrang as logistics bases. These bases would sustain an army division that General Westmoreland proposed to send into active combat in the strategic central highlands inland to "defeat" the Vietcong who were seizing control there.

General Westmoreland said that he wanted the 17 battalions and their initial supporting elements in South Vietnam by June and indicated that more troops might be required thereafter if the bombing failed to achieve results.

The Saigon military commander and General Johnson were not alone in pressing for American ground combat troops to forestall a Vietcong victory, the study points out.

On March 20, the Joint Chiefs as a body had proposed sending two American divisions and one South Korean division to South Vietnam for offensive combat operations against the guerrillas.

Secretary McNamara, the Joint Chiefs and Ambassador Taylor all discussed the three-division proposal on March 29, the study relates, while the Ambassador was in Washington for the forthcoming White House strategy conference.

The Ambassador opposed the plan, the study says, because he felt the South Vietnamese might resent the presence of so many foreign troops—upwards of 100,000 men—and also because he believed there was still no military necessity for them.

The Joint Chiefs "had the qualified support of McNamara," however, the study continues, and was one of the topics discussed at the national security council meeting.

Concern With Deployment

Thus, the study says, at the White House strategy session of April 1–2, "the principal concern of Administration policy makers at this time was with the prospect of major deployment of U.S. and third-country combat forces to SVN."

A memorandum written by McGeorge Bundy before the meeting, which set forth the key issues for discussion and decision by the President, "gave only the most superficial treatment to the complex matter of future air pressure policy," the Pentagon analyst remarks.

The morning that Ambassador Taylor left Saigon to attend the meeting, March 29, the Vietcong guerrillas blew up the American Embassy in Saigon in what the study calls "the boldest and most direct Communist action against the U.S. since the attacks at Pleiku and Quinhon which had precipitated the Flaming Dart reprisal airstrikes."

Admiral Sharp requested permission to launch a "spectacular" air raid on North Vietnam in retaliation, the narrative continues, but the "plea . . . did not fall on responsive ears" at the White House.

"At this point, the President preferred to maneuver quietly to help the nation get used to living with the Vietnam crisis. He played down any drama intrinsic in Taylor's arrival" and refused to permit a retaliation raid for the embassy bombing.

"After his first meeting with Taylor and other officials on March 31, the President responded to press inquiries concerning dramatic new developments by saying: "I know of no far-reaching strategy that is being suggested or promulgated."

"But the President was being less than candid," the study observes. "The proposals that were at that moment being promulgated, and on which he reached significant decision the following day, did involve a far-reaching strategy change: acceptance of the concept of U.S. troops engaged in offensive ground operations against Asian insurgents. This issue greatly overshadowed all other Vietnam questions then being reconsidered."

The analyst is referring to the President's decision at the White House strategy conference on April 1–2 to change the mission of the Marine battalions at Danang from defense to offense.

McGeorge Bundy embodied the decision in National Security Action Memorandum 328, which he drafted and signed on behalf of the President on April 6. The analyst says that this "pivotal document" followed almost "verbatim" the text of another memorandum that Mr. Bundy had written before the N.S.C. meeting to outline the proposals for discussion and decision by the President.

The Pentagon study notes that the actual landing of 3,500 marines at Danang the previous month had "caused surprisingly little outcry."

Secretary of State Rusk had explained on a television program the day before the marines came ashore that their mission was solely to provide security for the air base and "not to kill the Vietcong," in the words of the study. This initial mission for the marines was later to be referred to as the short-lived strategy of security that would apply only to this American troop movement into South Vietnam.

"A Dead Letter" Quickly

The President's decision to change their mission to offense now made the strategy of base security "a dead letter," the study says, when it was less than a month old.

At the April 1–2 meeting, Mr. Johnson had also decided to send ashore two more Marine battalions, which General Westmoreland had asked for in a separate request on March 17. Mr. Johnson further decided to increase support forces in South Vietnam by 18,000 to 20,000 men.

The President was "doubtless aware" of the general's additional request for the equivalent of two divisions, and of the Joint Chiefs' for three divisions, the Pentagon account says, but Mr. Johnson took no action on them.

"The initial steps in ground build-up appear to have been grudgingly taken," the study says, "indicating that the President . . . and his advisers recognized the tremendous inertial complications of ground troop deployments. Halting ground involvement was seen to be a manifestly greater problem than halting air or naval activity.

"It is pretty clear, then, that the President intended, after the early April N.S.C. meetings, to cautiously and carefully experiment with the U.S. forces in offensive roles," the analyst concludes.

National Security Action Memorandum 328 did not precisely define or limit the offensive role it authorized, and Ambassador Taylor, who had attended the National Security Council meeting during his visit to Washington, was not satisfied with the guidance he received from the State Department. Therefore, on his way back to Saigon on April 4, the Ambassador, formerly President John F. Kennedy's military adviser and Chairman of the Joint Chiefs, sent a cable from the Honolulu headquarters of the commander of Pacific forces to the State Department, saying:

"I propose to describe the new mission to [Premier Pham Huy] Quat as the use of marines in a mobile counter-insurgency role in the vicinity of Danang for the improved protection of that base and also in a strike role as a reserve in support of ARVN operations anywhere within 50 miles of the base. This latter employment would follow acquisition of experience on local counter-insurgency missions."

Ambassador Taylor's 50-mile limit apparently became an accepted rule-of-thumb boundary for counterinsurgency strikes.

And so, the analyst sums up, with the promulgation of National Security Action Memorandum 328, "the strategy of security effectively becomes a dead letter on the first of April," and the strategy of enclave begins.

PART VII

Covert Intervention, Overt Neglect

Introduction to
James Risen's

"Secrets of History: The C.I.A. in Iran"

THE 1953 CIA-LED COUP that resulted in a change of leadership in Iran is crucial to understanding current U.S.–Iranian relations. "The coup was a turning point in modern Iranian history and remains a persistent irritant in Tehran-Washington relations," writes James Risen, who published a front page exposé of the coup in *The New York Times*. He had obtained a copy of the agency's classified secret history of the 1953 coup that set the stage for the 1979 revolution and a generation of anti-American hatred.

Mohammed Mossadegh, the elected prime minister of Iran, had angered the British and the Americans by trying to nationalize the oil industry. The role of the U.S. government in the 1953 coup that overthrew Mossadegh and restored Shah Mohammed Reza Pahlevi to power had been argued for years. In his 1981 book *Inside the Iranian Revolution*, State Department official John D. Stempel on one hand quotes Iranians who described the U.S. role as "minimal," and on the other hand quotes CIA critics who claimed that the agency "masterminded the putsch." The secret history clearly proves that the CIA and British intelligence played pivotal roles in the coup.

As an irony of history, General H. Norman Schwarzkopf, the father of the Persian Gulf War commander, was enlisted by the CIA to persuade the shah to sign decrees, written by the agency, changing the Iranian leadership.

Donald Wilber, who planned the coup and wrote the secret history for the CIA, was a Middle East architecture expert whose years of wandering through sites gave him the perfect cover for a clandestine life.

James Risen covers national security for *The New York Times*. He was a member of the team that won the Pulitzer Prize for explanatory reporting in 2002 for coverage of the September 11 attacks and terrorism.

ADDITIONAL SOURCES

Kinzer, Stephen. *All the Shah's Men: An American Coup and the Roots of Middle East Terror*. Hoboken, N.J.: John Wiley and Sons, 2003.

Stempel, John D. *Inside the Iranian Revolution*. Bloomington, Ind.: Indiana University Press, 1981.

Related articles can be found in *The New York Times*, April 16, 2000.

James Risen

"Secrets of History: The C.I.A. in Iran—A Special Report"

THE NEW YORK TIMES, APRIL 16, 2000

FOR NEARLY FIVE DECADES, America's role in the military coup that ousted Iran's elected prime minister and returned the shah to power has been lost to history, the subject of fierce debate in Iran and stony silence in the United States. One by one, participants have retired or died without revealing key details, and the Central Intelligence Agency said a number of records of the operation—its first successful overthrow of a foreign government—had been destroyed.

But a copy of the agency's secret history of the 1953 coup has surfaced, revealing the inner workings of a plot that set the stage for the Islamic revolution in 1979, and for a generation of anti-American hatred in one of the Middle East's most powerful countries.

The document, which remains classified, discloses the pivotal role British intelligence officials played in initiating and planning the coup, and it shows that Washington and London shared an interest in maintaining the West's control over Iranian oil.

The secret history, written by the C.I.A.'s chief coup planner and obtained by *The New York Times*, says the operation's success was mostly a matter of chance. The document shows that the agency had almost complete contempt for the man it was empowering, Shah Mohammed Reza Pahlevi, whom it derided as a vacillating coward. And it recounts, for the first time, the agency's tortured efforts to seduce and cajole the shah into taking part in his own coup.

The operation, code-named TP-Ajax, was the blueprint for a succession of C.I.A. plots to foment coups and destabilize governments during the Cold War—including the agency's successful coup in Guatemala in 1954 and the disastrous Cuban intervention known as the Bay of Pigs in 1961. In more than one instance, such operations led to the same kind of long-term animosity toward the United States that occurred in Iran.

The history says agency officers orchestrating the Iran coup worked directly with royalist Iranian military officers, handpicked the prime minister's replacement, sent a stream of envoys to bolster the shah's courage, directed a campaign of bombings by Iranians posing as members of the Communist Party, and planted articles and editorial cartoons in newspapers.

But on the night set for Prime Minister Mohammed Mossadegh's overthrow, almost nothing went according to the meticulously drawn plans, the secret history says. In fact, C.I.A. officials were poised to flee the country when several Iranian officers recruited by the agency, acting on their own, took command of a pro-shah demonstration in Tehran and seized the government.

Two days after the coup, the history discloses, agency officials funneled $5 million to Iran to help the government they had installed consolidate power.

The outlines of the American role in the coup were disclosed in Iran at the outset and later in the memoirs of C.I.A. officers and other published accounts. But many specifics have remained classified, and the secret history obtained by *The New York Times* is the first detailed government account of the coup to be made public.

The C.I.A. has been slow to make available the Iran files. Two directors of central intelligence, Robert Gates and R. James Woolsey, vowed to declassify records of the agency's early covert actions, including the coup. But the agency said three years ago that a number of relevant documents had been destroyed in the early 1960s.

A C.I.A. spokesman said Friday that the agency had retained about 1,000 pages of documents related to the coup, besides the history and an internal account written later. He said the papers destroyed in the early 1960's were duplicates and working files.

The chief State Department historian said that his office received a copy of the history seven years ago but that no decision on declassifying it had yet been made.

The secret history, along with operational assessments written by coup planners, was provided to The Times by a former official who kept a copy.

It was written in March 1954 by Dr. Donald N. Wilber, an expert in Persian architecture, who as one of the leading planners believed that covert operatives had much to learn from history.

In less expansive memoirs published in 1986, Dr. Wilber asserted that the Iran coup was different from later C.I.A. efforts. Its American planners, he said, had stirred up considerable unrest in Iran, giving Iranians a clear choice between instability and supporting the shah. The move to oust the prime minister, he wrote, thus gained substantial popular support.

Dr. Wilber's memoirs were heavily censored by the agency, but he was allowed to refer to the existence of his secret history. "If this history had been read by the planners of the Bay of Pigs," he wrote, "there would have been no such operation."

"From time to time," he continued, "I gave talks on the operation to various groups within the agency, and, in hindsight, one might wonder why no one from the Cuban desk ever came or read the history."

The coup was a turning point in modern Iranian history and remains a persistent irritant in Tehran-Washington relations. It consolidated the power of the shah, who ruled with an iron hand for 26 more years in close contact with to the United States. He was toppled by militants in 1979. Later that year, marchers went to the American Embassy, took diplomats hostage and declared that they had unmasked a "nest of spies" who had been manipulating Iran for decades.

The Islamic government of Ayatollah Ruhollah Khomeini supported terrorist attacks against American interests largely because of the long American history of supporting the shah. Even under more moderate rulers, many Iranians still resent the United States' role in the coup and its support of the shah.

Secretary of State Madeleine K. Albright, in an address in March, acknowledged the coup's pivotal role in the troubled relationship and came closer to apologizing than any American official ever has before.

"The Eisenhower administration believed its actions were justified for strategic reasons," she said. "But the coup was clearly a setback for Iran's political development. And it is easy to see now why many Iranians continue to resent this intervention by America in their internal affairs."

The history spells out the calculations to which Dr. Albright referred in her speech.

Britain, it says, initiated the plot in 1952. The Truman administration rejected it, but President Eisenhower approved it shortly after taking office in 1953, because of fears about oil and Communism.

The document pulls few punches, acknowledging at one point that the agency baldly lied to its British allies. Dr. Wilber reserves his most withering asides for the agency's local allies, referring to "the recognized incapacity of Iranians to plan or act in a thoroughly logical manner."

The Roots:
Britain Fights Oil Nationalism

The coup had its roots in a British showdown with Iran, restive under decades of near-colonial British domination.

The prize was Iran's oil fields. Britain occupied Iran in World War II to protect a supply route to its ally, the Soviet Union, and to prevent the oil from falling into the hands of the Nazis—ousting the shah's father, whom it regarded as unmanageable. It retained control over Iran's oil after the war through the Anglo-Iranian Oil Company.

In 1951, Iran's Parliament voted to nationalize the oil industry, and legislators backing the law elected its leading advocate, Dr. Mossadegh, as prime minister.

Britain responded with threats and sanctions. Dr. Mossadegh, a European-educated lawyer then in his early 70s, prone to tears and outbursts, refused to back down. In meetings in November and December 1952, the secret history says, British intelligence officials startled their American counterparts with a plan for a joint operation to oust the nettlesome prime minister.

The Americans, who "had not intended to discuss this question at all," agreed to study it, the secret history says. It had attractions. Anti-Communism had risen to a fever pitch in Washington, and officials were worried that Iran might fall under the sway of the Soviet Union, a historical presence there.

In March 1953, an unexpected development pushed the plot forward: the C.I.A.'s Tehran station reported that an Iranian general had approached the American Embassy about supporting an army-led coup.

The newly inaugurated Eisenhower administration was intrigued. The coalition that elected Dr. Mossadegh was splintering, and the Iranian Communist Party, the Tudeh, had become active.

Allen W. Dulles, the director of central intelligence, approved $1 million on April 4 to be used "in any way that would bring about the fall of Mossadegh," the history says.

"The aim was to bring to power a government which would reach an equitable oil settlement, enabling Iran to become economically sound and financially solvent, and which would vigorously prosecute the dangerously strong Communist Party."

Within days agency officials identified a high-ranking officer, Gen. Fazlollah Zahedi, as the man to spearhead a coup. Their plan called for the shah to play a leading role.

"A shah-General Zahedi combination, supported by C.I.A. local assets and financial backing, would have a good chance of overthrowing Mossadegh," officials wrote, "particularly if this combination should be able to get the largest mobs in the streets and if a sizable portion of the Tehran garrison refused to carry out Mossadegh's orders."

But according to the history, planners had doubts about whether the shah could carry out such a bold operation.

His family had seized Iran's throne just thirty-two years earlier, when his powerful father led a coup of his own. But the young shah, agency officials wrote, was "by nature a creature of indecision, beset by formless doubts and fears," often at odds with his family, including Princess Ashraf, his "forceful and scheming twin sister."

Also, the shah had what the C.I.A. termed a "pathological fear" of British intrigues, a potential obstacle to a joint operation.

In May 1953 the agency sent Dr. Wilber to Cyprus to meet Norman

Darbyshire, chief of the Iran branch of British intelligence, to make initial coup plans. Assuaging the fears of the shah was high on their agenda; a document from the meeting said he was to be persuaded that the United States and Britain "consider the oil question secondary."

The conversation at the meeting turned to a touchy subject, the identity of key agents inside Iran. The British said they had recruited two brothers named Rashidian. The Americans, the secret history discloses, did not trust the British and lied about the identity of their best "assets" inside Iran.

C.I.A. officials were divided over whether the plan drawn up in Cyprus could work. The Tehran station warned headquarters that "the shah would not act decisively against Mossadegh." And it said General Zahedi, the man picked to lead the coup, "appeared lacking in drive, energy and concrete plans."

Despite the doubts, the agency's Tehran station began disseminating "gray propaganda," passing out anti-Mossadegh cartoons in the streets and planting unflattering articles in the local press.

The Plotting:
Trying to Persuade a Reluctant Shah

The plot was under way, even though the shah was a reluctant warrior and Mr. Eisenhower had yet to give his final approval.

In early June, American and British intelligence officials met again, this time in Beirut, and put the finishing touches on the strategy. Soon afterward, the chief of the C.I.A.'s Near East and Africa division, Kermit Roosevelt, a grandson of Theodore Roosevelt, arrived in Tehran to direct it.

The shah was a problem from the start. The plan called for him to stand fast as the C.I.A. stirred up popular unrest and then, as the country lurched toward chaos, to issue royal decrees dismissing Dr. Mossadegh and appointing General Zahedi prime minister.

The agency sought to "produce such pressure on the shah that it would be easier for him to sign the papers required of him than it would be to refuse," the secret history states. Officials turned to his sister for help.

On July 11, President Eisenhower finally signed off on the plan. At about the same time, C.I.A. and British intelligence officers visited Princess Ashraf on the French Riviera and persuaded her to return to Iran and tell her brother to follow the script.

The return of the unpopular princess unleashed a storm of protest from pro-Mossadegh forces. The shah was furious that she had come back without his approval and refused at first to see her. But a palace staff member—another British agent, according to the secret history—gained Ashraf access on July 29.

The history does not reveal what the siblings said to each other. But the princess gave her brother the news that C.I.A. officials had enlisted Gen. H. Norman Schwarzkopf in the coup campaign. General Schwarzkopf, the father of the Persian Gulf war commander, had befriended the shah a decade earlier while leading the United States military mission to Iran, and he told the agency "he was sure he could get the required cooperation."

The British, too, sought to sway the shah and assure him their agents spoke for London. A British agent, Asadollah Rashidian, approached him in late July and invited him to select a phrase that would then be broadcast at prearranged times on the BBC's Persian-language program—as proof that Mr. Rashidian spoke for the British.

The exercise did not seem to have much effect. The shah told Mr. Rashidian on July 30 and 31 that he had heard the broadcast, but "requested time to assess the situation."

In early August, the C.I.A. stepped up the pressure. Iranian operatives pretending to be Communists threatened Muslim leaders with "savage punishment if they opposed Mossadegh," seeking to stir anti-Communist sentiment in the religious community.

In addition, the secret history says, the house of at least one prominent Muslim was bombed by C.I.A. agents posing as Communists. It does not say whether anyone was hurt in this attack.

The agency was also intensifying its propaganda campaign. A leading newspaper owner was granted a personal loan of about $45,000, "in the belief that this would make his organ amenable to our purposes."

But the shah remained intransigent. In an Aug. I meeting with General Schwarzkopf, he refused to sign the C.I.A.-written decrees firing Mr. Mossadegh and appointing General Zahedi. He said he doubted that the army would support him in a showdown.

During the meeting, the document says, the shah was so convinced that the palace was bugged that he "led the general into the grand ballroom, pulled a small table to its exact center" and got onto it to talk, insisting that the general do the same.

"This meeting was to be followed by a series of additional ones, some between Roosevelt and the shah and some between Rashidian and the shah, in which relentless pressure was exerted in frustrating attempts to overcome an entrenched attitude of vacillation and indecision," the history states.

Dr. Mossadegh had by now figured out that there was a plot against him. He moved to consolidate power by calling for a national referendum to dissolve Parliament.

The results of the Aug. 4 referendum were clearly rigged in his favor; *The New York Times* reported the same day that the prime minister had won 99.9 percent of the vote. This only helped the plotters, providing "an issue on which Mossadegh could be relentlessly attacked" by the agency-backed opposition press.

But the shah still wouldn't move against Dr. Mossadegh.

"On Aug. 3rd," the secret history says, "Roosevelt had a long and inconclusive session with the shah," who "stated that he was not an adventurer, and hence, could not take the chances of one.

"Roosevelt pointed out that there was no other way by which the government could be changed and the test was now between Mossadegh and his force and the shah and the army, which was still with him, but which would soon slip away."

Mr. Roosevelt told the shah "that failure to act could lead only to a Communist Iran or to a second Korea."

Still haunted by doubts, the shah asked Mr. Roosevelt if President Eisenhower could tell him what to do.

"By complete coincidence and great good fortune," the secret history says, "the president, while addressing the governors' convention in Seattle on 4 August, deviated from his script to state by implication that the United States would not sit by idly and see Iran fall behind the Iron Curtain."

By Aug. 10, the shah had finally agreed to see General Zahedi and a few army officers involved in the plot, but still refused to sign the decrees. The C.I.A. then sent Mr. Rashidian to say Mr. Roosevelt "would leave in complete disgust unless the shah took action within a few days."

The shah finally signed the decrees on Aug. 13. Word that he would support an army-led coup spread rapidly among the army officers backing General Zahedi.

The Coup:
First Few Days Look Disastrous

The coup began on the night of Aug. 15 and was immediately compromised by a talkative Iranian Army officer whose remarks were relayed to Mr. Mossadegh.

The operation, the secret history says, "still might have succeeded in spite of this advance warning had not most of the participants proved to be inept or lacking in decision at the critical juncture."

Dr. Mossadegh's chief of staff, Gen. Taghi Riahi, learned of the plot hours before it was to begin and sent his deputy to the barracks of the Imperial Guard.

The deputy was arrested there, according to the history, just as proshah soldiers were fanning out across the city arresting other senior officials. Telephone lines between army and government offices were cut, and the telephone exchange was occupied.

But phones inexplicably continued to function, which gave Dr. Mossadegh's forces a key advantage. General Riahi also eluded the proshah units, rallying commanders to the prime minister's side.

Pro-shah soldiers sent to arrest Dr. Mossadegh at his home were instead captured. The top military officer working with General Zahedi fled when he saw tanks and loyal government soldiers at army head-quarters.

The next morning, the history states, the Tehran radio announced that a coup against the government had failed, and Dr. Mossadegh scrambled to strengthen his hold on the army and key installations. C.I.A. officers inside the embassy were flying blind; the history says they had "no way of knowing what was happening."

Mr. Roosevelt left the embassy and tracked down General Zahedi, who was in hiding north of Tehran. Surprisingly, the general was not ready to abandon the operation. The coup, the two men agreed, could still work, provided they could persuade the public that General Zahedi was the lawful prime minister.

To accomplish this, the history discloses, the coup plotters had to get out the news that the shah had signed the two decrees.

The C.I.A. station in Tehran sent a message to The Associated Press in New York, asserting that "unofficial reports are current to the effect that leaders of the plot are armed with two decrees of the shah, one dismissing Mossadegh and the other appointing General Zahedi to replace him."

The C.I.A. and its agents also arranged for the decrees to be mentioned in some Tehran papers, the history says.

The propaganda initiative quickly bogged down. Many of the C.I.A.'s Iranian agents were under arrest or on the run. That afternoon, agency operatives prepared a statement from General Zahedi that they hoped to distribute publicly. But they could not find a printing press that was not being watched by forces loyal to the prime minister.

On Aug. 16, prospects of reviving the operation were dealt a seemingly a fatal blow when it was learned that the shah had bolted to Baghdad. C.I.A. headquarters cabled Tehran urging Mr. Roosevelt, the station chief, to leave immediately.

He did not agree, insisting that there was still "a slight remaining chance of success," if the shah would broadcast an address on the Baghdad radio and General Zahedi took an aggressive stand.

The first sign that the tide might turn came with reports that Iranian soldiers had broken up Tudeh, or Communist, groups, beating them and making them chant their support for the shah. "The station continued to feel that the project was not quite dead," the secret history recounts.

Meanwhile, Dr. Mossadegh had overreached, playing into the C.I.A.'s hands by dissolving Parliament after the coup.

On the morning of Aug. 17 the shah finally announced from Baghdad that he had signed the decrees—though he had by now delayed so long that plotters feared it was too late.

At this critical point Dr. Mossadegh let down his guard. Lulled by the shah's departure and the arrests of some officers involved in the coup, the government recalled most troops it had stationed around the city, believing that the danger had passed.

That night the C.I.A. arranged for General Zahedi and other key Iranian agents and army officers to be smuggled into the embassy compound "in the bottom of cars and in closed jeeps" for a "council of war."

They agreed to start a counterattack on Aug. 19, sending a leading cleric from Tehran to the holy city of Qum to try to orchestrate a call for a holy war against Communism. (The religious forces they were trying to manipulate would years later call the United States "the Great Satan.")

Using travel papers forged by the C.I.A., key army officers went to outlying army garrisons to persuade commanders to join the coup.

Once again, the shah disappointed the C.I.A. He left Baghdad for Rome the next day, apparently an exile. Newspapers supporting Dr. Mossadegh reported that the Pahlevi dynasty had come to an end, and a statement from the Communist Party's central committee attributed the coup attempt to "Anglo-American intrigue." Demonstrators ripped down imperial statues—as they would again twenty-six years later during the Islamic revolution.

The C.I.A. station cabled headquarters for advice on whether to "continue with TP-Ajax or withdraw."

"Headquarters spent a day featured by depression and despair," the history states, adding, "The message sent to Tehran on the night of Aug. 18 said that 'the operation has been tried and failed,' and that 'in the absence of strong recommendations to the contrary operations against Mossadegh should be discontinued.'"

The Success:
C.I.A. and Moscow Are Both Surprised

But just as the Americans were ready to quit, the mood on the streets of Tehran shifted.

On the morning of Aug. 19, several Tehran papers published the shah's long-awaited decrees, and soon pro-shah crowds were building in the streets.

"They needed only leadership," the secret history says. And Iranian agents of the C.I.A. provided it. Without specific orders, a journalist who was one of the agency's most important Iranian agents led a crowd toward Parliament, inciting people to set fire to the offices of a newspaper owned by Dr. Mossadegh's foreign minister. Another Iranian C.I.A. agent led a crowd to sack the offices of pro-Tudeh papers.

"The news that something quite startling was happening spread at great speed throughout the city," the history states.

The C.I.A. tried to exploit the situation, sending urgent messages that the Rashidian brothers and two key American agents should "swing the security forces to the side of the demonstrators."

But things were now moving far too quickly for the agency to manage. An Iranian Army colonel who had been involved in the plot several days earlier suddenly appeared outside Parliament with a tank, while members of the now-disbanded Imperial Guard seized trucks and drove through the streets. "By 10:15 there were pro-shah truckloads of military personnel at all the main squares," the secret history says.

By noon the crowds began to receive direct leadership from a few officers involved in the plot and some who had switched sides. Within an hour the central telegraph office fell, and telegrams were sent to the provinces urging a pro-shah uprising. After a brief shootout, police headquarters and the Ministry of Foreign Affairs fell as well.

The Tehran radio remained the biggest prize. With the government's fate uncertain, it was broadcasting a program on cotton prices. But by early afternoon a mass of civilians, army officers and policemen overwhelmed it.

Pro-shah speakers went on the air, broadcasting the coup's success and reading the royal decrees.

At the embassy, C.I.A. officers were elated, and Mr. Roosevelt got General Zahedi out of hiding. An army officer found a tank and drove him to the radio station, where he spoke to the nation.

Dr. Mossadegh and other government officials were rounded up, while officers supporting General Zahedi placed "known supporters of TP-Ajax" in command of all units of the Tehran garrison.

The Soviet Union was caught completely off-guard. Even as the Mossadegh government was falling, the Moscow radio was broadcasting a story on "the failure of the American adventure in Iran."

But C.I.A. headquarters was as surprised as Moscow. When news of the coup's success arrived, it "seemed to be a bad joke, in view of the depression that still hung on from the day before," the history says.

Throughout the day, Washington got most of its information from news agencies, receiving only two cablegrams from the station. Mr. Roosevelt later explained that if he had told headquarters what was going on, "London and Washington would have thought they were crazy and told them to stop immediately," the history states.

Still, the C.I.A. took full credit inside the government. The following year it overthrew the government of Guatemala, and a myth developed that the agency could topple governments anywhere in the world.

Iran proved that third world king-making could be heady.

"It was a day that should never have ended," the C.I.A.'s secret history said, describing Aug. 19, 1953. "For it carried with it such a sense of excitement, of satisfaction and of jubilation that it is doubtful whether any other can come up to it."

Introduction to
John Dinges's

The Condor Years

O PERATION CONDOR WAS A shadowy Latin American military network created in 1975 by right-wing leaders in Chile, Argentina, Uruguay, Bolivia, Paraguay, and a year later by Brazil, and three years later by Peru and Ecuador with the intention of eliminating perceived enemies of the military governments. During their campaigns, thousands of people "disappeared" or were assassinated in Condor's anti-Communist crusade. Among the missions carried out by Condor were the murder of Orlando Letelier, foreign minister under Chilean President Salvador Allende, and his American colleague Ronni Moffitt in Washington, D.C., in 1976; the attempted assassination of Chilean Christian Democratic leader Bernardo Leighton and his wife in Rome, in 1975; the kidnapping and murder of Juan José Torres, a former president of Bolivia in Argentina, in 1976; and the murder of two Uruguayan legislators, Zelmar Michelini and Hector Gutierrez Ruiz in Argentina, in 1976. The demise of Operation Condor by 1981 was precipitated by the exposure of Condor after the Letelier assassination.

According to Dinges, who covered Latin America for *The Washington Post, Time,* and other publications, "The U.S. State Department and intelligence agencies had amazingly complete and intimate details about the functioning and planning of Condor." Unfortunately, Condor became a model for present U.S. covert action. "The echoes of the past," Dinges writes, "are already to be seen in the current war on terrorism: the massive pooling of intelligence, the compromised intelligence relationships, the gleaning of intelligence from the torture centers run by our allies, and even targeted, cross-border assassinations."

   Dinges was awarded the Maria Moors Cabot Prize for Latin American reporting and two DuPont-Columbia broadcast journalism awards as managing editor of NPR news. His previous books include *Assassination of Embassy Row* and *Our Man in Panama*. *Operation Condor* "is in large part underground history," he writes. "I have tried to bring together the documents and the interviews to achieve a laminate of maximum strength in reconstructing the once secret events."

ADDITIONAL SOURCES

Almada, Martín. *Paraguay: la carcel olvidada, el pais exiliado.* Panama: Asunción, 1978, 1993.

Dinges, John and Saul Landau. *Assassination on Embassy Row.* New York: Pantheon, 1980.

Propper, Eugene and Taylor Branch. *Labyrinth.* New York: Viking, 1982.

John Dinges

The Pursuit of Justice and
U.S. Accountability

THE CONDOR YEARS: HOW PINOCHET AND HIS ALLIES BROUGHT TERRORISM

TO THREE CONTINENTS, 2004

THE CONDOR YEARS demonstrated, two decades after the fact, that unresolved crimes of the past do not remain in the past. Operation Condor returned like a painful, inflamed carbuncle to plague the old age of those who conceived it and the officers who carried it out.

Condor's success turned out to be ephemeral. A decade later, none of the military governments was still in power. The Condor regimes' secret campaign to eliminate their democratic and guerrilla adversaries eventually was replaced by another kind of pursuit, to bring the military leaders themselves to justice. This time it was a campaign carried out in the light of day and in the arenas of international law.

The pursuit of justice, begun while the crimes were still being committed, would continue and gain strength for more than two decades. It was at first a slow and tedious process that for long years seemed doomed to futility by lingering military influence, legal setbacks, and national indifference. But as this is written, human rights prosecutions were reaching a crescendo, resulting in hundreds of extradition petitions, indictments, and imprisonment for many of the military officers who had enjoyed years of court-protected impunity.

The crimes of Operation Condor became the catalyst for an intense international prosecution that mirrored Condor's three-continent arena of activity. The cross-border Condor activities had been a relatively small portion of the mass violations of human rights committed by the military governments. Nevertheless, Condor took on unique significance, both symbolically and legally, in the effort to bring the military leaders to justice. The Condor crimes, by targeting high-profile public figures, especially military leaders and democratic politicians, attracted the extraordinary attention of zealous human rights lawyers, crusading judges, and persistent investigative reporters.

The international nature of the crimes expanded the jurisdictions that could prosecute them. The military leaders left behind amnesty laws, often negotiated with their civilian successors, but Condor presented a special problem. Because the military governments did not admit the existence of the international operations, the amnesty laws were drafted to cover only internal human rights abuses. The Letelier murder, for example, was explicitly excluded from Chile's amnesty law, passed in 1978. Thus in many cases the Condor operations left military leaders exposed to prosecution in neighboring countries for crimes protected by amnesties at home.

Condor's operations also left a trail of potential witnesses and other evidence in dozens of countries in Latin America, Europe, and the United States. While the Condor countries were fairly systematic about eliminating incriminating evidence about their own military activities, they were far less efficient in protecting their Condor partners, especially after the alliance had ended and civilian governments were in power. The evidence was of less importance to the country where it was discovered than to the countries it implicated in criminal activity. Thus pursuing investigators were able to uncover rich veins of evidence, including caches of documents in some cases.

Because of its nature as a massive intelligence undertaking, Condor generated a broad paper trail in the U.S. government as well. Condor involved at least six governments' intelligence services, and as such it was of immediate and crucial interest to the CIA and U.S. military intelligence. While there was no systematic U.S. attempt to gather information on human rights abuses or to place obstacles in the way of those committing them (at least until the Carter administration), intelligence reporting on Condor alliance enjoyed a high priority. It was relevant not only to U.S. policy but to overall counterintelligence and military liaison goals as well. Reporting on Condor was protected at the highest "codeword" level of classification.

To be sure, this is not to say that Condor was the only factor in unleashing of the recent breakthroughs in human rights prosecutions. It is my task here, however, to complete the account of the Condor years by showing how the international crimes of the military governments gave way to an increasingly successful campaign to document the crimes of the past in courts of law and to bring charges against the authors of those crimes.

No step was easy in the search for evidence and the pursuit of eventual justice.

Still, the first step was gigantic. The FBI investigation of the Letelier assassination led not only to indictments but to the gathering and eventual declassification of an enormous body of evidence about the Pinochet government's secret police and its international activity. That evidence, contained in thousands of pages of trial transcript and evidentiary documents measured in linear feet, was the first detailed exposure of Chile's secret apparatus of repression. It was that evidence, in particular the investigative work by the FBI's man in Buenos Aires, Robert Scherrer, that first publically revealed the existence of Operation Condor, in 1979. We now know, however, as described in Chapter 11, that the evidence was carefully selected to conceal crucial details about U.S. intelligence on Condor. Chile maintained an iron wall of silence about its own military crimes as long as Pinochet remained in power, refusing extradition of those indicted in the United States.

Argentina was the first country to attempt real investigations and real trials. The junta generals tumbled from power after an abortive invasion in April 1982 to wrest the bleak Falkland Islands off the southern coast from Great Britain. The armed forces that had pursued so relentlessly the war against terrorism against Argentina's own citizens were routed when their bluff was called by Britain's counterattack. Thousands of ill-equipped and badly led Argentine troops were captured with barely a fight, and at least 1,000 were killed. Junta president Leopoldo Galtieri resigned in disgrace. The new military leader, General Reynaldo Benito Bignone, was forced to begin the process of restoring civilian rule.

There was an immediate campaign, fiercely resisted by the military, to prosecute the crimes of what everyone now called the Dirty War. The newly elected president, Raúl Alfonsín, who had been a courageous human rights activist during military rule, created a commission, headed by writer Ernesto Sábato, to investigate the fate of the disappeared. The Sábato Commission conducted a hurried investigation and delivered its report, titled *Nunca Mas*—Never Again—in less than a year. It listed 8,961 names of disappeared, the bedrock minimum of documented victims of the regime's network of secret prisons and extermination centers.

The task of naming and trying the perpetrators was left to the courts. The Alfonsín government pushed through legislation sweeping aside the military government's "Self-Amnesty" decree enacted just before leaving power. Trials of the members of the military juntas lasted from April to December 1985 and ended in the conviction of the five top leaders, including Videla and navy chief Emilio Massera, who received sentences ranging from life to five years in prison. The trials created explosive anger among other military officers, who understandably concluded that they might be next to face trials. In fact, at least 1,700 additional prosecutions were in preparation in the months following the conviction of the top leaders.

For the next several years, the country roiled in unresolved conflict, including four armed rebellions by military units known as the *carapintados* for the camouflage paint they used on their faces. Alfonsín was forced to back down on prosecuting the lower ranking military. He agreed to set a deadline—called the *Punto Final*—after which no further charges could be filed against the military for human rights atrocities. Finally, in 1989, after a final bloody military revolt, Alfonsín's successor, Peronist President Carlos Menem, bought peace with the military by issuing presidential pardons for Videla and the other junta members.[1]

In the midst of the turmoil surrounding the trials and pardons, a young Chilean investigative reporter, Mónica González, arrived in Buenos Aires in pursuit of information about Chile's most famous unsolved murder: the 1974 assassination of Pinochet's predecessor, General Carlos Prats. There had been a perfunctory judicial investigation at the time that was quickly squelched by pro-military judges. González, a freelance reporter for a weekly magazine, wanted to study the Prats case files for a book she was writing.

After a frustrating week roaming the hallways of the majestic federal court building in downtown Buenos Aires, she had managed to read the official file of the case, but learned little. Most of the court employees and judges were holdovers from the military era, and the atmosphere in the court offices was unremittingly hostile.

By making herself and her quest visible, she finally got a break. A man she assumed was a court employee approached her in the hallway. "Señora, if you want to find something, don't waste your time [with the Prats case file]," he said. "Just look for the espionage trial of Enrique Arancibia Clavel, for when they arrested him in 1978. Just get ahold of those files."

González knew the name. Enrique Arancibia was a notorious right-wing civilian who had fled Chile in 1970 because of involvement in terrorist bombings around the time of the elections that brought Allende to power. After the coup, he had gotten a job in the Buenos Aires branch of the Chilean Banco de Estado. There had been a brief flurry of publicity surrounding his arrest as a spy in 1978, during a tense period in which Chile and Argentina had both mobilized their forces in a military stand-off over disputed territory in the southernmost tip of the continent, known as the Beagle Channel. But when the crisis between Chile and Argentina abated, thanks to papal mediation, the charges were dropped, and Arancibia resumed what appeared to be a quiet life as a restaurant owner. He was one of the people González had on her list to interview.

González learned that at the time of his arrest, Argentine police had searched Arancibia's apartment and his bank office and confiscated extensive files documenting his work as a Chilean agent. González looked up the case and located the judge in charge. The court files were supposed to be public records, but the judge had absolute control over who would be allowed to see them. He refused to give her access to the archive, or even to talk to her.

González had been ignored, brushed off, lied to, and threatened on this reporting trip, and she was no longer willing to take no for an answer. She decided to make herself a nuisance. She found out where the judge lived and set up a vigil, arriving by bus at 7 A.M. each morning on the street outside his house. For a week, she was there as he left his house in his chauffeur-driven car, trying to get his attention. The judge's wife came out and surveyed the spectacle with irate impatience.

"I heard her tell him, '*Nada mas*'—'No more.' This has to stop," González recalled. "Finally he had his driver pull up beside me. He just said, 'Get in,' and never said another word to me." The judge took her to his office and instructed a secretary to show her where the Arancibia documents were archived. She was allowed to read the documents, but she couldn't make copies.

The court archive was a sea of disorder. Ringed binders with ancient labels were arranged haphazardly on shelves. Boxes full of filings from long-forgotten cases covered most of the floor. The room appeared not to have been cleaned in years. The secretary located three closed boxes with files labeled "*Causa 949, Enrique Arancibia Clavel y otros . . . ,*" and left González alone.

González jerked the lid off one of the boxes, and let some of the loose contents spill out onto the floor. One of the first things that caught her eye was a small stack of Chilean identity cards. She recognized some of the names. They were Chilean political prisoners who had disappeared. In other boxes there were hundreds of pages of correspondence—original letters received from Santiago, and carbon copies of letters from Buenos Aires to Santiago. The correspondence started in October 1974, only a few days after the Prats assassination, and was arranged in chronological order up to the time of Arancibia's arrest in November 1978.

Note taking was too slow. González took out her tape recorder and spent the rest of the day reading the documents verbatim onto cassette tapes. She returned the next day and continued recording. It was astounding material of the kind few reporters or human rights investigator had ever seen. Arancibia had served as DINA's man in Buenos Aires for almost four years. The letters contained the day-to-day instructions from his superiors in Santiago as well as his intelligence reports back to DINA. There were code names and aliases, references to operations in Chile, Argentina, and Europe. There were long lists of names of people who had been kidnapped in Argentina and Chile. Some of it made sense. Much of it was uncharted territory. She didn't have time to record every document before time ran out.

Back in Chile, still under Pinochet's rule, she transcribed the material and turned it over to the Catholic Church's human rights organization, the Vicariate of Solidarity, which presented it as new evidence to keep the courts from closing the investigations of hundreds of cases of disappeared persons. González's most important story, in *Analysis* magazine and later in *La Nación* newspaper, was an exposé of one of DINA's pre-Condor propaganda operations, called Operation Colombo.

The operation, organized by DINA's Exterior Department in 1975, was intended to create a cover story for disappearances in Chile. In July 1975, two obscure publications, one in Buenos Aires and the other in the provincial Brazilian city of Curitiba, published lists of 119 Chileans with stories saying they had been killed in guerrilla activity in Argentina or in-fighting between leftist groups. Other stories showed pictures of dead bodies found in Argentina with placards saying they were MIR members. The ID cards with the bodies were Chilean, but the bodies were not. They belonged to Argentine victims of the AAA death squad. The stories were provided by an equally obscure Argentine news service and were picked up by Chile's pro-Pinochet press. One Chilean newspaper headlined its story "Chileans Exterminated like Rats."

All but four of the names appearing in the stories were of disappeared persons whose cases had been presented in a group habeas corpus filing by the Chilean Catholic Church in early 1975. The lists published in Buenos Aires and Brazil even reproduced the spelling errors contained in the Church's presentation to the court.

González's stories cited documents establishing that Arancibia, on DINA orders, had arranged for the publication of the false stories and lists, and that DINA Exterior Department officers had provided identity cards to be planted on the scene where the bodies were discovered. "Operation Colombo" was DINA's own name for the scheme.[2]

The Arancibia documents provide exclusive internal information on the whole range of security force activities from 1974 to 1978, and constitute a virtual road map of the joint operations between Chile, Argentina, and Paraguay that led to the formalization of Operation Condor. The documents were known publicly only in the form of González's transcripts for many years. Alerted to their existence, however, a Roman judge, Giovanni Salvi, traveled to Buenos Aires and obtained a complete copy from the court as evidence in his investigation of the assassination attempt against Bernardo Leighton. The author also obtained a complete set of the documents for use in this investigation—the only copy available outside judicial archives.

Uruguay, Bolivia, and Brazil all returned to civilian government in 1984 and 1985. In 1989, Paraguay's army unceremoniously dumped General Stroessner in a bloodless coup and called elections. Pinochet was also on his way out. He called a plebiscite designed to extend his presidency for eight more years, but was delivered a resounding "No" by the Chilean people. He tried to stop the vote count and reverse the result, but his own fellow junta members refused to go along with what in effect would be another military coup to prolong the dictatorship. The loss meant that free elections were allowed to go forward in December 1989, and Christian Democrat Patricio Alywin, backed by a coalition of parties that including Allende's Socialist Party, won a decisive victory.

Finally, all the Condor countries had shaken off the long military nightmare. Still, none had grappled successfully with the legacy of the past. Like Argentina, Uruguay had briefly attempted to investigate the crimes of the military junta, in a congressional commission, but the effort was aborted by an airtight amnesty law, ratified by majority vote in a national plebiscite. Uniquely among the Condor countries, Uruguay's Amnesty, called *"la ley de caducidad,"* renounced the right even to conduct criminal investigations of the human rights crimes.

Paraguay was the scene of the next major breakthrough in the pursuit of truth about the past.

Martín Almada was an accidental human rights hero. He was a teacher and fervent Colorado Party activist with a bright future. He studied at the University of La Plata in Argentina, and became Paraguay's first PhD in education. He returned to Paraguay in 1974 with the well-founded expectation he would advance in the small world of Paraguayan politics. He headed the local chapter of the teachers association, and was able to dispense minor patronage through his control of a government-funded project to provide subsidized housing to teachers. He was already asked to be an educational consultant for the government. There was talk of a ministry of education job.

In late 1974, when their lives changed forever, Almada and his wife, Celestina Pérez, were running a small private school in the town of San Lorenzo just outside of Asunción. On November 24, a squad of Paraguayan police came to his house and placed him under arrest. At the office of police intelligence chief Pastor Coronel, he was tortured and interrogated. There had been a car bomb attempt on President Stroessner's life, and the police had traced the plot to a group of young people, some of whom had studied at the University of La Plata at the same time Almada was there. The group had received training and support from the ERP, and Stroessner's archenemy, Dr. Augustín Goiburú, had obtained the bomb from Montonero contacts in Argentina and smuggled it into Paraguay himself.

Almada was totally innocent, according to those who were involved. One participant said they knew Almada in La Plata but decided not to approach him because he was on a government scholarship and was considered a loyal Colorado. "It was our fault he was arrested," said Dimas Piris Da Motta, who was the group's liaison between Argentina and Paraguay. But innocence was no protection in Stroessner's jails. Almada was savagely tortured for weeks. At one point he was placed on display in Pastor Coronel's office in front of a large group of officers, including foreigners, which he later would describe in public speeches as a "Condor tribunal."

During one of the torture sessions, the police called Almada's wife, Celestina. They questioned her and held the phone so that she could hear her husband's groans. A few days later, she collapsed and died of a heart attack. Almada's torture and his personal tragedy transformed a small-town schoolteacher into one of the most relentless pursuers of the military leaders of the Condor countries. Almada's experience gave him a unique vision of the inner workings of Operation Condor. He was in the same prison as JCR couriers Jorge Fuentes and Amílcar Santucho, and heard the story firsthand of their interrogations by Argentine and Chilean officers, and of Fuentes's transport back to his death in Chile. One of the Chilean officers, Colonel Jorge Otaiza, interrogated Almada at one point.

In 1978, after almost four years in prison, Almada was released and made his way into exile first in Panama, then in Paris, where he got a job as an education specialist in UNESCO. Determined to document what had happened to him and especially to find out how his wife had died, he began to research the personnel and structures of Stroessner's armed forces and police. When Stroessner fell in 1989, Almada was among the first exiles to return home, and he accelerated his quest for information.

Unlike the other Condor countries, there were no amnesties or special laws to protect the military. Stroessner fled into exile in Brazil and was joined by some of his followers. The most notorious torturers were put on trial and imprisoned, including Pastor Coronel, Police chief General Francisco Alcibiades Brítez, and intelligence chief General Benito Guanes, who had been Paraguay's representative to Condor. But Almada wanted the truth more than he wanted the punishment of his tormentors. Using a provision called "habeas data" of the newly passed constitution, Almada petitioned the courts for all public records concerning his arrest and imprisonment and the death of his wife. Habeas data was similar to the Freedom of Information Act and Privacy Act in U.S. law. It provided that any citizen could have access to any public document about himself or herself. Almada's petition was the first time the law had ever been used. In the hands of a sympathetic judge, it was a powerful tool.

Almada filed his request with a lower level criminal court judge, José Augustín Fernández, who sent a court order in December 1992 to the Paraguayan police. The police responded that the police archives containing records of Almada's arrest and imprisonment had been destroyed at the time of the coup against Stroessner.

Almada knew his country well and was undaunted. Among the vast network of people compromised by their work for Stroessner there were many who were jockeying for position with the new power holders, and there were many scores to settle. Almada put out the word in the press. A prominent human rights activist and Liberal Party congressman, Francisco de Vargas also got involved in the search. Within a few days they had some solid leads. A woman who was a friend of de Vargas brought her companion, a former policemen, to see him. The policeman knew where some documents had been hidden after the coup. They were in an obscure police facility outside Asunción, called the "Department of Production," he said. He had a small quid pro quo in mind. He needed a job for one of his sons. De Vargas was glad to oblige.

The woman also went to see Almada, and gave him a hand-drawn map. Almada arranged with Judge Fernández to go to the facility, in the town of Lambaré, just outside Asunción. The map showed which building at the site housed the hidden documents. Almada alerted a group of reporters and television cameramen, and they drove in a caravan to the police station, arriving at 10:30 in the morning of December 22, 1992. De Vargas lagged behind, nervous that nothing would be found.

With the press crowded behind him, Judge Fernández confronted the police official in charge of the facility. Policemen in Paraguay were used to taking orders only from their military superiors, not from judges. "I am the judge. At this moment I am empowered with the authority given to me by the Constitution, and I order you to let me enter," Fernández said. "I am your guarantee that nobody will harm you."

Once inside, Almada followed the map to a room on the second floor at the rear of the the complex of buildings. There was a formidable padlock on the door. Fernández ordered someone to get a crowbar. They broke the lock and pushed open the door, against the weight of something piled against it.

They were amazed by what they found inside. It was a medium-sized office with almost no furniture. Every horizontal surface was covered with stacks of papers. There were hundreds of ringed archive binders, bound chronological volumes of police interrogation reports, boxes of surveillance tapes and photos, jailhouse log books recording the arrival and departure of thousands of prisoners, correspondence with security forces from Chile, Bolivia, Argentina, Uruguay, Brazil, and the United States, "rap sheet" summary reports in alphabetical order with photos and fingerprints of thousands of Paraguayan and foreign prisoners, many of them on the lists of disappeared. Almada's rap sheet was there, and he also found interrogation reports and numerous other documents on his case.

Acting on another tip, searchers dug up other boxes of documents that had been buried in the courtyard. Among the findings were the yellowed and moldy remains of scores of ID cards of political prisoners who had been executed. The archive was so vast, it had to be transported in borrowed trucks to the Palace of Justice court building, where Judge Fernández had his office.[3]

Press reports at the time called the collection "The Archive of Terror" and the name stuck. Reporters estimated the weight of the documents at three or four tons. When years later the collection was microfilmed, the number of document pages was put at 593,000. It was quickly determined that the papers were the nearly complete records from the Department of Investigation of the Capital Police (DIPC), headed by Pastor Coronel. They were from Coronel's DIPC headquarters and jail located on a downtown street only blocks from Parliament. It was the jail where Jorge Fuentes and Amílcar Santucho were held and interrogated after their arrest in 1975, and their case is recorded in dozens of documents. Several telegrams and intelligence reports from 1976 and 1977 were labelled for distribution to "Condor." The researchers eventually found Manuel Contreras's original invitation to Paraguay to attend the founding Condor meeting, with the only copy anywhere of the agenda for the meeting. Many of the most important Phase Two Condor operations and prisoner exchanges are documented in dozens of memos and letters exchanged among all the Condor member countries.

Almada's[4] discovery is by far the largest collection of previously secret security force documents from any of the Condor countries. The Paraguay Archive forms a major part of the documentary backbone of this book, together with the Arancibia documents discovered by Mónica González and the declassification of Chile and Argentina documents ordered by the Clinton administration. Without these documents, the history of the Condor years could not be written.

THE DOCUMENT COLLECTIONS and the dogged investigations of pursuers like González, Almada, and human rights researchers in each of the countries laid the groundwork for an unprecedented series of human rights victories beginning in the mid-1990s. The first was in Rome. Investigating Judge Giovanni Salvi had been working since the early 1980s on the assassination attempt that left Bernardo Leighton and his wife seriously injured. Among the early leads was a 1979 article by the author, based on DINA sources in Chile, revealing for the first time that DINA had harbored a group of Italian terrorists, one of whom was identified as Stefano

Delle Chiaie, who had organized the Leighton assassination attempt. Judge Salvi prosecuted Delle Chiaie and the Chilean suspects through three trials over more than a decade. His was the first judicial investigation of DINA's European network, and he persuaded several of Delle Chiaie's rightist comrades to testify. He also traveled to Chile and Argentina. In Chile, he interviewed more than a dozen DINA personnel. In Buenos Aires, he became the only judge to enter SIDE headquarters, and came away with a complete copy of the Arancibia papers. The first trial, against Delle Chiaie, was premature—it was attempted without direct testimony from Michael Townley—and resulted in acquittal. Finally, Salvi reached an agreement with U.S. authorities to allow Townley to testify; during several days of secret depositions in 1992 and 1993 and personal testimony in Rome in 1995, Townley identified Delle Chiaie and his other coplotters in court for the first time. In June 1995, the court convicted Manuel Contreras and Exterior Department head Raúl Iturriaga Neumann in absencia and sentenced them to twenty and eighteen years respectively.

Chile refused the Italian extradition request, as it had done in response to earlier petitions from the United States in the Letelier case. But with a civilian government in power in Chile, the situation was changing quickly. After intense negotiations, the United States agreed to drop its extradition requests, dating from 1978, and Chilean courts began the first serious prosecution of the assassination case in Chile. The Letelier murder was the sole explicit exception to the amnesty law Pinochet's government had left in place. The trial, conducted by prosecuting Judge Adolfo Bañados, relied heavily on the evidence developed by the FBI, the testimony of Townley, and new evidence developed in Italy. In response to a Chilean *exhorto*—a request for cooperation—Judge Salvi delivered the voluminous body of testimony and documentary evidence he had gathered. The trial in Chile lasted four years, ending in spectacular public hearings in May 1995 and convictions of Contreras and operations chief Pedro Espinoza. Pinochet, still commander in chief of the armed forces, had rattled sabers against the civilian government before to prevent civilian action against the military, but this time he turned his back. After a few dramatic days of hiding out in military bases, Contreras gave himself up and began to serve a seven-year sentence in a special prison facility. Espinoza was locked up in the same facility to serve a six-year sentence. The prison was comfortable, but it did not mask the reality: for the first time, two of Pinochet's closet collaborators were serving time behind bars.

The Leighton and Letelier prosecutions were major tremors opening up cracks in the fortresses of military impunity, but the real shifting of the tectonic plates of international justice came with the arrest of retired general Pinochet in London in October 1998. That event is examined in detail in Chapter 3. Although Pinochet himself was able to slip away from personal accountability by claiming advanced age and mental disability, the Spanish case was followed quickly by other energetic prosecutions, first in Europe and finally in South America.

Judges in Rome and Paris fashioned investigations around carefully selected cases of binational victims—those with French or Italian passports in addition to their Latin American citizenship. The French judge, Roger Le Loire, centered his investigation, opened less than three weeks after Pinochet's arrest, on the disappearance of Jean Yves Claudet Fernández, one of the earliest Condor victims and part of the string of Condor kidnappings that started in Paraguay and included the capture in Argentina of MIR leader Edgardo Enríquez. Le Loire issued international arrest warrants for Pinochet and seventeen other Chilean and Argentine officials, including Batallion 601 operative José Osvaldo Riveiro, the "Colonel Osvaldo Rawson" of the Arancibia documents. Le Loire worked hand in hand with two other pursuers, lawyers William Bourdon and Sophie Thonon, representing the families of the victims. The judge brought his wide experience in espionage and terrorism prosecution to the investigation. He earlier had handled the questioning of Ilich Ramírez Sánchez—Carlos the Jackal—after his capture in Sudan in 1994. In May 2001, Le Loire served papers on Henry Kissinger, who was in Paris for a meeting, asking him to testify about his knowledge of Condor. Kissinger refused, but subsequently curtailed his international travel to avoid additional subpoenas.

Operation Condor was also the focus of the Italian case. Judge Giancarlo Capaldo, the Italian federal investigating judge, opened the case at the request of the Italian Justice Ministry within a few months of

Pinochet's arrest in London. He was asked to investigate evidence of other crimes against Italians committed by Pinochet, but he soon expanded the investigation to include the top military leaders and security force personnel of four Condor countries—Chile, Uruguay, Argentina, and Brazil. The new case, in effect, was the continuation of Judge Salvi's Leighton assassination case trials, and all of the evidence arduously gathered by Salvi—whose office was in the same court facility—was turned over to Capaldo.

The Rome investigation involved three Phase Two Condor operations: the Uruguayan-Argentine action against leaders of the Uruguayan Party for Victory guerrilla group in Buenos Aires in 1976; the 1977 Paraguayan-Argentine-Uruguayan interrogations of a group of Uruguayans and Argentines captured in Asunción and subsequently delivered by plane to Argentina; and the Argentine-Brazilian operation in 1980 to capture Montoneros trying to smuggle themselves back into Argentina (see descriptions of these cases in Chapter 13). The case was brought on behalf of eleven victims, all of Italian ancestry.

Even before Pinochet arrived back in Chile, courts in Argentina and Chile began to act with unprecedented vigor, resurrecting old cases and finding loopholes in the amnesty laws. The Prats murder investigation, taken over by a politically astute judge, María Servini de Cubria, cast its net across the Andes to Chile for the first time. Servini asked Chile to extradite Contreras and Espinoza, later adding DINA Exterior Department Raúl Eduardo Iturriaga, Iturriaga's brother, and DINA officer José Zara Holger. She included Pinochet in the list of suspects and asked for his extradition as a material witness. Arancibia, who had been in jail on Prats murder charges since 1996, was convicted in late 2001 and was sentenced to life in prison.

Chile's courts, which had hitherto ignored the Prats murder, were thus forced to give the case a fresh hearing. In December 2002, the Chilean Supreme Court ruled that the extradition case presented by Servini had merit. Instead of extradition, however, the court ordered the five defendants to be tried in Chile for the Prats murder. The court also found that the defendants could appeal for protection neither to Pinochet's amnesty law nor to the statue of limitations—referred to as "prescription" in Chilean law. Contreras and Iturriaga were immediately jailed.

By mid-2003, the amnesty in Chile had become an empty shell. The church sponsored human rights organization, FASIC, counted 247 separate ongoing indictments on human rights charges and was keeping track day to day on its Web site of which officers were currently in jail. Stopping short of a declaration of victory, the organization proclaimed:

> *Chile of 2003 is a profoundly different country in matters of human rights. From FASIC's point of view, the period 2000–2003 has been the most fruitful of the last 30 years. Never before has so much truth been achieved as now, never have there been more trials than now, and never before have we been in the presence of more propitious conditions to advance in the pursuit of justice in cases brought for violations of human rights.*

Meanwhile, in Argentina an even bigger case was launched, tailored to investigate the crimes of Operation Condor under organized crime statutes and to prosecute its perpetrators as members of an illegal criminal association. The case, under the direction of federal Judge Rodolfo Canicoba Corral, was far and away the most comprehensive judicial investigation of military crimes that had ever been attempted in Latin America. Its defendants were the top military leaders and intelligence officials of five of the six Condor countries (only Brazil was excepted). The list of victims, initially five, grew to include seventy-two people who disappeared in Condor operations in Paraguay, Chile, Argentina, and Uruguay. The charges went beyond the litany of crimes against humanity—torture, disappearance—to include violations of the right of asylum, extradition laws, and violations of each country's sovereignty. In addition to Argentine law—subject to the *Punto Final* laws restricting prosecution of Dirty War crimes—the Condor case established jurisdiction over the defendants in all the countries by citing the Nuremberg principles and other international precedents establishing universal jurisdiction in human rights cases.

In establishing the basic narrative of the creation of Operation Condor, the judge (citing as his source an article by the author in *La Nación* in August 1999) described the arrest of Jorge Fuentes and Amílcar Santucho in Paraguay in 1975 and how the three-country collaboration in that case can be traced with documents to the meeting in Santiago at which the security forces joined together in the new organization. The case continued to expand, adding the Michelini-Gutiérrez murders in late 2002, which had languished with little or no investigation either in Uruguay or Argentina for more than a decade.

In August 2001, Canicoba submitted an official request to the U.S. Justice Department, in accord with the Mutual Legal Assistance Treaty (MLAT) with the United States, seeking the testimony of Henry Kissinger on Operation Condor.

By indicating all of the top military leaders and seeking their extradition, the Condor case had the effect of nailing them in place in their own countries. None of the defendants could travel outside their own counties without fear of arrest on international warrants. The case also has a powerful, embarrassing effect on neighboring Uruguay, which was the one country that had conducted no human rights trials. Judge Canicoba demanded the extradition of four Uruguayan officers identified as working inside Argentina, in Condor operations based at Automotores Orletti, but Uruguay refused even to provide information. In addition to the Michelini-Gutiérrez case, the largest group of victims were the members of the Party for Victory who had been kidnapped in mid-1976 in Argentina. In late 2002, an Uruguayan judge finally allowed a criminal investigation of the Michelini and Gutiérrez murders to be opened. These were just the most important international investigations. Other European countries (Germany, Belgium, and Switzerland) opened investigations of their own citizens killed in the Condor countries.

The number of international warrants for military officials from the Condor countries had surpassed 200 as this book went to press. Retired military officers, even younger and lower-ranking officers pursuing lucrative business ventures, were at risk whenever they traveled abroad. In a major follow-up to the Pinochet precedent in June 2003, a Mexican court extradited a former Argentine navy officer, Ricardo Cavallo, to face charges of genocide and terrorism in Judge Baltasar Garzón's court in Spain. Cavallo had been running a small business in Mexico until his arrest in 2000. He was identified as a notorious torturer known as "Serpico" at the Navy's ESMA camp in Argentina. The legal procedure for his case was the same as that pioneered by Garzón in Pinochet's arrest in London, except that Cavallo was actually turned over to face trial in Spain. It was the first case in human rights law of a person arrested in one country being extradited to a second country for crimes committed in a third.

Condor, in its new incarnation as the central target of multicountry judicial investigations, had become the vehicle to ruin the peace and prosperity the military leaders were expecting in their declining years. Officers from Uruguay, where impunity still reigned at its most blatant, were prevented from taking the short trip to Argentina, and thus were cut off from their country's most active partner for business, cultural, and family connections. It became hard to keep track of which officials had been indicted in which countries, and who was currently in jail or under house arrest. As the cases advance from investigations to formal indictments, an increasing number of officials have actually found themselves in jail. Those consequences are a measure, albeit imperfect, of justice. In a larger perspective, there is a deep historical irony in the two incarnations of Condor. It once was the primary destroyer of international protections. Now two decades later its legal prosecution is the catalyst for a pioneering new era of international law. As a result of the Pinochet precedents set in Spain, followed by far-reaching prosecutions in the other countries, human rights protections were greatly strengthened, and for the first time since World War II, courts began to routinely honor the concept of universal jurisdiction as the last resort to prosecute the most powerful violators of human rights—those who enjoy impunity in their own countries. Just as Condor was created to mirror the international coordination of the JCR, Condor's international activities made it vulnerable to a multinational legal strategy to prosecute its leaders and operatives.

The Spanish have a saying that fits what happened to the military leaders who created Condor:

Criá cuervos, y te sacarán los ojos.
Raise a flock of crows and they will pluck out your eyes.

The CIA also has a term for it, "blowback"—the unintended consequences of U.S. policies kept secret from the American public. Here in the United States this era is undigested history. Only in the United States, whose diplomats, intelligence, and military were so intimately intertwined with the military dictators and their operational subordinates, has there been judicial silence on the crimes of the Condor years. No prosecutor has opened an investigation into the deaths in Chile of two American citizens, Charles Horman and Frank Teruggi, even after declassified documents produced promising new leads. The Letelier investigation has returned to a state of dormancy. For a while after Pinochet's arrest in London, the U.S. Justice Department began pursuing an energetic new approach to the solving of the still pending elements of the Letelier murder. There was talk of indicting Pinochet for giving the order to kill Letelier, but in the end, especially with the Bush presidency, the investigation seemed to be kept open more as a pretext for continued secrecy about unanswered questions in the case—such as those raised in this book—than a genuine effort to indict additional participants in the plot.

I have tried to establish the historical baseline of truth, at least of documented fact, about the United States government's relationship to the military personnel responsible for these mass international crimes. I have tried to balance my criticism of U.S. complicity with respect for the many U.S. officials who tried to keep their moral compass intact while implementing policies of deep moral ambiguity. Even after all these years, the toughest obstacle to this task continues to be U.S. official secrecy and a continuing will in some quarters to deceive, obfuscate, and even to cover up the extent of official U.S. connections to Operation Condor.

The Letelier assassination in Washington, D.C., was blowback. It was ordered by a close ally, a dictator the United States helped install, maintain, and defend in power; it was planned by an intelligence official who had been on the CIA payroll and who traveled frequently for consultation with CIA officials in Washington; it was carried out by DINA, a newly created security organization whose personnel were trained in Chile by a CIA team; it was detected in its initial operational stages not by alert spycraft but by the very chumminess of CIA officials with those planning the crimes.

Yet the U.S. ally carried out this major act of international terrorism on U.S. soil unimpeded. It is a major conclusion of this book that U.S. officials knew enough to have stopped the assassination, and that they launched a flawed and foreshortened effort to do so, then covered up their failure after Letelier and an American woman were murdered. Records declassified two decades later show that U.S. officials, including Secretary of State Kissinger, knew about Operation Condor's plans to assassinate nonviolent opposition leaders who were living in exile outside Latin America. Those same officials knew that Chile had attempted around the same time to send DINA agents clandestinely to the United States using false Paraguayan passports—one of Condor's standard operation procedures. The exact record of what happened next remains drastically censored, but we can know this much: Condor's assassination plans were taken so seriously that Kissinger himself sent a long cable to the ambassadors in the Condor countries, instructing them to take action to stop the Condor plans. Yet the instructions were not carried out and the assassination plans went forward.

The official story, promulgated at the time, was that U.S. intelligence knew about Condor only as a relatively innocent apparatus for international intelligence exchange. The Phase Three assassination plans were discovered only after Letelier was dead, according to this version. Therefore, U.S. officials could not have concluded an assassination was afoot. That version is starkly contradicted by documents declassified under President Clinton's executive order in 1999. The updated version of the cover story is that the Letelier assassination was not a Condor operation in the first place, that Operation Condor was barely visible on the radar screen of the busy officials surrounding Kissinger in the weeks prior to the Letelier assassination, but that, in any case, Kissinger, with his August 23 cable, spoke out against Condor.

This is the framework of Kissinger's official reply to Judge Canicoba's request for his testimony about Condor. The State Department letter to

Canicoba, on behalf of Kissinger, is the most authoritative statement the U.S. government has made about its involvement with Condor.

Some excerpts:

> *First, extremely serious crimes were committed in the name of Operation Condor by the Argentine military and security forces from 1976 to 1983. The questions address whether the United States knew of those crimes. The questions, furthermore, are directed to Dr. Kissinger's knowledge and acts while he was secretary of state. It is therefore important to state firmly and unequivocally in response to these questions that the United States was not complicit in Condor, neither in the last few months of Secretary Kissinger's service as Secretary of State in 1976, nor during the later years of its most intense activity. The 26,000 [sic] documents in the Chile Declassification Project and the newly released 4,700 documents in the Argentina Declassification Project support this fact and clearly demonstrate the opposition of the United States government to the activities of Operation Condor.*
>
> *Dr. Kissinger became aware of the existence of Operation Condor in 1976. As the documentary record shows, during that same year he spoke out publicly to the OAS General Assembly against human rights violations as a method of suppressing terrorism, and, on August 23, 1976, instructed U.S. ambassadors in the region to make clear to the highest government officials the "deep concern" of the United States over rumors of coordinated assassination plans, emphasizing that "if these rumors were to have any shred of truth, they would create a most serious moral and political problem. [Emphasis added.]*

In the manner of U.S. government denials, this one is carefully qualified. "Firm and unequivocal" are strong words, but the denial of U.S. complicity in Condor is restricted to the "last few months" of 1976 and thereafter. That period covers the period after which the Condor countries agreed to implement Phase Three assassination plans (June 1976, just after Kissinger's speech at the OAS meeting). But it excludes Condor's period of gestation in 1975, the founding of Condor at the Santiago meeting, and the early months of its intense Phase Two activity. During that period of more than a year, there were frequent contacts between Condor mastermind Manuel Contreras and the CIA, including at least three trips to Washington (January and July 1975 and July 1976) and a CIA payment to Contreras. There is also direct evidence of CIA and FBI access to interrogations under torture by Condor agents (the June 1975 letter from FBI officer Robert Scherrer concerning Fuentes and Santucho and the CIA report on two Chileans being held in Condor's secret Orletti detention center).

It is my argument, based on the declassified evidence, that the CIA and other U.S. agencies encouraged and supported the integration of the security forces of Chile, Argentina, Brazil, Uruguay, Paraguay, and Bolivia. This activity was applauded in Washington, not criticized, and was seen as a needed response to "international terrorism," especially the growing international organization of the JCR. The United States maintained liaison with Condor operations, provided training and material support to the Condor data bank and communications system, and received and disseminated intelligence generated by Condor kidnappings and torture. It is highly probable that Contreras informed his CIA contacts, including the Santiago station chief and CIA deputy director Vernon Walters, of his plans before convening the Santiago meeting, and that the CIA was immediately informed about the formation of Condor. I have established, based on the account of one of the intelligence officers present, that international assassinations were discussed at that meeting. Intelligence exchange and cross-border prisoner transfers (Phase One and Two) began immediately, and there is no evidence of U.S. "opposition" to those activies. Cooperation, liaison, acquiescence, and even complicity are words that would seem to accurately describe the relationship prior to the latter months of 1976.

The U.S. attitude changed from support to opposition, however, when our agents learned in June 1976 that Phase Three operations were being planned outside Latin America. Adding to the U.S.'s second thoughts were the assassinations in Argentina around the same time of prominent Bolivian and Uruguayan exiles, Juan José Torres, Zelmar Michelini, and Héctor Gutiérrez. The United States was not willing to support, even by acquiescence, the assassination of democratic, nonviolent leaders or to tolerate the launching of terrorist killings in Europe.

It was these Condor activities and plans that created a stir in the State Department when Latin American bureau officials learned about them from CIA reports. Kissinger's cable of August 23 did indeed order a strong expression of U.S. opposition to the Condor assassination. The obvious question left by Kissinger's response is why his instructions were not carried out. Why was his "deep concern" not conveyed to any of the three heads of state—Pinochet, Videla, and Alvarez—or to the security force chiefs who were planning the assassinations? It is inconceivable that lower-ranking State Department officials or ambassadors in the field would disobey a direct order from Kissinger. Yet the record shows that the order was not carried out, with tragic consequences.

I interviewed the principals in the Latin American bureau who handled the Condor matter for Kissinger. William Luers says he remembers being greatly concerned about Condor and personally pushed to try to stop it, but he was not able to consult still classified records to refresh his memory about why the warnings were not delivered. Harry Shlaudeman, the chief of the bureau at the time and the official whose name is on dozens of pages of documents about Operation Condor, now says he did not consider Condor important and does not remember why he sent word to the ambassadors to "take no further action" on Kissinger's instructions. Another Kissinger aide involved in Latin matters, William Rogers, said, "I don't have any recollection now of anything with regard to pulling our punches with respect to that cable." Both Shlaudeman and Rogers[5] asserted that the Kissinger warning, even if it had been delivered, would not have deterred Pinochet and Contreras from carrying out the assassination in Washington. No one knows the answer to that hypothetical question, but in my judgment such a supposition defies common sense. Contreras and Pinochet were American allies, not our enemies. They were running a terrorist organization, but they considered that Washington shared their strategic goals, to defeat world Communism. They were grossly mistaken to believe the United States government would tolerate the killing of a leftist exile leader in Washington, as shown by the persistent U.S. prosecution of those responsible. I find it impossible to believe they would have not called off the Washington operation if U.S. officials had told them in no uncertain terms, as Kissinger's démarche required, that their European assassinations plans were known and the United States officially opposed such activities.

The strongest evidence, of course, is what actually happened when the CIA got around to informing the French about the planned Paris operation. When French intelligence confronted the tri-national security forces (of Chile, Argentina, and Uruguay) planning the operation, they immediately called it off.

Kissinger's sidetracked expression of opposition to Condor should be seen in light of another series of events I have been able to document. At the same time Kissinger was sending the Condor démarche, the Argentine foreign minister was claiming that Kissinger had told him, not once but twice, that Argentine should step up its war on terrorism. Similar, though less blatant, messages were conveyed to Bolivia, Uruguay, and Chile. In the end, the red lights of opposition to atrocities were always dimmer than the green lights egging the military governments on in their war on terrorism.

The military governments were not only led to believe, they were told explicitly in secret meetings that U.S. human rights policy was public and tactical only and that United States sympathies were with the regimes that had overturned democracies and were killing thousands of their own citizens.

I DO NOT BELIEVE the United States set out to encourage the mass killings or the international terrorist missions carried out by our military allies in South America in the Condor Years. I believe that individual officers took courageous actions to lessen the violence and save lives in some cases. Our overall policies and actions on human rights, however, were so burdened by caution and ambiguity as to be meaningless to military leaders, such as Pinochet, Videla, and others. The result was in the end the same. "You are our leader," Pinochet said to Kissinger in the same month in which he, Pinochet, gave the go-ahead to commit an assassination in Washington, D.C. Looking to the United States for leadership, the military rulers found unequivocal support and public justifications for their war on Communism and terrorism. They therefore pursued that war in the way they thought was most effective.

What happened during the Condor Years was the first formalized international alliance to fight a war on terrorism. As such, they provide a template of pitfalls and tragedies that should be examined honestly and understood if we are to avoid complicity with similar human rights violations in future alliances and future antiterrorist campaigns. The cautionary lesson of Operation Condor and the massive military repression against their countries' own citizens is to be found in the way the United States exercises its leadership of the countries it gathers into its coalition against terrorism. The echoes of the past are already to be seen in the current war on terrorism: the massive pooling of intelligence, the compromised intelligence relationships, the gleaning of intelligence from the torture centers run by our allies, and even targeted, cross-boarder assassinations. Add secrecy, demands for internal loyalty among U.S. citizens and officials, and the dismantling of mechanisms of accountability. Combine with good intentions, high moral language, and the implacable will to prevail in a world struggle in which America's place in the world is perceived to be at stake. The echoes cannot be mistaken by those who care to listen.

All of these elements were present in the U.S. alliance with Condor countries in their war on terrorism. We aligned ourselves with our ideological, geopolitical allies. We divided the world into those who are with us or who are with the terrorists. We ended up in intimate embrace with mass murderers running torture camps, body dumps, and crematoriums, and who brought their terrorist operations to our own streets.

The history of the Condor Years is not one we are condemned to repeat.

[Editor's Note: Footnote numbers reflect notes published in the original at the bottom of a page.]

NOTES

1. Menem also pardoned 277 other officers who had been convicted for human rights crimes, misconduct in the Falklands War, and participation in the military revolts.

Page 375. *Arancibia case*: The case is identified, according to court documents, as "*Causa numero 949, Arancibia Clavel y otros por infracción arts 223 y 224 bis del Codigo Penal, que tramitara ante el Juzgado Nacional en lo Criminal y Correccional Fed-*

eral numero 5, Secretaria Numero 9." González said she did not remember the judge's name, but other documents list the judge as Dr. Ramon Montoya and his secretary as Dr. Juan A. Piaggio.

2. Operation Colombo was primarily a propaganda operation that should be included among the precursors to operation Condor. Arancibia and other Chilean participants in Colombo later had roles in Condor operations, but there is little evidence of formal participation by Argentine security forces.

Page 376. *Operation Colombo*: The author, with correspondent Rudolf Rauch, published one of the first investigative reports on the scheme, in *Time*, August 18, 1975. The article summed up the arrangement: "A working relationship would well serve the mutual interests of DINA and the AAA. DINA has a long list of names for which it needs bodies and the AAA has bodies for which it needs names." I expanded on the story in a two-part series in *National Catholic Reporter*, October 3 and 10, 1975. See also Mónica González, *La Nación*, July 5, 1990, "Descubiertos los archivos de la DINA en Buenos Aires."

Page 377. *Chilean plebiscite*: U.S. intelligence had firsthand reports of the coup plans and the dramatic actions by Air Force Commander Fernando Mattei to force him to back down. DIA, Top Secret, Chile: Government Contingency Plan, October 4, 1988; and DIA, Chilean Junta Meeting the Night of the Plebiscite, January 1, 1989 (Chile Project). See Peter Kornbluh (editor), *The Pinochet File: A Declassified Dossier on Atrocity and Accountability* (New York: The New Press, 2003), 426–32, for a more detailed account of these events based on U.S. documents.

Page 378. *Plot against Stroessner*: Interviews with survivors of the group Dimas Piris da Motta and Luis Alberto Wagner. Piris da Motta and Wagner's group was called *Ejército Popular Revolucionario* (also identified in some intelligence documents as Ejercito Paraguayo Revolucionario). Goiburú was the leader of a left-leaning faction of Stroessner's party called MOPOCO—Movimiento Popular Colorado. Goiburú and Piris Da Mota are mentioned in an intelligence report on the plot presented in a joint Brazil-Paraguay meeting of security forces, held May 3–6, 1976. See "*IV Conferencia bilateral de inteligencia entre los ejercitos de Paraguay y Brasil,*" undated 78:1674–86 (Paraguay Archive).

Page 378. *Almada arrest*: Interview with Martín Almada, September 7, 2001.

Page 378. *Almada's quest*: In Panama, Almada wrote a book about his prison experience, which he updated in 1993 with an account of the discovery of the archive: Martín Almada, *Paraguay: la carcel olvidada, el pais exiliado* (Panama 1978, Asunción 1993).

Page 380. *Scene at Lambaré*: Interviews with Martín Almada, Francisco de Vargas, and José Augustín Fernández.

3. The complete archive is housed in the eighth floor of the Palace of Justice in Asunción and is maintained by a small, dedicated staff, under the supervision of the Paraguayan Supreme Court. Its official name is Centro de Documnetación para la Defensa de los Derechos Humanos, directed by Luis María Benítez Riera and Rosa Palau Aguilar. The author initiated contact with the archive in 1999 and, with National Security Archive analyst Carlos Osorio, conceived of a project to catalog, microfilm, and digitize the complete collection. The project, in collaboration with Paraguay's Catholic University, received funding from AID and was launched in 2001. When completed, a catalog of 60,000 key documents will be available over the Internet. A preliminary

Web site, sponsored by UNESCO, is: http://www/unesco .org/webworld/paraguay/
documentos.html

4. Martin Almada was awarded the 2002 Right Livelihood Award, often referred to as "the
Alternative Nobel Prize," ". . . for his outstanding courage and persistent efforts to expose
and bring to account the torturers and to set his country on a new course of democracy,
respect for human rights and sustainable development." Almada has traveled extensively
in recent years and has testified in all of the major Condor investigations, including those
in Spain, Rome, Paris, and Argentina described in this chapter and in Chapter 3. The
prize committee said "the 'Archive of Terror' has proved the most important collection of
documents of state terror ever recovered. It is important not just for Paraguay but for the
whole of Latin America and, indeed, for the world."

Page 381. *Paraguay Archive*: The discovery of the archive went virtually unreported in the
mainstream U.S. press until after General Pinochet was arrested in London in
1998. Three books using the documents merit mention: Alfredo Boccia Paz, Myr-
ian Angélica González, and Rosa Palau Aguilar, *Es mi informe: Los archivos secre-
tos de la policia de Stroessner* (Asunción-CDE, 1994); Stella Calloni, *Los Años del
Lobo: Operación Condor* (Buenos Aires, 1999); and Alfredo Boccia Paz, Miguel H.
López, Antonio V. Pecci, and Gloria Giménez Guanes, *En los sotanos de los gen-
erales: Los documentos ocultos del operativo Condor* (Asunción, 2002).

Page 381. *Italians in Chile*: See John Dinges, "Chile's Global Hit Men," *The Nation,* June 2,
1979; and John Dinges, "Anatomia di un'Anonima omicidi," *La Repúbblica,* May
25, 1979.

Page 382. *Salvi at SIDE headquarters*: Interview with Salvi, January 2001. He said the papers
had been returned to SIDE by the federal court. Later they were placed again under the custody of the Argentine federal court.

Page 383. *Paris case victims*: George Klein, Chile, September 11, 1973; Alfonso Chanfreau, July
3, 1974, Chile; Etienne Pesle, September 19, 1973, Temuco, Chile; Jean Yves Clauder
Fernández, November 1, 1975, Buenos Aires; Marcel Rene Amiel, February 9, 1977,
Mendoza, Argentina.

Page 384. *Rome case victims*: The victims listed in the Rome case, with date and place of capture:

Daniel Alvaro Banfi Baranzano, September 13, 1974, Buenos Aires; Gerardo
Francisco Gatti Antuña, June 9, 1976, Buenos Aires; Maria Emilia Islas Gatti de
Zaffaroni, September 27, 1976, Buenos Aires; Armando Bernardo Arnone
Hernández, October 1, 1976, Buenos Aires; Juan Pablo Recagno Ibarburu, Octo-
ber 23, 1976, Buenos Aires; Dora Marta Landi Gil, March 29, 1977, Alejandro José
Logoluso, March 29, 1977, Asunción; Andrés Humberto Domingo Bellizzi Bel-
lizzi, April 19, 1977, Buenos Aires; Héctor Giordano Cortazzo, June 7–9, 1978,
Buenos Aires; Horacio Domingo Campiglia Pedamonti, March 12, 1980, Rio de
Janeiro; and Lorenzo Ismael Viñas Gigli, July 26, 1980, Uruguayana, Brazil.
Landi, Logoluso, Campiglia, and Viñas are Argentine citizens; the rest are
Uruguayan. Banfi and Bellizzi were arrested in separate operations in Argentina.

Page 385. *Prats indictments*: Also included in the indictment were Jorge Iturriaga Neumann,
Raul's civilian brother, and José Zara Holger, also of the Exterior Department.

Page 385. *Chile is profoundly different*: Statement July 2003, FASIC (Fundacion de Ayuda
Social de Iglesias Cristianas), text dated July 26, 2003, obtained from Web site,
www.fasic.org.

Page 385.	*Condor case defendants (titles before retirement):* **Argentines:** Jorge Rafael Videla, lieutenant general, former president and member of the military junta; Carlos Guillermo Suárez Mason, general, former commander of the First Corp of the military; Eduardo Albano Harguindeguy, general, former interior minister. **Chileans:** Augusto Pinochet Ugarte, general, member of the military junta, president; Manuel Contreras, general, chief of Dina; Pedro Espinoza, coronel, DINA. **Paraguayans:** Alfredo Stroessner, division general, president of the Republic of Paraguay; Francisco Brítez, general, chief of police; Pastor Coronel Milcíades, head of the Department of Investigations of the Capital Police; Benito Guanes, colonel, chief of the Military Intelligence Service. **Uruguayans:** Julio Vadora, Armed Forces commander in chief; Guillermo Ramírez, colonel; José Nino Gavazzo, major; Manuel Cordero, major; Enrique Martínez, major; Jorge Silveira, capitán; Hugo Campos Hermida, police commissioner. **Bolivian:** Hugo Banzer, president.

Page 385.	*Judge Canicoba Condor case victims:* Seventy-two Condor case victims: Agustín Goiburú Jiménez, Fausto Augusto Carrillo, Juan José Penayo, Federico Jorge Tatter, Dora Marta Landi Gill, Esther Ballestrino de Careaga, Antonio Maidana, Emilio Roa Espinosa, Alejandro José Logoluso, Gustavo Edison Insaurralde, Raúl Edgardo Borelli Cattáneo, Nelson Rodolfo Santana Scotto, José Luis Nell, Juan Alberto Filártiga Martínez, Ary Cabrera Prates, Elba Lucia Gándara Castroman, León Duarte Luján, Juan Pablo Recagno Ibarburú, Ruben Prieto González, Cecilia Susana Trías Hernández, Washington Cram González, Daniel Pedro Alfaro Vásquez, Adalberto Soba, Armando Bernardo Arnone Hernández, Rafael González Lezama, María Emilia Islas Gatti de Zaffaroni, Carlos Federico Cabezudo Pérez, Miguel Angel Moreno Malugani, Washington Domingo Queiro Uzal, Raúl Tejera, Carlos Alfredo Rodriguez Mercader, Eduardo Efraín Chizzola Cano, Jorge Zaffaroni Castilla, Ileana García Ramos de Dossetti, Edmundo Sabino Dossetti Techeira, Casimira María del Rosario Carretero Cardenas, Claudio Epelbaum, Lila Epelbaum, Mónica Sofia Grinspon de Logares, Claudio Ernesto Logares, José Hugo Méndez Donadío, Francisco Edgardo Candia Correa, Juan Pablo Errandonea Salvia, Simón Antonio Riquelo, Miguel Angel Río Casas, María Asunción Artigas Nilo de Moyano, Alfredo Moyano, Alberto Cecilio Mechoso Méndez, Horacio Domingo Campiglia, Susana Pinus de Binstock, Norberto Armando Habegger, Erasmo Suárez Balladores, Juan Carlos Jordán Vercellone, Graciela Rutila Artes, Luis Stamponi Corinaldeci, Oscar Hugo González de la Vega, Efraín Fernando Villa Isola, Edgardo Enríquez Espinosa, Miguel Ivan Orellana Castro, José Luis de la Masa Asquet, Manuel Jesús Tamayo Martínez, Carmen Angélica Delard Cabezas, José Luis Appel de la Cruz, Gloria Ximena Delard Cabezas, Cristina Magdalena Carreño Araya, Jara Angel Athanasiú, Frida Elena Laschan Mellado, Pablo Germán Athanasiú Laschan, Luis Enrique Elgueta Díaz, Carlos Patricio Rojas Campos, Alexis Vladimir Jaccard Siegler, María Claudia Iruretagoyena.

Page 386.	*Condor narrative:* Court filing dated April 11, 2001, referring to John Dinges, "Los Archivos de Condor," *La Nación* (Argentina), August 8, 1999.

Page 386.	*Kissinger questioning:* Judge Le Loire was the first to seek to question Kissinger. His request was voluntary, and Kissinger rejected it out of hand. Canicoba's request had the authority of the MLAT agreement and produced the only official response. Judges in Brazil and Chile have also sought to question Kissinger, to no avail. Kissinger called off a planned trip to Brazil to avoid the possibility of being served with an embarrassing subpoena while in that country.

Page 386. *Uruguayans sought*: The officers are José Nino Gavazzo, Manuel Cordero, Jorge Silveira, and police officer Hugo Campos Hermida. Campos Hermida died of cancer in 2001, just weeks after he told the author he wished to testify about the Argentine missions, which he said he knew about but denied partipating in.

386. *Military travelers*: Le Loire, as only one example, issued international warrants for 150 Page officers he wanted for questioning. Another Argentine officer, Jorge Olivera, was arrested in August 2000 and held briefly pending extradition to face charges in Le Loire's court in Paris.

5. Rogers, of the powerful Washington law firm of Arnold and Porter, represents Kissinger in fending off a lawsuit brought by the family of assassinated General René Schneider. An assistant secretary from Latin America, he was with Kissinger in the meeting with Pinochet in June 1976. In a statement seemingly at odds with the declassified record and other officials' statements, he said it was "not at all" U.S. policy to support and defend Pinochet at that time.

Page 393. *Plans were known*: Rogers and Shlaudeman, who coordinated their responses to author's questions, also asserted that the phrase "no further action" in the September 20, 1976, cable does not exclude the possibility that the Kissinger démarche was delivered prior to September 20. If that were the case, it would certainly be documented in cables in which the ambassadors reported back to Kissinger on the meetings he ordered them to seek. Both Rogers and Shlaudeman have the security clearances necessary to see cables still kept secret from the public, and would be able to back up their argument with evidence if it existed.

Introduction to
Peter Kornbluh's

The Pinochet File

IN OCTOBER 1998, while traveling in England, former Chilean ruler General Augusto Pinochet was arrested under an international warrant that included ninety-four counts of torture, issued by Judge Baltasar Garzón of Spain. After a sixteen-month legal battle, the House of Lords, the highest court in England, ruled that extradition could proceed. But after questions were raised about the former dictator's alleged fragile health, Home Secretary Jack Straw decided that Pinochet could be returned to Chile. Pinochet's seizure reverberated throughout the international community as it set a precedent for arresting human rights violators outside the borders of their own countries.

After overthrowing Salvador Allende, Chile's elected president, in 1973, Pinochet became one of the world's most brutal dictators. During his ruthless seventeen-year dictatorship, the Chilean military was responsible for the murder or disappearance of some 3,197 citizens, according to the Chilean Commission on Truth and Reconciliation. Thousands more were subject to torture, incarceration, forced exile, and other forms of state-sponsored terror.

In March 2005, the Chilean supreme court refused to strip Pinochet of his special immunity as a former president, enabling him to avoid trial for the murder of former Chilean General Carlos Prats who was assassinated in 1974 in Buenos Aires. But Pinochet still faced charges concerning a murder and nine abductions relating to Operation Condor (see above).

Peter Kornbluh, director of the National Security Archive's Chile Documentation Project, draws on 24,000 newly declassified records to expose

Pinochet's activities and the extent of American complicity in his crimes—
the American government and Henry Kissinger, in particular, turned a
blind eye to the atrocities Pinochet's government committed. Kornbluh
provides new details about the brutal murders of Frank Teruggi, a twenty-
four-year-old American graduate student who was studying in Santiago,
and Charles Horman, a thirty-one-year-old Harvard graduate who had
gone to Chile with his wife to experience firsthand the economic and social experiments of the Allende government. The efforts of the painful
search for Horman by his family became the subject of the film *Missing*.

ADDITIONAL SOURCES

Hauser, Thomas. *The Execution of Charles Horman: An American Sacrifice*. New York: Har-
court, Brace Jovanovich, 1978.
Hersh, Seymour. *The Price of Power: Kissinger in the Nixon White House*. New York: Summit
Books, 1983.
Guzman, Patricio, director. *The Pinochet Case*. First Run/Icarus Films.

Peter Kornbluh

American Casualties

THE PINOCHET FILE: A DECLASSIFIED DOSSIER ON ATROCITY AND
ACCOUNTABILITY, 2003

> [The assistant secretary] raised this subject [of mur-
> dered Americans] in the context of the need to be care-
> ful to keep relatively small issues in our relationship
> from making our cooperation more difficult.
> —*Memorandum of conversation between Assistant*
> *Secretary of State Jack Kubisch and Junta Foreign*
> *Minister Ismael Huerta, February 1974*

ON JUNE 8, 1976, the very day that Henry Kissinger commended General Pinochet for his "service" to the West, a Chilean intelligence officer met with reporters from CBS News and the *Washington Post* told them about the regime's post-coup execution of an American citizen. The meeting took place in a small, dark room in the Italian embassy where the officer, Rafael Gonzalez, had sought asylum in an attempt to leave Chile. Speaking passable English, Gonzalez recounted to the journalists that a few days after the coup, he had been summoned to the ninth floor of the Army's Military Intelligence Service (SIM) building to translate during the interrogation of an American prisoner named Charles Horman. "I was told . . . this guy knew too much . . . Horman, you know," as Gonzalez recounted the conversation with his superior, General Augusto Lutz, "and that he was supposed to disappear." According to a transcript of the recorded interview, Gonzalez added that he believed an American agent was in the room during Horman's interrogation—based on "the way that he behaves, his dressing, the shoes, you know and everything." "I wouldn't say the trigger was pulled by the CIA," he told the reporters. "But that the

CIA was mixed up in this . . . yes. It was the Chileans that get [rid] of him, but the CIA was behind that."[1]

These dramatic accusations transformed Charles Horman into the most famous American victim of the Pinochet regime; his case eventually became the subject of an Oscar-winning Hollywood movie, *Missing*. The film starred Jack Lemmon as Charles's father and Sissy Spacek as his wife; it portrayed his family's painful search for him in Santiago through an obstacle course of callous U.S. officials and a pro-coup U.S. policy.[2]

Horman was, however, the first of four U.S. citizens to be murdered by Chilean military. Another American, Frank Teruggi, also was seized by security forces at his home in Santiago nine days after the coup, and, like Horman, taken to the National Stadium where he was interrogated and executed. In January 1985, a military patrol detained a University of Pennsylvania mathematics professor named Boris Weisfeiler while he was hiking in southern Chile; Weisfeiler subsequently disappeared. In Washington D.C., Ronni Karpen Moffitt was killed in September 1976 by a car bomb planted by agents of the Chilean secret police, becoming an American casualty of the Pinochet regime's most infamous act of international terrorism. Years after they were committed, each of these horrific crimes would remain unresolved. Each would be defined by blatant cover-ups on the part of the Pinochet regime—and the concealment of evidence, negligence and/or simple disinterest on the part of the U.S. government.

Charles Horman

When Rafael Gonzalez's allegations about Charles Horman appeared in the *Washington Post,* they generated yet another scandal of potential U.S. misconduct—the premeditated murder of an American citizen, with alleged U.S. collusion, by a military actively influenced, and supported by the Nixon-Ford White House. For almost three years, the Pinochet regime had insisted that "extremists" of the left impersonating the military had murdered Horman, as well as Teruggi, to embarrass the new Junta. Even though the embassy had abundant evidence that this explanation was false, the U.S. government adopted and promoted such specious pronouncements. Only days after Chilean authorities privately conceded to his father that Charles had been shot in the National Stadium, a State Department spokeswoman told the press that Horman might have been killed by left-wing groups masquerading as soldiers—"really wicked people who would kill him just to make the military look bad."[3] Now, these revelations generated renewed demands from Horman's family for a complete accounting—his family filed a wrongful death lawsuit and legal demands for release of all relevant records—as well as a slew of angry letters from Capitol Hill, and public allegations of an official cover-up. "It now appears," stated a *Washington Post* editorial on June 27, 1976, that "American diplomats withheld from Mr. Horman's family crucial information about the circumstances of his death."

The U.S. government did withhold substantive information from the family—before June 1976, and for more than twenty years thereafter. Following the Gonzalez revelations, two State Department Latin American bureau officers did a cursory file review and quickly discovered a litany of liability: during his family's desperate search for him in Santiago after the coup, U.S. officials had failed to inform them that a credible source had told the embassy within days of his execution that Horman had been murdered in the National Stadium, and that they had undertaken no substantive actions in response to this information. Instead, U.S. officials passed on specious rumors that Charles was in hiding, or was making his way out of the country through a leftist "clandestine pipeline." Unbeknownst to the family, at least one of the U.S. consulate officials providing this information, James Anderson, was a CIA agent operating under diplomatic cover. The embassy never informed the family that the Chilean military seemed to have ready intelligence on Horman and Teruggi's leftist activities, and that U.S. officials had failed to pursue the question of how, and from where, the regime had obtained such information.

Indeed, the U.S. government's oft-repeated claims to be actively investigating the Horman-Teruggi murders were misleading, the State Department officials concluded. "We keep telling the families and the press that we are diligently pursuing every lead, doing everything to develop the circumstances surrounding the deaths of these Americans," the Chile desk officer Rudy Fimbres reported in a memorandum to Assistant Secretary for Inter-American Affairs, Harry Shlaudeman. "This is overdrawn."[4]

In their preliminary review of the files, mid-level ARA officials concluded that the Chilean military had executed Horman and that there was a possibility that U.S. intelligence agents in Chile had played some role in his death. "This case remains bothersome," three officers reported in a secret memorandum to Shlaudeman "Subject: Charles Horman Case" on August 25, 1976. "The connotations for the Executive are not good. In the Hill, academic community, the press, and the Horman family the intimations are of negligence on our part, or worse, complicity in Horman's death." Based on the files, they wrote, "we are persuaded that:"

> —*The GOC sought Horman and felt threatened enough to order his immediate execution. The GOC might have believed this American could be killed without negative fall-out from the USG.*
> *There is some circumstantial evidence to suggest:*
> —*U.S. intelligence may have played an unfortunate part in Horman's death. At best, it was limited to providing or confirming information that helped motivate his murder by the GOC. At worst, U.S. intelligence was aware the GOC saw Horman in a rather serious light and U.S. officials did nothing to discourage the logical outcome of GOC paranoia.*

The State Department deliberately hid these conclusions from the family. No U.S. official briefed the Hormans at the time; and when this pivotal document was first declassified in early 1980 pursuant to the family's lawsuit against U.S. officials, its content was completely censored. (Doc 1) Then, when the State Department declassified the document again in 1982 as part of continuing legal efforts around the Horman case, that specific section was blacked out, along with all other references to the CIA, on the grounds of "State Secrets" and "Executive Privilege."[5] (Doc 2) Only seventeen years later, in October 1999 when the Clinton administration released this memo intact among thousands of other documents relating to the United States and Chile, did the Horman family finally learn that, in 1976, at least a few U.S. officials had shared their suspicion of a possible role by U.S. covert operatives in Charles's murder. (Doc 3)

CHARLES HORMAN, along with Frank Teruggi, became two of an estimated 2,800 U.S. citizens caught in the cross fire of the Chilean coup.
About half the Americans in Chile were part of the business and diplomatic community and supported the coup; but many others were graduate students, like Teruggi, who had come to do research on Chile's social
revolution, or social activists like Charles and Joyce Horman who wanted
to experience the Allende experiment firsthand. When the new Junta labeled them, and hundreds of others who had come from abroad to Chile
during the Allende years as "foreign extremists" and began rounding
them up en masse, they received little sympathy from the Nixon administration, whose paramount goal was to embrace the new regime, and avoid
attracting attention to its bloodletting.

Top U.S. officials in Washington were well-aware that foreigners were
being targeted for repression. On September 20, Kissinger chaired a meeting of the Washington Special Actions Group in the White House Situation Room to establish a date for U.S. recognition of the new regime and
arrange emergency assistance. According to the secret minutes of the
meeting, Assistant Secretary Jack Kubisch briefed Kissinger on the desperate situation of foreigners trying to get out of Chile:

> *Most are third-country nationals who fled their own countries and got
> caught up in this thing. The government's holding about 5,000 in the
> stadium. They have been very candid about this. They intend to treat
> them in accordance with military courts. If innocent, they will be free
> to [go]. If guilty, the Junta intends to deal with them harshly.*[6]

"There are few Americans caught up in it," Kubisch informed the secretary. The memorandum of conversation does not record any further discussion of their situation before officials turned to evaluating a Chilean
military request for 1,000 flares and helmets to use in mopping-up operations.

The embassy "engaged in an all-out effort to ensure the welfare of . . .
Americans in Chile," the State Department would submit to Congress in

December 1973. But while other countries, most notably France, Sweden, the Netherlands, Belgium, and Venezuela flung open their embassy doors to provide refuge for their citizens and aggressively sought to secure their safety if they were detained, the United States did neither. A special investigation conducted by the U.S. General Accounting Office titled "An Assessment of Selected U.S. Embassy-Consular Efforts to Assist and Protect Americans Overseas During Crisis and Emergencies" concluded that the U.S. embassy and consulate buildings in Santiago had been specifically designed and equipped to house up to 450 persons for a three-day period in order to be responsive to a situation exactly like the Chilean coup. But requests for refuge were denied on the grounds that "the facilities were not adequate to permit them to stay overnight." U.S. officials also dragged their feet on aggressively interceding with Chile's new military authorities to protect detained U.S. citizens from abuse, failing to adhere to the Vienna Convention on consular relations by waiting to formally protest and demand their security until adverse media coverage forced them to do so. "In Chile," GAO investigators concluded:

> *Prompt and effective protests by high-level U.S. officials on behalf of arrested and detained Americans in accordance with the international Vienna Convention on Consular Relations, were not always made. . . . Formal written protests were made only in response to press publicity and Congressional interest.*

Some twenty-nine U.S. citizens were arrested and jailed in the days following the coup and at least fifteen imprisoned at the main detention-torture-execution center, the National Stadium. One, a Methodist priest named Joseph Doherty, was detained along with another Methodist, Francis Flynn, on September 16 and spent eleven horrific days there. On September 19, Doherty, who kept a detailed journal recording the beatings, torture and murders taking place around him, asked a Dutch embassy official who had gained access to prisoners to contact the U.S. consul "as neither of us had heard from them."[7] But Doherty did not have any contact with the U.S. consul, Frederick Purdy, until September 26 when he, Flynn and six other U.S. citizens were finally released into the custody of U.S. officials. "Mr. Purdy informed us that the condition of our release was that we had to leave the country," the Methodist pastor recorded in his journal. "Mr. Purdy informed us that if we did not accept this condition we could go back into the Stadium at which time the United States consulate would not be responsible for us."

CHARLES HORMAN, detained on the evening of September 17 and reportedly executed on or around September 20, was one of those Americans "caught up" in the coup. His friends described him as "a highly intelligent, liberal, mild-mannered, gentle individual." As a thirty-one-year old Phi Beta Kappa graduate of Harvard University, he had come to Santiago with his new wife Joyce in the late fall of 1972 to try his hand at writing and filmmaking. During the last year of his life, Charles, along with Frank Teruggi, worked as an editor of a small news service known as the North American Information Sources—which clipped, translated, and distributed U.S. news articles on Chile through a small progressive pamphlet called *FIN*. He also produced animated children's cartoons and was writing a book on the Allende government's effort to transform Chilean political society. According to his wife, at the time of the coup he was investigating the October 1970 assassination of General René Schneider.

The mysterious circumstances of his murder amidst the bloodshed of the Chilean coup have been catalogued in Thomas Hauser's compelling book, *The Execution of Charles Horman: An American Sacrifice*. On September 11, 1973, Horman happened to be visiting the scenic seaside town of Vina del Mar with Terry Simon, a vacationing family friend from New York. They found themselves trapped at their hotel, without access to news, phones or transportation back to Santiago. In search of other Americans with information, they met a U.S. navy engineer named Arthur Creter. "I'm here with the United States navy," he informed them. "We came down to do a job and it's done."[8]

Horman and Simon also met one of Creter's supervisors, Lt. Col. Patrick Ryan, deputy chief of the United States Naval Mission in Valparaiso, and one of the U.S. military attachés most ardently supportive of the coup. They pressed him for information on the coup and on the

UNCLASSIFIED

PAGE 01 STATE 058819

42
ORIGIN SCSE-00

INFO OCT-01 ISO-00 /001 R

DRAFTED BY SCA/SCS/DCANDEY:EJH
APPROVED BY SCA/SCS/DCANDEY
---------------------   069851

R 231453Z MAR 74
FM SECSTATE WASHDC
TO MR. AND MRS. EDMOND C. HORMAN
31 EAST 76TH STREET
NEW YORK NEW YORK TELEPHONE 212-744-2339

UNCLAS STATE 058819

E.O. 11652: N/A
TAGS: CDES, CI (HORMAN, CHARLES)
SUBJECT: DISPOSITION OF HORMAN REMAINS

THIS IS TO CONFIRM THE TELEPHONE CONVERSATION OF MARCH 21
BETWEEN MRS. HORMAN AND D.S. CANDEY OF THE DEPARTMENT
INFORMING YOU OF THE GOVERNMENT OF CHILI'S DECISION TO
APPROVE YOUR REQUEST FOR THE RELEASE OF THE REMAINS
OF CHARLES HORMAN FOR RETURN TO THE U.S. IN ORDER FOR
THE AMERICAN EMBASSY AT SANTIAGO TO ARRANGE SHIPMENT
YOU WILL RECALL THAT A DEPOSIT OF NINE HUNDRED DOLLARS
(900) IS REQUIRED TO COVER THE ESTIMATED COST FOR
PREPARATION OF THE REMAINS AND TRANSPORTATION TO
NEW YORK CITY. ADDITIONALLY, PLEASE PROVIDE THE NAME
OF THE FUNERAL HOME WHERE YOU WANT THE REMAINS TO BE
SHIPPED. FUNDS AND INSTRUCTIONS SHOULD BE SENT TO THE
OFFICE OF SPECIAL CONSULAR SERVICES, DEPARTMENT OF STATE.
PLEASE ACCEPT OUR DEEPEST CONDOLENCES IN THIS TRAGIC
AFFAIR.

DIRECTOR, SPECIAL CONSULAR SERVICES
DEPARTMENT OF STATE
WASHINGTON, D.C.   KISSINGER

UNCLASSIFIED

NNN

Chile Project (#S199900006)
U.S. Department of State
√ Release __Excise __Deny __Declass
Exemption(s)_____

State Department cable concerning Charles Horman's remains (note spelling error "Chili's").

possibility of getting back to Santiago. "I was approached by subject couple who identified themselves as American tourists and requested, at that time essentially a SITREP [situation report]," Ryan wrote in an October 5, 1973, summary of his contacts with Horman. "I gave them what info I considered appropriate, promised to keep them posted and also to lend them money if their stay in Vina proved lengthy. I also directed them not to leave the hotel."[9]

The two were forced to stay at the hotel for four days, until Lieutenant Colonel Ryan arranged for them to be transported back to Santiago with the head of the U.S. military group, Captain Ray Davis (one of the only U.S. officials with clearance to travel freely in Chile in the aftermath of the coup). At the embassy, Davis told them that the United States had no provisions for getting Americans out of the country. When Horman and Simon returned to the embassy on the afternoon of September 17 in an effort to secure safe passage out of the country for themselves and Joyce, they experienced a rude brush-off from a secretary. She told them it was "not our job" to help Americans leave Chile and that they would have to go to the U.S. consulate a mile away. By then it was late afternoon and Charles determined he should return home to avoid being caught out after curfew; so Simon met alone with a consulate official. As she recalled, that official also informed her they would have to wait till the borders opened and that "we're not responsible for people who want to leave, and I have no information about the necessary procedures."[10]

Horman arrived at his home on Vicuna MacKenna street around 5:00 P.M.[11] (His wife was not home; caught by the curfew, Joyce was forced to spend a terrifying night outside in the cold, huddled in a doorway across town.) A summary State Department report records what happened:

> According to the neighbors, between 1600 and 1700 on September 17, a private non-military truck came to 4126 Vicuna MacKenna. Ten to 15 men in Chilean Army uniforms led by a man wearing Captain's or Lieutenant's insignia got out, tried the gate and, finding it locked, jumped the fence and broke the lock. They entered the house, removed Horman and a box of books and papers from the house, and loaded

them on the truck. At about 2300 the same day, the same truck and
two other trucks returned to 4126 Vicuna MacKenna, carried out some
suitcases and a large box from the house, loaded them on the trucks
and departed towards downtown Santiago.

From the outset there was overwhelming evidence that Charles had
been detained and placed under interrogation by SIM, the Chilean Army
Intelligence Service headed by General Augusto Lutz. A witness from the
neighborhood had seen the truck carry Charles toward the National Stadium.[12] At 8:00 A.M. the next morning, a former neighbor of Horman's
received a call from a military intelligence officer who stated that "SIM
had detained a gringo with a beard," according to the State Department
report. She was also asked if she "knew that the gringo worked in pictures,
and if she was aware that the gringo was a leftist extremist."[13] A second
call was placed to the house of a Horman friend, Warwick Armstrong,
stating that an American who "makes films" had asked Armstrong to
speak on his behalf and ordered him to proceed to a local police Station.

From reports on both phone calls, the U.S. embassy learned of Horman's detention and the SIM inquiries on September 18.[14] A chronology
on the Horman case kept by the U.S. Consul, Fred Purdy, recorded that on

18 September—*Consulate received report of Horman's detention from*
one of its local employees one of whose relatives know Horman. Few
details given.

   —*Later also received call from Mr. Armstrong, also telling that*
Horman missing since late 17 September when reportedly detained by
military.[15]

On September 19, Joyce met with one of Purdy's consulate deputies,
John S. Hall, and informed him that her home had been ransacked, and
her husband taken away by the military. He queried her on what type of
information the soldiers might have found at the Horman residence, and
she described to him her husband's research on General Schneider's assassination.[16] Later that day, Terry Simon called the head of the U.S. Mil-
Group, Captain Davis, and asked him for help in locating Charles. Over

the next several days, both consulate and U.S. military officials made a series of informal inquiries to the Chilean police and military and intelligence offices; all denied detaining or holding Horman. Purdy went several times to the National Stadium to check the lists of detainees but "Horman's name did not appear as such or under any of several variants," Ambassador Nathaniel Davis cabled on September 25. "Embassy continues try locate him and all other amcits [American citizens] with full resources at its disposal."

Yet, the very next day Ambassador Davis refused Joyce Horman's plea to escalate the profile of U.S. efforts to find Charles by personally visiting the stadium. "She asked him to go to the Stadium with her," noted a report by the head of the U.S. MilGroup who attended the meeting.[17] "He declined and provided rationale for the negative response." According to Joyce Horman's recollection, Ambassador Davis told her, "We really can't do that. If we ask special favors of the ruling forces, everyone else will want them too. That might damage our relations with the new government."[18]

Inside the embassy, some U.S. officials had already concluded that Charles Horman was dead. "People were being killed in those days," Vice Consul Dale Shaffer recalled. "We thought Horman was dead," the head of the AID mission, Judd Kessler remembered. "We had asked the Chileans to tell us where he was and they hadn't, so we figured they were probably stalling to cover up." On or around September 30, a Chilean source named Enrique Sandoval informed Kessler that, in fact, Horman had been executed in the National Stadium.

Sandoval, a Ministry of Education official under the Allende government who had been briefly imprisoned in the Estadio Chile after the coup, met with Kessler twice. During the first meeting, around September 23, Kessler sought information on human rights atrocities, and told Sandoval that two Americans, Horman and Teruggi, were among the missing. Several days later, as Kessler recounted in a memo to the Chile desk officer on July 19, 1976, "I spoke with Sandoval again at which time he told me that someone he knew in the Chilean military had said that Horman had been in the National Stadium and either 'that he had been killed there,' or 'was dead.' " Kessler wrote no formal memorandum about this conversation; instead he informally passed it on to the chief consular officer, Fred Purdy during a hallway conversation in the U.S. embassy.[19] "I'll bet that's right," as Kessler remembers Purdy's response.[20] The consul general, whose job is the welfare of U.S. citizens, took no steps to follow up; inexplicably, Purdy neglected to pursue the leads Sandoval's story and his sources appeared to offer, failed to protest to the Chilean authorities, and withheld this information from Joyce Horman, and Charles's father when he flew from New York on October 5 to search for his son.

By the time Ed Horman arrived in Santiago, Frank Teruggi's body had been discovered at the morgue—not by the embassy, but by an American friend who insisted on looking for him there. The government of Chile claimed Teruggi had been picked up for curfew violations, taken to the National Stadium, released the next day and later found shot in the street. On October 3, the Foreign Ministry provided a virtually identical statement to the embassy on Horman: he had been detained at the National Stadium on September 20 for violations of curfew but released on September 21 "for lacking of merit to any charges against him," and the military was "checking into his whereabouts."[21] These events gave U.S. officials ever more reason to discount the regime's denials regarding the Horman case. In a meeting with Edmund Horman the day he arrived, however, Ambassador Davis never mentioned the regime's acknowledgement that his son had been in the stadium; instead the ambassador reiterated all of the Chilean military's disclaimers and then offered a theory that lent credence to them. "Davis said that the embassy feeling was that Charles probably was in hiding," as Horman recorded the commentary.[22]

Between October 5 and October 18 Ed and Joyce Horman conducted a poignant and desperate search for Charles. For two weeks they and, at Ed's demand, the embassy, pursued a set of inquiries that U.S. officials had failed to undertake: investigating detention centers other than the National Stadium; checking all foreign embassies where Charles might have sought asylum; a fingerprint check on all unidentified bodies at the morgue; issuing a press release to all Chilean newspapers; and publication of a reward for information leading to the whereabouts of Charles Horman. (When Ed requested that the CIA Station also be directed to utilize its resources to find Charles, however, Ambassador Davis sternly, and mendaciously, denied that any such thing existed in Chile.) Ed and Joyce traversed Santiago, searching hospitals and refugee centers, meeting anyone who might be helpful, and enduring useless questioning by low-level Chilean officials going through the motions of an investigation. With the embassy's help, they gained access to the inside of the stadium where, using a microphone, they called for Charles to come forward—a dramatic and wrenching scene depicted in the film *Missing*.

In the late afternoon of October 16, Purdy invited them to the embassy to meet with vice-consul/CIA Station operative James Anderson and a British journalist named Timothy Ross. Ross informed them he had a contact who claimed that Charles was "alive and well," and making his way through an underground "escape pipeline;" he was now in northern Chile and would soon be out of the country. At the end of the meeting, "following instructions from the ambassador," Anderson took Ed Horman aside and told him, "if you put any credence on this information you may wish to consider that any continuing embassy pressure in this case may be double-edged."[23]

The bizarre, unlikely, and contradictory nature of Ross's information— witnesses had seen Horman taken away by the military; military intelligence officials had clearly interrogated him and called his neighbors and friends the next day; and he had been missing for an entire month without a single communication—appeared to be lost on the embassy officials who found Ross credible enough to subject the Hormans to this meeting. The very next day, during a visit at the Ford Foundation's Santiago office, Ed Horman received a far more believable account of his son's fate: Charles "had been shot to death in the National Stadium on or before September 20." Although third-hand, this information rang true: it had been provided to a Foundation staffer, Lowell Jarvis, by an official in the Canadian embassy in Santiago who was close to a Chilean who, in turn, had obtained this information from high-ranking Chilean military sources.

Unbeknownst to the Hormans at the time, the source of this information was Enrique Sandoval, who had shared the identical story with the U.S. embassy almost three weeks earlier. In an effort to leave Chile and seek refuge for his family in Canada, Sandoval contacted the first secretary of the Canadian embassy, Mark Dolguin,[24] for assistance in early October, and told him the same thing he had told AID official Judd Kessler at the end of September. Then, Purdy had ignored this information; but now that Ed Horman pressed him to verify it, the embassy took less than twenty-four hours to confirm that Charles Horman was dead. In a terse cable to Washington, "subj: Deaths; Charles E. Horman," Ambassador Davis reported that

> *Embassy informed afternoon October 18, 1973 that previously uniden-*
> *tified male body which delivered to morgue on September 18, 1973 and*
> *given autopsy number 2663 had been identified through fingerprints as*
> *being that of Charles E. Horman. Unidentified body delivered to San-*
> *tiago Cemetery on October 3 and apparently interred thereafter. Cause*
> *of death was bullet wound. (Doc 4)*

The cable concluded that "Embassy advising wife and father."

When they returned to New York City, an angry and grieving Edmund Horman and his daughter-in-law both wrote highly negative reports on their experience in Santiago to the chairman of the Senate Foreign Relations Committee, William Fulbright. The embassy's handling of his son's case, Ed Horman charged in his letter, had been derelict:

> *The American Embassy did nothing to verify the evidence which had*
> *been placed in their hands on September 18th and which proved to be*
> *the key to the truth. From October 5th to the very end, their "efforts"*
> *produced no results beyond their repeated statements that they had*
> *contacted the Chilean government right up to General Pinochet, and*
> *had been told that the Chileans knew nothing about Charles or his*
> *whereabouts.*

"I do not know the reason underlying the negligence, inaction and failure of the American Embassy," Horman concluded. "Whether it was incompetence, indifference or something worse, I find it shocking, outrageous and, perhaps, obscene."

In the search for a missing American the embassy indeed produced no information beyond what the military Junta decided to tell them. Initially, embassy officials made multiple, informal and low-level inquiries and visits—to police Stations, the National Stadium, army military intelligence, and regime officials—and readily accepted repeated denials that the Chilean military was responsible for his disappearance. "Since we had received denials from military intelligence that they had any knowledge of Horman, we had seen no reason to follow this point further," as Purdy explained why he didn't actively pursue persuasive evidence that Horman was under the control of the Army's Military Intelligence Service.[25] One week after Horman's seizure, Washington requested a more substantive search. "Given Congressional and other high-level interest in this case," Kissinger's office cabled the embassy on September 24, "would appreciate Embassy redoubling its efforts locate Horman, including possibility he may be detained by Chilean authorities." Only then did Ambassador Davis elevate the case to the level of a bilateral issue by discussing it with the regime's foreign minister, and other ministry officials. "I raised Teruggi and Horman cases, pointing out public relations implications of any continuance of the present situation where circumstances of their disappearances remain unexplained," Davis reported to Washington on a September 27 meeting with Chile's new ambassador to the United States. "It would be helpful if the GOC were able to clear up the mysteries involved in the cases of the two missing or deceased Amcits," Davis told a high foreign ministry official on October 3.[26] During a meeting with Pinochet himself on October 12 to discuss substantive U.S. assistance to the new regime, Davis eluded to the "political problems we are encountering"—among them the Kennedy amendment and the Horman-Teruggi cases.

Washington chose not to exercise the considerable leverage, influence, and power it had at its disposal. At a time when the Nixon administration was laying the groundwork for formal recognition of the new regime, expediting tens of millions of dollars in emergency economic assistance to Chile, and covertly assisting the formation of its intelligence apparatus, U.S. policy makers led by Secretary of State Kissinger refrained from linking avid support to satisfactory action, resolution, and justice in these cases. Only in the wake of adverse media coverage and Congressional outrage over the handling of the Horman case, did department officials prod their Chilean counterparts to address the murders of two Americans. Assistant Secretary for Inter-American Affairs Jack Kubisch reflected the administration's attitude when, during a February 1974 meeting with Junta Foreign Minister Ismael Huerta, he broached the Horman and Teruggi cases. "Kubisch raised this subject," according to a memorandum of the conversation, "in the context of the need to be careful to keep relatively small issues in our relationship from making our cooperation more difficult."[27]

Congress, not the executive branch, finally used U.S. assistance to leverage Chilean military cooperation in the Horman case. When the Hormans left Chile on October 20, they asked for the prompt repatriation of Charles's remains. "Our purpose," as Ed Horman would remind the State Department, "was to verify identity, determine time and method of death, [and] find any evidence of torture."[28] As the U.S. government feigned impotence for five months the Pinochet regime stalled on relinquishing the body—rendering impossible any autopsy that could tie the Chilean military to Horman's death.[29] In early March 1974, at a time when the Chilean navy was seeking TOW missiles from the U.S., the powerful senator from New York, Jacob Javits, moved to block further shipments of military equipment to Chile until the remains were returned. Almost immediately a Chilean counterintelligence official informed the U.S. MilGroup that "he had authority to effect the return," according to Department summary of the case.[30] "We had to send him fast out of here because Senator Javits said that he will not approve [military equipment] in the Congress," Rafael Gonzalez recalled to the U.S. reporters in his June 1976 interview. On March 21, Gonzalez went to the U.S. consulate and asked James Anderson—the embassy officer who, Gonzalez stated, had a "dual role" in Chile as a consulate and CIA official—to accompany him to the general cemetery to locate and remove Horman's body. Gonzalez stated quite clearly why he had been picked for this assignment: "I could ID . . . identify Horman when he was dead because I saw him alive."

One more obstacle, and one more example of official U.S. callousness, remained: obtaining payment from the Horman family for sending the body—in a slatted wooden crate—back to the United States. On March

22, the State Department began repeatedly calling and cabling Horman's parents and widow for a deposit to cover the costs of transshipment. On March 23, 1974, a telegram signed by Kissinger arrived at the home of Horman's parents:

> *In order for the American embassy in Santiago to arrange shipment you will recall that a deposit of nine hundred dollars (900) is required to cover the estimated cost for preparation of the remains and transportation to New York City. . . . Funds and instructions should be sent to the Office of Special Consular Services, Department of State. Please accept our deepest condolences in this tragic affair. Kissinger (Doc 5)*

Four days later, his widow received a cablegram advising her that "to date we have received neither instructions nor funds to cover the estimated costs" and "urgently need . . . a deposit of dols 900 to cover estimated expenses." The State Department warned her of the possibility that "if instructions are not soon received the Government of Chile will order remains re-interred for health reasons." In a phone call the next day, a bureaucrat from the Consular Services Office gave her until the morning of March 30 to wire the money. Such official determination and pressure, from the family's perspective, contrasted sharply with the State Department's restrained response to Charles's disappearance six months earlier. "I pointed out," Ed Horman would tell the consular official who called again to request the nine hundred dollars, "that if certain employees of the Department of State had displayed the same sense of urgency at the right time, my son might still be alive."[31]

Frank Teruggi

U.S. officials considered the murders of Charles Horman and Frank Teruggi to be "closely linked." As the only two Americans killed by the regime following the coup, their special cases bear numerous similarities. Both of them worked on the publication of the small radical magazine-newsletter called *FIN*. Both were seized at home by Chilean military personnel who ransacked their houses, carting away books and papers considered to be evidence of a pro-Allende inclination. Both were taken to the National Stadium where Chilean authorities attempted to cover up the fact they had been there by keeping their names off lists shown to U.S. embassy officials. One additional commonality, as an internal State Department summary noted, was that "the Junta clearly had or quickly acquired derogatory information on Horman and Teruggi and frequently mentioned it to Embassy personnel."

The main apparent difference in their cases was that unlike Horman, Teruggi had not crossed paths with U.S. military or intelligence officers. Horman's experience, particularly in Vina del Mar, raised the suspicion that U.S. personnel might have "fingered him" for the Chilean military but there was no evidence that Teruggi had ever been on the U.S. radar screen. At least that is what his family was led to believe for more than twenty-five years after his death.

At the time of the coup, Frank Teruggi was a twenty-four-year-old graduate student studying Chile's economic transition under the Allende government. In October of 1971, after graduating from the California Institute of Technology, he enrolled in the School of Political Economy at the University of Chile in Santiago. He lived at a group house at 2575 Hernan Cortes St., frequented by Chilean militants, along with his American roommate David Hathaway.

At approximately 9:00 P.M. on the evening of September 20, according to a one-page summary of his case titled "Deceased United States Citizen," a squad of Chilean Carabinero police arrested Teruggi and Hathaway at their home:

> Both were taken to the Escuela de Suboficiales "Macul" of the Carabineros where they were detained overnight and then taken the morning of September 21, 1973 to the National Stadium. No reason for the detention was given. A note from the Chilean Foreign Office dated October 3, 1973 stated that Mr. Teruggi had been arrested on September 20 for violation of curfew and had been released for lack of merit on September 21, 1973. . . . According to Mr. Hathaway, the afternoon of September 21 an officer separated Mr. Teruggi from the other U.S.

citizens detainees based upon a list of names he was carrying. Mr.
Teruggi was not seen alive again. (Doc 6)

Hathaway's Chilean fiancée, Irena Muñoz, was at the house and witnessed the arrest. In a debriefing with vice-consul/CIA operative James
Anderson, she observed that a unit of 15–20 police agents arrived and
spoke to a neighbor outside who denounced Teruggi and Hathaway as
"foreigners." She also told Anderson that during a search of Teruggi's bedroom, the squad had found the complete works of Karl Marx and accused
him of "contaminating his mind." The police took the literature and other
materials, along with the two Americans.

The U.S. embassy learned of Teruggi's detention on September 24,
when a close friend, Steve Volk, reported them detained and missing. A
"Chronology of Information Relevant to Frank Randall Teruggi," put together by the State Department, suggested that Purdy was told by Chilean
authorities later that day that Teruggi was "being held at the National Stadium"; and during a visit to the facility the next morning a volunteer humanitarian worker told Purdy that Teruggi's interrogation had been
"completed." In the late afternoon of September 25, however, Purdy received a call from the general morgue stating "that body of Frank Randall
Teruggi, born 14 March, 1949, in United States had been brought to
morgue dead of bullet wounds on 22 September."[32] The consul took
Teruggi's roommate, David Hathaway, to the morgue on September 27,
the day after Hathaway's release from the stadium. Hathaway was forced
to examine over 150 bodies lined up in rows; but he could not positively
identify the corpse tagged with Teruggi's name. At this point, the State
Department called Teruggi's family in Des Plaines, Illinois, and told his
parents that there was some "confusion" about the fate of their son. Finally
on October 2, Steve Volk made a positive identification.[33]

In diplomatic note number 15126, dated October 3, the Chilean Foreign Office advised the embassy that Teruggi had been detained for curfew violations on September 20—a statement clearly contradicted by the
facts—and released the next day for lack of evidence. How, then, did he
die? "It is possible that Mr. Teruggi might have been wounded fatally by
curfew control patrols or by civilian criminal elements," according to the

diplomatic note, "and later recovered and taken to the morgue." During an October 15 meeting with the the U.S. Defense Attaché, Col. William Hon, the Chilean head of SIM, General Augusto Lutz, was far less diplomatic. "His theory," Hon reported in a memorandum of conversation, "is that Teruggi was picked up by his friends and ultimately disposed of."[34] As for Horman, Lutz theorized "that during this particular time of his disappearance groups of robbers or extremists dressed in soldier uniforms were making searches and robberies of houses known to be occupied by North-Americans and foreigners with the purpose of finding dollars or other saleable merchandise."

General Lutz also informed Hon that the Chilean military had obtained incriminating information on Teruggi's activities. "Gen. Lutz said they have knowledge that Teruggi was here in Chile to spread false rumors to the outside world relating to Chile and the situation."[35] This theme dominated the one and only substantive statement that Pinochet's military provided to the United States on the Horman and Teruggi cases. On October 30, General Lutz sent the U.S. defense attaché an unsigned memorandum on the "Antecedents [facts] on two North American citizens' Decease." (Doc 7) In "special deference to the American Embassy," the report stated, the Chilean Military Intelligence Service had "accurately investigated" the fate of Teruggi and Horman:

> Available information on both persons leads to the conclusion that they were involved in extreme leftist movements in our country, which they supported both materially and ideologically. It is necessary, furthermore, to indicate that available and well supported data evidence existence of an organization linked to North American residents in our country, with connections in the rest of the countries in the Continent and led from the U.S., which has undertaken an offensive campaign [against the Junta]. This situation is related with the citizens Horman and Teruggi since there are concrete reasons to believe that at least [Teruggi] belongs to said organization.

U.S. officials did not share these allegations of subversive activities with the Teruggi or Horman families at the time; but later a number of

State Department officials focused on them as a possible lead in resolving these murders. Did such evidence exist? If so, where did the Chilean military get it? What was the basis for their conclusions? In a compilation of known evidence and unanswered questions put together by Bureau of Inter-American Affairs officers in the summer of 1976 called "Gleanings," the authors noted that "the October 30 memorandum from Army Intelligence to Colonel Hon may have been based on information provided by U.S. intelligence."

In the Horman case, that supposition derived from a statement by the key source, Enrique Sandoval, that his contact inside the Chilean military "had seen an abundant dossier on Horman's U.S. activities in the United States."[36] In the case of Teruggi, whose activities seemed to attract the regime's attention even more than Horman's, speculation came to focus on one top secret and closely guarded CIA document.

In March 1975, Teruggi's father, Frank Teruggi, Sr., initiated a Freedom of Information Act request to the CIA for all documents relating to his son and his death. "Our representative in Santiago advises that there are no documents in his files pertaining to your son," the CIA responded in May. The Agency did, however, acknowledge that it found "a single document which pertains to your son" at Langley headquarters; this document could not, however, be declassified because of national security considerations. More than a year later, the CIA informed an ACLU lawyer representing the Teruggi family that "the document was furnished to representatives of this Agency by an intelligence service of a foreign country. [It] was not obtained from the Government of Chile or any other South American country. Also it contains no derogatory information on Frank Randall Teruggi and does not concern his death in September 1973."[37]

The document did, in fact, contain derogatory information on Teruggi and worse—the address of his home at 2575 Hernan Cortes in Santiago. In July 1972, one of West Germany's intelligence agencies provided a report to the CIA on their surveillance of an American living in Heidelberg who was allegedly engaged in activities to foster desertion and dissent among U.S. servicemen stationed in Europe. This individual published a series of underground newsletters and sought contributing writers and editors from other parts of the world. Through an informant, West German intelligence operatives obtained information that the name of Frank Teruggi, along with his address in Santiago, had been provided to this individual as "an important contact" to have in his newsletter network.[38]

The Germans also shared this information with the U.S. army's 66th Military Intelligence Group based in Munich. That unit forwarded a report to the FBI in October 1972. "According to information received by source, Teruggi is an American residing in Chile who is closely associated with the Chicago Area Group for the Liberation of the Americas," noted the FBI memorandum. (Doc 8) The FBI then opened a file—No. 10053422—subject: "FRANK TERUGGI SM-SUBVERSIVE and ordered its Chicago office to "conduct appropriate investigation to identify subject . . . and submit results of investigation in [a] form suitable for dissemination." (Doc 9) By December, agents were filing reports on his affiliations and attendance at conferences, while conducting background checks and interviews with former colleagues and acquaintances.

Routing information on the documents does not indicate that the FBI disseminated this information to Chile. The key question was, and remains, whether the CIA did so. When the Agency refused to declassify the document, the staff of the Senate Select Committee on Intelligence sought access to it; eventually they were shown a strategically censored copy. In a secret memo to the Directorate of Operation's South American division in November 1976, the CIA's legislative counsel noted that the staffers had posed the obvious question: "did CIA, or the service which originally obtained it, pass the document to [Chilean intelligence]; or to another Latin American intelligence service which might have passed it to [Chilean intelligence]?" The Directorate of Operations responded that it had conducted a "thorough check that fails to reveal any evidence that the Central Intelligence Agency released or passed the information on Frank Teruggi Jr . . . to any Latin American liaison service, including [Chile's]," according an internal CIA memorandum. Nevertheless, the Agency continued to withhold from release even a sanitized version of the German intelligence report and any of the routing sheets that would have accompanied it that would allow verification of this statement.

Pursuing the Truth

Until the Gonzalez allegations generated a new public and political uproar in mid-1976, the U.S. government took very little action to resolve
the Horman and Teruggi murders. Under pressure from the families and
Capitol Hill, the embassy submitted a series of mildly worded diplomatic
notes listing unanswered questions and requested an inquiry to determine the circumstances of their deaths—requests the military regime ignored, obfuscated, or simply denied. In a July 24, 1974, letter to Congress
on the Horman case, the State Department reported that "competent" authorities of the Chilean government "consider it highly probable that the
death was due to the action of snipers or extremists using military uniforms" and that the United States was "unable to establish a legal basis for
attributing an international wrong to the Chilean government for the
death of Mr. Horman."[39] During the period when the United States had
the most leverage in its bilateral relations with the Pinochet regime, it
never once took the position that these Americans had been deliberately
killed by the military, nor demanded that the regime identify, prosecute
or extradite the commanding officers and personnel responsible.

Both families made an energetic attempt to keep the investigation alive.
In February 1974, Teruggi's father, Frank Teruggi Sr., traveled to Santiago
with a group called the Chicago Commission of Inquiry and met with U.S.
embassy and Chilean military officials. "Is this case closed?," he pressed the
new ambassador David Popper, during a meeting at the embassy. Declassified meeting minutes record their exchange:

*Ambassador Popper: we have repeatedly tried to determine the facts in
this case and we will continue to do what we can to clear up these discrepancies. In all honesty I cannot be very optimistic about getting a
fuller story at this date and after this lapse of time.*
*Mr. Teruggi: . . . it is difficult for [my] family to understand how the
USG can be helping the Government of Chile when they don't even answer our questions.*

In the broad scheme of U.S.–Chilean relations, State Department officials made clear, resolving this murder was not a priority. Both the embassy, and the Bureau of Inter-American Affairs, as one internal memorandum noted in June 1974, "now indicate that they believe further pressure in this regard will be of no avail and merely further exacerbate bilateral relations for no benefit."

For twenty-five years neither the U.S. nor the Chilean governments provided any new evidence in the case relating to the circumstances of Frank Teruggi's death. Only one piece of noteworthy information emerged—from a source outside the United States. In November 1975, a Belgian government official named André Van Lancker provided a sworn affidavit to the U.S. consulate in Brussels relating to his harrowing imprisonment in the National Stadium from September 17 and November 8, 1973. Between September 20 and 22, 1973, he recalled, "I got knowledge of the attendance among us of a United States citizen, named Frank, a university man who had been arrested." During a brutal interrogation at the hands of uniformed police officers, Van Lancker was severely injured and taken to a hospital tent where Red Cross workers intervened to save his life. When he was returned to his cell, "fellow prisoners told me what happened to Mr. Frank:"

> The military took him for interrogation the same days as me i.e. about the 20th to the 23rd of September 1973 to the "caracol", a kind of corridor of the velodrome (the cycle-racing track next to the football stadium where personalities could not enter). An officer whose identification was "Alfa-1" or "Sigma-1," I do not remember anymore, was in charge of the interrogation where Frank was heavily tortured by blows and electricity shocks. Finally Frank was in such a bad condition that the officer commented that he (the officer) had gone too far and he shot him with a burst of machine gun—as used in such cases. Afterward, fellow prisoners told me the military commented among themselves, their fear of having troubles with the government of the U.S.A., [and] that is why they did not want to recognize Frank's presence in the stadium.

The scent of scandal from Rafael Gonzalez's account of the Horman murder brought renewed attention to both cases, and forced the State Department, at least temporarily, into a more activist mode. To obtain the truth of the Horman and Teruggi cases, the Chile desk officer Rudy Fimbres warned, a comprehensive "probe" would be required accessing evidence from the files of the U.S. intelligence agencies that likely knew more about the case than they admitted. The Chile desk was "unconvinced the total U.S. role is honestly and accurately reflected in the records available to the [State] Department," he informed Assistant Secretary Harry Shlaudeman, who was known to be close to the CIA.[40] In August, Fimbres and his colleagues wrote to Shlaudeman, "we find it hard to believe that the Chileans did not check with [the CIA Station] regarding two detained Americans. . . ." [The CIA Station's] lack of candor with us on other matters only heightens our suspicions."[41]

Assistant Secretary Shlaudeman promised the Senate Foreign Relations Committee that the department would do "everything possible" to investigate the unresolved murders of Horman and Teruggi and determine whether any official had initiated, condoned or was negligent in Horman's detention and execution. Instead, Shlaudeman simply assigned one lone career diplomat, Frederick Smith, Jr., who happened to be in Washington awaiting his next embassy posting, to do a "thorough examination" of department records. In the fall of 1976, Smith recalled, he spent several weeks sifting through files and drafting a detailed twenty-six-page report entitled "Death in Chile of Charles Horman."[42]

Like his colleagues, Smith understood that the answers to the mystery of Horman's fate were likely to be found elsewhere. "I see no other alternative if we want to satisfy ourselves—and others—that we have done all we can to determine the truth of the matter," he wrote in a cover memo to Shlaudeman, but to make a "high-level approach to the U.S. intelligence community." As Smith noted: "If one concludes—as I do—that the GOC was directly responsible for Horman's (and Teruggi's) death, it is difficult to believe that the GOC would have felt sufficiently secure in taking such drastic action against two American citizens without some reason, however unjustifiably inferred or inadvertently given, to believe that it could do so without substantial adverse consequences vis-à-vis the USG."[43] The final paragraph of his report recommended that

> *high-level inquiries be made of intelligence agencies, particularly the CIA, to try to ascertain to what extent, if any, actions may have been taken or information may have been furnished, formally or informally, to representatives of the forces that now constitute the GOC, either before or immediately after the coup, that may have led the Junta to believe it could, without serious repercussions, kill Charles Horman and Frank Teruggi.*

Neither declassified State Department nor CIA files indicate that any such "high-level" inquiry was ever undertaken. Unlike the Pentagon, which ordered a written debriefing of all U.S. military personnel who came in contact with Horman or were involved in efforts to find him, the CIA apparently did not officially question its key Station operatives— James Anderson, Ray Warren, John Devine, and Donald Winters among others—about their contacts with Chilean military officials in the days following the coup, or any discussions they might have had regarding Americans in Chile. Nor do the documents reflect any information on what effort the Agency (which had the best contacts inside the Chilean military) made to ascertain what happened to Horman and Teruggi after they were detained. The lack of documentation suggests no such effort was made.

The State Department did pursue two avenues of inquiry: a new set of questions for Rafael Gonzalez including, as Smith wrote, "if he knows of any information (pre or post coup) provided by U.S. sources [to Chile] regarding Horman or Teruggi or other American citizens"; and an effort to find and question Enrique Sandoval, the original source of the information that Horman had been killed in the stadium. On August 2, 1976, Fimbres tracked down Sandoval in exile in Montreal, Canada. "He confirmed he told Judd Kessler that 'Horman was dead, and not to look for him alive,'" Fimbres reported to the U.S. embassy, but he would not reveal his source:

I said I felt I must continue to pursue this line of inquiry because the information he provided had proven to be accurate. Better late than never. To his protestation that there was no point now in pursuing this matter, I explained that in simple justice to Horman's parents and in response to the many inquires regarding the circumstances of the deaths of the two Americans, we had vigorously to pursue every lead. He said he saw a threat in this. . . . He volunteered that his primary sources (sic) "uniformed persons," were in jail. He implied they would be at the mercy of Chilean security if it was revealed that that "they" had passed on to us information on Horman.

The State Department had concluded, quite incorrectly, that Sandoval's source was his brother, who they soon identified as "most likely Colonel Guillermo Sandoval Velasquez."[44] For this reason, Fimbres confessed to being confused at Sandoval's repeated references to multiple sources. "His use of the plural 'uniformed persons' is confusing," Fimbres wrote, "perhaps deliberately so. But more than once he implied throughout the conversation that he had more than one source."[45]

Indeed, Sandoval repeatedly stated that his information came from more than one person. In an interview with Hauser in 1976, he claimed he had three separate sources, among them a "close relative" serving inside the stadium and a military officer who said he was present when Horman was led away to be executed.[46] In a private meeting in Manhattan with Joyce Horman in March 1975, Sandoval confided that he had two sources: a relative and a "military fiscal"—an army lawyer—who were working inside the stadium.

Sandoval's sources represented the only direct witnesses able to identify those Chilean military officers responsible for murdering an American. But, having misidentified his informant as his brother, and now concerned about the personal security of this source, U.S. officials decided to abandon this avenue of inquiry. Any approach in Chile, as Fimbres and two colleagues wrote to Shlaudeman, would "have to be made with considerable discretion," and would be "terribly sensitive. We are skeptical that anything positive can be accomplished through this line of inquiry." (See Doc 3.) In his own final report to Shlaudeman in December, Frederick Smith also recommended against pursuing the Sandoval lead: "To do so might seriously endanger his source (his brother) and confirmation of Horman's presence at the National Stadium or other information we might obtain from him would seem at this point to be marginal to our main concern."[47] And U.S. ambassador to Santiago, David Popper, opposed pursuing Sandoval's sources, or any other inquiry to identify Horman's killers. "The U.S. cannot conduct a full investigation on the territory of another sovereign nation," he wrote to Fimbres. "Somewhere along the line we will have to take the position that we have gone as far as we can."[48]

A Final Missed Opportunity

There would be one more example of U.S. government irresponsibility in the Horman case—publicly unknown until the declassification of documents in June 2000—extending the long pattern of official disinclination, and simple inability, to bring the most famous crime against an American citizen in Chile to legal and historical closure. On March 11, 1987, an informant with credible ties to the Chilean secret police appeared at the U.S. embassy and requested to speak to Ambassador Harry Barnes, or the deputy chief of mission, George Jones. Instead he was referred to a junior political officer, David Dreher. In this initial meeting the informant—his name remains deleted from declassified files—said he knew what had happened to Charles Horman and wanted to come clean. "He knows who ordered the killing of Horman and that some of these people are currently top officials," Dreher reported. "He says he will name names."[49]

The State Department's Southern Cone desk, headed by David Cox, characterized this information as "intriguing," but took a remarkably reserved position on pursuing it. "It occurs to us, just as it probably has to you, that this could be a setup, by the extreme left or the GOC," Cox informed Ambassador Barnes. Rather than recommend that the informant be turned over to a high-level officer or even the FBI, the department recommended handling him at a very low level. "You are the best judge on who should meet with him," Cox wrote, "but from our vantage point, it would seem best at this stage to treat this as a consular matter."

On April 20, the informant returned to the embassy and spent ninety minutes discussing Horman's fate, providing for the first time new names of Chilean military officers involved in his seizure and death. According to the story he related to Dreher,

Horman was seized by Intelligence Units acting on information provided by [General Hugo] Salas, current CNI head. He was taken to the Escuela Militar and interrogated. From there he was transferred to the National Stadium for additional questioning. Documents seized from his residence indicated that Horman was an "extremist." He was therefore considered a foreigner/extremist and the order was given to execute him. [The informant] said that Horman spoke little Spanish and the troops that had him were unaware that he was an American. Instead, they thought that he was a Brazilian, Italian, etc . . . The record indicating that he was an American arrived at the stadium after the execution. He was forced to change clothes and then shot three times. The body was dumped on the streets to indicate he had been killed in a confrontation. The news of his death got lost in the confusion of those days and later was suppressed as it was known that he was an American.[50]

The source stated that Horman was among "several hundred people perished at the stadium." The person "who made the decision on who was to die," he said, naming names, was Col. Pedro Espinoza, who soon joined the secret police, DINA.[51] "[He] does not feel that the embassy did very much to help the Horman family," Dreher reported in a cable that went to the White House Situation Room. "[He] was highly critical of the Consul General at the time and also of the Military group for not acting to help a fellow citizen. He also said that he was getting the impression that the Embassy still was not very interested."[52]

Indeed, the embassy's handling of this informant reflected the same ambivalence about aggressively pursuing the Horman case that had dominated U.S. officialdom from the start. Here was a potential witness to the controversial murder of an American citizen—the first to step forward since Rafael Gonzalez in 1976. Yet the State Department seemed more focused on his motivations than evaluating what evidence he had to offer. "I don't understand his motivation. Why after fourteen years has he finally decided to tell his story?" Dreher complained in the report on the second meeting. When the informant returned to the embassy for a third and pivotal meeting on April 24, he said that he felt his family was being threatened and "insisted" that he had to get out of Chile and get his family to the United States. "[Deleted name] could be part of a GOC plot to compromise Embassy officials," the embassy noted in a comprehensive summary of the informant meetings. "On the other hand he could be on the level and have useful information." [Doc 10]

How to respond? If the United Stated did nothing it could create "the worse case scenario," in Dreher's assessment: the informant could be killed under mysterious circumstances and "it becomes known that he came to us for help after giving us new information on the Horman case [and] our reaction was to take the information lightly and to deny him any protection or aid. The press would crucify us." But stalling him was no longer an option. "We are going to have to decide what to do with this guy."[53]

After internal discussions, embassy officials simply decided to turn the informant away. When he returned for the fourth time on April 27 seeking some form of asylum, the informant was told that "the U.S. would not grant his request: transportation for subject and family to the United States and some form of subsistence for an indefinite period of time." He then left.[54]

Eighteen days later, after conferring with the Justice Department and FBI, the State Department partially changed its mind. Now officials in Washington took the position that "the Department has a fundamental interest in determining circumstances of deaths abroad of U.S. citizens, even thirteen years after the fact." Moreover, "we would consider it a very serious matter if senior GOC officials had been aware of the circumstances of Horman's death and attempted to conceal this information from the USG and Horman's family." Even so, the State Department was unwilling to send an investigative team to Santiago to establish the informant's bona fides. Instead it instructed the embassy to tell the informant that

*Before we could consider the possibility of his travel to the United
States, we would have to interview him more thoroughly. This cannot
be done in Chile. If [informant] is willing to travel at his own expense
to Montevideo, US officials Stationed there will interview him and
make a determination as to his credibility. [Informant] should understand the USG cannot offer him special assistance, financial or otherwise. . . . If we find [informant] is fully truthful after questioning in
Montevideo, including polygraph test, we would be willing to consider
the possibility of his subsequent travel to the United States.*

This unattractive offer was never delivered, and the new information
on the Horman case never pursued. The embassy had identified the informant and obtained biographic data on him—"we verified he was who he
said he was," one internal memo noted—but U.S. officials professed to be
unable to find him. "Although Emboff asked [informant] to keep in
touch, he has made no further attempt to contact us," the embassy complained.[55] "For our part we have no means of contacting subject as he
steadfastly refused to provide us with an address or telephone numbers,"
Ambassador Barnes cabled the department on June 17, 1987. Unsatisfied
with the embassy's lack of effort, on July 14 the State Department ordered
a "mission-wide effort," including the use of U.S. intelligence operatives,
to recontact this individual. A month later, the embassy sent back a brief,
and final, status report: "Post unable to locate [informant]."

NOTES

AMERICAN CASUALTIES

1. CBS News reporter Frank Manitzas, accompanied by the *Washington Post*'s Southern
Cone correspondent, Joanne Omang, taped their interviews with Gonzalez; in August,
Manitzas provided the tape to the State Department where it was transcribed as "The
Second Interview, Tuesday, June 8, 1976, in the Italian Embassy." Omang's story on the
interview appeared in the *Washington Post* on June 10, 1976; a follow-up *Post* story titled
"The Man Who Knew Too Much," appeared on June 20. Gonzalez's taped comments
were also cited by Thomas Hauser in his comprehensive book on the Horman case, *The
Execution of Charles Horman: An American Sacrifice* published by Harcourt, Brace, Jovanovich in 1978, reissued in paperback under the title *Missing*.
2. *Missing,* based on the Hauser book and directed by Costa-Gavras, premiered in February

1982. The movie received an Academy Award nomination for best picture and won the Oscar for best screenplay. In January 1983, former ambassador Nathaniel Davis, U.S. consul Fred Purdy and U.S. naval attaché Ray Davis sued Hauser, Costa-Gavras and Universal Pictures for $150 million for defamation of character. In July 1987 the libel claim was dropped after the judge in the case ruled that there were no legal grounds to bring it, and Universal and Costa-Gavras agreed to a joint statement saying that *Missing* was "not intended to suggest that Nathaniel Davis, Ray Davis or Frederick Purdy ordered or approved the order for the murder of Charles Horman—and would not wish viewers of the film to interpret it this way."

3. "He was shot in the stadium. I'm sorry. Things like this should not happen," a Chilean officer told Ed Horman on October 19. See "Victim's Father is Bitter at U.S. Handling of Case," *New York Times*, November 19, 1973. Pinochet's Defense and Foreign Ministries later denied they had ever admitted murdering Charles Horman.

4. Rudy Fimbres to Harry Shlaudeman, "The Charles Horman Case," July 15, 1976.

5. An October 26, 1978, memorandum from McNeil to Assistant Secretary Viron Vaky indicates that State Department lawyers wanted to keep secret the conclusion that the Chilean military had executed Horman to assist the legal defense of former U.S. officials being sued by the Horman family for wrongful death. McNeil forcefully recommended that the U.S. government "discharge our responsibility to be more responsive to these American citizens" and issue an official statement that "there is evidence to suggest that they died while in custody" of the Chilean military. Such a statement was never issued. The lawyers also objected to declassifying the suggestion that CIA and/or DOD intelligence agents might have played a role in Horman's death on the grounds that it was speculative opinion. In a December 28, 1978 memorandum, McNeil suggested "the Department of State is better off releasing everything it possibly can now, rather than be forced to release later and so appear to be 'covering up.' Lastly, the material in question is natural speculation that has occurred to almost everyone who has contact with the case," he added. "It may indeed anger some in the CIA and the military, but the speculation exists and is very much in public print. (Moreover, keeping the CIA and DOD happy is not grounds for FOI [Freedom of Information Act] refusals)." McNeil was overruled and the passage was deleted and kept hidden from the families for another twenty-one years.

6. See Washington Special Action Group Meeting, Subject: Chile, September 20, 1973.

7. Father Doherty's journal, which he later provided to State Department officials, recording the graphic details of abuse and torture inside the stadium, for Chileans and numerous foreigners from at least twenty-five different nations jailed with him. Soldiers, he wrote, formed a gauntlet outside his cell. "Men were made to run this gauntlet and as they did so they were beaten by soldiers with rifle butts. One man fell down from a blow he received and was shot in the chest by a soldier . . . he died five minutes later. The soldier who shot the man blew off the end of his rifle and laughed." He also recorded hearing an hour of machine-gun and pistol fire at the far end of the stadium between 4:00 and 5:00 A.M. on the morning of September 20. "I guessed that people were being executed and that those who had not died were being [given] the coup d' grace."

8. Horman interpreted Creter's comment as an admission of U.S. involvement in the coup. Terry Simon recalled that he told her that night that "We've stumbled upon something very important." But the U.S. embassy and Creter insisted he was referring to his naval engineering assignment in Chile, which, if real, was far more mundane. A cable from the

commander of the U.S. military group in Chile Captain Ray Davis, dated August 21, 1973 to Fort Amador in the Panana Canal Zone, requested the Creter be prepared to "assist Chilean Navy in following areas" among them: "producing their own CO_2 for recharging shipboard fire extinguishers" and "recommendations concerning installation of fluorescent lighting in living spaces aboard all Chilean ships." In an interview with author Thomas Hauser several years later Creter conceded that those jobs had not been accomplished when he met Charles and Terry in Vina del Mar. Hauser also obtained through a FOIA request a consulate file card on Charles Horman that indicated that Creter had sought and provided intelligence to the embassy on Horman's visit to Vina. The card noted: "Art Creeter—15 ND [Naval Division]/ 2 checked into Miramar Hotel, Rm. 315, 2300 on 10 Sept./ used 425 Paul Harris address/ said 'escritor' left 15 Sept." Hauser interviewed Creter about his strange document and noted: "One would not normally expect to find a 'naval engineer' leafing through hotel records, and Creter has no explanation for his conduct." See *The Execution of Charles Horman*, p. 234.

9. See "Resume of Naval Mission Contacts with Charles Horman and Terry Simon during the Period 11 September–15 September 1973 Valparaiso, Chile" signed by Patrick J. Ryan, LTCOL, USMC.

10. Simon recounted this episode to author Thomas Hauser as well as wrote about it in a short memoir in the magazine *Senior Scholastic*. See *The Execution of Charles Horman*, p. 94; and *Senior Scholastic*, "American Girl in Chile's Revolution," December 6, 1973.

11. One of the peculiar aspects of the Horman case is the fact that Joyce and Charles had moved to this home on September 7, only four days before the coup—too recently for their new address to be available to Chilean or U.S. authorities. (For reasons that are unclear, Charles used his prior address when registering at the Hotel Miramar in Vina.) None of their old neighbors reported anyone looking for them prior to September 17. It is possible, as in the case of other Americans arrested, that their move on September 7 attracted the attention of coup supporters in the neighborhood who denounced them as foreigners to the new military authorities and resulted in the house being targeted for a military raid.

12. The daughter of one of Horman's neighbors happened to be leaving after visiting her mother at the time he was taken by the military. Her car followed the truck all the way to the National Stadium and she later told Joyce Horman that she saw the truck go through the stadium gates.

13. Frederick Smith, Jr., "Death in Chile of Charles Horman," p. 3. The former neighbor was a courageous woman named Isabella Carvajal. In a Spanish-language statement her husband, Mario Carvajal, stated that the military official had referred to Horman as a *Norteamericano*. According to the statement, the SIM officer ended the telephone conversation by threatening her with death if what she had told him on the phone about Horman turned out not to be true.

14. Carlotta Manosa, a close friend of the Hormans at whose home Joyce stayed on September 18 after she found her own house ransacked and Charles missing, asked a relative who worked at the embassy to inform Purdy about the SIM phone call.

15. See "Victim's Father is Bitter at U.S. Handling of Case," *New York Times*, November 29, 1973.

16. Hall was one of several vice-consuls at the embassy. His meeting with Joyce is recorded in Hauser's *The Execution of Charles Horman*, pp. 117, 118. When she asked to stay at the consulate he told her, "we have no accommodations."

17. Captain Ray Davis, head of the MilGroup, took notes on the meeting and included them in a six-page draft chronology of his contacts with Charles and Terry, and his ostensible efforts to help Joyce.

18. *The Execution of Charles Horman,* p. 133. Joyce told Hauser that the ambassador had asked: "Just what do you want us to do—look under all the bleachers?" She recalls responding, "That's exactly what I want you to do, and I see nothing wrong with it."

19. See Kessler's memorandum to Rudy Fimbres, "Diuguid Article on Horman Case," July 19, 1976, and his undated letter to Frederick Purdy, written soon after.

20. *The Execution of Charles Horman,* p. 217.

21. After Horman's body was found on October 18, and the regime concocted the story that he had been shot in the street on September 18, the Foreign Ministry withdrew its October 3 statement as "an error."

22. In a rebuttal cable to Washington, Davis wrote that Purdy, and the U.S. military attaché, Colonel Hon, had a different recollection of his remarks. "According to their recollection, the Ambassador certainly never said 'that the Embassy feeling was that Charles probably was in hiding.' He may have mentioned this as a possibility." Davis himself did not offer an opinion on what he said.

23. Anderson wrote this "memorandum to the files" on October 17.

24. Dolguin lived next door to the Ford Foundation's Lowell Jarvis. Jarvis identified him to Horman only as an official from an English-speaking embassy with whom Jarvis played tennis.

25. Purdy made this statement in an unvarnished draft response to the letter Edmund Horman wrote to Congress in late October, complaining about how the embassy handled his son's case. The draft, dated November 17, 1973, was subsequently rewritten and sent as a rebuttal to the Horman letter signed by deputy chief of mission Herbert Thompson. See "Senator Javits' Interest in Horman Case," November 18, 1973.

26. State Department cable, confidential, "Approach to Foreign Office on Missing American Citizens Horman and Teruggi," October 3, 1973.

27. Ambassador Davis cabled a summary of this conversation to Washington. See "Kubisch Meeting with Minister Huerta," February 24, 1974.

28. Quoted from Horman's letter to Charles Anderson at the Office of Special Consular Services, March 27, 1974.

29. In an October 27, 1973, cable on "Disposition of Remains," the embassy reported that Sanitation officials "advises embassy that it cannot authorize shipment in present state, and that alternatives are cremation (and shipment of ashes) or reduction to skeleton (and shipment of bones). Sanitation says there is no possibility of exemptions." After two months of that argument, the minister of interior, General Bonilla, told the embassy he had "delayed authorization to ship Horman remains out of concern that release be so timed as to minimize use of event to detriment of Chile in U.S. media and public opinion."

30. "Death in Chile of Charles Horman," p. 6.

31. Quoted from Ed Horman's letter to Charles Anderson at the Office of Special Consular Services, March 27, 1974. In a follow-up letter to Charles Horman's widow on April 4, the chief of the State Department's Division of Property Claims, Estates and Legal Documents, Larry Lane, advised her that "Congress has not appropriated funds for payment of these expenses for private American citizens who die abroad and they must necessarily be met by the estate or relatives of the deceased."

32. State Department, "Chronology of Information Relevant to Frank Randall Teruggi," October 5, 1973. The Chilean medical examiner was apparently able to match fingerprints from Teruggi's application for Chilean identification card to the fingers on the body.

33. Hathaway called Volk as he was leaving Chile to ask him to look again at the body at the morgue and see if he could identify it. When Volk, now a history professor at Oberlin College, went to the consulate, he spoke with James Anderson. "I don't care what Hathaway told Volk. He told me that it wasn't Teruggi and that's the end of it." Anderson returned to tell Volk that they would not visit the morgue again because "we don't want to pressure the new government by asking for too many favors." The next day Purdy apparently changed his mind.

34. Defense Department, Memorandum for the Records, from Colonel W. M. Hon, Defense Attaché, October 16, 1973.

35. Ibid.

36. *The Execution of Charles Horman,* p. 244. Sandoval presumed, as he told Hauser, that this file "came from your CIA or Department of State."

37. CIA letter to Edna Selan Epstein, "Re: Freedom of Information Act Request of Frank F. Teruggi for Information Concerning his Son Frank Randall Teruggi," May 7, 1976.

38. FBI memorandum from Legat Bonn to Acting Director, [deleted] SM-Subversive, November 28, 1972.

39. Quoted in *The Execution of Charles Horman,* pp. 192, 195.

40. Rudy Fimbres to Harry Shlaudeman, "The Charles Horman Case," July 15, 1976.

41. See Document 3. When the August 25, 1976, Fimbres, Driscoll, and Robertson memo was released to the Horman family in 1979, this paragraph on the CIA's lack of candor was also censored.

42. I interviewed Smith in October 1999 and arranged for him to meet Joyce Horman for the first time. He made it clear that he did not consider his report to be a substantive investigation of the Horman case. His report is undated but was prepared in November–December 1976 and given to Shlaudeman near the end of the year.

43. This paragraph was deleted when the Smith report was first released to the Horman family in early 1980 on the grounds that it contained "thoughts intended for internal State Department deliberations," according to court records.

44. Fimbres misidentified Sandoval's source through a series of misassumptions and suggestions from a *Washington Post* reporter, Louis Duiguid. Years later, when Joyce Horman told Sandoval about the State Department's conclusions he made it clear that he didn't have a brother. Col. Sandoval Velasquez, who was tracked down by a researcher for U.S. television network in 2000, also denied he was Sandoval's brother—or his source.

45. Fimbres letter to Ambassador David Popper, August 4, 1976.

46. Hauser, *The Execution of Charles Horman,* p. 217.

47. See Smith's cover memo of his report to Shlaudeman, "Further Steps in the Case of Charles Horman," ca. December 26, 1976.

48. See Popper's letter to Fimbres on further investigation of the Horman case, August 17, 1976.

49. David Dreher, "Subject: Charles Horman case," March 11, 1987.

50. See Dreher's memo to the DCM, subject [deleted], April 20, 1987.

51. Col. Pedro Espinosa, convicted as a DINA co-conspirator in the Letelier-Moffitt assassination, has never been linked to the atrocities at the National Stadium. While it is possible he

played a role, it is also possible his name has been confused with that of the top military commander at the Stadium, Jorge Espinosa Ulloa. It is possible that the informant confused the two in his comments or that Dreher himself simply assumed the Espinosa he referred to was Pedro and put that in his memorandum of conversation.

52. See Dreher's memo to the DCM, subject [deleted], April 20, 1987.

53. See Dreher's memo to the DCM, subject [deleted], April 24, 1987.

54. This information is reported in a secret Embassy cable, "Horman Case: Embassy Views on Credibility of Source," June 15, 1987. The cable also reports that during a trip to the Embassy the informant left "a written document" with the Consul General, Jayne Kobliska, a typed four-page overview of events in September-October 1973 detailing his knowledge of Horman's fate. This important record was not included in the declassified files on the Horman case.

55. At that point the Department decided to inform Joyce Horman of this new development. In a brief phone call, an official named Peter DeShazo told her that the validity of the information the informant had shared "was difficult to ascertain," and "the informant was seeking certain monetary favors from the USG, a fact which also colors his motives for providing more information if not the story itself."

[Editor's Note: The revised paperback edition, published in mid-2004, contains an updated version of this chapter. The key witness in the case of Charles Horman, a Chilean intelligence agent named Rafael Gonzalez, was arrested in Chile in December 2003 and charged as an accessory to his death. Gonzalez retracted his original story that there was an American official in the room when Charles Horman was being interrogated after he had been detained. As of mid-2005, a Chilean judge is continuing a full investigation into those responsible for the murder of Charles Horman.]

Introduction to
Philip Gourevitch's

"The Genocide Fax"

IN THE SPRING AND early summer of 1994 at least eight hundred thousand people were massacred in Rwanda in a bloodbath that pitted the ruling Hutu tribe against the Tutsi, their long-time adversaries whom they perceived had been favored under colonial rule. "Two weeks after the slaughter of the Tutsis began, General Romeo Dallaire, the Canadian commander of the U.N. force in Rwanda, had announced that he could end the genocide with between five thousand and eight thousand troops," wrote Philip Gourevitch. "Instead, the Security Council cut Dallaire's existing force, of two thousand five hundred to two hundred and seventy." Three months before the state-sponsored genocide, Dallaire had sent a fax to high U.N. officials, notifying them of preparations for the extermination campaign. Dallaire's fax was a confidential document that remained secret until its existence was revealed in the London *Observer* in November 1995. Digging deeper into the story, Gourevitch sought to find out how high up in the U.N. hierarchy Dallaire's request had traveled before it was refused. Did it reach Kofi Annan, then under-secretary-general for peacekeeping operations? Or Secretary General Boutros Boutros-Ghali? Or the Security Council?

At the time of the extermination, the Clinton administration did nothing to stop the slaughter, acknowledging only that "acts of genocide may have occurred." When Gourevitch's articles appeared a few years later, detailing the crisis, President Clinton was shocked and wrote in the margin: "How did this happen?" (Clinton later "apologized" for his inaction on a visit to Rwanda in 1998.)

After Gourevitch's "The Genocide Fax" was published, media attention increased on the situation in Rwanda. Annan, who had by then become U.N. Secretary General, gave in to pressure and appointed an independent inquiry that eventually criticized him and the U.N. for the way it had handled the crisis.

Since 1997, Gourevitch has been a staff writer for *The New Yorker* where he has written several articles about the Rwanda genocide, receiving a citation from the Overseas Press Club. He has been a finalist for the National Magazine Award and is the author of *We wish to inform you that tommorow we will be killed with our families: Stories from Rwanda,* winner of the National Book critics Circle Award. He is also the author of *A Cold Case,* about a prosecutor who reopens a murder investigation after three decades.

ADDITIONAL SOURCES

Dallaire, Roméo A. *Shake Hands with the Devil: The Failure of Humanity in Rwanda.* New York: Carroll and Graf, 2004.

Gourevitch, Philip. *We wish to inform you that tomorrow we will be killed with our families: Stories from Rwanda.* New York: Picador, 1999.

Power, Samantha. *"A Problem from Hell": America and the Age of Genocide.* New York: Basic Books, 2002.

Philip Gourevitch

"The Genocide Fax"

THE NEW YORKER, MAY 11, 1998

WE WERE SURPRISED," a Rwandan diplomat told me after the Secretary-General of the United Nations, Kofi Annan, announced that he would be visiting Rwanda this week. "Many people in my country are not happy with Mr. Annan. He was the head of U.N. peacekeeping when U.N. peacekeepers allowed a genocide in Rwanda. But let him come, and he can hear about it directly." In fact, Annan's staff say, the Secretary-General plans to acknowledge the United Nations' sorry record in Rwanda, in the hope of establishing his credibility there. The Rwandan diplomat wondered whether Annan would also answer some questions. "There is the affair of the fax—the famous fax," he said. "Many people have heard of it, and everyone would like to know more."

The famous fax is dated January 11, 1994—three months before the state-sponsored genocide, in which members of the Hutu majority massacred at least eight hundred thousand people from the Tutsi minority and also tens of thousands of Hutus who opposed the genocidal regime. The fax, headed "Request for Protection for Informant," was sent by Major General Roméo Dallaire, the U.N. force commander in Rwanda, to peacekeeping headquarters in New York, and it reported in startling detail the preparations that were under way to carry out precisely such an extermination campaign.

Dallaire's informant was a former member of the security staff of President Juvénal Habyarimana, Rwanda's Hutu dictator. At the time of the fax, the informant was being paid about a thousand dollars a month—a kingly wage in Rwanda—by Habyarimana's political party to compile lists of Tutsis and to train the militiamen known as the *interahamwe* ("those who attack together") to kill them.

Dallaire, a Québécois, wrote as he speaks, in a clipped military English, and his telegraphic prose underscored the urgency of his message. The peace that his U.N. blue helmets were in Rwanda to keep was a fiction. Throughout the early nineties, government-sponsored massacres of Tutsis had become a regular occurrence, and Habyarimana's political and military cronies, whose ideology was known simply as Hutu Power, wanted them to continue. Their plan, according to Dallaire's informant, was once again to "provoke a civil war," and, as part of that plan, Belgian troops, who formed the backbone of the U.N. force, "were to be provoked and if Belgian soldiers resorted to force a number of them were to be killed and thus guarantee Belgian withdrawal from Rwanda." In the meantime, Dallaire's informant had been "ordered to register all Tutsi in Kigali," and Dallaire wrote, "He suspects it is for their extermination. Example he gave was that in twenty minutes his personnel could kill up to a thousand Tutsis."

As it happened, everything Dallaire's informant told him came true three months later. "He believes the President does not have full control over all elements of his old party/faction," Dallaire wrote, and, sure enough, on April 6, 1994, Habyarimana was assassinated—a move that created a pretext for the most radical elements of Hutu Power to seize control of the state and implement their program. The next morning, Rwandan troops captured, tortured, murdered, and mutilated ten Belgian blue helmets, whereupon Belgium—Rwanda's former colonial ruler—called the rest of its force home, triggering the collapse of the U.N. mission. During the hundred days that followed Habyarimana's death, an average of more than five Tutsis were murdered every minute in Rwanda, and it became clear that Dallaire's informant had not exaggerated the industrial killing capacity of the *interahamwe*.

Why had Dallaire's source told him so much? Because, Dallaire wrote, "he disagrees with anti-Tutsi extermination." The informant had offered to assist the U.N. force in raiding *interahamwe* weapons caches, and all he asked in return was U.N. protection for himself, his wife, and their four children. Dallaire was eager to act. He announced his intention to raid an arms cache within thirty-six hours, and he recommended that his superiors in New York help the informant be "evacuated out of Rwanda."

DALLAIRE'S FAX was, of course, a confidential document, and it remained secret until November of 1995, when it was described in the London *Observer*. A copy of the fax was then published in Belgium, where the news that the United Nations had known for months of Hutu Power's intention to massacre Belgian troops caused a furor.

Dallaire had labelled his fax "most immediate," addressed it to his superior in peacekeeping—Major General Maurice Baril, a fellow-Québécois—and signed off in French: *"Peux ceque veux. Allons-y."* ("Where there's a will there's a way. Let's go.") Reports soon appeared in the Belgian press explaining that the response from U.N. headquarters had been: Let's not. Dallaire, the reports said, had been expressly instructed to refrain from taking any direct preventive action. But the document containing these instructions failed to surface, and its author remained unidentified, so it was impossible to determine how high in the U.N. hierarchy Dallaire's fax had gone. Had it reached the Under-Secretary-General for Peacekeeping Operations, Kofi Annan? The Secretary-General, Boutros Boutros-Ghali? The Security Council?

With Annan's elevation to the office of Secretary-General last year, the questions only intensified, causing Annan's spokesman, Fred Eckhard, to complain, "We're taking a bum rap on this." But somebody with access to U.N. files disagreed with Eckhard, and one day my fax machine rang and a copy of the missing response to Dallaire spun into my office. It bore the same date as Dallaire's fax, it was also labelled "most immediate," and its subject was "Contacts with Informant." It had been sent under the name of Kofi Annan, bearing the signature of Iqbal Riza, who was Annan's deputy in the peacekeeping office and is now his chief of staff.

"New York," as U.N. people call headquarters, told Dallaire that the "operation contemplated" in his fax—and the extension of protection to the informant—could not be allowed under the Rwanda peacekeeping mandate imposed by the Security Council. Instead, Dallaire was instructed that if he was "convinced that the information provided by informant is absolutely reliable" he should share it with President Habyarimana, and inform him that the activities of the *interahamwe* "represent a clear threat to the peace process" and a "clear violation" of the "Kigali weapons-secure area." Dallaire was also told to share his information with the Ambassadors to Rwanda from Belgium, France, and the United States—the primary foreign sponsors of Rwanda's so-called peace process.

Never mind that Dallaire's informant had explicitly described the plans to exterminate Tutsis and assassinate Belgians as emanating from Habyarimana's court: the mandate said that peace-treaty violations should be reported to the President, and New York advised Dallaire, "You should assume that he"—Habyarimana—"is not aware of these activities, but insist that he must immediately look into the situation."

Dallaire did as he was told, and—but for the genocide—that might have been the end of the matter. Not surprisingly, Dallaire's informant stopped informing, and last year, when the Belgian Senate established a commission to sort out the circumstances under which some of its soldiers had been slaughtered while on duty for the U.N., Kofi Annan refused to allow General Dallaire to testify. In a letter to the Belgian government, Annan explained that past and present U.N. officials were protected by diplomatic immunity, and he did not see how waiving that immunity was "in the interest of the Organization."

"THE ISSUE HERE is a lack of judgment and historical memory," Alain Destexhe, a Belgian senator, who has written several books about the international response to the Rwandan genocide, told me recently. "I would like to know if ever before, in the years since 1945, the U.N. has received a fax or a cable announcing an extermination. Look at that word: 'extermination'— registering Tutsis, killing a thousand Tutsis in twenty minutes. You should be alarmed by that. You should think of the Jews. I really don't understand it. President Clinton is obliged to justify himself for fund-raising phone calls from the White House and alleged sexual harassment, and we're talking about a million people killed, so I think the U.N. should be accountable. How can anyone sensibly think of reporting the crimes of the President of Rwanda to the President of Rwanda and pretend that he has dealt with this matter responsibly? How could such a fax not be passed on immediately to the Security Council and all the member states? How can we be left to wonder whether even the Secretary-General"—Boutros-Ghali—"saw it?"

Last year, I read Dallaire's fax to one of Boutros-Ghali's closest aides, who said that he had never heard of it before. "It's astonishing," he said, "an amazing document, incredibly dramatic. I never heard of anything like that, and I find it incredible to imagine that it could not reach the Secretary-General. This is all at a level of drama that I don't remember experiencing except once or twice in the last five years at the U.N. It's just incredible that a fax like that could come in and not be noticed."

In fact, by 1996 Boutros-Ghali was at least aware of Dallaire's fax, because he referred to it, in an introduction to a volume on Rwanda, saying, "Such situations and alarming reports from the field, though considered with the utmost seriousness by United Nations officials, are not uncommon within the context of peace-keeping operations."

When I read Boutros-Ghali's words to Destexhe, I could almost hear him shuddering over the phone from Brussels. "Not uncommon?" he said. "Extermination? No no no." Last week, I asked Iqbal Riza, Annan's deputy, whether Boutros-Ghali would have seen the correspondence. "He should have," Riza said, adding that according to "standard practice every code cable or every fax of this nature will be copied to the Secretary-General's office" and then sorted by "a staff that decides what paper goes to him."

Boutros-Ghali's aide told me that he was certain "Boutros didn't see the actual document," but that it was likely he had "heard the essence of it, in summary." Riza said, "That's credible." During that period, daily cable traffic was "a stack about a foot high," Riza explained, and Dallaire's fax "was not a report on a serious incident, where there were casualties, or something like that," but "something that was forecast." If the forecast had come true "a week later or something," Riza said, then "I think they would have said, 'Yes, there is this fax, and this is what happened.'"

THE FACT THAT Kofi Annan's name is printed atop the reply to Dallaire's fax suggests that he was its author, or at least the one ultimately responsible for its contents. But Riza, whose signature appears on the response to Dallaire's fax, claims that that wasn't the case. At the time, he said, the United Nations was overseeing seventeen peacekeeping missions, and there was no way that one person could look after them all." So duties in New York were divided, and Riza found himself in charge of Rwanda. "I was responsible," he said, adding, "This is not to say that Mr. Annan was oblivious of what was going on. No. Part of my responsibility was to keep him informed and, in fact, to ask for guidance when I felt that was necessary. So he would have seen this paper, maybe, you know, whenever he had time—two or three days later, when he went through his copies. So that takes care of that question."

In hindsight, Riza told me, "you can see all this very clearly—when you are sitting with your papers before you, with your music on, or whatever, and you can say, 'Ah, look, there's this.' When it's happening in the heat of the moment, it's something else." He described the Dallaire fax as just one piece of an ongoing daily communication. "We get hyperbole in many reports," he said, adding that, in the months that followed, "incidents continued, but there was no sign to corroborate" Dallaire's warning.

Riza reminded me that the Belgian, French, and United States Embassies in Rwanda had been advised of Dallaire's information. "If those governments, especially the Belgians, had serious fears about what was going to happen, do you think they would have kept quiet?" he asked. "They would have battered down our doors." On the other hand, Riza stressed that the caution with which the Rwanda peacekeeping mandate was interpreted had to be understood in the context of the moment—and the context was "the shadow of Somalia."

During 1993, dozens of peacekeepers died in Somalia. In the two most spectacular incidents, twenty-three Pakistanis serving with the U.N. and eighteen American soldiers serving under their own command were killed. The American deaths occurred in October, and Riza said, "If we had gone to the Security Council three months after Somalia, I can assure you no government would have said, 'Yes, here are our boys for an offensive operation in Rwanda.'" How could he be so sure? Because, one of his aides told me, even in April of 1994, when the body count in Rwanda was leaping from the tens of thousands to the hundreds of thousands, the Security Council did not see fit to act. And another U.N. staffer said, "You do understand, I hope, that when we are talking about Rwanda and we speak of member states, we are speaking in particular about Washington."

It was true that the Clinton Administration had lost its appetite for peacekeeping operations after Somalia. In the wake of that debacle, the White House produced a document called Presidential Decision Directive 25, which amounted to a checklist of reasons to avoid involvement in U.N. peacekeeping missions. It hardly mattered that no American troops were involved in Rwanda; when the genocide began, the Administration's policy was that the U.N. should get out of Rwanda completely, and the original force of two thousand five hundred men was reduced to an ineffectual squad of two hundred and seventy. Dallaire begged for reinforcements, and his pleas were seconded by Boutros-Ghali, but, as the dead piled up in Rwanda, the United States successfully obstructed the Security Council from heeding their call.

"We—the international community—should have been more active in the early stages of the atrocities in Rwanda," Secretary of State Madeleine Albright said last December on a visit to Africa, setting the stage for President Clinton's more forceful apology, this spring in Kigali. In the same spirit, Annan's staff are fond of saying, "The whole world failed Rwanda." Annan himself recently told the French newspaper *Libération*, "I remember saying at the time, 'If a genocide does not push us to intervene, what can make us budge?'" It was a good question. Once the current round of mea culpas is over, we will still be left to wonder whether the genocide might have been thwarted before it had begun.

ON MAY 2, 1994, when the extermination of Tutsis was at its peak in Rwanda, Kofi Annan travelled to Washington to address a Senate hearing on U.N. peacekeeping operations. In the course of his testimony, he said, "Under our rules of engagement, they"—peacekeepers—"have the right to defend themselves, and we define self-defense in a manner that includes preemptive military action to remove those armed elements who are preventing you from doing your work. And yet our commanders in the field, whether in Somalia and Bosnia, have been very reticent about using force."

In the light of Dallaire's fax, Annan's failure to mention Rwanda is striking. After all, Dallaire hadn't asked for the permission that Annan denied him, to take preëmptive action against the Hutu Power arsenals; he simply announced his plan to raid weapons caches. Dallaire has said that he considered such action to be entirely consistent with his rules of engagement, and he has repeatedly stated that with five thousand well-equipped men he could have saved hundreds of thousands of lives in Rwanda.

Last September, Dallaire went on Canadian television and said of his tour in Rwanda, "I'm fully responsible for the decisions of the ten Belgian soldiers dying, of others dying, of several of my soldiers being injured and falling sick because we ran out of medical supplies, of fifty-six Red Cross people being killed, of two million people being displaced and made refugees, and about a million Rwandans being killed—because the mission failed, and I consider myself intimately involved with that responsibility." But Dallaire resisted "passing the buck" to the U.N. system. Instead, he passed it on to the member states of the Security Council and the General Assembly. If, in the face of a genocide, governments fear placing their soldiers at risk, "then don't send soldiers, send Boy Scouts," he said.

"I haven't even started my real mourning of the apathy and the absolute detachment of the international community—particularly the Western world—from the plight of Rwandans," Dallaire went on. "Because, fundamentally, to be very candid and soldierly, who the hell cared about Rwanda? . . . We know the genocide of the Second World War because the whole outfit was involved. . . . Who really comprehends that more people were killed, injured, and displaced in three and a half months in Rwanda than in the whole of the Yugoslavian campaign, in which we poured sixty thousand troops and more. The whole of the Western world is there—we're pouring billions in there, and we're still in there trying to solve the problem. Who is really trying to solve the Rwandan problem? Who is grieving Rwanda and really living it and living with the consequences? I mean, there are hundreds of Rwandans whom I knew personally, whom I found slaughtered with their families complete—and bodies up to here—villages totally wiped out. . . . And we made all that information available daily and the international community kept watching."

Dallaire was in uniform as he faced the camera; his graying hair was closely cropped; he held his square jaw firmly outthrust; his chest was dappled with decorations. He said, "The root of it is: What does the international community really want the U.N. to do?" He said, "The U.N. simply wasn't given the tools." And he said, "We did not want to take on the Rwandan Armed Forces and the *interahamwe.*"

Listening to Dallaire, I wondered, What would happen if a fax like his were to arrive at U.N. headquarters today?

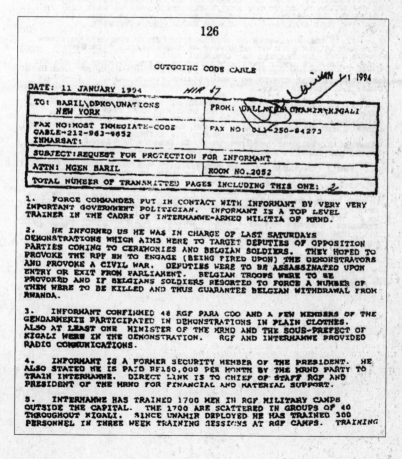

126

OUTGOING CODE CABLE

JAN 11 1994

DATE: 11 JANUARY 1994   *HIR 67*

TO: BARIL\DPKO\UNATIONS NEW YORK   FROM: DALLAIRE\UNAMIR\KIGALI

FAX NO:MOST IMMEDIATE-CODE CABLE-212-963-9852 INMARSAT: FAX NO: 011-250-84273

SUBJECT:REQUEST FOR PROTECTION FOR INFORMANT

ATTN: MGEN BARIL   ROOM NO.2052

TOTAL NUMBER OF TRANSMITTED PAGES INCLUDING THIS ONE: 2

1.   FORCE COMMANDER PUT IN CONTACT WITH INFORMANT BY VERY VERY IMPORTANT GOVERNMENT POLITICIAN. INFORMANT IS A TOP LEVEL TRAINER IN THE CADRE OF INTERAHAMWE-ARMED MILITIA OF MRND.

2.   HE INFORMED US HE WAS IN CHARGE OF LAST SATURDAYS DEMONSTRATIONS WHICH AIMS WERE TO TARGET DEPUTIES OF OPPOSITION PARTIES COMING TO CEREMONIES AND BELGIAN SOLDIERS. THEY HOPED TO PROVOKE THE RPF BN TO ENGAGE (BEING FIRED UPON) THE DEMONSTRATORS AND PROVOKE A CIVIL WAR. DEPUTIES WERE TO BE ASSASSINATED UPON ENTRY OR EXIT FROM PARLIAMENT. BELGIAN TROOPS WERE TO BE PROVOKED AND IF BELGIANS SOLDIERS RESORTED TO FORCE A NUMBER OF THEM WERE TO BE KILLED AND THUS GUARANTEE BELGIAN WITHDRAWAL FROM RWANDA.

3.   INFORMANT CONFIRMED 48 RGF PARA CDO AND A FEW MEMBERS OF THE GENDARMERIE PARTICIPATED IN DEMONSTRATIONS IN PLAIN CLOTHES. ALSO AT LEAST ONE MINISTER OF THE MRND AND THE SOUS-PREFECT OF KIGALI WERE IN THE DEMONSTRATION. RGF AND INTERAHAMWE PROVIDED RADIO COMMUNICATIONS.

4.   INFORMANT IS A FORMER SECURITY MEMBER OF THE PRESIDENT. HE ALSO STATED HE IS PAID RF150,000 PER MONTH BY THE MRND PARTY TO TRAIN INTERAHAMWE. DIRECT LINK IS TO CHIEF OF STAFF RGF AND PRESIDENT OF THE MRND FOR FINANCIAL AND MATERIAL SUPPORT.

5.   INTERAHAMWE HAS TRAINED 1700 MEN IN RGF MILITARY CAMPS OUTSIDE THE CAPITAL. THE 1700 ARE SCATTERED IN GROUPS OF 40 THROUGHOUT KIGALI. SINCE UNAMIR DEPLOYED HE HAS TRAINED 300 PERSONNEL IN THREE WEEK TRAINING SESSIONS AT RGF CAMPS. TRAINING

2/2

FOCUS WAS DISCIPLINE, WEAPONS, EXPLOSIVES, CLOSE COMBAT AND TACTICS.

6.   PRINCIPAL AIM OF INTERHAMWE IN THE PAST WAS TO PROTECT KIGALI FROM RPF. SINCE UNAMIR MANDATE HE HAS BEEN ORDERED TO REGISTER ALL TUTSI IN KIGALI. HE SUSPECTS IT IS FOR THEIR EXTERMINATION. EXAMPLE HE GAVE WAS THAT IN 20 MINUTES HIS PERSONNEL COULD KILL UP TO 1000 TUTSIS.

7.   INFORMANT STATES HE DISAGREES WITH ANTI-TUTSI EXTERMINATION. HE SUPPORTS OPPOSITION TO RPF BUT CANNOT SUPPORT KILLING OF INNOCENT PERSONS.   HE ALSO STATED THAT HE BELIEVES THE PRESIDENT DOES NOT HAVE FULL CONTROL OVER ALL ELEMENTS OF HIS OLD PARTY\FACTION.

8.   INFORMANT IS PREPARED TO PROVIDE LOCATION OF MAJOR WEAPONS CACHE WITH AT LEAST 135 WEAPONS.   HE ALREADY HAS DISTRIBUTED 110 WEAPONS INCLUDING 35 WITH AMMUNITION AND CAN GIVE US DETAILS OF THEIR LOCATION.   TYPE OF WEAPONS ARE G3 AND AK47 PROVIDED BY RGF HE WAS READY TO GO TO THE ARMS CACHE TONIGHT-IF WE GAVE HIM THE FOLLOWING GUARANTEE.   HE REQUESTS THAT HE AND HIS FAMILY (HIS WIFE AND FOUR CHILDREN) BE PLACED UNDER OUR PROTECTION.

9.   IT IS OUR INTENTION TO TAKE ACTION WITHIN THE NEXT 36 HOURS WITH A POSSIBLE H HR OF WEDNESDAY AT DAWN (LOCAL).   INFORMANT STATES THAT HOSTILITIES MAY COMMENCE AGAIN IF POLITICAL DEADLOCK ENDS.   VIOLENCE COULD TAKE PLACE DAY OF THE CEREMONIES OR THE DAY AFTER.   THEREFORE WEDNESDAY WILL GIVE GREATEST CHANCE OF SUCCESS AND ALSO BE MOST TIMELY TO PROVIDE SIGNIFICANT INPUT TO ON-GOING POLITICAL NEGOTIATIONS.

10.   IT IS RECOMMENDED THE INFORMANT BE GRANTED PROTECTION AND EVACUATED OUT OF RWANDA.   THIS HQ DOES NOT HAVE PREVIOUS UN EXPERIENCE IN SUCH MATTERS AND URGENTLY REQUESTS GUIDANCE.   NO CONTACT HAS AS YET BEEN MADE TO ANY EMBASSY IN ORDER TO INQUIRE IF THEY ARE PREPARED TO PROTECT HIM FOR A PERIOD OF TIME BY GRANTING DIPLOMATIC IMMUNITY IN THEIR EMBASSY IN KIGALI BEFORE MOVING HIM AND HIS FAMILY OUT OF THE COUNTRY.

11.   FORCE COMMANDER WILL BE MEETING WITH THE VERY VERY IMPORTANT POLITICAL PERSON TOMORROW MORNING IN ORDER TO ENSURE THAT THIS INDIVIDUAL IS CONSCIOUS OF ALL PARAMETERS OF HIS INVOLVEMENT. FORCE COMMANDER DOES HAVE CERTAIN RESERVATIONS ON THE SUDDENNESS OF THE CHANGE OF HEART OF THE INFORMANT TO COME CLEAN WITH THIS INFORMATION.   RECCE OF ARMED CACHE AND DETAILED PLANNING OF RAID TO GO ON LATE TOMORROW.   POSSIBILITY OF A TRAP NOT FULLY EXCLUDED, AS THIS MAY BE A SET-UP AGAINST THE VERY VERY IMPORTANT POLITICAL PERSON.   FORCE COMMANDER TO INFORM SRSG FIRST THING IN MORNING TO ENSURE HIS SUPPORT.

13.   PEUX CE QUE VEUX.   ALLONS-Y.

The Dallaire "Genocide Fax."

PART VIII

Health and
the Environment

Introduction to
Roy Norr's

"Cancer by the Carton"

I N 1938, Dr. Raymond Pearl, a biologist at Johns Hopkins University, presented a paper to the New York Academy of Medicine reporting on the scientific results of a study of the life histories of 7,000 people, concluding that tobacco smokers do not live as long as nonsmokers. Dr. Pearl's startling conclusion should have generated headlines across the country—the Associated Press, United Press, and reporters from New York newspapers all covered Dr. Pearl's presentation—but the story appeared in only a few papers, buried in a paragraph or two.

Three years later, *In Fact: An Antidote to Falsehoods in the Daily Press,* a newsletter written by press critic and investigative reporter George Seldes, published a story about Dr. Pearl's findings, noting that newspapers had ignored the story out of fear of offending tobacco advertisers. At the time, Seldes was one of the only writers publishing articles on the harmful effects of tobacco. In 1950, for example, after writing over thirty articles on the subject for his newsletter, he published a story entitled "Cancer and Tobacco News Suppressed." *In Fact* had more subscribers at its peak in 1947 than *The Nation* and *The New Republic* combined. But what was the reaction to his tobacco stories? Indifference.

Then in December 1952, after *In Fact* had ceased publication, a two-page article, by Roy Norr entitled "Cancer by the Carton," condensed from *The Christian Herald,* appeared in the *Reader's Digest.* With a circulation of seven million, *Reader's Digest* was America's most widely read publication—and it carried no advertising. The short article had a powerful impact. The following year cigarette smoking declined in America for

the first time in twenty years. Two years after the article, tobacco companies formed the Tobacco Industry Research Council to counter what they
regarded as a serious threat to their business. This resulted in "safer" cigarettes such as cigarettes with filters and low tar. *Time, Newsweek,* and
other publications began to report scientific studies on the health costs of
tobacco products.

Finally, in 1964, the Surgeon General of the United States issued a
landmark report on "Smoking and Health," which concluded: "Cigarette
smoking is a health hazard of sufficient importance in the United States
to warrant appropriate remedial action." "Cancer by the Carton" is a stunning example of a secret history that broke through the popular press bar-
rier and thereby led to improved health for countless people. Nevertheless,
for years after, the cigarette industry continued lying to the public about
addiction and the harmful effects of smoking.

ADDITIONAL SOURCES

Holhut, Randolph T., ed. *The George Seldes Reader: An Anthology of the Writings of America's
Foremost Journalistic Gadfly.* New York: Barricade Books, 1994.
Mann, Michael, director. *The Insider.* Touchstone Pictures, 1999.
Seldes, George. "Tobacco Shortens Life," *In Fact,* January 13, 1941.
———. "Tobacco and Cancer," *In Fact,* November 17, 1947.
———. "Cancer and Tobacco News Suppressed," *In Fact,* October 2, 1950.

Roy Norr

"Cancer by the Carton"

READER'S DIGEST, DECEMBER 1952

CONDENSED FROM *THE CHRISTIAN HERALD*

FOR THREE DECADES the medical controversy over the part played by smoking in the rise of bronchiogenic carcinoma, better known as cancer of the lung, has largely been kept from public notice. More than twenty-six years ago the late Dr. James Ewing, distinguished pathologist and leading spirit in the organization of the American Association for Cancer Research (now the American Cancer Society), pleaded for a public educational campaign.

"One may hardly aim to eliminate the tobacco habit," he wrote in his famous essay on cancer prevention, "but cancer propaganda should emphasize the danger signs that go with it."

No one questions that tobacco smoke irritates the mucous lining of the mouth, nose and throat, or that it aggravates hoarseness, coughing, chronic bronchitis and tonsillitis. It is accepted without argument that smoking is forbidden in cases of gastric and duodenal ulcers; that it interferes with normal digestion; that it contracts the blood vessels, increases the heart rate, raises the blood pressure. In many involvements of heart disease, the first order from the doctor is to cut out smoking immediately.

But what gives grave concern to public-health leaders is that the increase in lung-cancer mortality shows a suspicious parallel to the enormous increase in cigarette consumption (now 2,500 cigarettes per year for every human being in the United States).

The latest study, which is published in *The Journal of the American Medical Association* (May 27, 1952), by a group of noted cancer workers headed by Dr. Alton Ochsner, former president of the American Cancer Society and director of the famous Ochsner Clinic in New Orleans, discloses that, during the period 1920 to 1948, deaths from bronchiogenic carcinoma in the United States increased *more than ten times,* from 1.1 to 11.3 per 100,000 of the population. From 1938 to 1948, lung-cancer deaths increased *144 percent.* At the present time cancer of the mouth and respiratory tract kills 19,000 men and 5,000 women annually in the United States.

"It is probable that bronchiogenic carcinoma soon will become more frequent than any other cancer of the body, unless something is done to prevent its increase," is Dr. Ochsner's conclusion. "It is frightening to speculate on the possible number of bronchiogenic cancers that might develop as the result of the tremendous number of cigarettes consumed in the two decades from 1930 to 1950."

A survey recently published by the United Nations World Health Organization cites the conclusion of an investigation carried out by the Medical Research Council of England and Wales that "above the age of forty-five the risk of developing the disease increases in simple proportion with the amount smoked, and may be fifty times as great among those who smoked twenty-five or more cigarettes daily as among nonsmokers."

A study of 684 cases, made by Ernest L. Wynder and Evarts A. Graham for the American Cancer Society and published in the AMA *Journal,* May 27, 1950, stated this conclusion: "Excessive and prolonged use of tobacco, especially cigarettes, seems to be an important factor in the induction of bronchiogenic carcinoma."

More recently Wynder, now associated with Memorial Cancer Center in New York, expanded the statement: "The more a person smokes the greater is the risk of developing cancer of the lung, whereas the risk was small in a nonsmoker or a light smoker."

In his summary *Some Practical Aspects of Cancer Prevention,* Wynder lists tobacco as the *major factor* in cancer of the larynx, the pharynx, the esophagus and the oral cavity. "In 1926," he points out, "Ewing wrote that 'though a great body of clinical information shows that many forms of cancer are due to preventable causes there has been little systematic research to impress this fact on the medical profession or to convey it to the public.' This was true then, as it is today."

After a study of world-wide medical opinion, Wynder reaches the same conclusion arrived at by Ewing twenty-six years ago. "Cancer of the lung," he reports, "presents one of the most striking opportunities for preventive measures in cancer."

Cancer workers want something done, and done now on the basis of present clinical knowledge, to alert the smoking public.

Introduction to
Greg Palast's

"A Well-Designed Disaster"

O N MARCH 24, 1989, the oil tanker *Exxon Valdez,* owned by the Exxon Shipping Company, ran aground on Bligh Reef in Prince William Sound, just twenty-five miles from Valdez, Alaska. Eight cargo tanks ruptured, spewing about eleven million gallons of crude oil into the sound. By the time the ship was refloated twelve days later, over a thousand miles of shoreline were polluted by oil, and thousands of fishermen were out of work. It was the largest tanker spill affecting American shores in U.S. history.

The disaster was blamed on Captain Joe Hazelwood, who had a record of drunk driving arrests. He was charged with criminal mischief, driving a watercraft while intoxicated, reckless endangerment, and negligent discharge of oil. He was found guilty of the last count, fined $51,000 and sentenced to 1,000 hours of community service in lieu of six months in prison.

After repairs, the *Exxon Valdez* itself reentered service in 1990, loading oil in the Persian Gulf. Exxon agreed to pay $1 billion to settle civil and criminal charges related to the case. But a lawsuit brought by fishermen, property owners, businesses, and communities who said they were harmed by the oil spill was still being appealed by Exxon some fifteen years after the incident.

Greg Palast is an investigative journalist who has reported for a number of publications and TV outlets including *The Guardian* in London and BBC Television's *Newsnight.* After three years of research, Palast found "a twenty-year train of doctored safety records, illicit deals between oil company chiefs, and programmatic harassment of witnesses. . . . Our summary of evidence ran to four volumes. Virtually none of it was reported: The media had turned off its radar. Here's a bit of the story you've never been told."

ADDITIONAL SOURCES

Davidson, Art. *In the Wake of the* "Exxon Valdez": *The Devastating Impact of the Alaska Oil Spill.* New York: Random House, 1990.

Keeble, John. *Out of the Channel: The* Exxon Valdez *Oil Spill in Prince William Sound.* Cheney, Wash.: Eastern Washington University Press, 1999.

Ott, Riki. *Sound Truth and Corporate Myth$: The Legacy of the* Exxon Valdez *Oil Spill.* Seattle, Wash.: Dragonfly Sisters Press, 2005.

Greg Palast

A Well-Designed Disaster:
The Untold Story of the Exxon Valdez

THE BEST DEMOCRACY MONEY CAN BUY: THE TRUTH ABOUT CORPORATE

CONS, GLOBALIZATION, AND HIGH-FINANCE FRAUDSTERS, 2004

O N MARCH 24, 1989, the *Exxon Valdez* broke open and covered twelve
hundred miles of Alaska's shoreline with oily sludge.

The official story remains "Drunken Skipper Hits Reef." Don't believe it.

In fact, when the ship hit, Captain Joe Hazelwood was nowhere near
the wheel, but belowdecks, sleeping off his bender. The man left at the
helm, the third mate, would never have hit Bligh Reef had he simply
looked at his Raycas radar. But he could not, because the radar *was not
turned on*. The complex Raycas system costs a lot to operate, so frugal
Exxon management left it broken and useless for the entire year before
the grounding.

The land Exxon smeared and destroyed belongs to the Chugach natives
of the Prince William Sound. Within days of the spill, the Chugach tribal
corporation asked me and my partner Lenora Stewart to investigate allegations of fraud by Exxon and the little-known "Alyeska" consortium. In three
years' digging, we followed a twenty-year train of doctored safety records,
illicit deals between oil company chiefs, and programmatic harassment of
witnesses. And we documented the oil majors' brilliant success in that old
American sport, cheating the natives. Our summary of evidence ran to four
volumes. Virtually none of it was reported: The media had turned off its
radar. Here's a bit of the story you've never been told:

- We discovered an internal memo describing a closed, top-level
  meeting of oil company executives in Arizona held just ten

months before the spill. It was a meeting of the "Alyeska Owners Committee," the six-company combine that owns the Alaska pipeline and most of the state's oil. In that meeting, say the notes, the chief of their Valdez operations, Theo Polasek, warned executives that containing an oil spill "at the mid-point of Prince William Sound not possible with present equipment"—exactly where the *Exxon Valdez* grounded. Polasek needed millions of dollars for spill-containment equipment. The law required it; the companies promised it to regulators; then at the meeting the proposed spending was voted down. The oil company combine had a cheaper plan to contain any spill—don't bother. According to an internal memorandum, they'd just drop some dispersants and walk away. That's exactly what happened. "At the owners committee meeting in Phoenix, it was decided that Alyeska would provide immediate response to oil spills in Valdez Arm and Valdez Narrows only"—not the Prince William Sound.

• Smaller spills before the Exxon disaster would have alerted government watchdogs that the port's oil-spill-containment system was not up to scratch. But the oil group's lab technician, Erlene Blake, told us that management routinely ordered her to change test results to eliminate "oil-in-water" readings. The procedure was simple, says Blake. She was told to dump out oily water and refill test tubes from a bucket of cleansed sea water, which they called "the Miracle Barrel."

• A confidential letter dated April 1984, fully four years before the big spill, written by Captain James Woodle, then the oil group's Valdez Port commander, warns management that "Due to a reduction in manning, age of equipment, limited training and lack of personnel, serious doubt exists that [we] would be able to contain and clean up effectively a medium or large size oil spill." Woodle told us there was a spill at Valdez *before* the *Exxon Valdez* collision, though not nearly as large. When he prepared to report it to the government, his supervisor forced him to take back the notice, with the Orwellian command, "You made a mistake. This was not an oil spill."

Slimey Limeys

The canard of the alcoholic captain has provided effective camouflage for a party with arguably more culpability than Exxon: British Petroleum, the company that in 2001 painted itself green (literally: all its gas stations and propaganda pamphlets now sport a seasick green hue). Alaska's oil is BP oil. The company owns and controls a near majority (46 percent) of the Alaska pipeline system. Exxon (now ExxonMobil) is a junior partner, and four other oil companies are just along for the ride. Captain Woodle, Technician Blake, Vice President Polasek, all worked for BP's Alyeska.

Quite naturally, British Petroleum has never rushed to have its name associated with Alyeska's recklessness. But BP's London headquarters, I discovered, knew of the alleged falsification of reports to the U.S. government *nine* years before the spill. In September 1984, independent oil shipper Charles Hamel of Washington, DC, shaken by evidence he received from Alyeska employees, told me he took the first available Concorde, at his own expense, to warn BP executives in London about scandalous goings-on in Valdez. Furthermore, Captain Woodle swears he personally delivered his list of missing equipment and "phantom" personnel directly into the hands of BP's Alaska chief, George Nelson.

BP has never been eager for Woodle's letter, Hamel's London trip and many other warnings of the deteriorating containment system to see the light of day. When Alyeska got wind of Woodle's complaints, they responded by showing Woodle a file of his marital infidelities (all bogus), then offered him payouts on condition that he leave the state within days, promising never to return.

As to Hamel, the oil shipping broker, BP in London thanked him. Then a secret campaign was launched to hound him out of the industry. A CIA expert was hired who wiretapped Hamel's phone lines. They smuggled microphones into his home, intercepted his mail and tried to entrap him with young women. The industrial espionage assault was personally ordered and controlled by BP executive James Hermiller, president of Alyeska. On this caper, they were caught. A U.S. federal judge told Alyeska this conduct was "reminiscent of Nazi Germany."

Cheaper Than Manhattan

BP's inglorious role in the Alaskan oil game began in 1969 when the oil group bought the most valuable real estate in all Alaska, the Valdez oil terminal land, from the Chugach natives. BP and the Alyeska group paid the natives *one dollar*.

Arthur Goldberg, once a U.S. Supreme Court justice, tried to help the natives on their land claim. But the natives' own lawyer, the state's most powerful legislator, advised them against pressing for payment. Later, that lawyer became Alyeska's lawyer.

The Alaskan natives, the last Americans who lived off what they hunted and caught, did extract written promises from the oil consortium to keep the Prince William Sound safe from oil spills. These wilderness seal hunters and fishermen knew the arctic sea. Eyak Chief-for-Life Agnes Nichols, Tatitlek native leader George Gordaoff and Chenega fisherman Paul Kompkoff demanded that tankers carry state-of-the-art radar and that emergency vessels escort the tankers. The oil companies reluctantly agreed to put all this in their government-approved 1973 Oil Spill Response Plan.

When it comes to oil spills, the name of the game is "containment" because, radar or not, some tanker somewhere is going to hit the rocks. Stopping an oil spill catastrophe is a no-brainer. Tanker radar aside, if a ship does smack a reef, all that's needed is to surround the ship with a big rubber curtain ("boom") and suck up the corralled oil. In signed letters to the state government and Coast Guard, BP, ExxonMobil and partners promised that no oil would move unless the equipment was set on the tanker route and the oil-sucker ship ("containment barge") was close by, in the water and ready to go.

The oil majors fulfilled their promise the cheapest way: They lied. When the *Exxon Valdez* struck Bligh Reef, the spill equipment, which could have prevented the catastrophe, wasn't there—see the Arizona meeting notes above. The promised escort ships were not assigned to ride with the tankers until *after* the spill. And the night the *Exxon Valdez* grounded, the emergency spill-response barge was sitting in a dry dock in Valdez locked in ice.

When the pipeline opened in 1974, the law required Alyeska to maintain round-the-clock oil-spill-response teams. As part of the come-on to get hold of the Chugach's Valdez property, Alyeska hired the natives for this emergency work. The natives practiced leaping out of helicopters into icy water, learning to surround leaking boats with rubber barriers. But the natives soon found they were assigned to cover up spills, not clean them up. Their foreman, David Decker, told me he was expected to report one oil spill as two gallons when two thousand gallons had spilled.

Alyeska kept the natives at the terminal for two years—long enough to help Alyeska break the strike of the dock workers' union—then quietly sacked the entire team. To deflect inquisitive inspectors looking for the spill-response workers, Alyeska created sham emergency teams, listing names of oil terminal employees who had not the foggiest idea how to use spill equipment, which, in any event, was missing, broken or existed only on paper. When the *Exxon Valdez* grounded, there was no native spill crew, only chaos.

The Fable of the Drunken Skipper has served the oil industry well. It transforms the most destructive oil spill in history into a tale of human frailty, a terrible, but onetime, accident. But broken radar, missing equipment, phantom spill personnel, faked tests—all of it to cut costs and lift bottom lines—made the spill disaster not an accident but an inevitability.

I went back to the Sound just before the tenth anniversary of the spill. On Chenega, they were preparing to spend another summer scrubbing rocks. A decade after the spill, in one season, they pulled twenty tons of sludge off their beaches. At Nanwalek village ten years on, the state again declared the clams inedible, poisoned by "persistent hydrocarbons." Salmon still carry abscesses and tumors, the herring never returned and the sea lion rookery at Montague Island remains silent and empty.

But despite what my eyes see, I must have it wrong, because right here in an Exxon brochure it says, "The water is clean and plant, animal and sea life are healthy and abundant."

Go to the Sound today, on Chugach land, kick over a rock and you'll get a whiff of an Exxon gas station.

EVERYONE'S HEARD OF THE big jury verdict against Exxon: a $5 billion award. What you haven't heard is that ExxonMobil hasn't paid a dime of it. It's been a decade since the trial. BP painted itself green and ExxonMobil decided to paint the White House with green: It's the number-two lifetime donor to George W. Bush's career (after Enron), with a little splashed the Democrats' way. The oil industry's legal stalls, the "tort reform" campaigns and the generous investment in our democratic process has produced a Supreme Court and appeals panels that look more like luncheon clubs of corporate consiglieri than panels of defenders of justice. In November 2001, following directives of the Supremes, the Ninth Circuit Court of Appeals overturned the jury verdict on grounds the punishment was too dear and severe for poor little ExxonMobil.

The BP-led Alyeska consortium was able to settle all claims for 2 percent of the acknowledged damage, roughly a $50 million payout, fully covered by an insurance fund.

And the natives? While waiting for Exxon to make good on promises of compensation, Chief Agnes and Paul Kompkoff have passed away. As to my four-volume summary of evidence of frauds committed against the natives: In 1991, when herring failed to appear and fishing in the Sound collapsed, the tribal corporation went bankrupt and my files became, effectively, useless.

Coda: Nanwalek Rocks[1]

At the far side of Alaska's Kenai Fjord glacier, a heavily armed and musically original rock-and-roll band held lockdown control of the politics and treasury of Nanwalek, a Chugach native village.

According to not-so-old legend, rock came to the remote enclave at the bottom of Prince William Sound in the 1950s when Chief Vincent Kvasnikoff found an electric guitar washed up on the beach. By the next morning, he had mastered the instrument sufficiently to perform passable covers of Elvis tunes. Of all the lies the natives told me since I began work there in 1989, this one, from the chief himself, seemed the most benign.

When I first went to work there in 1989, I sat with the chief in his kitchen, across from an elaborate Orthodox altar. Russian icons were spread the length of the wall. It was a golden day, late summer at the end of the salmon run, but the chief's eighteen-year-old nephew hung out in the bungalow watching a repeating loop of Fred Astaire movies on the satellite TV.

Fishing was just excellent, the chief assured me. He'd taken twelve seals that year. I didn't challenge the old man, legless in his wheelchair. Everyone knew he'd lost his boat when the bank repossessed his commercial fishing license.

The village once had eight commercial boats, now it had three. Besides, all the seal had been poisoned eight years earlier, in 1989, by Exxon's oil.

It took an entire month for the oil slick from the *Exxon Valdez* to reach Nanwalek. Despite the known, unrelenting advance of the oil sheet, Exxon had not provided even simple rubber barriers to protect the inlets to the five lakes that spawned the salmon and fed the razor clams, sea lions, bidarki snails, seals and people of the isolated village on the ice. But when the oil did arrive, followed by television crews, Exxon put virtually the entire populace of 270 on its payroll.

"The place went wild," Lisa Moonan told me. "They gave us rags and buckets, $16-something an hour to wipe off rocks, to baby-sit our own children." In this roadless village that had survived with little cash or store-bought food, the chief's sister told me, "They flew in frozen pizza, satellite dishes. Guys who were on sobriety started drinking all night, beating up their wives. I mean, all that money. Man, people just went berserk."

With the catch dead, the banks took the few boats they had, and Chief Vincent's sister, Sally Kvasnikoff Ash, watched the village slide into an alcohol- and drug-soaked lethargy. Sally said, "I felt like my skin was peeling off." Nanwalek's natives call themselves Sugestoon, Real People. "After the oil I thought, this is it. We're over. Sugestoon, we're gone unless something happens."

Sally made something happen. In August 1995, the village women swept the all-male tribal council from office in an electoral coup plotted partly in the native tongue, which the men had forgotten. Sally, who's Sugestoon name Aqniaqnaq means "First Sister," would have become chief if Vincent, she says, hadn't stolen two votes. The rockers, Chief Vincent's sons, were out—so was booze (banned), fast food and the band's party nights in accordance with the new women's council cultural revolutionary diktats. The women returned native language to the school and replaced at least some of Kvasnikoff 's all-night jam sessions, which had a tendency to end in drunken brawls, with performances of the traditional Seal and Killer Whale dances.

They put the village on a health-food regimen. "We're fat," says First Sister, who blames the store-bought diet which, since the spill, must be flown in twice weekly from city supermarkets. To show they meant business on the alcohol ban, the women arrested and jailed Sally's disabled Uncle Mack for bringing a six-pack of beer into the village on his return from the hospital.

On good friday 1964, the snow-peaked mountains of Montague Island rose twenty-six feet in the air, then dropped back twelve feet, sending a tidal wave through the Prince William Sound. At the village of Chenega, Chugach seal hunter Nikolas Kompkoff ran his four daughters out of their stilt house, already twisted to sticks by the earthquake, and raced up an ice-covered slope. Just before the wall of water overcame them, he grabbed the two girls closest, one child under each arm, ran ahead, then watched his other two daughters wash out into the Sound.

Chenega disappeared. Not one of their homes, not even the sturdier church, remained. A third of the natives drowned. Survivors waited for two days until a postal pilot remembered the remote village.

Over the following twenty years, Chenegans scattered across the Sound, some to temporary huts in other Chugach villages, others to city life in Anchorage. But every Holy Week, these families sailed to the old village, laid crosses on the decaying debris, and Kompkoff would announce another plan to rebuild. Over the years, as the prospect of a New Chenega receded into improbability, Nikolas became, in turn, an Orthodox priest, a notorious alcoholic and failed suicide. He survived a self-inflicted gunshot to the head; however, he was defrocked for the attempt.

In 1982, Nikolas convinced his nephew, Larry Evanoff, to spend his life savings building a boat that could traverse the Sound.

Evanoff has four long scars across his torso. These wounds from Vietnam helped him get a government job as an air traffic controller in Anchorage, but he was fired when his union went on strike. Larry had lost both his parents in the earthquake and tidal wave.

Larry's boat was not finished until the subarctic winter had set in. Nevertheless, he sailed to remote Evans Island with his wife and two children, aged nine and fourteen. They built a cabin and, for two years, without phone or shortwave radio, one hundred miles from any road, lived off nearby seal, bear and salmon while they cleared the land for New Chenega. Over the next seven years, twenty-six of Chenega's refugee families joined the Evanoffs, built their own homes and, with scrap wood from an abandoned herring saltery, built a tiny church with a blue roof for Nikolas, whom they still called "Father."

On March 24, 1989, the village commemorated the twenty-fifth anniversary of the tidal wave. That night, the *Exxon Valdez* oil tanker ran aground and killed the fish, smothered the clam beds and poisoned all the seal on which Chenegans subsisted.

In mid-century, the average life expectancy for Chugach natives was thirty-eight years. They had next to nothing by way of cash and the state moved to take even that away. In the 1970s, new "limited entry" laws barred natives from selling the catch from their traditional fishing grounds unless they purchased permits few could afford. The natives did have tenuous ownership of wilderness, villages and campsites. In 1969, America's largest oil deposit was discovered on Alaska's north slope. The Chugach campsite on Valdez Harbor happened to be the only place on the entire Alaska coast that could geologically support an oil tanker terminal. Their strip of land grew in value to tens or even hundreds of millions of dollars. In June of that year, Chief Vincent's father, Sarjius, representing Nanwalek, and Father Nikolas, representing the nonexistent Chenega, agreed to sell Valdez to British Petroleum and Humble Oil (later called Exxon)—for the aforementioned one dollar.

The one-dollar sale was engineered by the Chugach's attorney, Clifford Groh. Before he moved on to his next gig as an oil company lawyer, Groh transformed the Chugach utterly and forever. No longer would Chugach be a tribe; Groh *incorporated* them.

The tribe became Chugach Corporation. The villages became Chenega Corporation and English Bay (Nanwalek) Corporation. The chiefs' powers were taken over by corporate presidents and CEOs, tribal councils by boards of directors. The Sound's natives, once tribe members, became shareholders—at least for a few years until the stock was sold, bequeathed, dispersed. Today, only eleven of Chenega's sixty-nine shareholders live on the island. Most residents are tenants of a corporation whose last annual meeting was held in Seattle, two thousand miles from the island.

I first met the president of Chenega Corporation, Charles "Chuck" Totemoff, soon after the spill when he missed our meeting to negotiate with Exxon. I found the twenty-something wandering the village's dirt pathway in soiled jeans, stoned and hungover, avoiding the corporate "office," an old cabin near the fishing dock.

Years later, I met up with Chuck at Chenega Corporation's glass-and-steel office tower in downtown Anchorage. The stern, long-sober and determined executive sat behind a mahogany desk and unused laptop computer. Instead of photos of the village, a huge map of Chenega's property covered the wall, color-coded for timber logging, real estate subdivision and resort development.

He had penned a multimillion-dollar terminal services agreement with the Exxon-BP pipeline consortium. For Chenega Island, a forty-six-room hotel was in the works.

In 1997, I returned to Chenega. It was the worst possible day for a visit. Larry was out on "pad patrol," leading a native crew cleaning up tons of toxic crude oil still oozing out of Sleepy Bay eight years after the *Exxon Valdez* grounding. They'd already lost a day of work that week for Frankie Gursky's funeral, an eighteen-year-old who had shot himself after a drink-fueled fight with his grandmother.

Larry and his team continued to scour the oil off the beach, his family's old fishing ground, but it wasn't theirs anymore. The day before, the corporation had sold it, along with 90 percent of Chenega's lands, to an Exxon-BP trust for $23 million.

"Corporation can't sell it," Larry said, when I told him about the check transfer. "People really can't own land." He rammed a hydraulic injector under the beach shingle and pumped in biological dispersants. "The land was always here. We're just passing through. We make use of it, then we just pass it on." Nanwalek also sold. Chief Vincent's son, leader of the Nanwalek Village rock band and director of the corporate board, arranged to sell 50 percent of the village land to an Exxon trust.

I was in corporate president Totemoff 's office the day Exxon wired in the $23 million. When Totemoff moved out of the village, he announced, "I hope I never have to see this place again." Now he doesn't have to. I asked Chuck if, like some city-dwelling natives, he had his relatives ship him traditional foods. "Seal meat?" He grinned. "Ever smell that shit? Give me a Big Mac any time."

NOTE

1. This diary of life in the native villages of the Prince William Sound was nearly censored out of *Index on Censorship*. The magazine had hired a guest editor for the "Tribes" issue, an amateur anthropologist. He'd been to the same group of Alaskan villages where I worked. The natives performed their special ceremony for him. Among themselves they call it "Putting on the feathers," in which they provide those quaint and expected lines that so please earnest white men with 16mm Airflex cameras and digital tape recorders. The great white anthropologist wrote down "healing poems" about "our friend the bear." I imagined him with helmet and pukka shorts preserving in his leather notebook the words of the ancient, wizened Injuns. Stanley Livingstone meets Pocahontas.

It was my terrible, self-inflicted misfortune to spoil this delicate idyll of the Noble Savage by my reporting that Alaskan natives are, in fact, very much like us, if not more so.

PART IX

Abuses of Power

Introduction to
"The Nixon White House Tapes"

IN FEBRUARY 1971, President Nixon secretly installed a voice-activated taping system in the Oval Office, on which he recorded thousands of hours of conversations with his staff, members of Congress, and others who were unaware that the conversations were being taped. The recording system was publicly revealed for the first time by a White House aide during the hearings into the Watergate break-in, and the taped evidence revealed that Nixon knew about the break-in and the subsequent cover-up. The evidence was the crucial factor in forcing Nixon to resign as president in August 1974.

In the first selection, Nixon talks about retaliating against major contributors to the Democratic party—whom he perceives as Jews—as a response to the questioning of evangelist Billy Graham, Nixon's friend, by the Internal Revenue Service. In the other tapes, Nixon discusses the so-called Huston Plan, named after presidential aide Tom Charles Huston, which called for the White House to coordinate an inter-agency program of domestic intelligence aimed at so-called dissidents utilizing such tactics as wiretapping and burglaries. Discussing the Huston Plan, which they justify as a response to the riots and demonstrations of the late 1960s and early 1970s, Nixon and Chief of Staff Alexander Haig reveal a lack of understanding of the causes of the civil discontent and exhibit a near total disregard for civil liberties.

Throughout the tapes, Nixon remains concerned primarily about his image rather than the nation's welfare. Most of the tapes revolve around the question: Does this hurt or help me politically? Similarly, a following segment reveals that FBI Director J. Edgar Hoover rescinded the Huston Plan not because of legal concerns but because he thought it would hurt his own reputation.

Nixon, Haig, and Buzhardt spend a great deal of effort trying to find documents and witnesses to prove that the Huston Plan, in fact, was canceled after two days. In their discussions, among other things, they suggest that illegal government activity, such as "black bag jobs," (burglaries) occurred in previous administrations with Hoover's knowledge and participation.

Nixon's language throughout is startling. He is crude, vulgar, and obscene. Even "the president's congressional allies, his friends, and friendly columnists were appalled," writes historian Stanley I. Kutler. Instead of lucid reasoning, articulate expression, and noble goals—what one hopes for in a president—the tapes reveal fuzzy thinking, unseemly language, and a preoccupation with petty concerns.

ADDITIONAL SOURCES

Nixon White House Tapes. U.S. National Archives and Records Administration, Web site: www.archives.com, e-mail for archive staff: Nixon@nara.gov

Kutler, Stanley I. *Abuse of Power: The New Nixon Tapes.* New York: The Free Press, 1997.

———. *The Wars of Watergate: The Last Crisis of Richard Nixon.* New York: Alfred A. Knopf, 1990.

"The Nixon White House Tapes"

(U.S. National Archives and Records Administration)

September 13, 1971, President Richard Nixon, H. R. (Bob) Haldeman, chief of staff, 4:36–5:05 p.m., Oval Office.

Nixon: . . . But Billy Graham tells an astonishing thing. The IRS is battering the shit out of him. Some sonofabitch came to him and gave him a three hour grilling about how much he, you know, how much his contribution is worth and he told it to Connally [former Texas Democratic governor and Nixon supporter]. Well, Connally took the name of the guy. I just got to get that nailed down to Connally when you get back. He didn't know it.

Now here's the point. Bob please get me the names of the Jews, you know, the big Jewish contributors of the Democrats. . . . All right. Could we please investigate some of the cocksuckers? That's all.

Now look at here. Here IRS is going after Billy Graham tooth and nail. Are they going after Eugene Carson Blake [president of the National Council of Churches]? I asked, you know what I mean is, Goddamn. I don't believe. I just don't know whether we are being as rough about it. That's all. . . .

Haldeman: Yeh.

Nixon: You call Mitchell [John Mitchell, the attorney general]. Mitchell could get—stick his nose in the thing. . . . Say now Goddamnit, are we going after some of these Democrats or not? They've gone after Abplanalp [Robert Abplanalp, friend of the president]. They've gone after Rebozo ["Bebe" Rebozo, another friend]. They've gone after John Wayne. They're going after, you know, every one of our people. Goddamnit, they were after me. . . .

May 16, 1973: The president, General Alexander M. Haig, Jr., then chief of staff, and J. Fred Buzhardt, counsel to the president, 4:55–5:22 p.m., Oval Office.

Nixon: . . . But basically the worst kind of thing is, frankly, the Plumbers operation.

Buzhardt: Yes.

Nixon: That looks like one of these Goddamn clowns hired a bunch of people here. But here you've got the CIA, the DIA, FBI, all working together on something.

Buzhardt: And Internal Revenue.

Nixon: Huh?

Buzhardt: And Internal Revenue.

Nixon: They in it, too?

Buzhardt: Yes.

Nixon: There you are, all working on something like this. Well, Goddamnit. Now, they all get together and get together a paper for the president of the United States that's something, that's pretty Goddamn important, isn't it? That's what's involved here. And it involves groups that were engaging in violence, disruption, unbelievable hell around this place. The trouble is we didn't do much good with it, did we? Had a riot the next year. Let's see Cambodia was in '70, '71. Yeah. May Day. That's what we've gotta handle with these progressive bastards. . . . But I don't think the country is going to get excited about a damn plan that was drawn up by agencies to control the Goddamn riots. That's all this is. . . .

Haig: There's no way. There's no way. In fact, most people will say *thank God*. Again, if we had done less we would have been irresponsible. You know this is the farce of the whole thing. Goddamn.

Nixon: I know.

Haig: We're doing what's right for the people in the country. You develop these vulnerabilities. It's just something . . . well, if they get into a big charge of suppression of civil liberties. . . . Goddamn. . . . There were some in the White House here that wanted more, that wanted to keep the army in.

Nixon: Keep the army in?

Haig: Yeh, but they didn't. They did just the opposite. And it's probably Huston [Tom Charles Huston, presidential aide, author of inter-agency domestic intelligence plan], coming in to keep this thing going.

Nixon: Well, that may be a separate issue. But don't let us start getting all upset about this thing. This will be another story. That's all, in my view. In my view when this busts, it will be another Goddamn story. The president authorized a super-duper activity in 1970 and so forth for the purpose of doing that which involves burglary, et cetera, and wire-tapping. There's your story. And what we plan to say, just say you're Goddamn right, however, we rescinded it. I mean, we, it did not prove operable and so forth and so on and it was deal with a specific problem at a specific time, and it was discontinued and was discontinued at such and such a time. I think we're gonna find discontinuance someplace in this damn government. . . . You see, with Dean [John W. Dean III, counsel to the president] gone the sonofabitch wouldn't put that in his file. Oh, the incredible treachery of that sonofabitch.

May 16, 1973: President Richard Nixon, Alexander Haig, and J. Fred Buzhardt, 8:45–9:33 p.m., Oval Office.

Nixon: . . . We have to realize they're not after Bob [Haldeman] or John [Mitchell] or Henry [Kissinger] or [Alexander] Haig or Ziegler [Ronald L. Ziegler, press secretary]. They're after the president. Shit. That's what it's all about. You know that. . . . They want to destroy us.

Haig: What they're hung up on. They're really in a dilemma up there. They want to get you and yet they don't and that's tough for them, too. . . . Some of those things came about from J. Edgar Hoover. He insisted on tapping . . . and some came from Henry.

Nixon: I know. A hell of a lot came from Henry. . . .

Nixon: You know, it's ridiculous that the president of the United States has to spend his time for the last—almost two months—worried about this horse's-ass crap. Unbelievable. Come in. Hi Fred.

Buzhardt: Yes, sir.

Nixon: You've had a hard night. I hope you got something to eat . . .

Buzhardt: Not yet. I'll get something. It's confirming out very well.

Nixon: Really?

Buzhardt: . . . There are no documents. Apparently Huston was wrong. There was no document turning it on in the first place.

Nixon: What is this document you've got in the file there?

Buzhardt: That was from Haldeman telling Huston that the answer was yes that you had made the decision. . . . It presents the picture and the recommendation. There was no action memorandum, though, to tell the people to go into business.

Nixon: I see.

Buzhardt: Whatsoever. They've all checked memories of people. He did it by telephone call.

Nixon: Haldeman?

Buzhardt: Huston. Huston apparently.

Nixon: Oh yeh?

Buzhardt: You see the procedure to turn it on is not described in Haldeman's memorandum. He said instead of using the procedure you suggested, use the one I explained to you. If this doesn't work, come back. That was obviously to call them and to tell them to go.

Nixon: Right. I don't want to piss on Haldeman damnit.

Buzhardt: You know, that's nothing. It was, subsequently they were told no go. They all got the message.

Nixon: Now wait a minute. Was there a no go order?

Buzhardt: Yes sir.

Nixon: I haven't heard that before.

Buzhardt: Yes sir, we've got the people who remember the no go order.

Nixon: Who?

Buzhardt: We've got Bill Sullivan [William Sullivan, former FBI official, critic of Hoover] and we'll get the details from him. I still haven't had a lengthy conversation with him. Lou Tordella [Louis W. Tordella, de facto head of the National Security Agency] got the message it was off.

Nixon: From Haldeman?

Buzhardt: No sir, none of them got it from Haldeman.

Nixon: Whom did he get the no go from?

Buzhardt: Huston gave it to Sullivan and Sullivan called everybody else.

Nixon: I see.

Buzhardt: And said no work. We're out of business. Huston, I mean, Sullivan was furious. They had convinced Hoover to go with it. They had a two and half hour meeting. They had the decision. He signed off. They sent it in to you. Unanimous recommendation. You approved it. It was unanimous. No dissents.

Nixon: I know.

Buzhardt: Then what I'm told is that Tolson [Clyde Tolson, J. Edgar Hoover's deputy] found out about it and got to Hoover.

Nixon: Clyde Tolson, right?

Buzhardt: Clyde Tolson said, this will ruin your image. Hoover then took his copy, footnoted it, screamed at Mitchell, got the issue raised. I think he may even have seen you. They are under the impression he did.

Nixon: I think he did, yeah.

Buzhardt: And you suspended the operation. That's the word they used. You suspended it out.

Nixon: When?

Buzhardt: It was within two days of it being issued to the best of their recollection.

Nixon: Jesus Christ [Laughs.] . . .

Buzhardt: It just took Hoover a reaction time. Tolson got to him. It came right back. Sullivan thinks he has notes that will give us the precise times. . . .

Now the history goes on from there. The question was raised subsequently once or twice it never went anywhere. I mean, you know, to show that it wasn't going on they made the pitch again. They never really got a bite and they never got a handle on it until Pat Gray [L. Patrick Gray, acting director and later nominee for director of the FBI] was appointed.

Nixon: Shit.

Buzhardt: No, we didn't have a problem but we came close, we came close. Pat went out to visit NASA, took four of his assistants with him, and he told Lou Tordella, "I understand we used to do some things for you that were very helpful." Lou said, "Yes that's true." He said, "I understand that we've cut them off." He said, "I'd like for you, why the hell were they, did they never go?" Well, Lou didn't know. All guys sat around the table, and he said well maybe some of your own people can tell you. But Lou finally told him, I said that I understand that Tolson finally got to Hoover and convinced him to scream because it would hurt his image. One of the guys at the table verified it.

Nixon: I know.

Buzhardt: Then Pat said, "Well damn well think we ought to try to put it back, we ought to review the situation, weigh the risks, the advantages, and see what's done." They started that process. Pat was putting back together the assets.

Nixon: Sullivan told you this?

Buzhardt: Tordella told me this.

Nixon: Oh Tordella. Thank God he's around.

Buzhardt: Then they thought that Pat was going to run with it. It went about six weeks, Pat trying to reassemble the assets cause it was real rusty now see. It had been since 1967, and then I forget what it was that happened that turned off the whole damn thing but something happened with respect to Pat's appointment or approval or something of this type it was all dead. . . .

Nixon: What is the situation then? Then they didn't burglarize anything?

Buzhardt: No burglarizing, no sir. . . .

Nixon: Then what in the hell does Dean mean? Dean must be relying on something he got from March, '72. He didn't know what the hell he had. . . .

Buzhardt: You see . . . all Dean's documents show is that there was an affirmative decision. By virtue of the memo from Haldeman to Huston. That's all he has.

Nixon: That's right.

Buzhardt: He doesn't know.

Nixon: How do we handle the fact that that was turned off?

Buzhardt: We tell them bluntly it was turned off. It was never done.

Nixon: Forty-eight hours later?

Buzhardt: Yes sir, and we'll have to check these logs and get the precise times, Mr. Secretary, I mean Mr. President, we can do that. We'll get that right down. I told Lou to go back and work on his notes, I want precision.

Nixon: Get the notes. Get it within a matter of hours or days I don't care if it was forty-eight days. Just so it was turned off. And nothing was done.

Buzhardt: And nothing was done.

Nixon: The contingency plan was presented, approved. I only approved the Goddamn policy. I didn't approve to burglarize this or that. You know what I mean. Neither did Haldeman.

Buzhardt: And I talked to Bob again. Bob just doesn't remember.

Nixon: I know.

Haig: We were talking about things that were done in 1960, up until 1967.

Buzhardt: They were done up until 1967.

Haig: (Laughs.)

Nixon: The question is whether we renewed things that were done in 1967.

Buzhardt: That is correct. We had one increment in there Mr. President in that document that was not previously done in 1967.

Haig: Which one was that?

Buzhardt: Well it was not recently, not as recently as 67. And that was a black job, black bag job on internal security targets. . . . Now, we both know how that system worked. . . . And how Hoover in the early days, Hoover participated. . . .

Nixon: Yep.

[Editor's Note: Sections marked by ellipsis (. . .) were withdrawn either for reasons of privacy or national security by the government or by the editor for being unintelligible or unrelated to the topic.]

Introduction to
Bob Woodward and Carl Bernstein's

"Watergate"

THE STORY OF HOW two young reporters, Bob Woodward and Carl Bernstein, broke open the Watergate scandal and brought down the president of the United States is an American legend. At the very least, most people are familiar with their portrayal by Robert Redford and Dustin Hoffman in the film, *All the President's Men*. Their efforts to uncover the truth behind the Watergate break-in has over time come to occupy a seminal position in American investigative or secret history. The tidal wave of media coverage following W. Mark Felt's admission that he was "Deep Throat" demonstrates the ongoing interest in the riddle of Watergate.

The events are quite simple. On June 17, 1972, five men were arrested for breaking into and attempting to place listening devices in the headquarters of the Democratic National Committee in the Watergate office building in Washington, D.C. Bob Woodward and Carl Bernstein were assigned by *The Washington Post* to cover the story. In a series of articles, Woodward and Bernstein, for a time the only journalists who pursued the story, gradually uncovered links between the burglars and the Committee to Reelect the President, and ultimately to White House payoffs, intimidation, cover-ups, and other abuses of power. Their articles played a crucial role in forcing Richard Nixon to resign as president in August 1974.

In addition, the Watergate scandal eventually led to new financial disclosure laws by government officials, changes in campaign financing, and amendments broadening the Freedom of Information Act, which provides public access to the records of federal agencies. The following selections include the first "Watergate" article in which Woodward and

Bernstein shared a byline and three other articles that carried the investigation to new plateaus.

In 1973, *The Washington Post* won the Pulitzer Prize for Public Service for Woodward and Bernstein's reporting on the Watergate break-in. Woodward was again the lead reporter for the *Post's* articles on the aftermath of 9/11 for which the paper received the Pulitzer Prize for national reporting in 2002. He has written a number of best-selling books, including the recent *Bush at War* and *Plan of Attack*. Together, Bernstein with Woodward described their role and the end of the Nixon presidency in *All the President's Men* and *The Final Days*.

ADDITIONAL SOURCES

Bernstein, Carl and Bob Woodward. *All the President's Men*. New York: Simon and Schuster, 1974.

Woodward, Bob and Carl Bernstein. *The Final Days*. New York: Simon and Schuster, 1994.

Woodward, Bob. *Shadow: Five Presidents and the Legacy of Watergate*. New York: Simon and Schuster, 2000.

Bob Woodward and Carl Bernstein

"Watergate"

"GOP Security Aide Among 5 Arrested in Bugging Affair"

THE WASHINGTON POST, JUNE 19, 1972

O NE OF THE five men arrested early Saturday in the attempt to bug the Democratic National Committee headquarters here is the salaried security coordinator for President Nixon's reelection committee.

The suspect, former CIA employee James W. McCord, Jr., 53, also holds a separate contract to provide security services to the Republican National Committee, GOP national chairman Bob Dole said yesterday.

Former Attorney General John N. Mitchell, head of the Committee for the Re-Election of the President, said yesterday McCord was employed to help install that committee's own security system.

In a statement issued in Los Angeles, Mitchell said McCord and the other four men arrested at Democratic headquarters Saturday "were not operating either in our behalf or with our consent" in the alleged bugging attempt.

Dole issued a similar statement, adding that "we deplore action of this kind in or out of politics." An aide to Dole said he was unsure at this time exactly what security services McCord was hired to perform by the National Committee.

Police sources said last night that they were seeking a sixth man in connection with the attempted bugging. The sources would give no other details.

Other sources close to the investigation said yesterday that there still was no explanation as to why the five suspects might have attempted to bug Democratic headquarters in the Watergate at 2600 Virginia Ave. NW, or if they were working for other individuals or organizations.

"We're baffled at this point . . . the mystery deepens," a high Democratic party source said.

Democratic National Committee Chairman Lawrence F. O'Brien said the "bugging incident . . . raised the ugliest questions about the integrity of the political process that I have encountered in a quarter century.

"No mere statement of innocence by Mr. Nixon's campaign manager will dispel these questions."

The Democratic presidential candidates were not available for comment yesterday.

O'Brien, in his statement, called on Attorney General Richard G. Kleindienst to order an immediate, "searching professional investigation" of the entire matter by the FBI.

A spokesman for Kleindienst said yesterday. "The FBI is already investigating . . . Their investigative report will be turned over to the criminal division for appropriate action."

The White House did not comment.

McCord, 53, retired from the Central Intelligence Agency in 1970 after 19 years of service and established his own "security consulting firm." McCord Associates, at 414 Hungerford Drive, Rockville. He lives at 7 Winder Ct., Rockville.

McCord is an active Baptist and colonel in the Air Force Reserves, according to neighbors and friends.

In addition to McCord, the other four suspects all Miami residents, have been identified as: Frank Sturgis (also known as Frank Fiorini), an American who served in Fidel Castro's revolutionary army and later trained a guerrilla force of anti-Castro exiles; Eugenie R. Martinez, a real estate agent and notary public who is active in anti-Castro activities in Miami; Virgilio R. Gonzales, a locksmith; and Bernard L. Barker, a native of Havana said by exiles to have worked on and off for the CIA since the Bay of Pigs invasion in 1961.

All five suspects gave the police false names after being arrested Saturday. McCord also told his attorney that his name is Edward Martin, the attorney said.

Sources in Miami said yesterday that at least one of the suspects—

Sturgis—was attempting to organize Cubans in Miami to demonstrate at the Democratic National Convention there next month.

The five suspects, well-dressed, wearing rubber surgical gloves and unarmed, were arrested about 2:30 a.m. Saturday when they were surprised by Metropolitan police inside the 29-office suite of the Democratic headquarters on the sixth floor of the Watergate.

The suspects had extensive photographic equipment and some electronic surveillance instruments capable of intercepting both regular conversation and telephone communication.

Police also said that two ceiling panels near party chairman O'Brien's office had been removed in such a way as to make it possible to slip in a bugging device.

McCord was being held in D.C. jail on $30,000 bond yesterday. The other four were being held there on $50,000 bond. All are charged with attempted burglary and attempted interception of telephone and other conversations.

McCord was hired as "security coordinator" of the Committee for the Re-election of the President on Jan. 1, according to Powell Moore, the Nixon committee's director of press and information.

Moore said McCord's contract called for a "take-home salary" of $1,209 per month and that the ex-CIA employee was assigned an office in the committee's headquarters at 1701 Pennsylvania Ave., NW.

Within the last one or two weeks, Moore said, McCord made a trip to Miami Beach—where both the Republican and Democratic National Conventions will be held. The purpose of the trip, Moore said, was "to establish security at the hotel where the Nixon Committee will be staying."

In addition to McCord's monthly salary, he and his firm were paid a total of $2,835 by the Nixon Committee for the purchase and rental of television and other security equipment, according to Moore.

Moore said that he did not know exactly who on the committee staff hired McCord, adding that it "definitely wasn't John Mitchell." According to Moore, McCord has never worked in any previous Nixon election campaigns "because he didn't leave the CIA until two years ago, so it would have been impossible." As of late yesterday, Moore said. McCord was still on the Re-Election Committee payroll.

In his statement from Los Angeles, former Attorney General Mitchell said he was "surprised and dismayed" at reports of McCord's arrest.

"The person involved is the proprietor of a private security agency who was employed by our committee months ago to assist with the installation of our security system," said Mitchell. "He has, as we understand it, a number of business clients and interests and we have no knowledge of these relationships."

Referring to the alleged attempt to bug the opposition's headquarters, Mitchell said: "There is no place in our campaign, or in the electoral process, for this type of activity and we will not permit it nor condone it."

About two hours after Mitchell issued his statement, GOP National Chairman Dole said, "I understand that Jim McCord . . . is the owner of a firm with which the Republican National Committee contracts for security services . . . If our understanding of the facts is accurate," added Dole, "we will of course discontinue our relationship with the firm."

Tom Wilck, deputy chairman of communications for the GOP National Committee, said late yesterday that Republican officials still were checking to find out when McCord was hired, how much he was paid and exactly what his responsibilities were.

McCord lives with his wife in a two-story, $45,000 house in Rockville.

After being contacted by *The Washington Post* yesterday, Harlan A. Westrell, who said he was a friend of McCord's, gave the following background on McCord:

He is from Texas, where he and his wife graduated from Baylor University. They have three children, a son who is in his third year at the Air Force Academy, and two daughters.

The McCords have been active in the First Baptist Church of Washington.

Other neighbors said that McCord is a colonel in the Air Force Reserve, and also has taught courses in security at Montgomery Community College. This could not be confirmed yesterday.

McCord's previous employment by the CIA was confirmed by the intelligence agency, but a spokesman there said further data about McCord was not available yesterday.

Several address books seized from the suspects contained mostly

Spanish names with Miami addresses. Police sources said all of the names in the books were being checked.

In Miami, *Washington Post* Staff Writer Kirk Scharfenberg reported that two of the other suspects—Sturgis and Barker—are well known among Cuban exiles there. Both are known to have had extensive contacts with the Central Intelligence Agency, exile sources reported, and Barker was closely associated with Frank Bender, the CIA operative who recruited many members of Brigade 2506: the Bay of Pigs invasion force.

Barker, 55, and Sturgis, 37, reportedly showed up uninvited at a Cuban exile meeting in May and claimed to represent an anticommunist organization of refugees from "captive nations." The purpose of the meeting, at which both men reportedly spoke, was to plan a Miami demonstration in support of President Nixon's decision to mine the harbor of Haiphong.

Barker, a native of Havana who lived both in the U.S. and Cuba during his youth, is a U.S. Army veteran who was imprisoned in a German POW camp during World War II. He later served in the Cuban Buro de Investigaciones—secret police—under Fidel Castro and fled to Miami in 1959. He reportedly was one of the principal leaders of the Cuban Revolutionary Council, the exile organization established with CIA help to organize the Bay of Pigs Invasion.

Sturgis, an American soldier of fortune who joined Castro in the hills of Oriente Province in 1958, left Cuba in 1959 with his close friend, Pedro Diaz Lanz, then chief of the Cuban air force. Diaz Lanz, once active in Cuban exile activities in Miami, more recently has been reported involved in such right-wing movements as the John Birch Society and the Rev. Billy James Hargis' Christian Crusade.

Sturgis, more commonly known as Frank Fiorini, lost his American citizenship in 1960 for serving in a foreign military force—Castro's army—but, with the aid of then-Florida Sen. George Smathers, regained it.

Contributing to this story were Washington Post *Staff Writers E. J. Bachinski, Bill Gold, Claudia Levy, Kirk Scharfenberg, J. Y. Smith and Martin Weil.*

"Bug Suspect Got Campaign Funds,"

THE WASHINGTON POST, AUGUST 1, 1972

A $25,000 CASHIER'S CHECK, apparently earmarked for President Nixon's re-election campaign, was deposited in April in a bank account of one of the five men arrested in the break-in at Democratic National Headquarters here June 17.

The check was made out by a Florida bank to Kenneth H. Dahlberg, the President's campaign finance chairman for the Midwest. Dahlberg said last night that in early April he turned the check over to "the treasurer of the Committee (for the Re-election of the President) or to Maurice Stans himself."

Stans, formerly Secretary of Commerce under Mr. Nixon, is now the finance chief of the President's re-election effort.

Dahlberg said he didn't have "the vaguest idea" how the check got into the bank account of the real estate firm owned by Bernard L. Barker, one of the break-in suspects. Stans could not be reached for comment.

Reached by telephone at his home in a Minneapolis suburb, Dahlberg explained the existence of the check this way:

"In the process of fund-raising I had accumulated some cash . . . so I recall making a cash deposit while I was in Florida and getting a cashier's check made out to myself. I didn't want to carry all that cash into Washington."

A photostatic copy of the front of the check was examined by a *Washington Post* reporter yesterday. It was made out by the First Bank and Trust Co. of Boca Raton, Fla., to Dahlberg.

Thomas Monohan, the assistant vice president of the Boca Raton bank, who signed the check authorization, said the FBI had questioned him about it three weeks ago.

According to court testimony by government prosecutors, Barker's bank account in which the $25,000 was deposited was the same account from which Barker later withdrew a large number of hundred-dollar bills. About 53 of these $100 bills were found on the five men after they were arrested at the Watergate.

Dahlberg has contributed $7,000 to the GOP since 1968, records show, and in 1970 he was finance chairman for Clark MacGregor when MacGregor ran unsuccessfully against Hubert H. Humphrey for a U.S. Senate seat in Minnesota.

MacGregor, who replaced John N. Mitchell as Mr. Nixon's campaign chief on July 1, could offer no explanation as to how the $25,000 got from the campaign finance committee to Barker's account.

He told a *Post* reporter last night: "I know nothing about it . . . these events took place before I came aboard. Mitchell and Stans would presumably know."

MacGregor said he would attempt this morning to determine what happened.

Powell Moore, director of press relations for the Committee for the Re-election of the President, told a reporter that Stans was unavailable for comment last night. Mitchell also could not be reached for comment.

In a related development, records made available to *The Post* yesterday show that another $89,000 in four separate checks was deposited during May in Barker's Miami bank account by a well-known Mexican lawyer.

The deposits were made in the form of checks made out to the lawyer, Manuel Ogarrio Daguerre, 68, by the Banco Internacional of Mexico City.

Ogarrio could not be reached for comment and there was no immediate explanation as to why the $89,000 was transferred to Barker's account.

This makes a total of $114,000 deposited in Barker's account in the Republic National Bank of Miami, all on April 20.

The same amount—$114,000—was withdrawn on three separate dates, April 24, May 2 and May 8.

Since the arrest of the suspects at 2:30 a.m. inside the sixth floor suite of the Democratic headquarters in the Watergate, Democrats have tried to lay the incident at the doorstep of the White House—or at least to the Nixon re-election committee.

One day after the arrests, it was learned that one of the suspects, James W. McCord Jr., a former FBI and CIA agent, was the security chief to the Nixon committee and a security consultant to the Republican National Committee. McCord, now free on bond, was fired from both posts.

The next day it was revealed that a mysterious White House consultant, E. Howard Hunt Jr., was known by at least two of the suspects. Hunt immediately dropped from sight and became involved in an extended court battle to avoid testimony before the federal grand jury investigating the case.

Ten days ago it was revealed that a Nixon re-election committee official was fired because he had refused to answer questions about the incident by the FBI. The official, G. Gordon Liddy, was serving as financial counsel to the Nixon committee when he was dismissed on June 28.

In the midst of this, former Democratic National Chairman Lawrence F. O'Brien filed a $1 million civil suit against the Nixon committee and the five suspects charging that the break-in and alleged attempted bugging violated the constitutional rights of all Democrats.

O'Brien charged that there is "a developing clear line to the White House" and emphasized what he called the "potential involvement" of special counsel to the President, Charles Colson.

Colson had recommended that the White House hire Hunt, also a former CIA agent and prolific novelist, as a consultant.

While he was Nixon campaign chief, Mitchell repeatedly and categorically denied any involvement or knowledge of the break-in incident.

When first contacted last night about the $25,000 check, Dahlberg said that he didn't "have the vaguest idea about it . . . I turn all my money over to the (Nixon) committee."

Asked if he had been contacted by the FBI and questioned about the check, Dahlberg said: "I'm a proper citizen. What I do is proper."

Dahlberg later called a reporter back and said he first denied any knowledge of the $25,000 check because he was not sure the caller was really a reporter for *The Washington Post*.

He said that he had just gone through an ordeal because his "dear friend and neighbor," Virginia Piper had been kidnapped and held for two days.

Mrs. Piper's husband reportedly paid $1 million ransom last week to recover his wife in the highest payment to kidnapers in U.S. history.

Dahlberg, 54, was President Nixon's Minnesota finance chairman in 1968. The decision to appoint him to that post was announced by then-Rep. MacGregor and Stans.

In 1970, Mr. Nixon appointed Dahlberg, who has a distinguished war record, to the board of visitors at the U.S. Air Force Academy.

A native of St. Paul, Minn., Dahlberg has apparently made his money through Dahlberg Electronics, Inc., a suburban Minneapolis firm that sells miniature hearing aids.

In 1959, the company was sold to Motorola, and Dahlberg continued to operate it. In 1964, he repurchased it.

In 1966, the company established a subsidiary to distribute hearing aids in Latin America. The subsidiary had offices in Mexico City. Three years later, Dahlberg Electronics was named the exclusive United States and Mexican distributer for an acoustical medical device manufactured in Denmark.

Active in Minneapolis affairs, Dahlberg is a director of the National City Bank there as well as the American National Bank & Trust Co. of Fort Lauderdale. In 1969, he was named Minneapolis' "Swede of the Year."

"Spy Funds Linked to GOP Aides"

THE WASHINGTON POST, SEPTEMBER 17, 1972

FUNDS FOR THE Watergate espionage operation were controlled by several principal assistants of John N. Mitchell, the former manager of President Nixon's campaign, and were kept in a special account at the Committee for the Re-election of the President, *The Washington Post* has learned.

The Mitchell assistants, all of whom still hold policy-making positions on a high level in President Nixon's re-election campaign, were among 15 persons who had access to the secret fund of more than $300,000 earmarked for sensitive political projects.

Included in those projects was the espionage campaign against the Democrats, for which seven persons—including two former White House aides—were indicted Friday by a federal grand jury.

It could not be learned whether the Mitchell aides, who include persons who once worked at the White House, knew that funds would specifically be expended for the purpose of illegal electronic surveillance. However, associates told *The Post* that the aides were aware that the money would be spent generally on gathering information about the Democrats.

Some of the Mitchell aides are among the persons named by a self-described participant in the Watergate operation as recipients of confidential memos based on the tapped telephone conversations of Democratic Party officials.

A spokesman for President Nixon's re-election committee, informed of *The Post*'s story, said late yesterday afternoon that "there have been and are cash funds in this committee used for various legitimate purposes such as reimbursement for expenditures for advances on travel. However, no one employed by this committee at this time has used any funds (for purposes) that were illegal or improper."

The Post's information about the funds and their relationship to the Watergate case was obtained from a variety of sources, including investigators, other federal sources and officials and employees of the Committee for the Re-election of the President.

The $300,000 fund also was used for travel and entertainment that campaign officials did not want known outside the campaign organization. One source said the money was in part used for routine and legal intelligence gathering about Democrats.

The fund was kept in the safe of former Secretary of Commerce Maurice H. Stans, finance chairman of the President's campaign. It is presumably the same money that the General Accounting Office cited in an Aug. 26 report as a violation of the new campaign disclosure law, because it had not been properly accounted for. The GAO, the investigative arm of Congress, said the fund contained $350,000.

Sources said that Stans had no previous knowledge of the Watergate bugging—a position he has taken in public on numerous occasions, though he has not answered reporters questions directly.

Stans, according to the sources, was aware of the existence of the secret fund and knew that large amounts of money had been withdrawn in the names of Mitchell aides.

Only one accounting of the special fund—a single piece of lined ledger paper listing the names of 15 persons with access to the money and the amount each received—was maintained. It was purposely destroyed shortly before April 7, the date that the new campaign finance law requiring detailed accounting of election funds took effect, the sources told the *Post*.

A spokesman for the Nixon re-election committee denied late yesterday that such a list ever existed.

On the day it was destroyed the list showed that the largest individual sums of money were distributed to a handful of campaign aides closest to Mitchell, then still the President's campaign manager.

It was from those withdrawals that Nixon committee money was used for the espionage campaign against the Democrats, according to sources.

Mitchell, formerly Attorney General, resigned as the President's campaign manager on July 1, saying it was because his wife, Martha, insisted he leave politics.

She said at the time that "I love my husband very much, but I'm not going to stand for all those dirty things that go on." The former Attorney General has repeatedly denied any knowledge of the Watergate bugging.

The Mitchell aides who received money from the secret account include individuals who reportedly were sent confidential memos containing information obtained from a tapped telephone at Democratic headquarters.

The names of those Mitchell aides also appear in an account of the espionage operation told by Alfred Baldwin, a self-described participant in the Watergate affair who has been interviewed by both the FBI and lawyers for the Democratic Party.

Baldwin reportedly was granted immunity from prosecution in the Watergate case, in exchange for telling the federal grand jury his version of the espionage conspiracy. He has described himself as a former FBI agent who was hired as a security guard for Martha Mitchell and subsequently was assigned to monitor conversations intercepted from the telephone of a Democratic official with offices in the Watergate.

Yesterday the FBI said the only agent who ever worked for the Bureau with the same name is Alfred C. Baldwin III, age 37, who was an agent from 1963 to 1965. Meanwhile, a spokesman for the Nixon re-election committee confirmed that an Alfred Baldwin "worked briefly" as a security guard for Mrs. Mitchell, though his name does not appear on the committee's payroll.

In his account to the Democrats, Baldwin said that one of the men indicted Friday in the Watergate case—James W. McCord Jr., the former security coordinator of the Nixon re-election committee—sent memos and transcripts of the bugged conversations to a White House aide and several high officials in the Nixon campaign—including the Mitchell aides.

According to Baldwin's account, McCord brought him into the espionage operation as a wiretap monitor on May 10 or 11 and told him that he would be assigned the same task in Miami during the Democratic

National Convention. Baldwin also said he was assigned by McCord to infiltrate Vietnam Veterans Against the War for the purpose of "embarrassing the Democrats" if the veterans demonstrated at the Republican convention.

The secret fund that supplied the money for Baldwin's Watergate activities and other aspects of the intelligence-gathering campaign was managed by the "political side" of the Nixon re-election committee—that part directly under Mitchell's control—but physically kept on the financial side, headed by former Commerce Secretary Stans.

In some cases, individual aides to Mitchell received nearly $50,000 from the secret account. Except for ex-White House aide G. Gordon Liddy, the former finance counsel of the Nixon campaign who was indicted in the Watergate Friday, no other officials of the finance operation are known to have obtained money from the account.

The actual distribution of money from the fund to the intelligence operation was described to *The Washington Post* as being an "extremely complex transaction." It was designed to eliminate the possibility of tracing any of the funds to their original source—thought to be campaign contributions—or to reveal the point of distribution in the Finance Committee for the Re-election of the President.

In the interest of secrecy only one person was assigned to maintain the single-sheet list of transactions. Usually, the money was distributed by Liddy, the sources said.

Besides the Mitchell aides "very few people" knew that the funds were used for intelligence-gathering and political espionage, according to one source. However, others at the Nixon committee knew of existence of a secret fund earmarked for sensitive political projects.

On June 18, "when we read about the Watergate break-in in the papers," said another source, "we put two and two together."

"Vast GOP Undercover Operation Originated in 1969"

THE WASHINGTON POST, May 17, 1973

THE WATERGATE BUGGING and the break-in into the office of Daniel Ellsberg's psychiatrist were part of an elaborate, continuous campaign of illegal and quasi-legal undercover operations conducted by the Nixon administration since 1969, according to highly placed sources in the executive branch.

There are more instances of political burglaries, buggings, spying and sabotage conducted under White House auspices that have not yet been publicly revealed, according to the sources.

Although the undercover operations became most intense during the 1972 presidential campaign, such activities as the Watergate bugging and the break-in in the Ellsberg case, which previously had appeared to be isolated, were regarded in the White House as components of a continuing program of covert activity, according to the sources.

The clandestine operations, the sources said, were at various times aimed at radical leaders, student demonstrators, news reporters, Democratic candidates for president and vice president and the Congress, and Nixon administration aides suspected of leaking information to the press.

The sources said that many of the covert activities, although political in purpose, were conducted under the guise of "national security," and that some of the records relating to them are believed to have been destroyed. Some of the activities were conducted by the FBI, the Secret Service and special teams working for the White House and Justice Department, according to the sources.

Most of the activities were carried out under the direct supervision of members of President Nixon's innermost circle, among them former White House deputies H. R. (Bob) Haldeman, John D. Ehrlichman and John W. Dean III; former Attorney General John N. Mitchell, and former Assistant Attorney General Robert C. Mardian, the sources said.

Although most of the clandestine operations are still shrouded in secrecy, they are known to include:

- The use of the Secret Service to obtain information on the private life of at least one Democratic presidential candidate in 1972.
- The possession of Sen. Thomas Eagleton's confidential health records by Ehrlichman, former White House domestic affairs chief, several weeks before the information was leaked to the news media.
- The use of paid provocateurs to encourage violence at antiwar demonstrations early in the first Nixon administration, and again in the 1972 presidential campaign.
- Undercover political activities against persons regarded as opponents of the Nixon administration conducted by "suicide squads" in the FBI. The term is a bureau euphemism for teams of agents engaged in sensitive missions which, if revealed, would be disavowed by the FBI and the White House.
- The use of paid-for-hire "vigilante squads" by the White House and Justice Department to conduct illegal wiretapping, infiltrate radical organizations for purposes of provocation and engage in political sabotage.

The "vigilante squads" included professional wiretappers and ex-CIA and ex-FBI agents.

One such "vigilante squad," under the supervision of former White House aides E. Howard Hunt Jr. and G. Gordon Liddy, conducted the Watergate bugging in 1972 and the break-in at the office of Daniel Ellsberg's psychiatrist in 1971. The Watergate grand jury reportedly is examining other undercover activities by the squad, including another burglary that the team is suspected of committing.

According to one highly placed source in the executive branch, undercover operations by the Hunt-Liddy squad were transferred from the White House to the Committee for the Re-election for the President under an arrangement worked out by Haldeman, then chief of the White House staff, and John N. Mitchell, then Attorney General.

The transfer of the squad from the White House to the re-election committee in late 1971 and early 1972 was made to gear up for the upcoming presidential campaign in which "dirty tricks," spying and deceptions represented a basic campaign strategy.

Two persons occupying high positions in the Nixon administration have told *The Washington Post* that other "vigilante squads" were established by the White House and Justice Department to conduct supersecret political operations long before the Watergate bugging.

Some records relating to the Nixon administration's broad program of covert activities are believed to have been destroyed in the immediate wake of the Watergate bugging arrests last June 17. Other records were destroyed last month, when it became apparent that some of the activities might come to light in the renewed grand jury investigation of the bugging and related matters, according to one source.

To prevent further disclosure of the activities, the sources reported, the White House has promulgated "national security" guidelines for use in the Watergate investigation that are designed, at least in part, to prevent testimony about the undercover operations by those with knowledge of them.

Haldeman and Ehrlichman, the President's two principal deputies until April 30, when they resigned, invoked both executive privilege and "national security" considerations in refusing to answer certain questions before the federal grand jury investigating the Watergate and related matters, according to a reliable source.

Their actions, the source reported, amounted to a claim that the questions involved confidential White House business or national security matters that are beyond the grand jury's power to investigate.

Some sources who have previously supplied details on the Watergate scandal to *The Washington Post* have recently refused to discuss certain "potentially illegal" activities they say they have knowledge of, on grounds that to do so might violate "national security" regulations.

Two sources said that some of the White House documents submitted to the Watergate trial judge by former presidential counsel John Dean provide information about previously unreported covert political activities, conducted under the guise of "national security" by the Nixon administration.

Several sources described the political espionage and sabotage conducted by the President's re-election committee, including the Watergate bugging, as the logical extension of covert operations established long before by the Nixon administration.

"Watergate was a natural action that came from long-existing circumstances," one high-level participant in many of the undercover activities observed. He added: "It grew out of an atmosphere. This way of life was not new . . . There have been fairly broad (illegal and quasi-legal) activities from the beginning of the administration. I didn't know where 'national security' ended and political espionage started."

According to this source, the activities were aimed at whatever individual or groups the White House perceived as a threat at any given moment. "First it was radicals," he said, "then it was reporters and leaking White House aides, then the Democrats. They all got the same treatment: bugging, infiltration, burglary, spying, etectera."

As one example, this source cited the 1971 FBI investigation into the background of CBS News correspondent Daniel Schorr. The investigation, the source said, was personally ordered by Haldeman.

At the time that it was publicly revealed that the correspondent was under investigation, the White House said that Schorr was being considered for a job in the administration—an assertion that administration officials have since conceded was untrue.

In addition to the use of the FBI for such intelligence-gathering purposes, the White House used the Secret Service in the 1972 campaign to investigate the private life of at least one Democratic presidential candidate, according to reliable sources.

The sources reported that the Secret Sevice—or perhaps a single agent acting alone—provided the White House with regular reports on private activity of the candidate.

In addition to receiving Secret Service reports on such matters, the White House twice considered leaking stories in the news media about the activity, the sources said.

A spokesman for former White House special counsel Charles W. Colson has acknowledged that Colson received such information on a candidate's private life but denied that the data came from the Secret Service.

The Secret Service's role in collecting such information represents the second time that agency has been reported to have engaged in intelligence-gathering against political opponents of the White House.

On Nov. 4, *The New York Times* reported that Nixon campaign aides and the White House received information about confidential meetings held by Sen. George McGovern with potential financial backers.

Jack Warner, spokesman for the Secret Service, said last week that an investigation last year concluded that there was no evidence to support *The Times* report.

"If you have new information," Warner said, "let us have it and we will reopen our investigation. This type of activity would be unprecedented, and if at any time an investigation reveals that a Secret Service agent was identified with this activity, he would be judged unsuitable for the Secret Service."

Seven investigative sources and Nixon administration officials have told *The Washington Post* recently that Colson and Haldeman were the prime movers behind the extensive undercover campaign mounted on behalf of President Nixon's 1972 re-election, although other high officials were also involved.

Much of that secret campaign of spying, sabotage, deception and other "dirty tricks" was designed to help secure the Democratic presidential nomination for Sen. McGovern, considered by the White House to be President Nixon's least formidable opponent.

One former high official in the Nixon administration said: "It was a campaign that went astray and lost its sense of fair play. Secrecy and an obsession with the covert became part of nearly every action. It all turned to mud, and I'm sorry to have been a part of it."

As examples of the other secret, but apparently legal, tactics employed in the Nixon campaign, sources in the White House, the Committee for the Re-election of the President and investigative agencies have cited the following:

- Well before they were leaked to the news media, former presidential adviser Ehrlichman obtained copies of Sen. Thomas Eagleton's health records. It could not be determined how Ehrlichman obtained the records, which Eagleton, as Democratic vice presidential candidate, refused to supply even to his running mate, Sen. McGovern.

  According to *The Post*'s sources, Ehrlichman had received copies of the records which showed that Eagleton had received electric shock treatment for nervous exhaustion in 1960, 1964 and 1966.

  (Former Attorney General Ramsey Clark has said that Eagleton's health records were in the FBI files, and reliable sources said that material from the FBI files was provided to White House and Nixon campaign aides during last year's election campaign by former Assistant Attorney General Mardian.)

- Fred V. Malek, a former White House aide and deputy manager of the Nixon re-election committee, ordered establishment of a network of persons to gather information in nearly all of 50 states on the campaign of Sen. McGovern.

  Field operatives in the project had a code-word contact—the name "Viola Smith"—at the Nixon committee for transmitting the information by telephone to a group at Nixon campaign headquarters known as the "McGovern Watch." In addition, written reports would be mailed to the Nixon committee on forms marked "confidential" and containing space for details about staff changes, speeches and polls in the McGovern campaign.

  Malek acknowledged he wrote a memorandum on "Intelligence on Future Appearances of McGovern and Shriver" but denied that the memo was intended to set any covert activities into motion. The memo, obtained by *The Washington Post*, advises persons in the field to call "Viola Smith at 202-333-7220 to advise her of information that you learn of."

  DeVan L. Shumway, a spokesman for the Committee for the Re-election of the President, acknowledged yesterday that he requested two reporters to supply information about Sen. McGovern's campaign schedule to the Nixon committee.

Shumway said that the two reporters, whom he declined to identify, turned down the request because "most of my friends in the news business are honorable." He said he approached the reporters under orders from Jeb Stuart Magruder, the former deputy Nixon campaign director.

- Colson organized at least 30 groups of Nixon supporters to "attack" network news correspondents through write-in, telephone and telegram campaigns to their local stations, according to Tom Girard, a former Nixon committee press aide.

Girard, now a correspondent for Westinghouse Broadcasting, Inc., said he quit the Nixon committee last May because he was "appalled" at Colson's proposal, made during an election strategy meeting on May 3, 1972. Republican sources in two states said they actually participated in a phone-in campaign to complain about an ABC commentary that was critical of President Nixon.

- One Democratic presidential contender sought legal advice after he established that members of his family were being investigated and followed. A former official in President Nixon's campaign acknowledged that the Committee for the Re-election of the President was responsible for ordering the surveillance.

- Watergate conspirator Hunt had phony flyers printed advertising a free-beer rally for New York City Mayor John Lindsay, a Democratic presidential candidate during the Florida primary election last March. The flyers were distributed in the black neighborhoods in Florida. Hunt also had reprints made of a *Newsweek* article critical of Sen. Edmund Muskie's wife. The reprints were distributed in New Hampshire before the primary there.

- Former Assistant Attorney General Mardian, who became political coordinator of the Nixon campaign, had two spies in the McGovern campaign who reported directly to him, according to other campaign officials. In addition, two Nixon campaign aides on loan from the Republican National Committee posed regularly as newsmen to obtain routine data about McGovern trips and speeches.

- Ken W. Clawson, deputy director of communications for the White House, assisted a reporter in locating the alcoholic brother of one of the Democratic presidential candidates—for a news story that apparently never was published.

- Magruder, the deputy Nixon campaign manager, offered from $5,000 to $10,000 to several writers in an attempt to persuade them to assemble a critical book about Sen. McGovern's early life in South Dakota. The project was eventually abandoned, according to several sources.

- William Rhatican, a former assistant to Colson, said that he is "sure" telegrams of support were sent by the Nixon committee to the White House after Dr. Henry A. Kissinger's Oct. 26 "peace at hand" speech declaring that the Vietnam war was virtually over.

     Rhatican, now an aide to White House press secretary Ronald L. Ziegler, said he also understood that Colson used campaign funds to set up Vietnam veteran groups to support the President. The groups had the appearance of being volunteer organizations. Mel Stevens, a consultant to the Veterans Administration, was lent to Colson to set up a pro-Nixon, veterans group that also used government money, according to White House and Veterans Administration officials.

What has been described by Nixon committee sources as an "obsession" with secrecy and manipulation, apparently extended even to the minutest details of the campaign. "Nothing was left to chance," one former White House aide observed.

As an example, several Nixon campaign officials cited White House orchestration of the Republican National Convention last August.

"We couldn't control what the (television) networks did completely," one official said, "but we came close. When they weren't paying attention to what was going on at the speaker's platform, we'd shut off the lights in the convention hall to force the cameras to the podium."

Introduction to
Greg Palast's

"Florida's Ethnic Cleansing of the Voter Roles"

IN THE WAKE OF the many irregularities associated with the 2000 presidential election, Greg Palast, one of the world's leading investigative journalists, discovered that of more than 57,000 "felons" purged from the voter roles in Florida by Secretary of State Katherine Harris and Governor Jeb Bush, at least 90 percent of those on the "scrub" list were, in fact, not felons. The majority of the individuals who were barred from the polls were Black and Hispanic—likely Democratic voters. Had these votes been counted, George Bush would not have won Florida by a plurality of 537 votes and Al Gore would have become president.

Palast broke the story in *Britain's Observer* while the election was still being adjudicated in the courts, but his revelations were ignored by the American media except for Salon.com, which was the first American outlet to reveal his findings, and later *The Nation*. Finally, in June 2001, *The Washington Post* reported Palast's account of how the presidential election of 2000 was stolen.

Given Florida's role in the national election, why hadn't the American media blanketed its pages and screens with Palast's startling news? In *The Best Democracy Money Can Buy*, Palast explains that he freely offered some leads to CBS. The next day the producer called him and said, "I'm sorry, but your story didn't hold up." Palast asked: "How was this determined?" The producer said, "We called Jeb Bush's office."

Palast's experience proves that uncovering secret history requires a skeptical mind, extensive research, dogged interviewing, patience, and avoiding sources who are the objects of investigation until a critical mass of independent information has been gathered.

ADDITIONAL SOURCES

Berry, Mary Frances, ed. *Voting Irregularities in Florida During the 2000 Presidential Election: Report and Appendix.* Collingdale, Pa.: Diane Publishing Co, 2003.

Palast, Greg. "How Jeb Bush Stole the 2000 Election for His Brother," *Harper's,* March 2002.

Whitman, Mark, ed. *Florida 2000: A Sourcebook on the Contested Presidential Election.* Boulder, Colo.: Lynne Rienner Publ., 2003.

Greg Palast

Florida's Ethnic Cleansing of the Voter Roles

THE BEST DEMOCRACY MONEY CAN BUY: THE TRUTH
ABOUT CORPORATE CONS, GLOBALIZATION, AND
HIGH-FINANCE FRAUDSTERS, 2004
(ORIGINALLY PUBLISHED ON *SALON.COM*, DECEMBER 4, 2000)

I F VICE PRESIDENT Al Gore is wondering where his Florida votes went, rather than sift through a pile of chads, he might want to look at a "scrub list" of 57,700 names targeted to be knocked off the Florida voter registry by a division of the office of Florida Secretary of State Katherine Harris. A close examination suggests thousands of voters may have lost their right to vote based on a flaw-ridden list of purported "felons" provided by a private firm with tight Republican ties.

Early in the year, the company ChoicePoint gave Florida officials the names of 8,000 ex-felons to "scrub" from their list of voters.

But it turns out none on the list was guilty of felonies, only misdemeanors.

The company acknowledged the error, and blamed it on the original source of the list—the state of Texas.

Florida officials moved to put those falsely accused by Texas back on voter rolls before the election. Nevertheless, the large number of errors uncovered in individual counties suggests that thousands of other eligible voters have been turned away at the polls.

Florida is the only state that pays a private company that promises to provide lists for "cleansing" voter rolls. The state signed in 1998 a $4 million contract with DBT Online, since merged into ChoicePoint, of Atlanta. The creation of the scrub list, called the central voter file, was mandated by a 1998 state voter fraud law, which followed a tumultuous year that saw Miami's mayor removed after voter fraud in the election, with dead people discovered to have cast ballots. The voter fraud law

required all sixty-seven counties to purge voter registries of duplicate registrations, deceased voters and felons, many of whom, but not all, are
barred from voting in Florida. In the process, however, the list invariably
targets a minority population in Florida, where 31 percent of all Black
men cannot vote because of a ban on felons.

If this unfairly singled out minorities, it unfairly handicapped Gore: in
Florida, 93 percent of African-Americans voted for the vice president.

In the ten counties contacted by Salon, use of the central voter file
seemed to vary wildly. Some found the list too unreliable and didn't use it
at all. But most counties appear to have used the file as a resource to purge
names from their voter rolls, with some counties making little—or no—
effort at all to alert the "purged" voters. Counties that did their best to vet
the file discovered a high level of errors, with as many as 15 percent of
names incorrectly identified as felons.

News coverage has focused on some maverick Florida counties that
rejected the scrub lists, including Palm Beach and Duval. The *Miami Herald* blasted the counties for not using the lists; but local officials tell
us they had good reason to reject the scrub sheets from Harris's office.
Madison County's elections supervisor, Linda Howell, had a peculiarly
personal reason for distrusting the central voter file. She had received a
letter saying that since she had committed a felony, she would not be
allowed to vote.

Howell, who said she has never committed a felony, said the letter she
received in March 2000 shook her faith in the process. "It really is a mess,"
she said.

"I was very upset," Howell said. "I know I'm not a felon." Though the
one mistake did get corrected and law enforcement officials were quite
apologetic, Howell decided not to use the state list because its "information is so flawed."

She's unsure of the number of warning letters that were sent out to
county residents when she first received the list in 1999, but she recalls
that there were many problems. "One day we would send a letter to have
someone taken off the rolls, and the next day, we would send one to put
them back on again," Howell said. "It makes you look like you must be a
dummy."

DIXIE AND WASHINGTON COUNTIES also refused to use the scrub list. Starlet Cannon, Dixie's deputy assistant supervisor of elections, said, "I'm scared to work with it because [a] lot of the information they have on there is not accurate."

Carol Griffin, supervisor of elections for Washington, said, "It hasn't been accurate in the past, so we had no reason to suspect it was accurate this year."

But if some counties refused to use the list altogether, others seemed to embrace it all too enthusiastically. Etta Rosado, spokeswoman for the Volusia County Department of Elections, said the county essentially accepted the file at face value, did nothing to confirm the accuracy of it and doesn't inform citizens ahead of time that they have been dropped from the voter rolls.

"When we get the con felon list, we automatically start going through our rolls on the computer. If there's a name that says John Smith was convicted of a felony, then we enter a notation on our computer that says convicted felon—we mark an 'f ' for felon—and the date that we received it," Rosado said.

"They're still on our computer, but they're on purge status," meaning they have been marked ineligible to vote.

"I don't think that it's up to us to tell them they're a convicted felon," Rosado said. "If he's on our rolls, we make a notation on there. If they show up at a polling place, we'll say, 'Wait a minute, you're a convicted felon, you can't vote.' Nine out of ten times when we repeat that to the person, they say 'Thank you' and walk away. They don't put up arguments." Rosado doesn't know how many people in Volusia were dropped from the list as a result of being identified as felons.

HILLSBOROUGH COUNTY'S ELECTIONS SUPERVISOR, Pam Iorio, tried to make sure that the bugs in the system didn't keep anyone from voting. All 3,258 county residents who were identified as possible felons on the central voter file sent by the state were sent a certified letter informing them that their voting rights were in jeopardy. Of that number, 551 appealed their status, and 245 of those appeals were successful. (By the rules established by Harris's office, a voter is assumed guilty and convicted of a crime and conviction unless and until they provide documentation certifying their innocence.) Some had been convicted of a misdemeanor and not a felony, others were felons who had had their rights restored and others were simply cases of mistaken identity.

An additional 279 were not close matches with names on the county's own voter rolls and were not notified. Of the 3,258 names on the original list, therefore, the county concluded that more than 15 percent were in error. If that ratio held statewide, *no fewer than* 7,000 voters were incorrectly targeted for removal from voting rosters.

Iorio says local officials did not get adequate preparation for purging felons from their rolls. "We're not used to dealing with issues of criminal justice or ascertaining who has a felony conviction," she said. Though the central voter file was supposed to facilitate the process, it was often more troublesome than the monthly circuit court lists that she had previously used to clear her rolls of duplicate registrations, the deceased and convicted felons. "The database from the state level is not always accurate," Iorio said. As a consequence, her county did its best to notify citizens who were on the list about their felony status.

"We sent those individuals a certified letter, we put an ad in a local newspaper and we held a public hearing. For those who didn't respond to that, we sent out another letter by regular mail," Iorio said. "That process lasted several months."

"We did run some number stats and the number of Blacks [on the list] was higher than expected for our population," says Chuck Smith, a statistician for the county. Iorio acknowledged that African-Americans made up 54 percent of the people on the original felons list, though they constitute only 11.6 percent of Hillsborough's voting population.

Smith added that the DBT computer program automatically transformed various forms of a single name. In one case, a voter named "Christine" was identified as a felon based on the conviction of a "Christopher" with the same last name. Smith says ChoicePoint would not respond to queries about its proprietary methods. Nor would the company provide additional verification data to back its fingering certain individuals in the registry purge. One supposed felon on the ChoicePoint list is a local judge.

While there was much about the lists that bothered Iorio, she felt she didn't have a choice but to use them. And she's right. Section 98.0975 of the Florida Constitution states: "Upon receiving the list from the division, the supervisor must attempt to verify the information provided. If the supervisor does not determine that the information provided by the division is incorrect, the supervisor must remove from the registration books by the next subsequent election the name of any person who is deceased, convicted of a felony or adjudicated mentally incapacitated with respect to voting."

But the counties have interpreted that law in different ways. Leon County used the central voter file sent in January 2000 to clean up its voter rolls, but set aside the one it received in July. According to Thomas James, the information systems officer in the county election office, the list came too late for the information to be processed.

According to Leon election supervisor Ion Sancho, "there have been some problems" with the file. Using the information received in January, Sancho sent 200 letters to county voters, by regular mail, telling them they had been identified by the state as having committed a felony and would not be allowed to vote. They were given thirty days to respond if there was an error. "They had the burden of proof," he says.

He says twenty people proved that they did not belong on the list, and a handful of angry phone calls followed on election day. "Some people threatened to sue us," he said, "but we haven't had any lawyers calling yet." In Orange County, officials also sent letters to those identified as felons by the state, but they appear to have taken little care in their handling of the list.

"I have no idea," said June Condrun, Orange's deputy supervisor of elections, when asked how many letters were sent out to voters. After a bit more thought, Condrun responded that "several hundred" of the letters were sent, but said she doesn't know how many people complained. Those who did call, she said, were given the phone number of the Florida Department of Law Enforcement so that they could appeal directly to it.

Many Orange County voters never got the chance to appeal in any form.

Condrun noted that about one-third of the letters, which the county sent out by regular mail, were returned to the office marked undeliverable. She attributed the high rate of incorrect addresses to the age of the information sent by DBT, some of which was close to twenty years old, she said.

Miami-Dade County officials may have had similar trouble. Milton Collins, assistant supervisor of elections, said he isn't comfortable estimating how many accused felons were identified by the central voter file in his county. He said he knows that about 6,000 were notified, by regular mail, about an early list in 1999. Exactly how many were purged from the list? "I honestly couldn't tell you," he said. According to Collins, the most recent list he received from the state was one sent in January 2000, and the county applied a "two-pass system." If the information on the state list seemed accurate enough when comparing names with those on county voter lists, people were classified as felons and were then sent warning letters. Those who seemed to have only a partial match with the state data were granted "temporary inactive status."

Both groups of people were given ninety days to respond or have their names struck from the rolls.

But Collins said the county has no figures for how many voters were able to successfully appeal their designation as felons.

CHOICEPOINT SPOKESMAN Martin Fagan concedes his company's error in passing on the bogus list from Texas. ("I guess that's a little bit embarrassing in light of the election," he says.) He defends the company's overall performance, however, dismissing the errors in 8,000 names as "a minor glitch—less than one-tenth of 1 percent of the electorate" (though the total equals 15 times Governor George W. Bush's claimed lead over Gore). But he added that ChoicePoint is responsible only for turning over its raw list, which is then up to Florida officials to test and correct.

Last year, DBT Online, with which ChoicePoint would soon merge, received the unprecedented contract from the state of Florida to "cleanse" registration lists of ineligible voters—using information gathering and matching criteria it has refused to disclose, even to local election officials in Florida.

Atlanta's ChoicePoint, a highflying dot-com specializing in sales of personal information gleaned from its database of four billion public and not-so-public records, has come under fire for misuse of private data from government computers.

In January 2000, the state of Pennsylvania terminated a contract with ChoicePoint after discovering the firm had sold citizens' personal profiles to unauthorized individuals.

Fagan says many errors could have been eliminated by matching the Social Security numbers of ex-felons on DBT lists to the Social Security numbers on voter registries. However, Florida's counties have Social Security numbers on only a fraction of their voter records. So with those two problems—Social Security numbers missing in both the DBT's records and the counties' records—that fail-safe check simply did not exist.

Florida is the only state in the nation to contract the first stage of removal of voting rights to a private company. And ChoicePoint has big plans. "Given the outcome of our work in Florida," says Fagan, "and with a new president in place, we think our services will expand across the country."

Especially if that president is named "Bush." ChoicePoint's board, executive suite and consultant rosters are packed with Republican stars, including former New York Police Commissioner Howard Safir and former ultra-Right congressman Vin Weber, ChoicePoint's Washington lobbyist.

Introduction to
Seymour M. Hersh's

"Torture at Abu Ghraib"

T HE HORRIFIC PHOTOS of Iraqi prisoners being tortured by Americans at the Abu Ghraib prison in Iraq have seared themselves into the world's consciousness. Taken clandestinely by individual servicemen while the torture was taking place, the photos eventually made their way to top officials at the Pentagon but were kept secret by the U.S. military until they were leaked. Several were first broadcast on CBS's *60 Minutes 2* in April 2004. Some of the most shocking photos, including that of a hooded man standing on a box, attached to wires, and another of a pyramid of naked men piled on top of each other, were published about a week later in *The New Yorker,* accompanying an article by investigative journalist Seymour Hersh.

He had obtained a copy of an internal army report that had never been made public. It revealed that Iraqi detainees at Abu Ghraib, a prison complex near Baghdad that had formerly been used for torture by Saddam Hussein, had been the victims of systematic torture by American soldiers and civilian interrogators. The report "amounts to an unsparing study of collective wrongdoing and the failure of army leadership at the highest levels," Hersh wrote.

Hersh's exposé reverberated around the world. In the United States, a Senate committee conducted hearings into the army's conduct but though charges were brought against soldiers of low rank, top officials who allegedly ordered the practices escaped censure. Secretary of Defense Donald Rumsfeld, who bore ultimate responsibility for the action of American troops, remained in his job and Alberto Gonzales, whose radical legal reasoning as White House counsel had helped provide a justification for the terrible abuses of prisoners at Abu Ghraib, was later appointed Attorney General by President Bush.

The Abu Ghraib story is the latest in a series of startling exposés by Hersh, who won a Pulitzer Prize in 1970 when he first gained national recognition by breaking the story of the massacre of Vietnamese civilians at My Lai. (See above.) Since then, Hersh has investigated a number of secret histories in articles and books which include *The Price of Power: Kissinger in the Nixon White House*, *The Target is Destroyed: What Really Happened to Flight 007 and What America Knew About It*, and *The Samson Option: Israel's Nuclear Arsenal and American Foreign Policy*.

In 2005, *The New Yorker* received a National Magazine Award for "Torture at Abu Ghraib" and two related articles written by Seymour Hersh.

ADDITIONAL SOURCES

Danner, Mark. *Torture and Truth: America, Abu Ghraib, and the War on Terror.* New York: *The New York Review of Books*, 2004.

Hersh, Seymour M. *Chain of Command: The Road from 9/11 to Abu Ghraib.* New York: HarperCollins, 2004.

Strasser, Steven, ed. *The Abu Ghraib Investigations: The Official Independent Panel and the Pentagon Report on the Shocking Prison Abuse in Iraq.* New York: Public Affairs, 2004.

Seymour M. Hersh

"Torture at Abu Ghraib"

THE NEW YORKER, MAY 10, 2004

IN THE ERA of Saddam Hussein, Abu Ghraib, twenty miles west of Baghdad, was one of the world's most notorious prisons, with torture, weekly executions, and vile living conditions. As many as fifty thousand men and women—no accurate count is possible—were jammed into Abu Ghraib at one time, in twelve-by-twelve-foot cells that were little more than human holding pits.

In the looting that followed the regime's collapse, last April, the huge prison complex, by then deserted, was stripped of everything that could be removed, including doors, windows, and bricks. The coalition authorities had the floors tiled, cells cleaned and repaired, and toilets, showers, and a new medical center added. Abu Ghraib was now a U.S. military prison. Most of the prisoners, however—by the fall there were several thousand, including women and teenagers—were civilians, many of whom had been picked up in random military sweeps and at highway checkpoints. They fell into three loosely defined categories: common criminals; security detainees suspected of "crimes against the coalition"; and a small number of suspected "high-value" leaders of the insurgency against the coalition forces.

Last June, Janis Karpinski, an Army reserve brigadier general, was named commander of the 800th Military Police Brigade and put in charge of military prisons in Iraq. General Karpinski, the only female commander in the war zone, was an experienced operations and intelligence officer who had served with the Special Forces and in the 1991 Gulf War, but she

had never run a prison system. Now she was in charge of three large jails, eight battalions, and thirty-four hundred Army reservists, most of whom, like her, had no training in handling prisoners.

General Karpinski, who had wanted to be a soldier since she was five, is a business consultant in civilian life, and was enthusiastic about her new job. In an interview last December with the St. Petersburg *Times,* she said that, for many of the Iraqi inmates at Abu Ghraib, "living conditions now are better in prison than at home. At one point we were concerned that they wouldn't want to leave."

A month later, General Karpinski was formally admonished and quietly suspended, and a major investigation into the army's prison system, authorized by Lieutenant General Ricardo S. Sanchez, the senior commander in Iraq, was under way. A fifty-three-page report, obtained by *The New Yorker,* written by Major General Antonio M. Taguba and not meant for public release, was completed in late February. Its conclusions

about the institutional failures of the army prison system were devastating. Specifically, Taguba found that between October and December of 2003 there were numerous instances of "sadistic, blatant, and wanton criminal abuses" at Abu Ghraib. This systematic and illegal abuse of detainees, Taguba reported, was perpetrated by soldiers of the 372nd Military Police Company, and also by members of the American intelligence community. (The 372nd was attached to the 320th M.P. Battalion, which reported to Karpinski's brigade headquarters.) Taguba's report listed some of the wrongdoing:

> *Breaking chemical lights and pouring the phosphoric liquid on detainees; pouring cold water on naked detainees; beating detainees with a broom handle and a chair; threatening male detainees with rape; allowing a military police guard to stitch the wound of a detainee who was injured after being slammed against the wall in his cell; sodomizing a detainee with a chemical light and perhaps a broom stick, and using*

military working dogs to frighten and intimidate detainees with threats of attack, and in one instance actually biting a detainee.

There was stunning evidence to support the allegations, Taguba added—"detailed witness statements and the discovery of extremely graphic photographic evidence." Photographs and videos taken by the soldiers as the abuses were happening were not included in his report, Taguba said, because of their "extremely sensitive nature."

THE PHOTOGRAPHS—several of which were broadcast on CBS's *60 Minutes 2* last week—show leering G.I.s taunting naked Iraqi prisoners who are forced to assume humiliating poses. Six suspects—Staff Sergeant Ivan L. Frederick II, known as Chip, who was the senior enlisted man; Specialist Charles A. Graner; Sergeant Javal Davis; Specialist Megan Ambuhl; Specialist Sabrina Harman; and Private Jeremy Sivits—are now facing prosecution in Iraq, on charges that include conspiracy, dereliction of duty, cruelty toward prisoners, maltreatment, assault, and indecent acts. A seventh suspect, Private Lynndie England, was reassigned to Fort Bragg, North Carolina, after becoming pregnant.

The photographs tell it all. In one, Private England, a cigarette dangling from her mouth, is giving a jaunty thumbs-up sign and pointing at the genitals of a young Iraqi, who is naked except for a sandbag over his head, as he masturbates. Three other hooded and naked Iraqi prisoners are shown, hands reflexively crossed over their genitals. A fifth prisoner has his hands at his sides. In another, England stands arm in arm with Specialist Graner; both are grinning and giving the thumbs-up behind a cluster of perhaps seven naked Iraqis, knees bent, piled clumsily on top of each other in a pyramid. There is another photograph of a cluster of naked prisoners, again piled in a pyramid. Near them stands Graner, smiling, his arms crossed; a woman soldier stands in front of him, bending over, and she, too, is smiling. Then, there is another cluster of hooded bodies, with a female soldier standing in front, taking photographs. Yet another photograph shows a kneeling, naked, unhooded male prisoner, head momentarily turned away from the camera, posed to make it appear that he is performing oral sex on another male prisoner, who is naked and hooded.

Such dehumanization is unacceptable in any culture, but it is especially so in the Arab world. Homosexual acts are against Islamic law and it is humiliating for men to be naked in front of other men, Bernard Haykel, a professor of Middle Eastern studies at New York University, explained. "Being put on top of each other and forced to masturbate, being naked in front of each other—it's all a form of torture," Haykel said.

Two Iraqi faces that do appear in the photographs are those of dead men. There is the battered face of prisoner No. 153399, and the bloodied body of another prisoner, wrapped in cellophane and packed in ice. There is a photograph of an empty room, splattered with blood.

The 372nd's abuse of prisoners seemed almost routine—a fact of army life that the soldiers felt no need to hide. On April 9th, at an Article 32 hearing (the military equivalent of a grand jury) in the case against Sergeant Frederick, at Camp Victory, near Baghdad, one of the witnesses, Specialist Matthew Wisdom, an M.P., told the courtroom what happened when he and other soldiers delivered seven prisoners, hooded and bound, to the so-called "hard site" at Abu Ghraib—seven tiers of cells where the inmates who were considered the most dangerous were housed. The men had been accused of starting a riot in another section of the prison. Wisdom said:

> SFC Snider grabbed my prisoner and threw him into a pile. . . . I do not think it was right to put them in a pile. I saw SSG Frederick, SGT Davis and CPL Graner walking around the pile hitting the prisoners. I remember SSG Frederick hitting one prisoner in the side of its [sic] ribcage. The prisoner was no danger to SSG Frederick. . . . I left after that.

When he returned later, Wisdom testified:

> I saw two naked detainees, one masturbating to another kneeling with its mouth open. I thought I should just get out of there. I didn't think it was right . . . I saw SSG Frederick walking towards me, and he said,

"Look what these animals do when you leave them alone for two seconds." I heard PFC England shout out, "He's getting hard."

Wisdom testified that he told his superiors what had happened, and assumed that "the issue was taken care of." He said, "I just didn't want to be part of anything that looked criminal."

THE ABUSES BECAME PUBLIC because of the outrage of Specialist Joseph M. Darby, an M.P. whose role emerged during the Article 32 hearing against Chip Frederick. A government witness, Special Agent Scott Bobeck, who is a member of the Army's Criminal Investigation Division, or C.I.D., told the court, according to an abridged transcript made available to me, "The investigation started after SPC Darby . . . got a CD from CPL Graner. . . . He came across pictures of naked detainees." Bobeck said that Darby had "initially put an anonymous letter under our door, then he later came forward and gave a sworn statement. He felt very bad about it and thought it was very wrong."

Questioned further, the army investigator said that Frederick and his colleagues had not been given any "training guidelines" that he was aware of. The M.P.s in the 372nd had been assigned to routine traffic and police duties upon their arrival in Iraq, in the spring of 2003. In October of 2003, the 372nd was ordered to prison-guard duty at Abu Ghraib. Frederick, at thirty-seven, was far older than his colleagues, and was a natural leader; he had also worked for six years as a guard for the Virginia Department of Corrections. Bobeck explained:

What I got is that SSG Frederick and CPL Graner were road M.P.s and were put in charge because they were civilian prison guards and had knowledge of how things were supposed to be run.

Bobeck also testified that witnesses had said that Frederick, on one occasion, "had punched a detainee in the chest so hard that the detainee almost went into cardiac arrest."

At the Article 32 hearing, the army informed Frederick and his attorneys, Captain Robert Shuck, an army lawyer, and Gary Myers, a civilian, that two dozen witnesses they had sought, including General Karpinski and all of Frederick's co-defendants, would not appear. Some had been excused after exercising their Fifth Amendment right; others were deemed to be too far away from the courtroom. "The purpose of an Article 32 hearing is for us to engage witnesses and discover facts," Gary Myers told me. "We ended up with a C.I.D. agent and no alleged victims to examine." After the hearing, the presiding investigative officer ruled that there was sufficient evidence to convene a court-martial against Frederick.

Myers, who was one of the military defense attorneys in the My Lai prosecutions of the nineteen-seventies, told me that his client's defense will be that he was carrying out the orders of his superiors and, in particular, the directions of military intelligence. He said, "Do you really think a group of kids from rural Virginia decided to do this on their own? Decided that the best way to embarrass Arabs and make them talk was to have them walk around nude?"

In letters and e-mails to family members, Frederick repeatedly noted that the military-intelligence teams, which included C.I.A. officers and linguists and interrogation specialists from private defense contractors, were the dominant force inside Abu Ghraib. In a letter written in January, he said:

> I questioned some of the things that I saw . . . such things as leaving inmates in their cell with no clothes or in female underpants, handcuffing them to the door of their cell—and the answer I got was, "This is how military intelligence (MI) wants it done." . . . MI has also instructed us to place a prisoner in an isolation cell with little or no clothes, no toilet or running water, no ventilation or window, for as much as three days.

The military-intelligence officers have "encouraged and told us, 'Great job,' they were now getting positive results and information," Frederick wrote. "CID has been present when the military working dogs were used to intimidate prisoners at MI's request." At one point, Frederick told his family, he pulled aside his superior officer, Lieutenant Colonel Jerry Phillabaum, the commander of the 320th M.P. Battalion, and asked about the mistreatment of prisoners. "His reply was 'Don't worry about it.'"

In November, Frederick wrote, an Iraqi prisoner under the control of what the Abu Ghraib guards called "O.G.A.," or other government agencies—that is, the C.I.A. and its paramilitary employees—was brought to his unit for questioning. "They stressed him out so bad that the man passed away. They put his body in a body bag and packed him in ice for approximately twenty-four hours in the shower. . . . The next day the medics came and put his body on a stretcher, placed a fake IV in his arm and took him away." The dead Iraqi was never entered into the prison's inmate-control system, Frederick recounted, "and therefore never had a number."

FREDERICK'S DEFENSE IS, of course, highly self-serving. But the complaints in his letters and e-mails home were reinforced by two internal army reports—Taguba's and one by the army's chief law-enforcement officer, Provost Marshal Donald Ryder, a major general.

Last fall, General Sanchez ordered Ryder to review the prison system in Iraq and recommend ways to improve it. Ryder's report, filed on November 5th, concluded that there were potential human-rights, training, and manpower issues, system-wide, that needed immediate attention. It also discussed serious concerns about the tension between the missions of the military police assigned to guard the prisoners and the intelligence teams who wanted to interrogate them. Army regulations limit intelligence activity by the M.P.s to passive collection. But something had gone wrong.

There was evidence dating back to the Afghanistan war, the Ryder report said, that M.P.s had worked with intelligence operatives to "set favorable conditions for subsequent interviews"—a euphemism for breaking the will of prisoners. "Such actions generally run counter to the smooth operation of a detention facility, attempting to maintain its population in a compliant and docile state." General Karpinski's brigade, Ryder reported, "has not been directed to change its facility procedures to set the conditions for MI interrogations, nor participate in those interrogations." Ryder called for the establishment of procedures to "define the role of military police soldiers . . . clearly separating the actions of the guards from those of the military intelligence personnel." The officers running the war in Iraq were put on notice.

Ryder undercut his warning, however, by concluding that the situation had not yet reached a crisis point. Though some procedures were flawed, he said, he found "no military police units purposely applying inappropriate confinement practices." His investigation was at best a failure and at worst a cover-up.

Taguba, in his report, was polite but direct in refuting his fellow-general. "Unfortunately, many of the systemic problems that surfaced during [Ryder's] assessment are the very same issues that are the subject of this investigation," he wrote. "In fact, many of the abuses suffered by detainees occurred during, or near to, the time of that assessment." The report continued, "Contrary to the findings of MG Ryder's report, I find that personnel assigned to the 372nd MP Company, 800th MP Brigade were directed to change facility procedures to 'set the conditions' for MI interrogations." Army intelligence officers, C.I.A. agents, and private contractors "actively requested that MP guards set physical and mental conditions for favorable interrogation of witnesses."

Taguba backed up his assertion by citing evidence from sworn statements to Army C.I.D. investigators. Specialist Sabrina Harman, one of the accused M.P.s, testified that it was her job to keep detainees awake, including one hooded prisoner who was placed on a box with wires attached to his fingers, toes, and penis. She stated, "MI wanted to get them to talk. It is Graner and Frederick's job to do things for MI and OGA to get these people to talk."

Another witness, Sergeant Javal Davis, who is also one of the accused, told C.I.D. investigators, "I witnessed prisoners in the MI hold section . . . being made to do various things that I would question morally. . . . We were told that they had different rules." Taguba wrote, "Davis also stated that he had heard MI insinuate to the guards to abuse the inmates. When asked what MI said he stated: 'Loosen this guy up for us.' 'Make sure he has a bad night.' 'Make sure he gets the treatment.' " Military intelligence made these comments to Graner and Frederick, Davis said. "The MI staffs to my understanding have been giving Graner compliments . . . statements like, 'Good job, they're breaking down real fast. They answer every question. They're giving out good information.'"

When asked why he did not inform his chain of command about the abuse, Sergeant Davis answered, "Because I assumed that if they were doing things out of the ordinary or outside the guidelines, someone would have said something. Also the wing"—where the abuse took place—"belongs to MI and it appeared MI personnel approved of the abuse."

Another witness, Specialist Jason Kennel, who was not accused of wrongdoing, said, "I saw them nude, but MI would tell us to take away their mattresses, sheets, and clothes." (It was his view, he added, that if M.I. wanted him to do this "they needed to give me paperwork.") Taguba also cited an interview with Adel L. Nakhla, a translator who was an employee of Titan, a civilian contractor. He told of one night when a "bunch of people from MI" watched as a group of handcuffed and shackled inmates were subjected to abuse by Graner and Frederick.

General Taguba saved his harshest words for the military-intelligence officers and private contractors. He recommended that Colonel Thomas Pappas, the commander of one of the M.I. brigades, be reprimanded and receive non-judicial punishment, and that Lieutenant Colonel Steven Jordan, the former director of the Joint Interrogation and Debriefing Center, be relieved of duty and reprimanded. He further urged that a civilian contractor, Steven Stephanowicz, of CACI International, be fired from his army job, reprimanded, and denied his security clearances for lying to the investigating team and allowing or ordering military policemen "who were not trained in interrogation techniques to facilitate interrogations by 'setting conditions' which were neither authorized" nor in accordance with army regulations. "He clearly knew his instructions equated to physical abuse," Taguba wrote. He also recommended disciplinary action against a second CACI employee, John Israel. (A spokeswoman for CACI said that the company had "received no formal communication" from the army about the matter.)

"I suspect," Taguba concluded, that Pappas, Jordan, Stephanowicz, and Israel "were either directly or indirectly responsible for the abuse at

Abu Ghraib," and strongly recommended immediate disciplinary action.

THE PROBLEMS inside the Army prison system in Iraq were not hidden from senior commanders. During Karpinski's seven-month tour of duty, Taguba noted, there were at least a dozen officially reported incidents involving escapes, attempted escapes, and other serious security issues that were investigated by officers of the 800th M.P. Brigade. Some of the incidents had led to the killing or wounding of inmates and M.P.s, and resulted in a series of "lessons learned" inquiries within the brigade. Karpinski invariably approved the reports and signed orders calling for changes in day-to-day procedures. But Taguba found that she did not follow up, doing nothing to insure that the orders were carried out. Had she done so, he added, "cases of abuse may have been prevented."

General Taguba further found that Abu Ghraib was filled beyond capacity, and that the M.P. guard force was significantly undermanned and short of resources. "This imbalance has contributed to the poor living conditions, escapes, and accountability lapses," he wrote. There were gross differences, Taguba said, between the actual number of prisoners on hand and the number officially recorded. A lack of proper screening also meant that many innocent Iraqis were wrongly being detained—indefinitely, it seemed, in some cases. The Taguba study noted that more than 60 per cent of the civilian inmates at Abu Ghraib were deemed not to be a threat to society, which should have enabled them to be released. Karpinski's defense, Taguba said, was that her superior officers "routinely" rejected her recommendations regarding the release of such prisoners.

Karpinski was rarely seen at the prisons she was supposed to be running, Taguba wrote. He also found a wide range of administrative problems, including some that he considered "without precedent in my military career." The soldiers, he added, were "poorly prepared and untrained . . . prior to deployment, at the mobilization site, upon arrival in theater, and throughout the mission."

General Taguba spent more than four hours interviewing Karpinski, whom he described as extremely emotional: "What I found particularly disturbing in her testimony was her complete unwillingness to either understand or accept that many of the problems inherent in the 800th MP Brigade were caused or exacerbated by poor leadership and the refusal of her command to both establish and enforce basic standards and principles among its soldiers."

Taguba recommended that Karpinski and seven brigade military-police officers and enlisted men be relieved of command and formally reprimanded. No criminal proceedings were suggested for Karpinski; apparently, the loss of promotion and the indignity of a public rebuke were seen as enough punishment.

AFTER THE STORY BROKE on CBS last week, the Pentagon announced that Major General Geoffrey Miller, the new head of the Iraqi prison system, had arrived in Baghdad and was on the job. He had been the commander of the Guantánamo Bay detention center. General Sanchez also authorized another investigation into possible wrongdoing by military and civilian interrogators.

As the international furor grew, senior military officers, and President Bush, insisted that the actions of a few did not reflect the conduct of the military as a whole. Taguba's report, however, amounts to an unsparing study of collective wrongdoing and the failure of army leadership at the highest levels. The picture he draws of Abu Ghraib is one in which army regulations and the Geneva conventions were routinely violated, and in which much of the day-to-day management of the prisoners was abdicated to army military-intelligence units and civilian contract employees. Interrogating prisoners and getting intelligence, including by intimidation and torture, was the priority.

The mistreatment at Abu Ghraib may have done little to further American intelligence, however. Willie J. Rowell, who served for thirty-six years as a C.I.D. agent, told me that the use of force or humiliation with prisoners is invariably counterproductive. "They'll tell you what you want to hear, truth or no truth," Rowell said. " 'You can flog me until I tell you what I know you want me to say.' You don't get righteous information."

Under the fourth Geneva convention, an occupying power can jail civilians who pose an "imperative" security threat, but it must establish a regular procedure for insuring that only civilians who remain a genuine security threat be kept imprisoned. Prisoners have the right to appeal any internment decision and have their cases reviewed. Human Rights Watch complained to Secretary of Defense Donald Rumsfeld that civilians in Iraq remained in custody month after month with no charges brought against them. Abu Ghraib had become, in effect, another Guantánamo.

As the photographs from Abu Ghraib make clear, these detentions have had enormous consequences: for the imprisoned civilian Iraqis, many of whom had nothing to do with the growing insurgency; for the integrity of the army; and for the United States' reputation in the world.

Captain Robert Shuck, Frederick's military attorney, closed his defense at the Article 32 hearing last month by saying that the army was "attempting to have these six soldiers atone for its sins." Similarly, Gary Myers, Frederick's civilian attorney, told me that he would argue at the court-martial that culpability in the case extended far beyond his client. "I'm going to drag every involved intelligence officer and civilian contractor I can find into court," he said. "Do you really believe the army relieved a general officer because of six soldiers? Not a chance."

PERMISSIONS